Let Them Paddle

Let Them Paddle

Coming of Age on the Water

Alan S. Kesselheim

FULCRUM
GOLDEN, COLORADO

Library of Congress Cataloging-in-Publication Data
Kesselheim, Alan S., 1962-
  Let them paddle : coming of age on the water / Alan S. Kesselheim
    p. cm.
  ISBN 978-1-55591-351-9 (pbk.)
1. Kesselheim, Alan S., 1962- 2. Canoeists--United States--Biography. 3. Canoes and canoeing--North America. 4. Family recreation--North America. I. Title.
  GV782.42.K47A3 2012
  797.122092--dc23
  [B]
                              2011053093

Printed in Canada
0 9 8 7 6 5 4 3 2 1

Maps and design by Jack Lenzo

Fulcrum Publishing
4690 Table Mountain Dr., Ste. 100
Golden, CO 80403
800-992-2908 • 303-277-1623
www.fulcrumbooks.com

I am glad I shall never be young without wild country to be young in. Of what avail are forty freedoms without a blank spot on the map?

—ALDO LEOPOLD, *A SAND COUNTY ALMANAC*

NUNAVUT

NORTHWEST
TERRITORIES

Kazan River

Seal River

SASKATCHEWAN

CANADA

MANITOBA

MONTANA

Yellowstone River

N. DAKOTA

Younts Peak (headwaters)

WYOMING

USA

TEXAS

Rio Grande

MEXICO

N

0   100   200   300 miles

0   200   400 km

Eli KAZAN RIVER

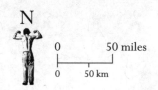

N

0   50 miles
0   50 km

NORTHWEST TERRRITORIES

put-in

ALBERTA

Lake Athabasca

Kasba Lake

flight

Athabasca Camp

SASKATCHEWAN

Baker Lake (take-out)

Baker Lake

flight

Thirty Mile Lake

Kazan Falls

Inuit grave site

musk ox encounter

Angikuni Lake

Yathkyed Lake

triple portages

blackfly nightmare

Kazan River

remony

Ennadai Lake

NUNAVUT

MANITOBA

HUDSON BAY

Churchill

train

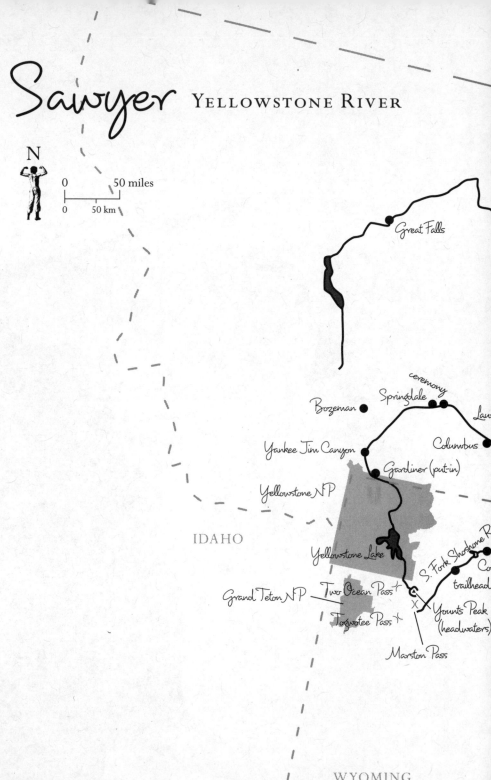

Sawyer   YELLOWSTONE RIVER

N

0   50 miles

0   50 km

Great Falls

ceremony

Bozeman   Springdale   Laur

Yankee Jim Canyon   Columbus

Gardiner (put-in)

Yellowstone NP

IDAHO

S. Fork Shoshone R

Yellowstone Lake   Coo

trailhead

Grand Teton NP   Two Ocean Pass

Younts Peak
(headwaters)

Togwotee Pass

Marston Pass

WYOMING

MONTANA

Missouri River

confluence (take-out)

Intake Diversion Dam

Glendive

windstorm camp

Yellowstone River

Pompeys Pillar

Miles City
(water stop)

N. DAKOTA

Billings

Bighorn River

S. DAKOTA

Ruby SEAL RIVER

N

0 — 50 miles
0 — 50 km

HUDSON BAY

NUNAVUT

MANITOBA

SASKATCHEWAN

N. Seal River

phone cabin

beluga whales

Button Bay

polar bear encounter

Churchill

S. Seal River

Little Sand Lakes portages

wolf pups

Churchill River

South Indian Lake (put-in)

shuttle

train

Thompson

highway

Rio Grande

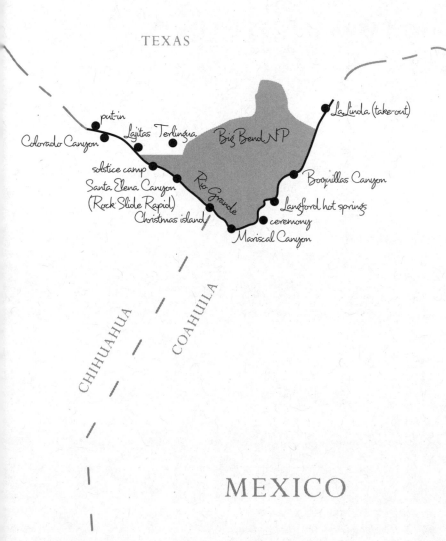

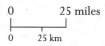

USA

TEXAS

0   25 miles

0   25 km

put-in

Colorado Canyon

Lajitas   Terlingua

Big Bend NP

LaLinda (take-out)

solstice camp

Santa Elena Canyon

(Rock Slide Rapid)

Rio Grande

Christmas island

Boquillas Canyon

Langford hot springs

ceremony

Mariscal Canyon

CHIHUAHUA

COAHUILA

MEXICO

PART I ELI
THE KAZAN RIVER

ELI READS IN THE WINDBREAK OF OVERTURNED CANOES.

One

Memory lane for Marypat and me. Landed at the same beach as we did in 1991... Water level is quite high this summer... Paddled off of Map #1. The kids were up for the push and Eli did some strong navigating. Camped on high ground where the bugs are intense.

—AL, GROUP JOURNAL

Unloading the Single Otter floatplane happens with shocking speed—a momentous transition accomplished with mundane efficiency. Two folding canoes, forty days' food, tent, sleeping bags, clothing duffels, everything that will support our family of five for almost six weeks in the tundra wilderness of Canada's Far North is passed from the open maw of the plane, down along the float, to a disorganized heap on the beach in minutes.

Cliff, our friend and a pilot, shrugs and turns back to the plane. I shake his hand. Marypat gives him a hug. He walks the float and climbs into the cockpit. He has a two-hour return flight, heading southwest over unpopulated boreal wilderness, to his fishing camp on Lake Athabasca, in northern Saskatchewan. He is concerned about strong winds aloft that ate an alarming amount of fuel on the way in.

"Watch out for bears," he calls and closes the door.

The engine coughs. The plane idles away from shore into deep water, roars off across the rumpled surface of Kasba Lake, and is a vanishing speck in the empty sky before I bend to open the first canoe bag. The sense of a door closing is palpable.

Blackflies ricochet off of my forehead. The kids pull on their bug shirts. Marypat rummages through a food pack. Small waves lap against the sand. A faint whiff of gas lingers. A breeze stirs through the stunted forest. It isn't silence that engulfs us on the wave-smoothed beach, but the absence of humanity.

Our human world, so immediate and familiar and safe moments earlier, evaporated with the disappearing plane. We have stepped into another dimension—one made up of wind and water and bugs in a wilderness larger than Alaska. Everything that will sustain and shelter us across nearly six hundred miles of Barren Lands vastness lies at my feet.

Kasba Lake spreads away to the horizon, blue, pure, frozen solid nine months of the year. The outlet of the Kazan River, the river we will paddle down, pours away around the corner. We are already deep into the wilds above 60 degrees latitude, across the border of Nunavut, formerly the District of Keewatin of the Canadian Northwest Territories. Over the next weeks we will dive deeper yet, entering and traversing the true tundra.

"Where's the can opener?" Marypat asks. She is hunched over an open pack, has lunch supplies scattered on a patch of mossy ground.

I remember putting the knife with can opener someplace handy, but damned if I know where. I check the dry box, my clothes bag, the equipment pack without success. Marypat finds an all-in-one tool in the repair kit, which has every conceivable gadget except for a can opener. She starts punching holes in the lunch-meat can with a screwdriver blade.

Fourteen years earlier, in late June 1991, Marypat and I unloaded another floatplane on this precise beach. We had already been out more than a year, having paddled some eleven hundred miles from southern Alberta and wintering in a remote cabin at Cliff's fishing camp on Lake Athabasca. We were in our late thirties, deeply held in the wilderness embrace, well along on our second transcontinental canoe expedition. We had been married for five years, together for more than a decade. At that moment of reckoning, poised to begin with gear scattered and Marypat wobbly with airsickness, she was six months pregnant with our first child.

That child, Eli, now thirteen years old, has retreated to the top of a nearby sandy rise to lie down. I can just see his size-ten feet poking up. Sawyer and Ruby, his younger siblings, are exploring on the beach. They stop to investigate a small stream. Cliff's parting words still echo in the air.

"Don't get out of sight," I call.

They are veteran campers, comfortable outdoors, eager to explore. Ruby is just ten, and Sawyer is twelve, but they have a resume of trips many adults would be proud of. The Yukon River, the Yellowstone, the Green and Colorado, the Salmon and Snake, not to mention dozens of day trips in the wilderness of the West near our home in Bozeman, Montana—climbing peaks, cross-country skiing, riding mountain bikes, running whitewater.

However, their impressive trip vitae doesn't guarantee an acceptance of camp chores. They are kids. The overriding circumstance, for them, is that this is a cool beach to check out, with wolf tracks in the sand. What they don't yet comprehend is that we've made a quantum leap. We have never taken on anything of this length or difficulty as a family. Nothing even close.

We may have landed—we can place ourselves on the map, in our memories—but we aren't here. It takes time to catch the pulse of wilderness time, to reclaim our skills and hone our judgment, earn our place here. First days are, by definition, sloppy and dangerous transitions.

I wrestle the first boat out of its bag, start the fabrication process that will render a pile of shock-corded aluminum poles, metal ribs, folding seats, and the limp boat skin into a functional seventeen-foot canoe. I succumb to the green-hazed filter of a head net to combat the blackflies, which seem worse than I remember.

Marypat brings me a tortilla-wrap sandwich. "I'll come help in a minute," she says. Her face is wan with the lingering effects of airsickness.

I quell an impulse of frustration with Eli, who is still reclining in the sun. Sawyer and Ruby are goofing around in the sand. You'd never know that half an hour earlier they'd both been retching into barf bags in the back of the plane. They'd be in the way if they tried to help, but that doesn't keep me from resenting their obliviousness.

Marypat is regaining her equilibrium. Bush planes are the worst parts of trips for her. She can get sick on a rock-smooth flight, and sometimes it takes her the better part of a day to recover. Our flight from Cliff's camp wasn't rock smooth, and it was more than two hours long. Cliff did his best to dodge the thunderheads, but Marypat spent more than half of the flight hunched over a plastic bag.

Nothing is elegant or efficient about our departure. The canoes take longer than they should to go together. We can't remember where we packed things. Dry bags don't fit in the hull. The biggest food pack must weigh 120 pounds. It takes two of us to heave it into the boat. The seat for the passenger is awkward. The spray covers won't fit over the load.

Only Day 1, but I am acutely aware of how tight we've cut the itinerary to fit it into a busy summer and of the average mileage we have to maintain. If this trip requires the entire forty days, we'll get home one day before school starts. Today is a good day to paddle. It's bad karma to squander these conditions.

We shove off, ragtag and disheveled. Ruby settles into the lumpy passenger berth, sitting on dry bags. The boys take up their paddles, look to the horizon, start the trip that has been, until now, a vague conversation among adults. The two boats labor around the point and aim for the outlet of the Kazan River. A quarter mile from shore I slip gears, back to that long summer day in late June 1991.

I am thirty-eight, soon to be a father. My pregnant wife is paddling in the bow. Our blades hit the water in sync. We have taken millions of strokes together, covering thousands of miles, and have been together in the wilds for a year. Yet, we are daunted by what we have taken on. The pregnancy changes everything.

Part of our load is the child we had tried for years to have. Then, when we had given up, halfway through the austere winter in a tiny log cabin hunkered in muffled winter silence, we succeeded. For months we agonized over whether to continue our expedition. Our families implored us to come home. One day we'd convince ourselves that to continue was folly; the next, we'd steel ourselves to go on. Our decision hung over us until the moment we loaded onto the bush plane and latched the door behind us.

Eli's birthright is that fetal journey down the Kazan River, an experience he felt through the walls of Marypat's womb. Part of his makeup is the mysterious mix of sensations and emotions communicated through her over the weeks spent traversing this wild expanse—her anxiety in rapids, the hunkered submission to thunderstorms, the reverie of sunsets, the fatigue at the end of a portage. An immersion he had no say in.

Ruby starts to sing. I am pulled back to this trip, this beginning. She sits on the tent dry bag, facing the stern. Sawyer paddles in the bow. A month earlier, Ruby graduated from fourth grade. She doesn't question our journey or our judgment. She has grown up on leaps of faith. The doubts are mine. I glance over at Eli, paddling bow in Marypat's canoe. He is almost six feet tall. He and I can trade shoes. He'll be fourteen in October; I'll be fifty-two in November. We are both on a coming-of-age journey.

Marypat and I hatched this scheme two years earlier, when it struck us that each of the kids had a birth river, a long trip they participated in from the womb. Eli's is the Kazan. Sawyer's is the Yellowstone, across Montana. Ruby's is the Rio Grande, along the border with Mexico.

What about returning to each river as a family to mark the transition to adulthood? we thought. Our society offers so little help with that leap. Isn't an adventure better than mall cruising or driver's ed? If we wanted something with the significance of a walkabout, we'd have to create it. Besides, it was an excuse for more trips. It was a quixotic notion, a bold plan, a cool idea, crazy enough to be compelling.

It wouldn't be the first time we fell prey to whimsy. In 1985 we set off on our first trans-Canadian canoe expedition. That trip was sparked by an offhand comment around a desert campfire in Utah. Marypat and I had been together for several years by then, and we had taken a number of northern canoe trips. Every time, even after a month in the bush, the trip ended before we were ready. We mourned the finish, resisted the return.

That morning in the desert we had been tossing around trip ideas, scheming adventures. One of us said something like, "What if we went north and stayed out for a really long time, like a year?" For a minute we were struck dumb by the idea. Why not? Where would we go? How would we pull it off?

Instead of passing by, the notion caught hold, stuck fast, wouldn't let go. Two years later, we set our overburdened canoe into the Athabasca River near Jasper, Alberta, the first day of a 420-day journey. We were alone. We had no idea where we'd spend the winter. Jostled by the frigid glacial melt of the Columbia Icefields, we wondered what the hell we'd done.

That yearlong trip led to my first book and the start of my writing career. It led to our marriage. It would lead to decades of subsequent journeys, and it established a life cemented by adventure, a life that eventually incorporated our three children. At the start of that trip, however, just as on this one, we were striking off into a blank map, a frontier of possibilities that could lead anywhere.

The problem with our current whimsy is that Eli's trip comes first, and it is far and away the most challenging of the three. We are asking Sawyer and Ruby to participate well before they come of age. The idea, though, was irresistible, romantic, full of heart. It gathered momentum. A year ago we started doing the things to make it happen—months of drying food, organizing logistics, saving money, collecting equipment, making contacts.

Now our canoes are furrowing the water, and the plane is a fading memory. It is all so familiar, the rippled surface of lake, being contained by the skin of a boat that holds everything, the rhythm of paddle strokes, the long-day sun. Dark green forest rims the shore, a spiky fringe of trees stitching a seam into the sky. A pair of mergansers skim away just above the water. The North, for me, so pregnant with memories and yet so brand new and fraught with unknowns for Eli. I watch him in the other canoe. He faces the horizon, full of youth and confidence and strength, at the verge of his voyage in life. He has the physique of a man, the grace and strength of a natural athlete, but he is still so unformed and young. His mop of hair hangs down his forehead. He wears his pants two inches below his boxers' waistband. He alternates between making me proud and driving me crazy.

I look down at my map, at the first rapid coming up around the bend. I remember it well. I have a good memory for that sort of thing, but I recall this spot particularly vividly because it was a dicey run the first time.

I know we need to hug the left bank around the inside of a sweeping curve. Last time we were pulled right, found nowhere to land and scout along the willowy banks, and had to paddle hard left to miss some scary water.

This rapid has been in my thoughts for months. It is one of the spots I've fixated on when I wake late at night, thinking about the trip and the things that might go wrong. Day 1 and we capsize, wreck a boat, lose gear. The images are sharp and the scenario utterly possible. Even at the start, this wilderness is remote in a way no wilderness is in Montana. There is no road five miles away. There is no road for two hundred miles in any direction.

It is the first little test to get past, the first gauge of the wisdom or foolishness of taking on a journey of this magnitude with our three children. I share nothing of this with the kids or with Marypat, only that we need to be hard left as we approach.

The Kazan is a brawny, large-volume river even at the start. It pulls us off the lake like a train gathering speed, and it has that same kind of unstoppable inertia and weight. Rocks flash past under the hull, a dizzy mosaic. I am in the lead boat and hang close against shore.

The river is much higher than I remember. Willowy shrubs along the bank wave in the current. An overflow channel breaks off abruptly. It takes me by surprise. My boat gets sucked in. Marypat is right behind me and can do nothing but follow. Ahead, the side channel braids into smaller branches weaving through flooded vegetation, narrow and fast. I consider banging my way through, but it's too thin. We hang up on a gravel bar.

"Damn! Let's hop out," I call.

Dutifully, without hesitation, Sawyer and Ruby step into the fast, icy current. Marypat and Eli are doing the same. We manhandle the boats through an opening back to the main river, work our way over slippery rocks into the deeper current. There are some boat-eating holes midriver and more intimidating whitewater downstream.

I pause, holding the canoe with the river rushing through my legs, and assess the rapid while Ruby and Sawyer climb back in. I line us up and hop into the stern. The river takes hold.

Sawyer is a strong paddler. He may only be twelve and barely a hundred pounds, but we have paddled dozens of rapids together. I don't have to say much. He sees where I'm heading and leans out with a draw stroke to shift our angle, then backpaddles through the big set of standing waves at the bottom to keep us from slamming into the hills of water and taking gulps of river over the bow. The boat wobbles through, but comes out dry.

I twist in my seat to see Marypat and Eli, their canoe bucking through the whitewater. They coast up to us and I catch Marypat's eye.

"Well, that was a pretty ignoble start," I say.

"No kidding," Marypat agrees. "This river is really high!"

We make a dismal first camp past the edge of the map I have labeled #1, more than a dozen miles in. It will be light most of the night at this latitude. The day is warm and the blackflies are fierce. The ground is rough and swampy, and the forest is a thin fur of spindly trees. The boulders are covered with caribou lichen and sphagnum moss.

Our tent goes up in a lumpy clearing between black spruce trees. Eli and I stagger up to the kitchen with the behemoth food pack. When I open the cooking pot bag, I discover the can opener–knife right where I'd thoughtfully packed it but lost in the blizzard of pretrip details. While Marypat finishes the tent, I kindle our fire, start cooking dinner. The kids lounge around, at loose ends, swatting at the insects that cloud their heads. They're used to river camps with swimming holes and sand beaches. I try not to read disgruntlement into their body language.

Shortly after dinner, the bugs drive us to our shelter. There, the five of us line up in the four-person tent, shoulder to shoulder. It's snug, but cozy, and it is a relief to strip clothes and stretch out.

I volunteer to make the first entry in the group journal that we will take turns writing in each day. I comment on the weather, the wildlife, the day's logistics, then add a brief summary paragraph. Everyone lies on their bellies and scribbles in their personal journals. Trip traditions begin. Afterward, Marypat reads from the just-released Harry Potter book we picked up at a midnight bookstore party in Calgary on the eve of our flight north to Lake Athabasca.

Scenes from the recent weeks flash through my thoughts. The mass of gear stacked in the basement and the astonishing pile of food required to power five people for forty days. Fixing a flat tire in Conrad, Montana, on the drive north, pulling a U-Haul with our minivan. The customs officer at the border asking how many gallons of bug dope we'd brought with us. Marypat, Ruby, and Sawyer all puking in the back of the plane while the dark green mass of wilderness crawled past below.

It is happening, I think. This trip that was so ephemeral and cerebral, until now. I wonder what we've forgotten in the abstracted frenzy of packing, all the details sandwiched between soccer games and work and clarinet lessons. I wonder if I'm asking too much of my children. I wonder if I'm asking too much of myself.

Sphagnum moss cushions my bed. I stretch out the soreness in my lower back, taking note of some unaccustomed stiffness in my left elbow—first-day tweaks. My clothes already smell of wood smoke. Mosquitoes cluster by the dozen on the mesh roof of the tent. A thrush calls in the forest.

I see Eli whittling a groove around the top of a willow stick he's peeled the bark off of.

"What's that?" I ask him.

"I'm marking off the days," he says.

Like a prisoner marks the days? I wonder.

"It's amazing that more trips don't end in disaster on the first day," I say instead.

Marypat puts the book down, looks across at me. "Yeah, it felt pretty clumsy."

We talk over the kids, who are all listening in.

"Is the bear spray in the tent?" I ask.

Two

On Tabane Lake we got lost in all the islands. We went one too many passages and had to cut through some islands to get back on track...When we got to camp we had a coming of age ceremony for me. I got a necklace and a bracelet

—ELI, GROUP JOURNAL

Weeks earlier I had been in the car with Eli, driving on some errand.

"Dad," he said, "I'm really scared about this trip."

"It's good to have some fear," I said, launching into a fatherly miniser-mon. "I'm actually glad to hear it. What we're doing is a pretty big deal and it shouldn't be taken lightly. This is bigger than any trip we've ever done as a family. I have some nervous moments myself."

"I'm not scared about that," he said, with a you-don't-get-it edge to his voice. "I'm scared about being away from my friends. Forty days. That's a really long time."

"Oh, that," I said. "It probably does seem long, but you know what? It's nothing. You'll come back and it'll be like no time at all. And, in the mean-time, you will have had this incredible experience that none of your friends can even imagine."

He wasn't buying it. I probably wouldn't have either, at his age.

"Is your girlfriend giving you a hard time?" I asked.

"She's mad at me for being gone so long."

"No doubt you'll make up for it with hours on the phone when you get back," I said.

"You're a lot of help, Dad."

"Don't mention it."

In some ways, Eli reminds me of myself, and it is not always a comfort-ing recognition. I had my first girlfriend at his age. I would meet her in the alley after her ballet practice and walk her home, holding hands, stopping to practice kissing. We murmured on the phone to each other for hours, back in the days when phones had cords and rotary dials.

I pulled away from my parents and family activities, just as Eli tends to. His agenda is about hanging with friends more than joining family out-ings. He tends to see himself as the black sheep, the kid who doesn't fit the mold the way his siblings do. I had more free time on my hands than Eli does, and I didn't pursue parentally sanctioned activities with that time. I smoked cigarettes, skipped classes, snuck out at night, dabbled in vandalism. I don't think Eli has the same opportunities for mischief—his time is scheduled more than mine was—but I recognize his impulses. That awareness gives our interaction a testiness, the friction of similar magnetic declinations. My appreciation for his character is spiced with the salt of apprehension and firsthand knowledge.

The map rests at my feet in a waterproof case when we leave camp the next morning. We have packed the load better this time. The boats are heavy, but trim, and we settle into a steady, if still labored, paddling rhythm. The day is pleasant—warm and calm, still buggy. The first mile slips by, then another.

We have two sets of maps, one in each boat, and they are always out. I study them closely many times a day, partly because I am a little obsessed with knowing my whereabouts, but more because I love the exploration. New things keep popping into focus. A connection to a neighboring drainage. A string of lakes I hadn't noticed before. Discoveries that are never revealed on a GPS screen.

The topographic quads we have along are 1:250,000 scale, four miles to the inch. One map sheet covers roughly a sixty-by-seventy-mile area, more than four hundred square miles. I prefer the big picture, the scope of surrounding topography. We'd go broke and have a pack full of nothing but maps if we bought small-scale quads for a trip of this length. The problem is that at this scale, a fair amount of detail gets left out. Navigation requires vigilance, and it doesn't take long to go astray.

For the most part, our route is a matter of going with the flow, but there are long lake sections, dead-end bays, lakes freckled with islands, convoluted bends, braided sections of current. It matters that we know where we are.

Marypat stowed her watch before she got up. From now on we're on trip time, a clock made of daylight and hunger and miles covered, but she made a point of mentioning that I was up starting the morning fire before 5 AM.

"Just giving you a benchmark," she said.

It is another of our rituals, this abandonment of clocks, a practice we started twenty-five years earlier, on our first trips together. Daylight lasts twenty hours or more. What matters is that we make our miles, keep track of progress, respond to conditions, pay attention to our physical status. The time of day, so critical in our town lives that it seems unimaginable to abandon it, becomes more and more meaningless.

Back in Montana, a friend is taking care of our house. The metronome keeps ticking—beating its rhythm to sports practices, music lessons, library board meetings, writing deadlines, daily exercise—but without us. Our house, with the aging roof we hope will last another season, waits. We are only days away from that world, but it seems as distant as Saudi Arabia.

Eli has the map out in the other canoe. For long moments he bends over it, glancing up at islands and pointing, putting it together. He surprises me by keeping accurate track of our location, even though he's never used this scale map before or taken more than a passing interest in map reading on our other trips. He knows the basics, can interpret the symbols, and he quickly catches on to the relationship between map scale and real ground. He starts making suggestions about the best route.

If he were presented with navigational problems as an academic exercise, like homework, it would be a far different scenario. Here, he knows that it is his energy expended if we blunder into a dead-end bay. We have discussed the mileage we need to average each day. Doing the math, measuring miles, using the compass—it all has the weight of real consequence.

On wilderness trips, and especially this one, all the skills and techniques carry consequences. None of them seem academic. Pitching the tent so we stay dry, building a fire for heat and cooking, tying knots that won't slip, developing an efficient paddle stroke. There are no grades for achievement, no motivational gold stars. Failure is fatiguing, uncomfortable, dangerous, and occasionally life threatening. All three of the kids are paying attention with an intensity schoolwork rarely merits.

On Tabane Lake, the route winds through a maze of islands, past a series of points and bays, before the Kazan empties out again. I concentrate hard on matching the map with landforms we paddle past. The higher water level I've noticed, if it is radically different from what it was when the maps were drawn, several decades earlier, will shift the appearance and size of islands and other topographic features.

"Hey, there's a moose!" Sawyer points up a narrow bay.

Sawyer is the noticer in the family. He has a sharp eye, catches movement, picks up the small details. He also has an uncanny ability to approach wildlife. Once, when he was younger, he walked off the sidewalk and picked up a pigeon from a lawn. On a family vacation in Mexico, when Sawyer was only five, he wandered off behind a food stall in a village and reappeared hugging a wild turkey to his chest.

On Tabane Lake, this bull is standing in shoulder-deep water. He plunges his head under. The wide antlers disappear. Only the hump of his back remains visible. Then he comes up, water and pondweeds streaming from his mouth. We pass the binoculars around.

By the time we start up again, I have to strain to regain my focus on the map and pinpoint the turn to the river outlet.

"I think we're going one point too far," Eli says.

I hunch close, pore over the map, then study the shore. "No, we turn around the next one, I'm pretty sure." Eli shrugs. He accepts my seniority, but it's clear he doubts me.

We paddle on, around the point, start up a broad finger of lake. I'm trying hard to reconcile things, but I realize that I'm getting pretty creative making things work out between the map and the landscape. I don't want to turn back, waste the morning retracing. I'm not at all confident Eli is right, but I'm losing confidence in my assessment with every stroke. I keep thinking things will snap into proper focus if we can just see around the next corner. They don't.

Instead, Tabane Lake suddenly looks like a geographic labyrinth. We might spend days going in and out of dead-end bays looking for the river outlet. It's remarkable how quickly my certainty bleeds away. I think of the early explorers in this country, floundering around without maps or route descriptions, feeling their way blind.

"There's some current here," Marypat breaks in.

Sure enough, the underwater weeds are pulled toward a narrow gap in the point. According to my map, there shouldn't be a gap there, but the current is undeniable and the opening may be the result of high water or further evidence that we're not where I think we are. Then again, the flow could be an anomaly, some eddying backwater in a bay that will seduce us further off course. I take heart in remembering that studying the underwater vegetation for hints of current was one of the most common navigational cues early explorers used.

We follow the weeds, waving below us like hair. The current is imperceptible, but it leads through the gap, down to the end of a bay, and there the Kazan funnels out in a short rapid.

Back on the river, we gunwale up together, let the current pull us along, break out some snacks. Eli gives me a hard I-told-you-so look, shakes his head. He doesn't have to say a thing.

Marypat starts reading the next chapter in *Harry Potter and the Half-Blood Prince*. I look over the map, the same one we used in 1991. Our old route, with camps and notes, are penciled in. Images of Marypat in her green overall maternity garb flash in my memory, camps where we waited out bad weather, an island where we stopped for lunch and a nap.

"Throw me the grouse turds, Elanor," Sawyer says.

Eli chucks the bag full of sesame sticks his way. Ruby leans back from the bow seat against a pack, stretches her hand back for her share. *The level of trust they grant us is overwhelming*, I think.

The Kazan is a classic pool-and-drop river. At Kasba Lake the elevation is roughly 1,100 feet. By the time it empties into Baker Lake, near Hudson Bay, 550 river miles to the northeast, it has fallen to 8 feet above sea level. Along the way, the drainage passes through a series of lakes, several of them significant. Angikuni and Yathkyed, for example, both among the largest in the Barrens, and Ennadai, which we paddle onto after lunch.

Ennadai is our first flatwater test, nearly sixty miles in length, and also where we make the transition from the northern fringe of boreal forest to the treeless expanse of tundra. A dozen miles up the lake, the spiky forests typical of the transition zone known as the Land of Little Sticks gives way to caribou lichen, sphagnum moss, willows a couple of feet high, and stunted, ground-hugging dwarf birch. It is a landscape of sweeping distance, much of it underlain by permafrost, scribed by heavily glaciated ridges, only rarely punctuated with pockets of undersized trees.

Between lakes, the Kazan gathers itself into a focused flow marked by emphatic rapids, miles of headlong current, banks of ice-wracked boulders. It is a river of greater volume and power than anything in Montana, yet it is just one of a dozen major rivers that flow through this part of the North with equal or greater volume—the Dubawnt, the Thelon, the Back—each of them connected to hundreds of smaller drainages.

The Barrens encompass a wilderness matched by few places on earth. Antarctica or the interior of Australia, perhaps. Maybe the Sahara. It is bounded on all sides by a continuation of wild country. To the south, hundreds of miles of forests cover the lightly populated northern tier of the Canadian provinces; farther north, the harsh island archipelago that the tortuous Northwest Passage winds through, held in the grasp of polar ice ten months of every year.

It is called barren because of the lack of trees. The tundra is treeless for the same reason that high mountains are treeless; the climate is too cold and dry to support large vegetation. To the east, tree line drops south all the way to northern Manitoba, near Churchill. Moving west, trees inch farther north in an upswept line, until, at the border with Alaska, they grow nearly to the Arctic Ocean.

The only major city in the Northwest Territories is Yellowknife, with a population hovering around ten thousand. In the interior, the only other year-round settlement is Baker Lake, an Inuit village of less than fifteen hundred people, some five hundred miles away as the bush plane flies. A handful of other communities, small and isolated villages, perch on the coasts of Hudson Bay and the Arctic Ocean. Away from the coastline, there is nothing in the way of development besides a couple of fly-in fishing camps scattered across the Alaska-sized land. No fences, no roads, no railroad tracks, no villages. Nothing.

Only the throbbing vastness, restless with more freshwater lakes, ponds, streams, rivers, bogs, muskeg, swamps, and pools than anywhere on earth. Only the throngs of caribou that move, still, by the tens and hundreds of thousands in time to the ancient rhythms, pushing to the northern fringe of the continent every spring to calve, pulsing back south each winter, following the trails they have branded across the terrain ever since the last retreat of the glaciers. Swimming the rivers at crossings held in the synapses of genetic memory. Streaming across ridges, antlers limned against the summer sky.

The caribou, in turn, interact within a web of life that includes grizzly bear, musk ox, arctic fox, wolf, moose, migrating birds, swarms of insects, schools of fish. But it is the deer, *tuktu*, as the Inuit call them, that define the tundra and that made life possible for the traditional people of the interior, much as the buffalo defined the American West and were central to the survival and cultural integrity of aboriginal people.

Ennadai Lake begins as a narrows, bounded by a sandy esker ridge to the west and forested lowlands to the east. A finger of beach pokes out from the esker a few miles up. We stop there and the kids immediately start lobbying to camp.

The winds are calm, the weather sunny. We might have hours of good paddling to capitalize on, but we've made more than our fifteen-mile average and it's an attractive spot. There are some adjustments we need to make to the canoes. The kids don't have to work too hard before they talk us into it.

I notice that Eli's pants are pulled up, cinched tight around his waist. Baggy pants worn low may be the current fashion statement in middle school, but in blackfly country it is a grievous tactical error. In less than a day, Eli's waist was ringed with a band of bites, dozens and dozens of them—red, itchy, bleeding welts. The pants came up. The belt tightened.

We all wear our pant legs tucked into our socks. The kids spend the day in hooded bug jackets. We turn to face the insect-damping breezes like weather vanes. Little clouds of blackflies buzz behind our heads in the wind eddies.

AL AND ELI PADDLE THROUGH A RARE CALM DAY.

If you set out to create an ecosystem-sized petri dish with conditions ripe for insect life, you'd be hard pressed to improve on the design of northern tundra. Start with an inexhaustible and varied supply of water—flowing currents, lakes of every size, and stagnant water on a vast scale resting on permafrost in pools and puddles and ponds. Add warm summer temperatures, almost constant sunlight, and abundant herds of warm-blooded animals.

Sure, insects are essential. They feed millions of birds and fish and constitute the foundation of the food chain, but on the tundra, the sheer volume and density of bug life seems more than strictly necessary.

Mosquitoes are a nuisance, but blackflies are the truly demonic resident. They land and crawl until they find an opening. They go up your nose, in your ears. When they find exposed flesh, they excrete an enzyme in their saliva that breaks down skin layers until blood starts to pool, then they lap it up. Their bites itch and scab over. They seem especially numerous these first days.

"What's going on with your elbow?" Marypat asks me when I pass her a pack from the boat.

"I don't know. It's a little sore, but no big deal."

"It's pretty swollen," she says, coming over to look.

"Looks like tennis elbow," I say, twisting to get a better look. "That's never happened before."

Marypat has another motive for stopping. After we unload the canoes and pitch the tent, she gathers us all into a circle, putting Eli in the center. She has put a lot of thought into this ceremony, a ritual to mark the passage in Eli's life. It feels contrived, because it is, but also weighty enough that everyone takes it seriously.

Marypat can get away with this sort of thing. The kids will follow her lead, even when they're doubtful, because, more often than not, she's more fun than anyone on the block. She's talked them into peak-climbing clubs, arduous bike rides, wearing goofy costumes, taking part in outrageous scavenger hunts, things I'd never be able to get them to do. Part of her power to persuade is that she is right there with them, having fun, looking silly, laughing her irrepressible laugh.

"I heard you were at school today," one of the kids will say.

"I never saw you there," she says.

"I know, I was upstairs. But I heard you laugh down in the office."

This is more somber. The kids circle up, ready to go. She has adapted elements from goddess worship, earth-based spirituality, totem spirits. It all feels a little over the top to me, but I hang in there, facing the compass directions, invoking the wind and earth and water, holding up symbolic feathers and sticks and rocks, repeating phrases.

It isn't that I don't accept earth-based spirituality. In fact, if I had to articulate my beliefs, they would be precisely those. If I replace the word *God* with the word *nature*, I am far more at ease with the whole religious enterprise.

In nature, and particularly in the depths of a wilderness such as the one the Kazan River carves its way through, I feel humility. I feel awe. I feel reverence and sanctuary and exultation and meekness and holiness, all the religious buzzwords. Here, I encounter the realm of the spiritual, the awareness of larger powers, the intersection with mystery in a tangible, daily way that I never once have felt coming from pulpits or holy books or in houses of God. Here, I am in church every moment of every day.

We take our children to the wilderness the way other parents take their offspring to Sunday services. This trip is our bar mitzvah, our Holy Communion, as well as our walkabout. When Jesus sought answers, he went to the desert for forty days. Our forty days in the North isn't fueled by religious quest, but the power and majesty of it, however it manifests itself, is precisely what we've come for.

It doesn't make the ceremony any less awkward for me. Marypat finishes up and presents Eli with a bracelet decorated in a wave pattern. She reaches up, holds his face, kisses him. It gives me a chill, watching them. It makes me remember her holding him in her arms when he was a baby, nursing, locking eyes. She hands out amulets for all of us, carved talismans from Africa that are supposed to protect us from watery dangers. We each knot the strings around our necks. I feel the light, angular weight of the stone carving against my chest. It comes from a continent of great rivers, rivers rife with power, not to mention crocodiles and hippos and carnivorous fish and parasitic worms. For some reason, this necklace, this sentiment for safe passage, carries more significance for me than anything else in the ceremony.

I'm not sure what Eli makes of it. He accepts the gifts, listens to the readings, takes part in the ritual. He is both solemn and self-conscious, shuffling from foot to foot in the center of our circle, smiling at us sheepishly, and seems a little relieved to be done with it. All of us take away something, give something, bear witness to Eli's becoming a man.

The real ceremony, the one made up of countless paddle strokes through weeks and down river bends across an empty map, has only just begun.

The next day, Eli drops our only pair of binoculars over the side of the canoe.

Three

We went one mile, found a camp. We read Harry Potter, made a village, and we're still waiting here for the wind to die down.

—RUBY, GROUP JOURNAL

"We have to stop!" Marypat yells.

It's windy. The red canoes rise and fall in the waves, wallow in the troughs, less than a mile from our sandy ceremony camp. Water splashes over the gunwales. As long as we were protected in the narrows, the going was fine, but as soon as the lake flared wide, the whitecapped rollers hit us broadside.

"I know. Let's get behind that island, out of the waves, and see what we can find."

The shoreline is rocky, dense with willows, and backed by thick forests of spruce. The boats finally bob in the half acre of relative calm behind the island, but there is no place to stop. Waves roll past, crash against rocky points in the distance, throw spray in the air. Everywhere the shore looks inhospitable.

I get the binoculars out of the dry box and start scanning. At the fringe of a bay, half a mile off, I make out a narrow strip of sand that might work.

"Let me see," says Eli. I hand him the binos.

Marypat asks for them next, and Eli hands them across. She grabs for them, but the strap catches on Eli's thumb, he lets go before she has hold, and they drop into the lake. Marypat makes a desperate grab as they disappear but misses. I fight the impulse to jump overboard after them. They are gone.

Gone, too, the ability to study distant landscape, find the gap of river outlet at the end of a lake, look at birds, discern musk ox from grizzly at half a mile, search the sky. It is so sudden, so irrevocable, so shocking that I say nothing.

Eli knows how big this loss is. Losing the binoculars will have daily consequences. All the more sobering because it happens so early in the trip. It makes me feel like things could unravel from here. Small mistakes, the lack of care, little accidents, and somewhere a tipping point is passed and things go badly wrong. Expedition history brims with tragedies built out of incremental missteps.

"I'm really sorry, Dad," Eli says when we start paddling toward the sand. His voice is sincere. Wind snatches the words. He is facing away from me, bending into his strokes.

Our first windbound camp is that strip of sand barely ten feet across. We pitch the tipi-style tarp on lumpy ground just off the beach. The tent site is a tiny opening in a stand of willows. Behind camp lies dense woods, swampy ground, game trails.

My sanguine assessment of our progress, just yesterday, fades with the passing day. The lake heaves, dotted with flashes of whitecaps. Wind beats at the tent fabric. We shelter under the tarp while rain squalls move through. There is no place to go exploring. The dense, wet forest is not inviting. So we read Harry Potter, keep a fire going, eat meals, until, eventually, it is time for bed.

"If I wake early and it's calm, let's think about going," I say in the tent.

"Dad, let me make you a pillow like mine," Eli says.

I've been making do with a wadded-up jacket, but Eli takes my clothing duffel, removes all the hard objects, and then zips my fleece coat around the outside. It's bulky, but I have to admit that it's pretty luxurious. It feels like Eli is making amends.

"Feels nice," I say. "Thanks, bud."

The next morning the weather has not improved, although I do my best to convince myself otherwise. The sky is that lingering pale dawn that follows a brief, twilit night, but it is full of scudding clouds. Marypat has a look out the tent window and lies back down. I go outside to assess. It could be October.

Back in my sleeping bag, I look across to Marypat. Her eyes funnel her energy. They dance with blue intensity, that fierce joy, her appetite for adventure, all there. The first time we met, I was shocked by the crackle of fire in her eyes. We have been in this dilemma with wind so many times together, on so many lakeshores and riverbanks, in so many forced camps. She snuggles back down in her bag, content to doze.

The first year after we met, before I moved to Montana to be with her, we spent a month in the canyonlands of Utah. Ever since, I've thought of it as our honeymoon. For weeks we walked the slickrock, camped under the stars, lounged over cups of morning coffee, filled canteens under the drips of seeps, made love in the desert air with white-throated swifts bombing past the cliff faces.

It was where we annealed the bond of wilderness at the core of our attraction. That first time in the desert, the recognition of shared intention, the compatibility of our styles, the realization that we complemented each other—all of it came clear. That connection has never waned. We have slept in tents, hunkered around fires, walked trails, endured appalling weather, paddled rapids, spent thousands of days together outdoors. It is the constant compass in our lives.

If things got really bad between us, if our relationship hung in the balance, my instinct would be to heal by isolating ourselves somewhere very wild. That was precisely what we were doing that year in the North when Eli was conceived.

Another day passes. More rain, cold wind, the dark, wild lake, miles lost. In camp, the kids busy themselves making elaborate sand sculptures, houses and pathways and walls, decorated with leaves and moss and careful mosaics of small rocks. They spend hours focused on the work.

From an early age they have had the capacity to invent games and competitions out of nothing. I remember them building forts out of driftwood piles on the Yellowstone River, and marking out complicated courts in the sand and creating a game with throwing sticks and scoring schemes. They'll set up target practice, leap off of sandbanks in their underwear, race sticks in the current, bury each other in the sand, rampage through the woods on fantasy quests, whacking at trees, shouting commands.

Here, in this limited space, they get ideas from each other as they shape the sand. Eli paves a walkway with tiny willow leaves. Sawyer finds a small fern to replicate palm trees. Ruby makes a fence out of driftwood twigs the size of matchsticks.

It is almost nightfall, after dinner, when the wind finally calms. The lake is still rough, the light going, but we strike camp and paddle away from the dreary prison. No telling how far we'll get, whether we'll have to bush out some mucky campsite half a mile away, but we go.

The lake calms. The water turns smooth and unruffled, undulating. Into the silence of twilight, with only the sounds of our strokes, the small splash of our bow waves, we cover barely four miles before it is too dark to make out landforms or read the map. It is probably near midnight, but it is an escape. Better yet, we gain the tundra. The island we stop at is barren on top, with a perfect tent site, flat and exposed and lovely.

"This is more like it!" I exclaim.

Only four miles, but it feels like a beginning, like we've passed through a barrier.

It takes nearly a week to cross what comes to be known as Endless Ennadai Lake, a distance we could accomplish in three reasonable paddling days.

Only one of those days is calm. Then, we never once get out of the canoes. We pee over the side. We eat lunch on board. We paddle across miles of exposed water, far from shore. We make time, until, exhausted and cramped, we make camp on another tundra island.

"It's the flatwater I've been dreading," Marypat confides. "I know I can't keep up. It's exhausting."

On our other trips, we have always been able to count on each other as paddling partners. We switch bow and stern each day. We paddle in sync, often going miles without words. On other family trips, we have enjoyed a preponderance of river current. Day after day of lake paddling is Marypat's nemesis.

She is an athlete, a passionate outdoorswoman, a person who relishes physical challenge, and she's not used to lagging behind. When we go on hikes or bike rides together, I'm usually the one watching her back as she pulls away uphill. It's a strange, novel twist for both of us, this disparity.

The all-day paddling rhythm is new for the kids too. They are used to rivers we can float along, stints of paddling alternating with relaxing miles or exhilarating whitewater. On Ennadai, we only rarely stop. They can be strong paddlers when they need to be, but this pace requires prolonged stamina, a willingness to harness up for the long haul. It is as much a mental challenge as a physical one, and they aren't there yet.

Many times each day I find myself chiding them. "Keep paddling," I say. "Nice, steady pace. Gotta keep it up."

I cringe as I hear myself. I wait for them to rebel. Even to me it feels more like work than fun. The ability to rise above fatigue and monotony is an adult mind-set. I wonder how I would have reacted at their age. I doubt I would have had their fortitude or willingness.

Calm conditions are a gift, but one that comes with its own price. Mile on mile, the lake is a mirrored stillness. The distant horizon line heaves into view in excruciating slow motion—the fuzzy green of faraway islands, a vague headland slowly sharpening into focus out of the heat shimmer.

It may be dead calm, but we are still zooming along at a top speed of three or four miles an hour. The fact that we can see to the horizon in every direction accentuates the sense of creeping forward. It takes the mental tenacity of a long-distance runner to overcome the repetitive, endless accumulation of strokes. Much as I appreciate the respite, there are times, on a dead-still day, when I crave the distraction of a little breeze.

When you're ten, twelve, and thirteen, that monotony is monumental. Hell, it's challenging enough when you're fifty.

Whoever rides as the passenger is charged with keeping conversations going. Eli and Ruby spend half an afternoon discussing the challenges and rewards of middle school. Ruby dissects her recent trip to Florida with a friend's family in minute detail, starting with what food was served on the flight and ending with their escape from the Pensacola airport on the last plane out before a hurricane struck.

We relive events, sing songs, make up stories, ask questions, probe for every detail. At one point Eli asks Ruby to count off sixty seconds while he counts paddle strokes. "I'm going to figure out how many strokes we'll take on this trip," he says.

One day of calm. On every other, wind harries us. Progress is a continual battle with headwinds and crossing winds. Rivers of air with nothing to stop them. Oceans of air.

I mark a boulder on shore, paddle hard for what seems a very long time, only to glance over and see no perceptible movement. Islands and points seem to retreat in front of us. Playing the wind is a game of chess. We study the map to gain advantage along the route, use islands for protection, cling to shore to maximize whatever buffer it might afford.

Crosswinds are worse than headwinds, because you are forced to paddle constantly on one side to keep from having to correct with every stroke. In some cases, both paddlers stroke on the same side in order to maintain course. There are days when my arm goes numb from overuse.

At every bay, every gap between islands, every open-water crossing, we pause to assess. The two canoes rock in the waves. We paddle constantly to hold our place, keep our angle, while we consider the space, the direction and size of waves, the density of whitecaps. Each decision flirts with disaster, calculates risk. Capsizing is not an acceptable outcome. Capsizing would be a dire blow to our trip at best, immediately life threatening at worst. These decisions are, at once, mundane and profoundly important. They come up half a dozen times a day.

Every morning I sit by the fire, feeding the flames with tiny driftwood, sipping coffee, and take the wind's measure. I feel for change, notice direction, study the waves, strategize a course on the map. No telling whether we'll be stopped after a mile or if we'll paddle for twenty.

At lunch stops, or when fatigue demands a break, we climb out of the hulls. Except for the one calm day, it is predominantly cold. Ruby usually demands a fire. It always seems like a hassle—collecting driftwood, finding tinder, getting a flame going in a gale—but it is always worth it.

The five of us jostle shoulders around the spark of flame, put a pot on for hot drinks, dry our socks. Ruby sings all the time. Songs she doesn't know the words to, old Beatles tunes, songs that aren't songs at all, only what she wants to say put to music. Harry Potter comes out. We stretch and bask in the flickering heat. The tiny circle of light, that primal energy, pulls us together. Against the sky, a long-tailed jaeger jousts in the gusts, hovering, coasting, whirling, looking for prey.

Sawyer is wracked by coughing fits several times a day. It has become clear that he probably has whooping cough. During the spring, an outbreak swept through the public schools in Bozeman. Sawyer developed some symptoms, but his test was negative. We put it down to viral infection. He continued to play soccer, go on runs. He has an inhaler that seems to help mitigate the attacks, but there are times when he is bent double, coughing so hard he pukes up bile, and it's been going on for months.

It crossed our minds to call off the trip because of his cough. Unfortunately, whooping cough is something you simply have to live through. There isn't much that can be done about it, no matter where you are. Also, we couldn't face calling off a trip that had taken so much to pull together, a trip that we'd likely never be able to recapture. Beyond that, Sawyer wouldn't have let us do it.

Six miles from the outlet on Ennadai, wind stops us again. It isn't the waves that force us to shore, but simple exhaustion, mental and physical. I pop four ibuprofen in my mouth. My elbow has a golf-ball-sized lump on it that won't go away.

When the kids were little, the first-aid kit bulged with Band-Aids to address the appalling number of "owies" that came along. These days, the dominant and most frequently used item is the large bottle of vitamin I.

The kids have discovered the immunity from injury offered by sphagnum moss. The land is carpeted by it, thick beds of soft, spongy, yielding ground, miles and miles on end. It is like living in a padded room.

They have taken to wearing their life jackets and running around, gang tackling each other. Sometimes the tackler has to be blindfolded. The rules are quite fluid. Five minutes after gaining shore, utterly spent and trudging into camp with the packs, they are scampering across the tundra, giggling maniacally, and piling on in writhing tangles of arms and legs.

Later, in the tent, I argue for a dawn dash.

"If it's calm when I wake up, we go. No breakfast, no fire. Let's get to the river, then stop to eat."

"Dad, you should check the watch before you wake everybody," Ruby says.

"Yeah, it's light at three o'clock," Sawyer agrees. "No getting up until at least four."

"Fair enough," I say. "But if it's good, let's really do it."

"I've got it!" Eli announces. He's been busy scribbling figures in his journal. "If we go forty days, we'll take 768,000 paddle strokes each."

Four

Today it felt like we paddled for 30 miles because of the huge headwind. The good thing was no mosquitoes. We stopped for about an hour waiting for the wind to settle down. We had a fire and read Harry Potter. Tonight we ate a big dinner of pesto.

—ELI, GROUP JOURNAL

The first thing I do when I wake is listen. The air is still, the tent fabric doesn't even flutter. Everyone else is deeply asleep, nestled in bags. Ruby has squirmed her way onto Marypat's sleeping pad. Three o'clock when I check the watch. I lie back, tuned to any change outside, calculating the day's challenges on the map I've studied enough to commit to memory.

This predawn hour is my weakest moment, my greatest time of doubt, the window through which what-ifs crawl in. What if we keep having to struggle this hard? What if the kids revolt? What if we pick wrong one time and a boat goes over? What if my elbow gets so bad I can't paddle?

At four o'clock I escape the mental torment and rouse the crew.

"It's totally calm, guys. Let's get off this lake!"

They all groan, but stir themselves, start pulling on long underwear.

"You sure, Dad?" Eli asks.

"Look how thick the bugs are on the door," I say. "No wind."

The bugs are fierce enough that we have camp struck and the boats loaded in record time. By now, every pack and dry bag has its niche. Rigging the boats, securing the gear, making sure things we need during the day are close to hand is a drill we handle as routinely as getting ready for school in the morning.

We angle across the same bay that was frothing whitecaps the night before. Mist lays against the water. A loon calls.

No one is very happy about the dawn dash. The kids are hungry, still drowsy, grumpy as hell, but the serene miles glide under the hulls. More to the point, by the time we land at the river outlet, where welcome current leads off around the corner, the air is stirring.

"Look at that," I say to Marypat. The lake is burred with gusts. Small waves start up. We look back to the horizon, think about the horizons beyond that, all the way back to the dropped binoculars at the start of End-less Ennadai.

"The dawn dash worked!" I crow.

Ruby is leaping from boulder to boulder on top of a rise overlooking the outlet. River-mauled rocks, glacially deposited rocks, lichen-scabbed rocks. She is outlined against the early day sky. Sawyer and Eli start after her, playing follow-the-leader, waiting for hot chocolate.

The Caribou Inuit who lived in this country called the Kazan River *Inuit Ku*, the "river of men." For thousands of years they sustained life here. They lived in small clusters, groups of a few dozen people made up of several extended families, strung out along the drainage. During the summer, they sheltered in tents of stitched-together caribou hides. In winter, they built igloos. They fished, they snared rabbits, they killed ptarmigan, they picked cranberries, but their lives were inextricably tied to the caribou.

Caribou provided the Inuit with their clothing, their food, the tallow they rendered into oil for cooking and light, their shelter, and many of their tools and implements—from sinew to bone buttons to kayak skins. *Tuktu* allowed these people to survive, and even flourish, in the center of subarctic austerity.

Other Inuit groups lived along the coasts, where their culture and lifestyle were wedded to the sea. For them, the caribou constituted only one facet of a livelihood based on an array of marine species. Their environment was harsh and difficult, but also diverse. For the Caribou Inuit, living wholly in the interior, it was the deer and the deer alone. Without caribou, life instantly became hollow and unsupportable.

From our vantage, their existence was rigorous beyond belief. They lived in a land without wood of any size, where they were utterly exposed to the elements. They were besieged by hordes of insects during the summers and overcome by unimaginable cold and dark through the long winters. They had to be cunning and resourceful, fashioning everything out of meager and fragile resources. Every single day was riveted to the most basic survival. If the deer didn't come one season, they starved.

Yet, by all reports, the traditional Inuit were people full of joy and generosity and humor. People who knew how to love and dance and feast and play. People of delicate artistry and grace, as well as toughness and endurance. They lived here, all around the shores we will paddle past—Ennadai Lake, Angikuni Lake, Yathkyed Lake, Forde Lake, Thirty Mile Lake. Their presence still whispers in the air, and their artifacts litter the land.

When the Europeans came, they arrived as fur traders, explorers, missionaries. Men of their time. Their appearance signaled the demise of the aboriginal lifestyle and threw the tenuous balance of existence off-kilter. It is a story we know so well, the story of modern western representatives armed with technological power and all manner of seductions, driven by concepts of property ownership and commerce that were utterly foreign, running smack into subsistence culture. The story of degradation, of duplicity, of trickery, of abiding ignorance, of sickness and alcohol and the empty solace of strange religions.

A story not of brotherhood, but of paternalism and dominance. Europeans did not come as equals, but as superiors. We offer you the hand of friendship, they said. We want to be partners in trade, to share your knowledge, to pay you to trap fur. We will help you. But our rules are now your rules.

The Caribou Inuit lived so remotely, at such a remove from the thrust of occupation and exploration, that the tragedy didn't finally play itself out until the mid-1900s. When I was born, half a century ago, the Inuit were still here, still living in the Stone Age, still clinging to a life woven from the land where the deer live.

In 1991, when Marypat was heavily pregnant with Eli, we paddled down a different arm of Ennadai Lake and descended a small, unnamed river flowing north. Our route that summer didn't regain the Kazan until Angi-kuni Lake. Only later did we learn that the river we followed was known to the Inuit as The River of the Dead, for all the people who perished of disease and starvation along it.

Marypat's pregnancy that summer made us appreciate the Inuit on a level we had only theoretically engaged before. They had embraced every aspect of life on the tundra—sickness, death, love, birth, starvation, flirta-tion, triumph. For us, being pregnant and vulnerable opened a window on that experience. Not the same, but a more profound connection than we had ever felt before.

We adopted what we called the Pregnancy Pace. When Marypat needed a nap, she laid back in the canoe and snoozed. On portages, we sauntered. In rapids, we always took the conservative route. The pregnancy erased the tendency to confront environmental challenges, to become adversarial, to take chances. We felt the presence of the Inuit around every bend.

Since that fork on Ennadai Lake, we have paddled new territory. As the pregnancy changed everything back then, our three young children do this time around. At the outlet, after a breakfast of hot cereal, the Kazan pulls us down the miles. There are small rapids we slap through, isolated pockets of stubby trees, strings of lakes peppered with tundra islands. Through all of it, the heady pulse of current we have so missed over the last week.

After the days of struggle, it feels like recess. We gloat over the miles going under us. We recline while the river does our work. Ruby entertains us by playing rock-and-roll air guitar.

During the afternoon, the river brings us alongside a large esker com-plex, a high set of sandy ridges deposited by the meltwater of retreating gla-ciers and winding across the tundra for miles, sinuous as giant snakes. Small pothole lakes rest on top of permafrost layers in the hollows. The kids run the crests with their arms out, like they are flying. Eli points out a snowshoe hare in a clump of vegetation.

"It looks as big as a donkey," he says.

He is falling prey to the strange lack of proportion that takes over in an environment without trees to provide relative scale. Sometimes a distant tree looks like a giant redwood, until you paddle up close and see that it's barely five feet tall.

"Look over here," Marypat says.

She has found a pile of rocks covering a cribwork of small logs. Along-side rests a weathered kayak paddle and some tent poles made of desiccated

SAWYER FLIES DOWN AN ESKER RIDGE DURING A FAMILY WALK AWAY FROM THE RIVER.

wood. We peer through gaps in the pile of rocks and make out human bones. A hip joint, some ribs, a femur.

"Someone is buried here," Marypat says. "This was their paddle. Whoever put them here spent a lot of time doing it. They carried all these rocks, found the wood, built this frame, picked out a spot overlooking the river. They left valuables here, things that meant something to whoever this was. Who knows how long it's been here."

Sawyer looks out across the space.

"It feels like a lonely place to be left," he says. "All by yourself, with nobody around who will visit."

"Where else should they be?" I say. "And it's powerful here. You could leave your bones in worse places."

By the end of the day the winds gust with such force that even on the current it's tough going. But we have gone some thirty miles, our biggest day yet. We've left Ennadai behind, made up for one of our windbound days.

It is with great satisfaction that we measure the day's route on the map with a piece of dental floss and write it into the group journal. Two or three of us go through the ritual to double-check accuracy. On the inside flap of the journal I've listed each day's mileage and am keeping a running tab of our average, a math lesson the kids pay close attention to.

The wind dies while we cook dinner. Predictably, the blackflies come out in swarms. We take up the mealtime bug posture. Each of us finds a rock to stand on, facing whatever breeze we can detect, gaining a bit of height, and shovels food from our bowls. Food that is spiced with little morsels of insect protein. In the first days we scrupulously plucked out the dead bugs, but anymore, they just go down the hatch.

Marypat and I clean dishes, stow everything, cover the gear with the tarp, scan the camp for odds and ends, check that the boats are tied up. Before we dive into the tent and smash the bugs that come with us, we pause to look around. The eskers we climbed gleam in the distance. The wide river powers around an upstream bend, rippling and muscular. A bank of dark cloud squats on the horizon, perhaps an ominous sign, but we leave the tent fly open for ventilation.

Much later, in the semidarkness that passes for night, we both wake to the sound of rain. Still rising to the surface of consciousness, I fumble out the screen door to zip the back of the fly closed. Marypat takes the front. All I can see in the momentary glance outside is solid gray sky.

This night we are next to each other. The kids have devised a sleeping rotation so that no one has to sleep against the tent wall on consecutive nights, and that allows each of them a turn between us. The upshot is that we get to snuggle together once every fourth night or so.

The kids are sound asleep. Marypat and I grope for each other through zippers and sleeping bag liners. There has been no opportunity for intimacy this trip, and little energy for it.

Outside, rain ticks against the tent fabric. Wind gusts through our camp. The river rustles past. I think of the life out there, taking cover, huddling together, or moving stoically about its business through the damp night. Sandhill cranes, arctic foxes, wolverines, grizzly, wolf, golden eagles. Each life—its intensity, its small, meaningful flame. Our lives, cupped under the storm in a shelter of sheer fabric.

We hold each other in the middle of the pile of our family, saying nothing. Our lovemaking is furtive, muffled, quick.

I think of all the stolen, crowded passion that goes on in the world. In the extended-family tenements of Kabul, in the sleeping rooms of Belize, the thatch huts of Cambodia. I think of the Inuit in their summer tents or on the snow sleeping benches in igloos under piled blankets of caribou hide.

After we met, when it became clear that we were serious about each other, Marypat set one of her conditions. "I'm going to have children," she said. When it came time to make good, however, we couldn't do it. That failure, lasting through years that were punctuated by miscarriages and the monthly emotional roller coaster of defeat, slowly debilitated us. We drifted through the seasons. Sadness seeped into the corners of our love.

Marypat is not ambitious about career or profession. She has her goals, the themes that form the foundation of her self-concept—art, adventure, friendship, exercise. She has more energy than almost anyone I can think of. But professional ambition has never been part of the equation. Ambition to have children, to be a mother, on the other hand, was fundamental. When we couldn't pull it off, it was like a trapdoor into despair opened beneath her.

I am convinced that what gave us Eli was another year spent in the wilds of the North. We took on that fourteen-month expedition because we didn't know what else to do, how to get off the cycle of frustration and sadness, how to move ahead. Halfway through the winter, it happened.

We knew better. We'd been down that road before. It had always led to miscarriage. We didn't even mention it to each other for the first three months. We didn't talk about names, plans, hopes, anything. But that time, it took. Months passed, the first trimester went by, Marypat's belly rounded out, she got nauseous in the mornings.

One morning that March, with the river barely starting to thaw a path into the bay and the jack pine forest still carpeted with snow, Marypat looked up from a drawing she was working on and into the huge, liquid eyes of a female otter. The otter had come all the way from the bay, sliding across the snow, up onto our porch, and reared up against the window frame to look at Marypat.

Three feet apart, without a sound, they looked into each other's eyes. Then the otter wallowed over to a neighboring vacant cabin and disappeared underneath. There, in the following weeks, she gave birth to her litter of pups, after first acknowledging Marypat's presence.

Coincidence? It didn't feel like it. It felt like recognition and congratulations.

The summer of Marypat's pregnancy we would lie together in the tent and feel the baby move. "Check this out," Marypat would say and take my hand to her belly, where the restless elbows and knees and feet of our child rummaged around. "It's really active tonight."

I remember feeling that urgent life, that insistent movement. Marypat was transformed by it, and not only physically. She developed an air of preoccupation, as if she were constantly listening, interacting, engaged in a way that rendered me a spectator.

I sensed the momentous change coming toward me, lying on the ground with my gravid partner while the raucous cries of arctic terns rang outside in the summer night.

Here, under the spitting sky, a decade and a half later, we hold each other close, flanked by our sleeping children. No telling what the morning will bring, but it is snug and delicious being buttoned up tight against a storm, drifting off to sleep in a tent anchored in the middle of tundra sea.

Five

It started raining in the middle of the night. Now it's a steady downpour with constant wind. We huddle under the tarp drinking hot drinks and getting ready to cook up a breakfast of eggs, sausage, and bannock. Al and I got up earlier and had a cup of coffee together, nice alone time. The rain continued nonstop all day, very gray. I hope we can move tomorrow, deeper into the barrens.

—MARYPAT, GROUP JOURNAL

As usual, I am first up. A little rain and cold isn't going to stop us. We'll snap the decks over the load, dress for it, keep our momentum going. I wrestle up the tarp to cook under, pile rocks on the stakes to guy it out. Wind bows the fabric, straining against the ropes.

When we calculated fuel supplies, we planned on wood cook fires for half the expedition, or twenty days. Even on the tundra there is dead willow, driftwood that comes downstream, sticks that line the high-water mark. The farther north we travel, the more tenuous fuel becomes, but cooking on fires saves us the substantial weight and bulk of a dozen stove canisters. It's this kind of strategic decision that avoids the prohibitive extra expense of a fly-in resupply. This morning, though, it's too wet to struggle with starting a fire and I want the protection of the tarp, so I set up the stove and start a pot of water.

I'm brewing the second cup of coffee by the time Marypat joins me. "Looks a little iffy," she says.

"I know it," I grumble. "Let's get the kids up in a bit, have a hot breakfast, then decide."

By the time that happens, the day is raw and cold. Wind punches at the tarp, roars across the river. Rain, almost sleet, drives sideways. The Kazan is the color of metal.

The five of us scrunch together under the creaking tarp fabric, leaning against packs, sitting on folding camp chairs. Another round of hot drinks—cocoa for the kids, coffee and tea for the adults. Everything has been carefully calculated in our menu, but it is already clear that we will be short on hot chocolate. Coffee, on the other hand, we have in relative abundance, a disparity the kids bring to our attention.

"Looks like there's three bags of coffee for every bag of cocoa," Eli says, after searching through the drink sack.

"Sorry, you guys," I say. It's a shortfall I feel guilty about. "Cocoa is really tough to estimate. It looks like a huge bag of the stuff, but it goes really fast."

We dried most of our food in the months before departure. The food dehydrator hummed almost constantly, week after week—tomato sauce, chili, dried fruit of every variety, eggs, jerky, vegetables, precooked meals. It saved us a tremendous amount of money. It also cut substantially the weight and bulk of food, although you'd never know it by the food packs. Equally important, it allows us to vary the menu and control meal ingredients.

Our summer menu rotates a series of seven or eight dinners, including corn chowder, chili and mashed potatoes, spaghetti, and pesto. At lunch, we choose between half a dozen different dried fruits that complement crackers and cheese, bannock and hummus, or peanut butter and jelly. Every four or five days, we get scrambled eggs for breakfast. For the most part, we eat as well as we do at home.

Despite an extra round of hot drinks, it is cold enough that after breakfast we bundle back into the tent and cozy into sleeping bags. Everyone has staked out one of the mesh pockets sewn into the tent fabric for their stash of personal supplies. Journals, books, maps, colored-pencil boxes, various treasures. Ruby has already amassed a bristling collection of feathers. Eli has a tiny caribou antler poking from his pouch.

Ruby asks me for my pocketknife. She has started to notch a stick to count the days, like Eli.

It is a testament to all the weather delays that we finish Harry Potter, a book I thought might last all trip. Eli immediately starts rereading it. We have taught the kids how to play cribbage on a small travel set. Sawyer takes two games out of three from me.

Whenever hunger insists or boredom builds, we return to the tarp, fire up the stove for hot drinks or another meal, take the day's measure. The storm is unrelieved. "This is no time to be on the water," I mutter, to no one.

Back in the tent, the kids start wrestling around, releasing energy. Now and then they bash against the walls.

"Listen, you guys," I shout. "I know it's hard to hang out, but this is the deal. There is nothing we can do about it. And you have to be careful. Imagine what it would be like if the zipper breaks. How would it be to have no place to escape the bugs? It's like dropping those binos—one little thing. Then the tent rips, or the zipper separates, or we lose a knife. This is not a place that will forgive our mistakes."

"Okay," says Marypat, when I've wound up my rant. "Let's start the next book."

Although the kids aren't avid readers in school, they love being read to. At home, we read out loud while they lie on the floor and draw. In the tent, they'll listen as long as someone will keep turning pages.

I've gotten to the point that I rarely bring a book along at all. On too many trips I've brought home books unopened. The trip experience is too involving for me to crave an escape. If I need diversion, I study the maps or write in my journal. A quadrant of topographic map has endless possibilities. For long periods I can sit still and do nothing but poke at the fire, look at the sky, watch the river flow past. It is a meditative state I am utterly incapable of in town.

The traditional Inuit had no concept of linear time analogous to our ticking clocks. For them, days blended together in a matrix of sunsets, storms, spring floods, winter blizzards, the coming and going of birds, feasts, starvation, birth. The passage of experience was fluid and layered. No second hand kept count of the rhythm of their lives.

Clocks emerged out of sedentary, agrarian cultures as a way to keep track of planting and harvests. Later, clocks were the mechanism by which industrial economies, demanding a workforce tied to an unbending, predictable, easy-to-manage daily schedule, were regulated.

In the slippery world of quantum physics, one of the things no one has been able to definitively prove is the existence of clock time. In that frontier where shapes shift and multiple events happen simultaneously, where things we assume are solid and immutable turn ephemeral and insubstantial, time does not punch a clock.

There are accounts of traditional Inuit enduring the long, cold, starving winter months by sliding into a state of semihibernation. Their breathing slowed, along with their heart rates. They didn't eat or drink. They slipped away, their forms sitting quiet in the dark corners of igloos. Days went past, weeks.

In that culture, there are stranger things still. The matter-of-fact acceptance of spirit travel, for example. Shape-shifting—the notion that a person's spirit might leave the shell of body and go places, perhaps inhabiting another form, such as a bear or a wolf or a walrus. They are said to put on the coat of another animal's skin.

A person's spirit might enter that space for a time, the body of a caribou, let's say, and exist there, learn lessons, and then return to share the wisdom in the human world. This is not hyperbole, not metaphor, but as real as boarding a plane and spending a weekend in Paris is for us. I don't pretend to understand it, but here, buffeted by wind, with the slide of current outside, the ticking of time is increasingly irrelevant.

So our day slips past in the grayness of storm, caught together in the shuddering tent. And another night. At first light it is still raining, but I am up anyway. The weather is the same. The wind-hammered tarp leans against me while I brew coffee.

Time may be ephemeral, perhaps contrived, but we have a deadline to keep, only so much food to sustain us, and a great many miles to cover.

The maddening thing about wind is its unpredictability. It might die in the time it takes me to make coffee. It might spring up out of calm from nowhere. It might last a week or an afternoon. We could load up and be blessed with calm for days or load up and become hypothermic around the corner. There is nothing to be gained from frustration, but frustration rises up.

Things are still uncertain when we pack up in a cold drizzle. Leaving has the feel of abandoning home. It requires overcoming the magnetism of the known. We have been warm and dry and relatively comfortable here, in spite of the weather. Packing up is strangely poignant and difficult, full of portent.

A few breaks tear through the clouds, but the wind is unabated. All of us wear long underwear, wool hats, full rain gear, neoprene paddling mitts. The river is dark and ruffled, our red boats the only splash of color in the muted world.

For six miles we struggle against a steady headwind down a flatwater narrows. The shoreline inches by, our arms grow leaden with the work, and we are still cold. At the end, a sharp rapid funnels out through a pinch of rock. We sneak the right side, staying clear of the chaotic waves and the most turbulent current.

At a low, waterworn point of rocks, the kids demand a break, and Ruby demands a fire. The five of us scatter, picking up driftwood, wrestling dead willow branches from the ground, finding wisps of dry tinder. The wood is wet, but with the help of the resinous bark of dwarf birch twigs, a flame gathers force, becomes a fire, and we circle round, warming hands, crowding close.

It is gray, cold, wet, and windy, but Ruby is singing. She breaks into an air guitar solo, jumping around the flames in her pink polka-dot rain gear.

"What I like about you," she yells, between riffs. "You really know how to dance. When you go up, down, jump around, Talk about true romance. Yeah!"

She adds some Elvis leg shimmy.

"Rock on, Ruby," Sawyer yells from his perch on a rock ledge.

"When you're whispering in my ear, Tell me all the things that I want to hear, Well it's true. It's what I like about you. Yeah, yeah, yeah yeah. It's what I like about you." She arches her back, throws in a final chord, bows low before us.

"Thank you, Detroit," intones Eli.

"Whaddaya bet that's the first time the ptarmigan around here have heard that one?" I say.

The day finally turns nice around evening, when it's time to stop. Just as we pull up to a broad, sandy point, Sawyer notices something on the opposite bank.

"There's either a bear over there, or a big, black cow," he says.

A dark shape moves along a band of willows. "If we had binos," I glance at Eli, "we could see what it is."

"Looks like a musk ox," says Marypat, "but it could be a bear too. Let's paddle over."

It is a musk ox, our first, and the most southerly sighting we've ever made. The shaggy beast feeds on the willows, rubs against the brush, oblivious to us. The canoes are ten feet from him before he turns. Marypat clicks photos. Sawyer starts to backpaddle. Even then, the prehistoric-looking animal, roughly the size of a bison, ambles along the sand, grazes here and there, finally heaves himself up the bank and walks off, stopping once or twice to gaze back at us.

Day 10, and by far our nicest camp. The sun comes out. The wind dies to a breeze. The bugs are light. We lay things out to dry, wash bodies and hair, air the sleeping bags. Ruby and Sawyer shed their clothes, brave the cold water, make cities of sand, run naked down the shore tossing driftwood at each other.

Eli stays aloof, reading his book. He is perfectly capable of goofiness, even seems tempted by it, but he has started to separate himself. After a while, he puts the book down and begins an elaborate sand structure. He has an artist's eye and that urge for creative expression. At home, he'll spend hours doodling a drawing in his room when he is supposed to be studying for a math test.

"What the Barrens need," says Marypat, "is children."

She's right. I have had the same thought. Their playfulness, their laughter, seems to fill a void. It sounds strange, but it feels as if the landscape responds to them. It feels as if that human innocence and joy is an energy the land rises up to embrace.

Watching my children, naked and laughing, splashing in the shallows, or sculpting sand, I conjure the ancient encampments, where Inuit children played their games, chased each other between skin tents, called across the space in the long summer night.

On other trips, adult trips, the Barrens have been powerful, awesome, grand, brutal, endless, forbidding, intense, magical. Never a land for play. This evening, though, it quickens in response, perks up, as if it has been aching for it.

There are times—like at our next camp, on a round, willow-encircled island partway down Dimma Lake, after another day beating for nearly twenty miles against a wind—when a kind of giddiness overtakes us.

Our canoes are pulled up, turned over. The lake spreads away, blends into the sprawling land. Clouds tow their shadows across the open miles. Two semipalmated plovers feed above the waterline.

We declare a cocktail hour, only our second one. Marypat goes off to pee and Ruby tries to sneak around behind her with the camera. The boys are casting Harry Potter spells on each other with wands of willow, dodging and ducking behind glacial boulders.

"*Expelliarmus!*" Eli shouts. Sawyer does a shoulder roll behind a rock.

We are in deep, hundreds of miles from anywhere civilized, having scratched our way across the trackless space. We are utterly alone, and feel that way. *Isolation* is too small a word for this. An unequivocal embrace of humility is the only possible response.

At the same time, we are full of ourselves, strangely exhilarated. We have come here by dint of our strengths and skills and paddle strokes. We have fought conditions, taken what the land and weather have granted us, made our way with competence—created fire and built shelter and traveled forward against adversity, found joy in our smallness. We are charged with our capabilities.

Power and humility, competence and meekness, that strange juxtaposition, and it makes us silly, proud, half drunk.

When we go to bed, I feel uncharacteristically reckless. Maybe it's the cocktail, but I don't even cover the gear with our tarp. I leave the tent fly wide open. I don't want to jinx it by saying anything, but I notice that the wind has shifted out of the south. If it holds, it will be a tailwind.

Six

This morning we woke up to misty fog. When we left the fog rose a lot, so that was good. Me and my dad got my multiplication down. I know all of them. We were on lake all the way, it seemed like. When we got to camp we got to see 10 musk ox from a ways away.

—RUBY, GROUP JOURNAL

The opposite of giddy is what I feel when I jolt awake to the sound of a hard rain shower and have to scamper, naked, outside to cover gear and secure the tent.

It doesn't help that one of my eyes is gunked shut. I've noticed some infection for a day or two, put it down to the irritation caused by one of many blackflies that have flown into my eyes or to the deet additive in our bug dope, some of which has certainly made its way under my eyelids.

We have some antibiotic drops in our first-aid kit, and I squeeze a couple in, lying back down between Sawyer and Eli, who are either sleeping deeply or doing a good job of faking it.

In late October 1991, two months after our return from our second trans-Canadian expedition and the pregnant summer on the Barrens, Eli was born in the bedroom of our home in Montana. It was snowing outside. Marypat had been in labor for most of twenty-four hours, through a long night. Our midwife, Vicki, stayed for it all. One of Marypat's sisters, Nancy, was there, along with our friend Ursula.

I had come to the point of not believing there was a baby in there, despite the periodic reassurance of a heartbeat check. I think Marypat had her doubts too. Hour after hour, the waves of contractions came and went. She moaned and turned, deep in the throes of this most personal trial.

But then the crown of head was visible, a whorl of hair, and that impossible magic act began, squeezing a human body out of an opening that starts out the size of a half-dollar coin.

Then his head, that tiny, glistening face emerging from the dark, muffled flesh into the dazzle of light and air.

"Here," Vicki said to me, after she'd made sure the umbilical cord wasn't wrapped around his neck. "Come hold the head. One more push will do it."

It felt both awkward and holy, putting my hand beneath the untouched skull of my child. It had no weight, sat in my palm, smaller than a softball. Then Marypat strained, arched her back, gave a final, desperate shout, and the body slithered out in a single, fast gush.

I think Marypat kept crying out in unintelligible relief. I held my son, still attached to the womb. He looked absolutely serene. He was not wizened or wrinkled. His face was smooth. He didn't cry. His blue eyes were open and steady. Vicki wrapped him in a soft towel, lifted him gently to Marypat's breast. He locked on to the blue eyes of his mother. Marypat was weeping and laughing, exhausted and energized, holding her child of the North.

No telling what Eli had made of those winter months in the sixteen-by-twenty-foot cabin on the shores of Lake Athabasca. The weeks of forty-below cold, the returning sun, the first calls of geese. Or what response he had, from inside Marypat, to the lift and sway of waves, the pumping adrenaline in whitewater, the strain of portages.

Who knows what impact all the miles in a canoe and nights on the ground and the subtle influence of our days together in the wilds had on this baby who had been thrumming along, burgeoning, at that remove. It meant something, how he was nurtured by our passage, something unquantifiable that will be played out in all the choices that come his way and in the matrix of who this boy is.

Now, Eli rolls over in his sleeping bag. He breathes his morning breath at me. He takes up almost as much floor space as I do. I can still beat him in an arm wrestle, but it's getting to be a close thing.

Awkward and holy is what it still feels like, this relationship.

The sky today is rowdy with giants. Dark-bellied thunderheads roll through, towering columns of cloud. Sunstruck and dazzling, black and brooding, charged with electricity, potent with wind.

Near the end of Dimma Lake, one of them hits us. We have been watching it come, hoping it might pass by but hurrying into rain gear all the same. Rain strikes in a sudden wallop, pounding the lake, pummeling our boats and bodies. It is deafening, an assault. The water turns black, waves spring up, slap at the hulls made of woven canvas and aluminum frames put together like Tinkertoys. We keep paddling, holding course, half blinded by the torrent. Sawyer hunches over in the bow, his head bent. He paddles on, but doesn't look up.

A mile later the sun is out, the land steams, we strip layers. A tailwind pushes us along. Everything is titanic. The land, the sky, the light, the clouds, the wind. At one point, we stop and raise the tarp to avoid being on the water in the presence of a lightning-filled monster, only to have it sail past—benign, beautiful, full of awful grace.

All day our canoes dodge under the jousting clouds. We are puny beyond thinking, yet we paddle almost thirty miles, camp on another island, make another willow twig fire, erect our shelter on another patch of moss, tie up the canoes for the night, mark our maps, make our notes, read out loud.

And the next day, the same.

At first light, the world is shrouded in mist. Everything drips, but I want the comfort of a fire. I go hunting for the innermost dead twigs of dwarf birch, sheltered at the center of low thickets. As I push through the wet undergrowth I think of bear, of caribou, of the women and children whose daily chore it was to wrest fuel from the meager land.

Black bears stick to the trees. Polar bears rarely come inland from Hudson Bay. The Barren Lands grizzly is the only species on this tundra. A smaller cousin to the grizzlies of Montana, they flourish here, living off of caribou calves, bird eggs, berries, fish. We have come across tracks and scat here and there, but haven't seen one. Bear spray comes into the tent every night, stays close to hand in the boats, but these grizzly are reclusive, shy, uncontaminated by human contact. They are certainly a danger, but the few I've seen on former trips were running the other way at a good rate. I feel less vulnerable in a larger group, and the way the kids make noise, it's hard to imagine sneaking up on animals.

But there are moments, like this, with dew dripping, the sky drawn down close, the day early and cloaked, when the possibility of a bear rising up out of a clump of vegetation or from a depression in the ground seems very real.

Bit by bit, a small fistful accumulates in my palm, tiny frail wands of wood wrapped in bark that take off like kerosene once you get them going. When I have a bunch the size of my head, I heap it carefully on the metal fire pan, cluster it loosely, and poke a match into the center. The pile steams and smokes, hisses. The flames are grudging, reluctant. I hunch over the flickering hope in fervent attention, as if in prayer.

Then the resin catches, the flames reach critical mass, roar into life, enough of a blaze to light the larger dead twigs of driftwood. When it is going strong, I lean back, find my folding backrest, organize the pile of wood close by, wait for coffee. I know that Marypat is smelling smoke and that she is reassured, comforted at the prospect. There is no solace like a warm fire and a simmering pot when the fog is down to the deck and the world is made of cloud.

The day brings more wind, more storm, more sky. The morning fog is swept away. The kids want to make Angikuni Lake, known to the Caribou Inuit as Great Lake. It feels like a benchmark in the trip, roughly a third of the way through.

Much of the day a side wind hinders us, so that Marypat and I have to paddle almost exclusively on one side of the canoes. My right arm starts to go numb during the afternoon. I try to switch but it's too hard to hold course. I get Eli to paddle on the same side when the winds are at their worst. I do my best to ignore the numbness, keep stroking. Long as I don't lose hold of the paddle shaft, I'm okay, I tell myself. I am on a pretty steady diet of ibuprofen at this point, along with eye drops a couple of times a day.

Several years back, I went over the handlebars of my bicycle when a car pulled out of an alley in front of me. I landed hard on my shoulder, separated the clavicle bone from the socket. Ever since, it has made some alarming sounds when I make certain motions. Perhaps the numbness, another symptom I've never experienced while paddling, has something to do with that injury. But maybe it's not that at all. Maybe it's nothing more than living with body parts that have fifty-two years' worth of mileage.

A mile from Angikuni, a lone musk ox appears on one shore and a herd of ten more dot the opposite hillside. We take it as a sign to stop. We're all very tired. The lake is in sight. We want grandstand seats to watch the wildlife.

By now, the drill is ingrained. One of us tends to the boats, turns them over, ties them up, stores paddles and life vests and other loose gear underneath. Two people set the tent up, blow up sleeping pads, arrange the bags according to the kids' strict rotation system. Two more set up the kitchen, hunt for wood, orient the fire pan to the wind, organize the food and cooking gear.

MUSK OX ALONG THE KAZAN, PREHISTORIC BEASTS IN THEIR ELEMENT.

All the while the musk ox forage across the broad slope, dark boulders of fur, unrecognizable intelligence. These animals live in the high latitudes, above tree line, year-round. They are made for the winter that goes on nine months of every year. Their fur, called qiviut, is the ultimate insulation, so effective that snow won't melt on their backs. Their only predator, besides man, is the wolf. A plate of horn as much as four inches thick is plastered across the fore-head, parted in the center, and sweeps out into lethal points on each side.

They look like relics of the Ice Age, contemporaries of the woolly mammoth. In fact, they were. Fossil evidence shows them mingling with saber-toothed cats and mammoths during the Pliocene. Members of the goat clan, musk ox once numbered in the hundreds of thousands and populated the high Arctic from Alaska to Greenland.

Then, in a period of less than a century, the musk ox were hunted nearly to extinction by explorers, whalers, and local hunters. Only a nation-wide ban on hunting saved the last remnants, just several hundred individu-als. Since then, musk ox populations have been rebounding. Estimates put their current numbers in northern Canada at roughly one hundred thousand.

The warming climate is bringing new challenges in the North. Para-sites that plague musk ox are enjoying longer life cycles and inflicting more-prolonged infections on herds, killing off weaker and older individuals. The shifting climate may also exacerbate the worst enemy musk ox face: thick crusts of ice. When thawing temperatures are followed by hard periods of frost, a thick rind of ice forms on the surface of winter snow. Musk ox can't paw through the armor to the sparse vegetation that sustains them through the rigors of winter. In a matter of weeks, they starve by the thousands.

We watch them all through dinner, while they move slowly across the hill. Several calves cavort among the cows. One or two of the adults lie down. Eventually the small herd files over the brow of the summit and out of sight.

Eli walks inland to a huge glacial erratic boulder. He climbs to the top and stands there against the sky—a bit of flesh-and-blood topography— looking at the lone musk ox bull on our side, still in view. He is wearing a wind shirt of mine that I've had for twenty-five years. It may be my favorite piece of outdoor gear, but it has gotten a tad snug. The faded fabric glows in the orange light of the long twilight.

I know exactly how the cuff of that wind shell feels against his wrist. I imagine the emotions stirring in him, that urgency of youth, the restlessness in the marrow, the plans that fire him, the thoughts crossing his mind as he looks out over the wilderness. Space and more space and more after that.

I can't say how crushing it is to rise to another day of wind. I have a little incantation I keep repeating to myself. *Take what the land gives you*, I think. So far, what we have been given is pretty damn meager.

Angikuni opens to the north, and it is flecked with whitecaps. We pad-dle into it anyway, seeing what we can do. There is a string of three islands that might provide shelter, as long as we can make the crossings between them. The decks are snapped over the load. We are wearing rain gear and long underwear.

The waves are high, but doable. We angle the canoes into them, quarter the wind, crab across the gap, the hoods of our coats snapping in the breeze. The sky is leaden and low. When we finally gain the lee of the first island, the wind is cut off. We stroke leisurely through the quiet water, another world. We forget the intensity of battle.

Then we emerge again, the waves rise. The canoes slam into the snarling march of water, white with foam. Three times we do this, alternating between unbelievable calm and full-pitched battle, until we round the corner of the final, large island and confront the unobstructed force of wind.

On another strip of rocky shore we climb stiffly out of the boat hulls, collect the odds and ends we need. The tarp goes up. We manage another fire. A drizzle falls on us. Marypat lies down to nap. I pore morosely over the map, study the stretch of open water to get across before current takes hold again, dozens of miles away. Only a few miles from our desultory bivouac we will rejoin the trail Marypat and I paddled that summer when Eli was our stowaway. A few miles that, now, are impossible.

Eli gets bored, leaves the shelter of the tarp, and starts building an *inukshuk*. *Inuksuit* are the rock cairns that dot this tundra landscape, left by the Inuit. They marked their trails, their grave sites, their favorite camps, the places where caribou crossed rivers. They are artistic, whimsical, enduring, and functional. The way the top rock leans might indicate the direction of travel. A window of rock might frame the distant objective. A line of rock piles constructed to resemble human profiles might be designed to spook herds of caribou to a specific ambush site.

Eli's is a tall spire with a top rock cocked at a jaunty angle. I snap a picture of him posed next to it, yellow rain gear against gray sky. Ruby is singing again. Sawyer finds some remarkable mushrooms with broad, flat tops. The three of them spontaneously develop a competition involving mushrooms decorated with bits of lichen, cranberry leaves, twigs. They bring their creations to the fire, set them on the grill as if they are culinary presentations, and ask me to judge them.

This silliness is irresistible. I stow the maps. They parade their "entrees" past me, grill them up as they extol their delectable qualities, line them up for judging, charge off to find more. Marypat naps through it all.

At some point, the sky seems to lighten. We convince ourselves that we can paddle on. It is never clear how much wishful thinking this decision making is infused with. I am much more prone to that seduction than Marypat is. She can nap a day away, curled up on the ground, cozy as a dog waiting for its daily walk.

This time the going is difficult, but just possible. We use the land to shelter us when we can, struggle along when we can't, arms tingling with the exertion.

"Mom and I camped right there," I point to a small island. "I remember how I had to help her out of the tent in the morning, give her a hoist."

"That was the hardest thing," Marypat says. "All that getting up off the ground. Once I was up, or in the boat, I was fine."

We don't make many miles. The waves are hills of water, freckled with white, rolling down the miles at us. Even if we can manage the danger, our progress is agonizing.

On the gravelly shore, just above the wave line, we unload the boats. Eleven grueling miles from the camp below the musk ox. Eleven stuttering miles to add to the lengthening column and figure into the average. Marypat and I find ourselves alone. The kids are humping packs up to the campsite. We face each other on opposite sides of a canoe.

"This is way harder than I ever thought it would be," Marypat admits.

I nod. "I don't remember it being such a battle," I agree. "And the bugs are worse than I ever recall."

"It's just hard," Marypat says. "The paddling is hard. The kids are great, but we end up doing most of the chores and cooking. Even when I was pregnant, it never felt like this much work. And I'm tired like I never was when we could paddle together."

"I don't even want to start on how creaky and sore I've been feeling," I say. "I don't like to admit it, but fifty-two isn't at all like thirty-eight."

We hear a shout from the kids.

"Look at those goofballs!"

All three of them are naked, perched on a rock over some deep water. It is Ruby's doing, no doubt. She has dunked in every lake, and this time she's talked the boys into it. One after another they cannonball into the water, whoop in shock, and clamber back out. They hotfoot around, shake themselves, scurry back into their long underwear.

"But we're making it," Marypat says, a tone in her voice that makes me think of her on the rugby pitch. "We're here again and we're making it!"

Eli makes the plunge into frigid water, at Ruby's insistence.

Seven

Started the day with more blackflies than ever. So many you couldn't see your clothing. It was a rainy, long day, so no new animals. We had a very long lunch after going 18 miles. The end of the day turned very windy and cold, but pleasant under the Megamid tarp.

—ELI, GROUP JOURNAL

"I'm making dinner," Eli announces.

"Really?" both Marypat and I chorus.

"Yeah, I want pesto and I'll make it," he says.

It's as if he overheard our private confession down by the canoes and has stepped up. Marypat and I decide it's time for another cocktail night. We recline in our chairs, open a bag of nuts, hover and offer advice as Eli goes about cooking the meal.

"This is the pattern of this trip," Marypat observes. "The mornings are terrible weather and the evenings are beautiful. In between it's a crapshoot. It's been that way the whole time."

Eli pulls dinner together with surprising competence, serves it up with a nonchalance that doesn't quite mask his pride. He even delivers our bowls to us and remembers to stoke the fire before he sits down to eat.

Ruby and Sawyer are not to be left out. They take on the after-dinner pot of tea and the dish-cleaning chore. Sawyer collects extra wood and stows it under the tarp for the morning fire. It is a small thing, this dinner two weeks in, but it feels like a breakthrough. And it is remarkable how our mood can swing as abruptly as the weather.

Better still, the next morning dawns benign and sunny, with the hint of a tailwind. It may be only the second or third day we've gone without long underwear. The downside is that the bugs are with us, even on the water. Much of the time we are forced to wear head nets. In all our trips north, the water has been a safe zone where bugs don't venture. Not this time. A mile from shore, blackflies keep at us, just enough that we can't do without netting.

Nobody complains. The miles go under the hulls. Once again we eat lunch in the canoes, at rest on the quiet lake, avoiding the intensity of bugs on land. The kids recline on the load. Marypat goes to her knees, leans across a pack in front of her to relieve her lower back.

Some people become more and more plain looking the longer they are out on an expedition. The strain shows in their faces. They lose the manufactured glow of daily showers, cosmetics, nice clothes. Marypat becomes more beautiful. She embraces this life. Her exuberance and joy flush her cheeks, light her eyes, make her laugh. She thrives here—even over the long haul, even when conditions become epic—and it shows.

For long stretches after lunch, while the shoreline unreels, I talk about what it was like to spend the winter in our little cabin on Lake Athabasca or about trips my family took when I was young. On a calm day, unrelieved monotony is the foe, the endless repetition of strokes, the sluggish scroll of landmarks going past.

We poke through a gap between low, rounded islands, then cross the mouth of a deep bay. I use a distant white patch of beach to aim at when no other landforms help me keep on track. Gulls fly overhead. The sun is warm against my skin. After lunch, I have to fight to keep my eyes open. I want nothing more than to lie down and nap.

At the same time, I have to keep myself in check. I want to push for miles, get all the way across. The wind could spring up at any moment. We make crossings, draw a straight line from point to point, greedy for progress. Marypat repeatedly falls behind. I know it is demoralizing to always play catch-up, but I have to force myself to lighten up, let her take the lead.

Then my canoe seat breaks. I shift my weight and one of the leg brackets, a plastic clip, snaps off. The seat suddenly sags. Marypat paddles up. We work at a repair with duct tape.

"You're hard on gear," she says.

"I just shifted in my seat!" I protest. "This shouldn't have snapped off."

We switch boats, paddle on. Marypat perches gingerly on the patched-together seat. I am focused on the far side of the lake. We will get there. But the kids are exhausted by the time we do. All of us are. Our butts are sore, our arms ache, Eli has been taking his share of ibuprofen for a sore shoulder. But we are within half a dozen miles of the river outlet and have made all the major crossings before we give in.

It's the warmest day we can remember. All of us strip down, brave the clouds of blackflies long enough to bathe. When camp is set, the five of us walk up through the hummocky ground to a glacially scraped bedrock ridge. Along the way we collect dead sticks, small, dried pieces of precious fuel.

An *inukshuk* marks the top of the ridge, another one squats on the horizon. Small lakes and streams dot the interior. I am always route finding through these vistas. Up that stream, across that lake, portage over that bridge of land, across another lake, and there you are—somewhere new and brimming with potential. All of it is country the Inuit tramped, perhaps where they located their summer camps, maybe along a caribou migration route. They connected all the dots.

Angikuni Lake stretches off, all the unruffled miles we stroked across and that seemed so unlikely one day earlier. The shimmering lake blends into a vague pastel horizon line. No one is out there. This was once the heart of Inuit culture, full of summer camps, this very lake. Today, but for our spot of color on one shore, it is empty of humanity.

As evening comes on, the bugs intensify. I don't know how bug cycles work, but it seems like this single warm day after all the cold and wind we've had has provoked an outburst, as if millions of blackflies have been hunkering in the mosses just awaiting their chance to come out and play. They have been bad before, but never like this. They coat the arms of our jackets, the legs of our pants.

Eating is almost impossible. They ping off our faces, fly into the food, crawl everywhere, looking for an opening. Even with my head net on, they crawl in through the little gaps in the elastic and fill the inside of the netting. I keep grabbing the mesh and making a fist, collecting piles of blackfly carcasses I have to dump out.

The routine for getting into the tent requires one person to dive in, kill the dozens of bugs that came with, make sure everything is organized, and then station him or herself at the zipper. One at a time, the rest of us line up about twenty feet off, do our best to shake off bugs, then sprint for the tent. The insider zips the door open just long enough for each of us to dive through, then zips it shut again. Despite the system, by the time all of us make the dive, the bug life inside is only slightly diminished from the clouds outside.

For the next twenty minutes, we each take a quadrant of tent and go into bug-killing mode, until the corpses litter the floor and the tent fabric is smeared with pureed blackfly guts. Finally we can strip off clothes and relax, mark our progress on the maps, gloat over the good day.

Everyone lies on their bellies, writing in journals. Eli has started drawing birds, copying illustrations from the field guide in colored pencil. He has some artistic talent. All the kids are more prone to draw than to write.

"I'm going to do a caribou with a big rack and put birds all over the antlers," Eli says.

On the outside of the tent fabric, blackflies congregate in moving mats, coating entire sections of the fly in solid masses. They make little continents of single-minded obsession all over the tent.

"Where else would you ever experience bugs like this?" Marypat says, trying to manage some positive spin on this remarkable onslaught. Nobody even responds.

The next day we are weatherbound again. It is cold, squalls gust through, waves pound against the shore. The bugs may be beaten down, but we don't even discuss going on. The topic in the tent is what route we will follow for the remainder of the trip.

We have come prepared for several options. We can follow the Kazan out to Baker Lake, where it joins the drainage of the Thelon near Hudson Bay. The other option is to choose a route out of Yathkyed Lake that will allow us to cut south, across a low divide into the Maguse River, and, from there, make our way to Hudson Bay near the village of Arviat.

The Maguse has the lure of new territory for Marypat and me. It is also a section of the Barrens we have long looked at exploring. The problem is that the various routes to gain the Maguse all require a fair amount of portaging, as well as some long stints on lakes. We have all the maps, including some larger-scale quads for the traverse sections.

Pretty quickly we discard one of the crossings, which could require as much as fifteen miles of portaging. A second possibility would entail far less portaging and drop us into the Ferguson River, but the connection to the Maguse would take us across a great many miles of open lake.

I think it is the most doable of the Maguse options, but Marypat and the kids have no interest in that much lake paddling.

"I don't think so," Marypat says. "It would be a nightmare for me."

Option three involves a hop from Yathkyed Lake into the Kogtok River. If the Kogtok has enough water, it looks like the easiest traverse. If it doesn't, we could be in for a long stretch of portaging and dragging before gaining adequate current and making our way to the Maguse, after which there would still be some large lake sections to work across.

We measure the distance of each route, estimate the percentage of lake paddling versus river paddling, count up the portage miles and multiply by 1.5 to account for the double carry that would be required. All of us scrutinize the two-dimensional sheets and squeeze mental images of real terrain out of them, based on what we have traveled through already.

"The Ferguson route has too many lakes," Marypat declares.

"The big portage route is too long. Fifteen miles, most of it portaging. That doesn't sound like fun at all," says Ruby.

We all agree that the Kogtok is the most likely possibility.

"Problem is," I say, "if we paddle the south shore of Yathkyed Lake to get there, then spend several days exploring the portage, and then decide that there isn't enough water and we have to go down the Kazan after all, we'll really be behind schedule. As it is, we've barely managed to approach our fifteen-mile-a-day average because of the weather, and we haven't had a single portage yet."

"I think we should do the Kazan," Eli says. "We came here to do my river, right? That's what I want to do."

Sawyer is the last to give up the unknowns. He has always had the most enthusiasm for physical challenges. He and Marypat are the ones who are most often up for that blend of adversity and potential reward. In this case, though, Marypat seems less than wholehearted. For Sawyer, giving up this possibility is really difficult.

A few weeks before we left for the expedition, I took the two boys out to dinner. These boys' night out dates are a sporadic tradition with us. The boys like it because they get to go out for a rare restaurant meal. Then they suffer through whatever topic I bring to the table. Marypat and Ruby accuse us of going out to talk about girls, but they're only partly right. We talk about being brothers, about friendship and loyalty, about the dynamics of locker rooms, whatever.

At the preexpedition dinner I asked them both what their biggest fear about the journey was. Predictably, Eli's was being away from his friends. Sawyer said he was most nervous about the big portage.

Then I asked what trip thing they were most excited about. "The big portage," said Sawyer, without hesitation.

I can see him working out the images of portaging across miles of mucky tundra under the weight of a forty-pound dry bag, doubled over with coughing fits. He is visibly torn. I admire his stubborn tenacity and his flaming hope for unexpected, breakthrough adventure.

"You know what," I say, after a prolonged silence. "You guys are pulling off an epic trip. I'd be surprised if many kids your age have ever done an expedition like this. I really don't think we need to prove anything by adding another challenge."

No one says anything for a moment, but then Sawyer nods. The decision is made. We are committed to the Kazan. Ruby leans over and nuzzles against him.

The next morning is gray, shrouded in mist and drizzle. Temperatures have warmed, and the blackflies are back. I watch a sparrow, just under the eve of the tent fly, feed on the thick masses of blackflies that swarm on the mosquito netting. The little bird keeps making small hops, gleaning bugs off the fabric, but there aren't enough sparrows in the Arctic to make a dent in the blackfly population.

If it weren't for the bugs, I tell myself, I'd be out there hustling up breakfast. The weather isn't great, but it isn't bad either. We can't be stopped by bugs. The sparrow keeps flitting against the tent fly. The blackflies shift and jostle against each other. Maybe they've just congregated under the tent, I think. Once I get out they won't be so bad.

Usually I'm pretty good at the Zen of bug tolerance. I settle myself, find that inner calm, lose the agitation that seems to attract bugs. I can reach a kind of equilibrium.

But this morning the blackflies are just as intense outside as they were on the tent wall. It doesn't matter whether I'm under the tarp or out in the open, they coat everything. I start the stove, get some hot cereal out, fill a pot with lake water. While I wait for the water to boil, I sit in my folding seat and work for that calm center. Blackflies crawl on the inside of my head net. When I look at my arms, they are moving with black fur. Once in a while I smear a swatch of bugs on my sleeve or pant leg. It feels like grease under my hand, a thick slime, satisfying and disgusting.

"How is it?" Marypat calls from the tent.

"You don't want to know. Stay inside. I'll bring you guys breakfast."

Normally we would never eat food in the tent. In bear country, food in the tent is a mortal sin. But this is not a normal morning.

I get the pot of hot cereal done, ladle it onto plates, add butter and brown sugar and a sprinkle of raisins, and deliver them through a slit in the tent door zipper.

"Don't you dare spill," I hear Marypat admonish.

My portion is literally equal parts cereal and blackfly protein. I admit that I consume the bugs with a certain predatory relish.

When we break camp, it is a full-on emergency evacuation. It requires a constant level of mental reassurance, a constant refusal to submit to the panic that would erupt if we think too long about how horrendous the bugs are. I keep up an internal dialogue. I'm loading the boat now, I say to myself. I'm setting the packs in, clipping them into the canoe. Now I'm getting the tent into its dry bag. The mental prattle keeps me on task, keeps me from being pulled into the appalling frenzy of bug life that is pelting me.

The hulls of the canoes are black and moving. The tent poles are coated in a thick paste of bug puree. Marypat takes a quick picture of the three kids with the cloud of bugs swarming around their netted faces. That brief moment with her head net off, just long enough to focus and snap, almost pushes her over the edge.

"Jesus, Mary, and Joseph," she yells. "Let's get out of here!"

We hurl ourselves into the canoes, paddle feverishly for open water. The bugs follow us. They slowly diminish with distance, but the day is sultry and warm and the swarms stay with us for miles. Periodically I remove my head net, wad it up in my hands to kill the blackflies on the inside, turn it inside out to dump the fistful of corpses, shake my head like a wet dog, and put it back on.

No one says this, but everyone is thinking that if the bugs stay this intense, we might not be able to cope.

Eight

We woke up to wind and cold, so we are windbound again. We were in the tent most of the day. Sawyer and I made a wind block. It is sweet I got some soft bird feathers. I thought it was musk ox fur, but it wasn't. We had a good dinner and met some guys.

—RUBY, GROUP JOURNAL

Every feature of the Barrens is a legacy of the glacial era. For thousands of years, a continent of ice more than two miles thick squatted on this part of North America, pulsing back and forth in slow advances and retreats—so much ice that it literally weighed the crust of the earth down, pushing it into the molten mantle by its sheer mass.

Since it melted, less than ten thousand years ago, the crust has been rebounding, rising, sluggishly recovering its balance like a floating cork. The rind of the planet has been buoying up a couple of centimeters a century, which is fast-paced drama when it comes to geology. And it continues.

Sheets of ice not only pushed the crust down, but worked the landscape like a bulldozer on steroids. Mountains planed flat, ridges scraped smooth, sets of islands like so much clay, lined up with the direction of glacial movement. In the ebb and flow of episodes, ice rasped away at the bedrock, dug depressions destined to be lakes, dropped erratic boulders the size of buildings, left the sand ridges of eskers. Glaciers polished acres of rock glassy smooth, left piles of debris in moraine deposits, streamlined ridges into drumlins, and littered the continent with kames, outwash plains, kettle topography, pingos, and other landforms idiosyncratic of ice. On the Barrens, where the bedrock is either laid bare or thinly covered with peat and gravel, the ice sheets might as well have melted yesterday, geologically speaking.

What remains of the Ice Age, besides the distinctive landforms, are the layers of permafrost. Often less than a foot below the surface, the ground is frozen hard year-round. It was permafrost that prevented the Inuit from burying their dead. The frozen ground keeps many lakes from draining away into the soil, locks up large concentrations of carbon in ice, dictates the vegetation that can grow.

The Arctic and subarctic regions are largely deserts. Wet as the ground is, full of lakes and rivers as the terrain is, most of the North above 60 degrees latitude gets less than ten inches of precipitation each year. Precipitation may be meager, but evaporation is even less robust. In fact, in the equation P−E (the difference between the annual amount of precipitation and evaporation), precipitation wins out, hence the profligacy of water in the tundra.

The delicate balance between precipitation and evaporation (whether moisture comes in the form of rain or snow)—how long the highly reflective snow and ice lasts each winter, how quickly the permafrost is thawing, and how all of this impacts the dynamics of surface water and groundwater—all of it is in flux in the global drama of climate change.

When it comes to global warming, scientists consider the northern latitudes the canary in the coal mine, the part of the globe where effects are noticed first and are most dramatic. In Greenland, isolated communities have been completely cut off because fjords no longer freeze solid or glaciers have receded. On Herschel Island, near the Northwest Passage, graves erupted out of the topsoil because of thawing permafrost and subsequent frost heave. Sea ice is melting at such unprecedented rates that polar bears have to swim farther and farther to reach pack ice and are forced to spend greater parts of every year on the mainland. Instances of polar bears drowning have been recorded in recent years, a phenomenon never documented before.

Many scientists think it likely that there will be no pack ice left within the century, and their models keep speeding up the clock. The possibility of the tundra becoming a vast dry grassland is not out of the question.

Changes in the climate and hydrology will have ripple effects on tundra vegetation, mammals, migratory birds, Native communities, fisheries, everything. Whatever the reality turns out to be, over the next decades those effects will radiate outward, gather momentum, and impact the energy balance of the earth. The specifics of that change remain mysterious and unpredictable; that it will come, and that it will be profound, is no longer in doubt.

The land we paddle our canoes through is green with peat moss, caribou lichen, stubby willow, and dwarf birch. Rock ridges as broad and gray as whalebacks hump out of the earth. The rolling miles are littered with boulders first transported and then dropped willy-nilly by the melting ice.

The mix of land and water seems pretty even. On the maps, it often appears like there is more water than land. Perhaps there is. Every high point offers a view punctuated by lakes and ponds, seamed with rivers.

When we regain the Kazan, still plagued by clouds of blackflies, it gives us a rollicking ride down a wide stretch full of big standing waves. The canoes rise and fall, twist and buck. I kneel on the fabric floor, feel the sinews of water working through the flexible hull. The power of the Kazan is formidable. In these fast stretches, it rolls downhill like something molten, roiling, viscous, all of a piece. I glance back at Marypat. She and Sawyer are a speck of red engulfed by dark, fast water, and the water itself is engulfed by the green carpet of space it flows through.

It is late in the day when things change. The conditions shift from sultry and still to cold and blustery in the space of a river bend. A bank of fog moves over the water, shortens the horizon to a quarter mile. The blackflies vanish. A wind starts up. Every spot on the bank that looks like a promising camp from a distance turns lumpy and rocky close up. We skid along, approaching and then rejecting sites.

A low, scrubby island with a fringe of rocks lies ahead. We have to stop. Two willow ptarmigan waddle off, clucking like mad, when the canoes hit shore.

"Ptarmigan Island," Sawyer christens it.

The high point may be three feet above the river. The entire surface is made of round cobbles. At the upstream end, the island is ravaged by river ice, the vegetation torn and shredded, rocks scraped into small ridges. But we aren't going on.

"Hey, I'll take this over bugs anytime," says Eli.

Thinking of these conditions as a welcome reprieve is pushing it, but everyone agrees with him. All trip we have vacillated between good paddling but buggy conditions, or bug-free days with difficult or impossible traveling circumstances. Each feels like a relief at first.

The tent site is a small square of scraped ground, marginally flat, on top of rocks and a mat of low willows. It takes three of us to hang onto the tarp long enough to guy it out, where it flaps and strains in the gusts of wind.

"Wow," Marypat says when we've finally gotten everything battened down, piled fifty-pound rocks on the boat lines, and reconvened under the tarp. "We just jumped seasons in half an hour."

There is no way to get a fire going. We huddle in the drafty confines of the tarp, brew up drinks and dinner on the stove, keep shrugging into more clothes. The wind is strong enough that we don't trust the tarp to withstand the pressure. Before retreating to the tent, we drop the center pole and weigh the fabric down with heavy rocks.

The tundra is shrouded in tattered, wind-driven fog. A pair of arctic terns, looking natty and alert, hunch on some rocks at the river's edge. The river rolls by, sandpapered with wind gusts.

My eye infection is finally going away, and my lumpy elbow seems to have leveled off, not getting better, but not getting worse either. It still looks alarming, but it hasn't hindered my paddling much. As I crawl over rocks into the tent, I notice that my right knee is tender and sore.

"Just what I need," I grumble.

"What do you need?" Marypat asks.

"Nothing."

I know exactly what it is. Gout. The great physical indignity of my life.

I was diagnosed in my late twenties. Back then, I was running a lot. For a time I kept rationalizing the periodic swellings and pain to landing on a loose stone with the ball of my foot, or rolling my ankle on a hiking trail. But it was pain like I'd never had in my joints, along with red, inflamed swelling. There were times when the weight of a bedsheet on my foot was too much to stand.

When I visited the doctor, it took him less than a minute to diagnose it.

"What do you mean, gout?!" I protested.

"No question. Gouty arthritis. That's obviously what it is."

"You've hardly even looked at it, for crying out loud. I can't have gout. Gout is what fat English kings who ate too much rich food got!"

"Turns out that a lot of other people get it too. It's probably hereditary. It might have something to do with diet, but trying to control it that way is not usually effective. There are drugs you can take."

At that point, the pain was so great that I would have agreed to amputation. Bring on the drugs.

Ever since, I have done periodic battle with the affliction. Gout, a form of arthritis, is the result of elevated levels of uric acid. Mine are only slightly elevated. Once every so often the uric acid will crystallize in a joint, often the big toe, but it can settle in ankles, knees, even earlobes. When it does, it causes irritation and inflammation.

I've seen microscopic pictures of uric acid crystals. They look like needles of glass, which is exactly what they feel like. During an attack, the pain is throbbing, intense, unrelieved by either ice or heat. It is worst during the night. If it's an acute attack, it can be crippling.

I've taken drugs, but I hate the thought of hitching up to a lifetime of prescriptions, so I periodically wean myself from them, first cutting back, and then, if I don't have symptoms, stopping altogether. Years can pass without an attack, or with only minor bouts, which I can treat with anti-inflammatory drugs.

My tendency, when I feel the first twinge, is to ignore it, deny it. I have never quite reconciled this reality. By now, though, I know what this initial tenderness is forecasting, and it is nothing to take lightly. Before bed, I pop four ibuprofen, then try to ignore it.

"What's going on?" Marypat asks.

There are no secrets in our living quarters.

"My knee's a little sore," I say.

She gives me a look, says nothing. Only months later does she reveal that she was doing her own mental calculations as she watched me succumb to this series of physical setbacks. "I was thinking a lot about how we were going to keep going if you went down," she told me.

Our tent is cozy. The wind buffets the walls, but we have it guyed out to bomber rocks, zipped snug. I am sandwiched between Eli and Ruby. I take turns rubbing their faces. They lie on their backs, eyes shut, while I work their foreheads, back through their hair, around their eye sockets and cheekbones. I remember, as a child, how my mother would rub my head when I had a headache, how cool and soothing her hands felt, and how I visualized the pain receding back, pushed by her fingers, dissipating down my neck.

I don't sleep well. My knee aches. I lie for hours listening to the wind and, in the distance, the ripple of river parting around the island. I hear the ptarmigan again, and several times the terns keen shrilly at some affront.

The morning is sunny and cold, but the wind is stronger yet. Low cumuli scud across the blue sky. When I get up, I find that the rocks we weighted the tarp down with have abraded holes in the fabric, some of them large. Marypat retreats into the tent with the tarp and the repair kit, starts to sew patches. Between her patchwork and some duct tape, we manage a repair we hope will be sufficient. It's a piece of gear we can't afford to lose.

Even on the river, we are windbound. The gusts are strong enough that we have to lean against them to walk. The kids start fashioning a wall of rocks for a windbreak. I work at making a better repair of the canoe seat, using a willow stick for a splint. There is enough wood around, between driftwood pieces and dead willow, to build a good fire once the windbreak is done.

Much of the day we spend cooking, making batches of bannock bread, which we alternate with pilot biscuits for lunch, cooking up corn chowder, one of the kids' favorite meals, indulging rounds of hot drinks. The hot chocolate supplies are running low, so Sawyer and Eli go for coffee sweetened with brown sugar.

The terns hover around the island, parrying the wind with their saber-like wings, diving for minnows, resting on the tops of rocks. Sometime in the afternoon, Eli and I are sitting shoulder to shoulder, backs to the gale, sipping coffee, looking out across the wind-filled expanse, thinking our thoughts.

"Dad," he says. "I wouldn't choose to be anywhere else on earth right now."

"You mean that?" I say.

"Yeah. This is an incredible place."

"You're right about that," I look at him. "But that's about the last thing I would have expected you to say."

"Why?"

"Well, to be honest, what with the bugs and the wind and all the hard paddling, what with being stuck on this pissant lump of an island in the middle of the river…" Then I hesitate. "I just didn't expect that."

I can't be sure whether he's being genuine or saying something he knows I would like to hear. Or both. Maybe it doesn't matter. What matters is that none of the kids, not one of them at any point, has said anything that could be construed as whining. I keep waiting for it, assuming it will come. That when-can-we-go-home plea. God knows they've had some cause to bitch.

Like any parent, I'd like to believe that everything is equal when it comes to my feelings for and treatment of the kids. That I love them the same, that I am an impartial arbitrator. In general terms, it's true, but I have to watch myself with Eli. He's the oldest of the three, just as I was. Two brothers and a younger sister, just the same.

There were periods in my youth when I made use of my superior strength and age to rule with an iron fist over my siblings. Those are memories I am ashamed of, and I am deeply grateful to my siblings for overlooking those fits of subjugation and humiliation.

Eli is in the same position. He is stronger, able to enforce his rule, able to frustrate Sawyer to tears. At the same time, he is the model they follow. I find myself overreacting in response. I'll come down on Eli like a ton of bricks and tend to overlook Sawyer's contributions to the conflict. I weigh in to protect Sawyer more than I should, out of my lingering guilt. I know exactly the temptations Eli dances with, that seduction of tyranny. He is, in truth, far less prone to abuse his power than I was, but in heated moments I forget that and succumb to the tendency to scapegoat him.

I look over at him, sipping at a coffee cup roughened by wind, wearing my old coat. His tangled hair hangs in his eyes. He is already starting to get facial hair. He will probably forget his comment about wanting to be nowhere else on earth. To me, though, it is one of those indelible moments of parenthood, a gem to tuck away and hold tight.

The day sails past on the wind. The sun circles the dome of sky. Clouds stampede through the view. The river sucks at the island. The calm we hope for never comes.

Then, in the evening, a single canoe appears.

Nine

We spent a good part of the morning getting to the portages. It was very slow water and we went down the wrong bay, which was really frustrating. Finally we came to the rapids...It was hard going. All the big packs had waist belts that couldn't get small enough for any of us except Al. Everything today but strong winds—a little sunshine, a little cloud, a bit of rain, a tailwind. Saw our first caribou.

—MARYPAT, GROUP JOURNAL

For more than two hundred miles we haven't seen a soul. Except for an occasional high-flying jet, the Inuit artifacts, a few hints of other travelers—charcoal from old fires, a tea bag—we have been alone. Sometimes it takes a great mental leap to conjure up that world teeming with humanity.

Now, nearly three weeks in, a boat sprouts out of nowhere. We wait, feeling like Caribbean natives watching Columbus wade ashore, as the boat comes toward us.

"What the hell are you guys doing out in this wind?" I call, when the two men paddle near.

They skitter up against the end of the island. We gather round.

"We were desperate to move," one of them says. "A plane dropped us off at the outlet of Angikuni Lake yesterday. We only have a week to get to Yathkyed Lake before our pickup."

All of us shake hands. They are friendly and jovial. I notice how they look us over, taking in the kids. Their boat is piled high with a jumble of gear. They are both wearing full wet suits. It looks like they have a bigger load for a week than we have for six. They have that untested air about them, the way we did our first days out.

"How are you taking the portage?" the larger man asks.

"I think we'll stay right till we're past the falls, then maybe ferry across to make the last carry on river left," I say. "We might just take it all on the right. We have to look at it."

They don't stay very long. We discuss the rapids to come, the blackflies, the weather. They climb back in and push away from shore. The current catches hold. Their canoe recedes in the distance, moving crabwise in the wind, becoming a speck, vanishing into space like a stone through water.

The Kazan drops four hundred feet between Angikuni and Yathkyed Lakes, a distance of roughly one hundred river miles. A big chunk of that descent happens in a three-mile stretch known as the Triple Cascades. There the

Kazan roars through a rock gorge, pounding down three emphatic rapids. The middle drop is a bona fide falls, while the rapids above and below might as well be, if you have the misfortune to get pulled into them.

For days, every time I look at the map, my attention has been drawn to the rapids. It is a benchmark in the expedition. For eighteen days we have been eating our way through our supplies. The good news is that the gargantuan pack we could barely lift during the first week is now at least manageable.

Paddling toward the maelstrom from upstream, as we do in heavy air the next morning, you'd never know that all hell is about to break loose. The river pools for miles above the whitewater, the current barely perceptible, as if dammed. Only as we draw near do we pick out the strange break in the river horizon. Then the wisps of mist in the distance. Finally, the din of water, the roar of liquid tonnage falling down a jagged rock face.

We paddle against the right bank for a good mile before we get close. The canoes glide through the still, unruffled pool. But there, right in front of us, the glassy flow gathers speed, bends downhill, froths over the first drop into a chaos of white battering down the tortured ancient rock.

The bow of my canoe slices into mud within yards of the breaking water. Marypat noses in next to me. We pull the boats well up. The exhilaration of water applauds around our heads. The relief of standing on land makes us laugh.

The first carry is short. Eli volunteers to take one of the canoes. I set him up under the portage yoke and he lumbers away, strong but awkward. Sawyer and Ruby load themselves up, front and back, with dry bags. Neither one of them tips the scales at more than one hundred pounds. The packs dwarf them, but they are game enough to grab a few paddles and loose gear.

It takes two trips, but the pile is moved to the bottom of the first rapid in short order. Marypat takes pictures, all of us poised in front of rock-and-foam. The kids fish in the jostling eddy water without success.

On we paddle, hugging shore again, to the brink of the falls, where the river drops sheer through a craggy lip of rock and the roar is loud enough that we have to shout to each other.

My swollen knee is pretty wobbly. I'm not in much pain, thanks to repeated doses of vitamin I, but the joint feels loose. If I step wrong and my knee hyperextends, the pain is a jolt that can make me fall down, which would not be a good thing with a pack on my back and a canoe overhead.

The ground doesn't help matters. The tundra is hummocky and yielding, full of standing water and mucky spots. Caribou trails wind in a latticework of parallel tracks. Eli doesn't volunteer for a canoe this time. Marypat says she'll have a try, but the boat isn't set up right for the pack she's carrying, and she has to drop the canoe one hundred yards along.

Half a mile downstream, we descend again to the river below the falls. One of our options is to pick a spot to ferry the loaded canoes across the current between the falls and the final rapid in order to get to a steep, short portage over a ridge that shortcuts a bend in the river. The ferry maneuver involves paddling against the current at an angle, so the net effect is to move the boat sideways in the rapid without losing much ground, the same way a ferryboat angles against river or tidal current. If we can manage it, the crossing would save us probably a mile of portaging. The more we look at it, though, the more dubious it appears.

A large boulder and ledge jut into the river. The main current is pushy and full of cresting waves. The landing on the far side is complicated by some tricky-looking holes and ledges.

"I think we can do it," Eli says. "I really don't want to have to portage the whole thing."

"I think it's the second thing you said that's making your judgment call," I say.

Marypat looks doubtful. I run some very vivid mental images of trying to cross that water with kids on board and having something go wrong. None of them are scenarios I'd enjoy explaining to friends and family afterward.

"I don't like it," Marypat says. "Maybe at lower water it would be okay. Maybe if it was just us in the boat it might be okay, but looking at it right now, it sort of makes me want to puke."

We scramble downstream, climb up on rocks, get every vantage we can, and it never feels comfortable.

"Like they say," I put my arm around my partner, "nobody ever drowned on a portage."

"It's not worth it," she agrees.

The kids groan, but accept our call. One of Eli's strong points is that he is willing to listen and be convinced, and he won't hold a grudge. Even as a toddler he could be cajoled into accepting our edicts. Here, he takes a final wistful look at the shortcut, sighs, and turns away.

The portage lengthens by a mile. I return for the canoe Marypat dropped, and take it very slowly and carefully all the way across. Portaging requires a steady stamina, like paddling, only with more sweat and pain.

The first half is through swampy, lumpy tussocks. The boat grinds on my shoulders and against my neck. I assess every step before committing. I follow a caribou track until it leads off course, then go cross-country or switch to another narrow trail. My leg holds fine, as long as I don't rush things. Once in a while I slip and earn a twinge of pain that keeps me careful. Blackflies swarm under the hull. Sweat runs down my neck. I keep on, resisting the temptation to stop and rest, walking slow, feeling old. In my thirties, in trip shape, I used to pride myself on almost running across portages.

The kids occupy my thoughts. They have put up with unbelievable bugs, paddled through headwinds, spent days trapped in the tent. Now they bend like Sherpas under their loads. The things their friends complain about, that they have complained about at home, aren't even in the same universe when it comes to challenge.

The route rises through more hummocks and willow, which I push my way through, up over a rock lip greasy with lichen, across a flat bench where I can see the river open out, and finally descends to a ledgy platform of rock just below the final rapid, where the Kazan jostles and bumps before making a broad left turn and hurrying on. I walk steadily, methodically, ignoring the flies, the canoe creaking overhead.

At the end I drop the canoe on river-fluted rock, lift my head net, splash water on my face. The best thing about portaging is that feeling of weightlessness after you lift the canoe off. The river pours through a vise of rock just upstream, dark and bellowing with power. I lie on my belly to take a long drink, then head back for another load.

The portage takes up a big chunk of the day, punctuated by a lunch in the rocks next to the hurrying river. As lunch spots go, you could do a lot worse. Mist from the falls swirls in the breeze. Gulls land in the cliff walls, flashes of gray against the dark rock and blue sky. The rapids are like a black hole; they suck in our attention. The sweep of land and sky recedes in the racket and motion of waterworn canyon. We cluster together in the eye of this storm of noise, eat our ration of trail mix and dried fruit, jerky, cheese, and pilot biscuits.

The kids bear up under the strain, but I can see Sawyer thinking that he made the right choice in opting out of portage-filled trip revisions.

"Fifteen miles of portaging," he says, once, when I walk next to him. "Sheesh! What were you thinking, Dad?"

When I head back for a final load, I try to pick up all the odds and ends, as well as the last heavy pack.

"Dad! What are you doing? Drop that stuff!" Eli is swinging down the trail toward me. "We can take our share," he says. I feel a gush of gratitude as I watch him swing a pack onto his back, grab a paddle, and stride down the trail.

At the end, as we gather ourselves again, Sawyer and Eli cast lures into a narrow eddy. Right off, they start pulling in lake trout the size of their legs. Huge, lunker fish bigger by a quantum leap than anything they've ever had on a line before.

"Got another one!" they shout, by turns. The cheap rods bend and quiver, the fish come flapping out of the dark pool, heavy and strong and glistening. Most they release, but we have fish dinners planned as part of our menu, so they keep a couple in a pool above the river.

Ruby stands over the captured fish. She watches the alien, muscular water creatures gulping in the shallow water, periodically bashing against rock in a bid to escape, and it undoes her.

"I don't want the fish to die!" she wails. "I'm going to put them back."

"Ruby, we need them for dinner," I say, holding her.

She sobs against my chest. "I don't want them to die, Dad."

Meantime, Eli and Sawyer are wholly consumed by the thrill. They keep casting, reeling in massive fish. Eli hooks a stunning grayling, probably eighteen inches long. He holds it up, shimmering iridescence, flapping wildly.

"God, isn't it beautiful?" he says.

Ruby has retreated. She can't stand the sight of dying fish, of this beauty yanked out of its element. Marypat comforts her.

We pick two trout for dinner. The boys and I clean them, cut them into manageable hunks, put them in bags. "I don't want fish slime all over the boats, attracting bears," I say. "And I hope you guys know that you've just turned your sister into a vegetarian."

"I'm going to draw that grayling," Eli says. "And we're going to cook dinner. I know just how to do it."

Before that, there are more miles to make. The river canters on, big and fast, below the Triple Cascades. Miles of easy speed. After all the flatwater we've done, the pull of current beneath the hull always feels like heady hitchhiking. We take breaks, lean back, watch the banks whiz past.

The boys have a strategy for dinner. On the rocky island where we finally camp, they build a fire of driftwood twigs and branches of ice-battered willow. They grill the hunks of trout until tender, then shred the meat with their fingers and sauté the fish with Cajun spices in the Dutch oven before serving it over rice.

Eli under a canoe on one of the Triple Portages.

Seeing the fish reduced to bits of meat, Ruby manages to overcome her aversion. Even more, she hates being left out. She pitches in to help and eats her share when it comes time. The recipe is surprisingly tasty and there is enough to make it a feast.

After dinner, on a whim, I pull out the satellite phone.

It is not a gadget I like. All this time the phone has been another object in our load, cased in its dry box, clipped into the boats every day, carried here and there. Ignored.

I am not a technology geek. I'm no Luddite, but I don't like GPS, phones, laptops, the rest of the paraphernalia. I come to places like these precisely to escape all that junk. Telephones, voice mail, e-mail, beeps and electronic hums—it all belongs back there, through the portal that closed the moment the plane disappeared in the sky above Kasba Lake. I don't want its intrusion.

On the trips I've joined where these sorts of gadgets come along, I've found them an annoying distraction. People are forever gazing into tiny, pixilated display screens, punching in waypoints, making calls, playing with the technology, marveling at it.

Sure, there are moments when knowing a precise location is handy, or being able to make contact has helped with some logistical problem. On the whole, though, I'll trade some inconvenience and occasional geographic uncertainty for the claptrap of technology any day.

I've succumbed because I couldn't imagine myself justifying not having a satellite phone if something really went wrong.

One of our Bozeman friends, Scott, agreed to be our safety backup and emergency contact. Before we left, he and I went over the route, talked through the itinerary options. I gave him copies of the maps, a list of contacts, emergency numbers.

"Look," he said. "I know you don't like these phones, but you need to try and give me a call at some point. Otherwise, if something happens and you guys don't show up on schedule, we'll have to search that whole river. Sometime a few weeks in, just walk off behind camp and give me a call. You don't even have to tell anyone. Just let me know where you are, whether you're on track. That way I can eliminate a big chunk of the route."

In this camp there is nowhere to walk off to in secret, and I don't want to anyway. Ever since that moment of doubt Marypat and I shared on the shores of Angikuni Lake, when we questioned the whole premise of this trip, however briefly, our family has transformed into a team.

I realize that I haven't been treating the kids as my young children as much as I have been considering them trip mates. They've started to pull their weight. More and more, they pitch in and help without being asked. They paddle a full day without being nagged. They don't bitch and complain. To the contrary, as often as not they lift my mood with their antics. I find myself asking their advice on our position, on our best route, on campsites. They are, more and more, my partners. I'm not about to skulk off behind a bush to make a secret call.

Besides, I've never really believed that the phone will work.

Ten

We woke up to cold, windy weather. We had cold cereal and packed up to go. The first 8 miles were scouting and running rapids. The rest was good moving water with a few lakes, but there was a big headwind. We camped right in the middle of a rapid and tonight we had cinnamon rolls!! Later, we put a fishing hook on the reel, without a pole, and Eli still caught a fish. We went to bed in clammy sleeping bags.

—SAWYER, GROUP JOURNAL

"You know what you're doing, Dad?" Eli asks, when he sees me get the phone out of its cushioned case.

"Yeah, sure," I say. "The guy at the store showed me. And there's this instruction sheet. Shouldn't be too hard."

"Uh-huh, just the kind of thing you're really good at," he says. "You can barely handle the television remote."

I flip up the antenna like I make these calls all the time, push the power button. The screen comes to life, tells me it's looking for a satellite.

That's the iffy part. Since the majority of satellites orbit near the equator, the process of acquiring satellite signals and holding on to the connection at higher latitudes becomes problematic. The salesperson told me that this far north, we might have to wait up to ten minutes for a contact, and that we might lose our connection suddenly.

So I'm surprised when, in a matter of seconds, a little satellite symbol appears and the phone tells me to make my call. I dial Scott's number like I'm sitting in a motel room in Iowa. Nothing happens for a few seconds, then it rings. Rings again.

"Hello?" It's Scott's wife, Sue, and she could be one island downriver, the connection is so clear.

"Sue! It's Al!"

The connection may be clear, but I'm shouting into the phone as if I have to yell all the way from Canada. Marypat gives me a take-it-down-a-big-notch hand signal.

"Scott's not home," Sue says. "He's really going to be bummed."

"Listen, that's okay. I just want to let you know what's going on. I don't know how much time we've got with this phone, but here's the deal."

I give her our location, tell her the route we've decided on, that we're more or less on schedule. All of this conversation takes place at a pretty high decibel level. The connection holds. I start to relax. We talk about the bugs and weather, how great the kids are doing. She fills me in on some local news. The whole time I'm imagining her in her kitchen, making dinner for her daughters on a bugless Montana evening in their house on the outskirts of town.

"These calls aren't cheap," I say eventually. "Give Scott the update. We're thinking of you guys."

I put the phone back in its case. Sue's voice still lingers in my ear. Images of home are bright in my head, but I'm abruptly back on the Kazan. The thrill of making contact infuses all of us. I pace around on the rock while I relay every bit of the conversation, all the news. It's reassuring, in a strange way. That other life, the one we took leave of, is still motoring on. There are people back home meeting for coffee, talking on street corners, going to movies, playing soccer.

"Montana seems really, really far away," Eli says.

"Makes me a little homesick, I have to admit," Marypat adds.

The phone call is symptomatic of our schizophrenic lives, this schizophrenic culture, where we can leap like this between worlds and communicate back and forth from one to the other. Very strange stuff. The way we live, we keep bumping up against different realities. I find it disorienting as hell. We can fly across eight or ten time zones in less than a day, hop from a metropolitan downtown to deep wilderness in a couple of hours, but are we really there when we land?

In our town lifestyle, we participate fully in the social fabric of urban existence, school, and professional life. Like the rest of mainstream America, we watch DVDs, we fight over the telephone, we struggle paying the bills, we have a trampoline in the backyard. Marypat and I often feel like taxi drivers; on any given spring weekend, the kids could be scattered across five hundred miles on different soccer fields. The one thing we haven't given in on is cell phones, which Eli would very much like to have, like all his friends.

Then, for weeks at a time, sometimes longer, we dive into the wilds, enter the dimension where clocks have no bearing, where no music plays, where phones don't ring, and what the weather does matters a great deal. Twice in the last twenty years, Marypat and I have put onto a river and not come back for fourteen months. More than four hundred days together in deep wilderness, paddling across North America, wintering in the tiny cabin on the shores of Lake Athabasca. It was how we got Eli.

For better or worse, we're passing that legacy on to the kids. In this realm we sleep on the ground, notice the phase of the moon, eat dinner sitting on rocks, build fires, hear geese flying through the night.

"We're the one-percenters, Alan," a friend once said to me.

He is a passionate paddler who goes off for long stretches, has a perverse penchant for paddling hundreds of miles upriver, would rather spend the night camped on a riverbank than in any five-star hotel on the planet.

It sounded elitist at first, but I realized that he meant it as nothing but fact. He wasn't referring to income inequality but to adventure appetite. When it comes to that, he's probably overstating it by half. To a large extent, people like us have become anachronisms.

A great many people, and more all the time, live their entire lives without ever once sleeping out under the stars. It's entirely possible to pull off a full life span and never have to pee on a bush.

The modern concept of adventure embraces the silliness of "reality" television, which is about as far from real as it gets. Beautiful, scantily clad people eating bugs and dangling from helicopters, or meeting in some ersatz cave, lit by flickering propane torches—sets designed to summon up a primordial, *Lord of the Flies* ambience.

With the phone call home, we reached through the skin of experience and touched another world. All of us felt the contact, the reminder, the poignancy of it. To be honest, we all miss it to some extent. Here, the blackflies cloud the air, the river hurries by, our fire of willow twigs quickly turns to ash.

I told Sue that we were two solid days away from Yathkyed Lake, but the next morning it's not at all clear that it will be the first good day. A cold wind gusts up the river. I have trouble keeping the breakfast fire going long enough to boil water. This summer, it seems, we aren't allotted more than one day of good traveling at a time.

The rapids start several miles down. We have the decks snapped on, plenty of clothes layered under our life jackets. The whitewater goes on for miles, long sections punctuated by ledges, rocks, some big holes and waves. We stop to scout, river left, then sneak along that shore for a bit before paddling toward midriver and eventually make our way to the right bank, where we start leapfrogging down through a series of rapids.

It's a protracted process. Above some heavy water, we land the canoes, clamber out, hike to the top of the riverbank for the view, discuss our route and the paddling moves we'll need to make, look ahead to the next landing. Then, back to the canoes—girding up, kneeling, cinching up the spray skirts, keeping the sequence of obstacles and paddling strategy straight.

I am paddling with Eli, while Ruby perches in the load midcanoe. With one or two exceptions, none of the water along the shore is terribly difficult, as long as we execute the plan. In several places, though, we have to paddle far out to avoid big holes, and then slide back toward shore before getting pulled into the large waves and rocks in the main channel. The boats edge out into the river, skirt past the dangerous, snarling holes of water, and power back into the safe zone near shore before getting sucked into the big stuff.

I can tell Eli is getting frustrated with the process. It seems painstakingly slow, and none of the runs are all that tough. At his age, I would have been exasperated too. He trusts his physical capabilities and hasn't lived enough to leaven that confidence with judgment. For the most part, he doesn't know failure, and he excels at sports, has an easy knack for mastering challenges. He's the kid who will pick up a rock, wing it nonchalantly at an impossible target, and nail it. Also, what he doesn't truly comprehend, and can't comprehend, is how big a deal it would be to blow it. Losing gear, wrecking a canoe, getting injured in a swim—any one of those scenarios would transform our adventure immediately into a survival epic.

At the last section, though, I give in to his energy.

"Look, Dad, here's how we do it!" He pulls me to a point of rock and maps out his strategy. He can be very persuasive. It looks doable, a little more adventurous than we have allowed ourselves to be, but doable. The crux of his plan requires some quick sideslip maneuvering in order to hit a tongue of water. If we miss it, we'll smash into rocks or be in for a wild ride through waves.

Down below, the river slows and pools. Eli's energy is infectious. Marypat and Sawyer are game too.

In the bow, Eli responds first, putting in draw strokes or pointing to something we hadn't seen from shore. He is competent with the paddle, doesn't hesitate. The boat slides through a break in a ledge, just as we planned. Eli starts backpaddling to help ferry us away from rocks and into a deeper channel. Then he sees the slot, powers forward. I'm powering and bracing in the stern. We schuss through the gap, flanked by jagged rocks that would tear holes in the canoe hull, and ride out the train of waves into calm water. Sawyer and Marypat are on our tail. Sawyer holds his paddle over his head in triumph.

"Yes!" Eli whoops, but I can sense in his voice that he understands how small a mistake it would have taken for things to go wrong.

The rapids distracted us from the wind. Once through them, the day turns into a steady slog against air. River current is our ally. Whenever the wind seems to have stopped us cold, I look at the cobbles sliding by for reassurance.

The land, just here, seems particularly immense. Not that it hasn't been vast all along, but this day, the way the river loops around bends, the way the light fills the sky, how the bluster of air and current pushes at us, the scene is rendered huge.

A rounded hill rolls away, bathed in sunlight. It would take the rest of the day just to walk to the top of it. Tundra fields unfold, tapestries of dark and light green, mile after mile. Rock outcrops and ridges stand out in gray contrast. The sky is deep summer blue with cloud ships sailing through it. Bend after bend the river uncoils, with the specks of our boats on its back, through space that makes me breathe deep.

"Geez, just think how fast we'd be going without the wind," Marypat says when we stop for lunch, reclining against boulders above the river.

"Yeah, but think how we'd be going nowhere at all without the current," I say.

Everyone is game for making miles. We have a goal, a rapid and portage twenty-five miles from our last camp. No one says anything about stopping, even when we have to grind across a four-mile bulb of river with little current, into the teeth of the wind. The canoes slap through wind-driven waves. We say nothing, just bend into the strokes, stay close together, try to keep from marking our pitiful progress by looking at the shore.

"We earned every damn mile today," I say when we finally pull the canoes up on a ledge of rock partway through a powerful rapid, at the start of a short portage. "You guys should be proud."

The camp, perched on flat, mossy ground above the loud river marks the halfway point in our itinerary. Twenty days out. Eli takes the length of dental floss we've tied to the map case and measures our progress. Sawyer checks his measurement, as does Marypat. We pencil in our camp on the map with a little tipi symbol, scan back over the windy, rapid-hatched day.

I log our distance on the group journal tally. We are just under fifteen miles for our daily average. It's respectable, considering all the delays.

"I'm making cinnamon rolls tonight to celebrate," Marypat announces.

"And I'm burning my underwear!" I add.

Marypat is the acknowledged baker, both at home and on the trail. She hunkers over a bowl and makes a batch of dough out of supplies in our pantry bag, rolls it out on the griddle, sprinkles on a layer of cinnamon sugar and raisins. As she works, she brushes wisps of her hair off her face with the back of her hand. The bugs are out, but no one mentions them. The cinnamon rolls go into the Dutch oven. She rests it on a thin layer of coals and builds a small twig fire on top.

Once the rolls are safely baking on the side, I build the fire back up for the solemn ritual of burning a pair of my underwear. I've been promising to burn these particularly gnarly whitey tighties for days. The kids have been ridiculing them since the trip start, and the time is right. I wave them on a stick above the licking flames. They smolder and catch fire. The elastic band melts and drips. I intone some silliness about undergarment rights of passage, the reincarnation possibilities for dirty underwear, but my theatrics are a decided sideshow to the main event.

Rightly so, because when the lid is lifted on the rolls and Marypat drizzles on a sweet glaze, the underwear ceremony, the day's battle against headwinds, the fact that it is deep twilight at the end of a very long day—all of it is forgotten.

This small thing, a batch of cinnamon rolls made from our pantry supplies, is a magnificent event. The kids hover over Marypat's every move, and once served, the rolls last about thirty seconds.

"I could eat five of those babies," Eli says, looking wistfully at the empty Dutch oven. Then he turns to the dinner pack and starts putting things away.

He has adopted the task of food organization. Every evening he gets the next day's breakfast out. In the morning, he pulls out the lunch supplies and stashes them in the lunch pack. Periodically he'll consolidate the food packs and reorganize the dwindling load. By now, he knows what food is in what pack better than Marypat and I do.

"You're getting skinny, Dad," Ruby says in the tent that night. She pats my bare stomach.

"Yeah, you're getting chicken legs," Sawyer chimes in.

"Thanks for sharing," I say.

It always happens on these trips. Losing weight is a given for me. Halfway through, I've probably lost fifteen pounds. It's come to the point that I purposely take expedition pants that are snug, because I know they'll be hanging on me by the trip's end.

It isn't as simple as steady exercise and limited food, either. I also lose the compulsions that dog me back home. The tendency to snack when I don't need to, the tendency to drink more than I need to, the use of food as a procrastination device. On trips, those impulses don't even come up. Not that I could indulge them if they did, but the fact is that I don't even think of them.

We'll have cocktail night once a week. I don't find myself looking for seconds at dinner. I'm satisfied with a lunch that would seem skimpy back home on a day when I'm sitting in an office.

Part of it has to do with my preoccupation with the challenges of each day. My mind and energy is completely focused on the immediate prospect of making our distance, coping with rapids, reading weather, doing the chores. Food is fuel, nothing more or less.

That's not all of it, though. Whatever neuroses and habits drive those compulsions at home simply evaporate out here.

Eleven

Lovely morning in camp, followed by a very pleasant paddle all the way to Yathkyed Lake. Camped at a pretty spot above the lake on a bedrock outcrop. We're poised to deal with getting across Yathkyed, roughly 30 miles, depending on shortcuts. Everyone is pulling their weight, both in camp and in the boats. We're melding into an expedition team.

—AL, GROUP JOURNAL

Another morning. The winds are up enough that there is no rush to break camp. Yathkyed Lake gapes to the horizon. We've done well to get here. The winds may build more, making it impossible to go on, or they may calm. For once I'm not overly worried about it. Marypat turns out an extra batch of lunch bannock, and we cook an involved breakfast of scrambled eggs served over bread.

The transformation of eggs that we dried to powder at home months earlier, and that look like a slightly congealed, lumpy, watery mess in the bowl, is a marvel. Mixed with cheese and some chopped salami, fried up in the skillet, they morph into a pretty close approximation of fresh scrambled eggs. We spoon them over fried bannock, add a dash of hot pepper oil from the spice kit, and finish off with a round of hot drinks. I may not fixate on food in the wilds, but, on the other hand, I appreciate a good meal here like nowhere else.

Waves pile in against shore below our overturned boats. We stall some more, decide to walk to a ridge marked by a low *inukshuk*. Dozens of bird nests dot the ground nearby. They are empty now. The frenzy of claiming territory, mating, brooding, hatching is over already. In a few weeks, these birds will gird themselves for the return south. This year's hatchlings, only a couple of months old, will join the flocks, rise into the sky, get up to speed, or perish.

The abandoned nests are made of dead grass, circles the size of small hats, clusters of them lying on the peat by the dozen. We pick our way through them as in a graveyard, the frail tombs that symbolize the unbelievable efforts made every single year by all the birds that migrate here, only to flee the season again a few months later.

Humans are scarce on the Barrens, but birds congregate here by the millions every summer. Spotted sandpipers that start in the highlands of Guatemala, sandhill cranes from the Rio Grande valley, rough-legged hawks that winter on the plains of Colorado, arctic terns that manage an unbelievable yearly circuit from the Antarctic waters off of southern Africa back to the Arctic North, crossing the Atlantic on the way, a round trip of more than twenty thousand miles.

They stream up over the prairies, across the Great Lakes, across the Gulf of Mexico, riding thermals above the Rocky Mountains. Birds in great flocks and in solitude. Birds of land and water. Predators and prey. Longspurs, scoters, water pipits, grebes, loons, golden eagles, peregrine falcons, sanderlings—they throng north, find their niche, have babies, get those babies up to snuff, then escape again before winter, if all goes well. The next spring they do it again.

Even robins, those denizens of the backyard, come north. To see robins on the tundra is to cast them in a radically different light. Here, that prober for worms in the turf of subdivisions becomes something robust, rugged, and feral.

From the *inukshuk* ridge the view includes a flat bench below us where telltale circles of rocks mark the tent rings of an old summer camp. Marypat, Ruby, and Sawyer head down that way while Eli and I start back for another round of coffee.

"Hey, what's this?" Ruby says, stooping to pick up a wooden object.

She holds a fashioned piece of wood in her hand. It is maybe ten inches long, round, with a carved grip near one end. A simple design has been scribed into the surface of the wood.

Ruby discovers a drumbeater artifact near camp on Yathkyed Lake.

"What is it?" Ruby asks again.

"You know what this is," Marypat is suddenly certain. "It's a drumbeater. Remember, we saw these in the museum in Baker Lake. You hold it here." She takes it by the grip and demonstrates drumming against an imaginary skin drum held in her other hand. "That's exactly what this is."

We all hold the artifact. It is weathered but still functional, completely intact. Things take a long time to decay in this cold, arid environment. What hands held this? What dances did it beat the rhythm to? I think of an igloo, late winter, with the sun returning, full of Inuit in their bulky clothes, smiling with the warmth, thinking of spring and the coming of the deer. I hear the drum start up, the feet shuffling, the beat filling the space, filling the air, sending out a throbbing assertion of life.

Ruby lays the drumbeater back in the moss, into the perfect mold it has settled into. We turn and walk toward the canoes.

On a windy day when the going is torturous, the kids' strategy is to ask leading questions that have some chance of provoking one of us into a round of storytelling. The canoes are twisting through the gray waves, slapping into troughs. We hug shore, slowly creep past rocky islands. The next point takes an age to reach.

"So, Dad," Ruby says, "tell us what Christmas was like when you were our age."

"Christmas, eh?" Like I'm fooled by her innocent-sounding query.

Fact is, diving into these ad lib monologues can be a treat. How often do we get to dredge up these bits of personal history and family tradition and share them? I find myself relishing the memories of childhood, how we had to wait an excruciating time, until the dinner turkey was stuffed and in the oven, before we could open presents. How my grandfather, at some unexpected point, would pound loudly on the front door and then hide, so that when we got there we found only a toboggan piled with gifts. How we couldn't decorate the tree until Christmas Eve.

Whenever I reach some conclusion, the kids throw in another question, ask about a relative, or about the games we'd play. Pretty soon, a sizeable hunk of coast has gone past in the telling. Still, it's an endurance test. We have become strong, steady paddlers by now, but the wind forces us to favor one side, and the mental fortitude required is exhausting.

At the end of a shallow bay, we land on a gravel beach and collapse, stretch our backs and shoulders, break out lunch. We could stop. We might stop, but no one suggests anything yet, and by the time we've finished lunch, the wind has died. We always know when the wind goes down, because the blackflies come back.

The lake goes flat. We take a compass bearing and beeline for a distance-saving narrows between two islands. A lone caribou jogs along a willowy shoreline. We have seen a few of the deer, but not the big herds. This one runs inland when it senses us, antlers bobbing on the skyline. It looks very alone in all the space. Perhaps the main herd is just over the rise. There could be five thousand of them behind a ridge and we'd never know it.

I hear Eli, in the bow of Marypat's canoe, working on the lyrics of the oldie "I Think We're Alone Now." He's been getting this song down for the last couple of days.

CARIBOU, THE KAZAN, AND ENDLESS LANDSCAPE.

"Children behaaaave," he croons. "That's what they say when we're together..." It's really handy when the favorite songs of your offspring happen to be the ones you listened to at their age.

I find myself joining in the chorus. "So now we're running just as fast as we can...Holding onto one another's hand...Trying to get away, into the night. Then you wrap your arms around me and we tumble to the ground and then you say...I think we're alone now. There doesn't seem to be anyone arou-hound...I think we're alone now. The beating of our hearts is the only sou-hound..."

As I sing, I remember walking home from school at Eli's age, singing "Pretty Woman," my heart full of hormone-juiced longing, thinking about that seventh-grade girl I was stuck on.

Puberty struck Eli in sixth grade. We noticed when he needed new shoes roughly every third week. Body hair, acne, smelly socks. He agitated to move out of the kids' room into his own, and when he did, he turned it into a soccer and football shrine that started reeking of bad deodorant. In choir, that music elective for jocks, he went from soprano to tenor in less than a week. At lunch recess, he became the school arm-wrestling champion.

Girls started calling him on the phone. I don't remember that in my youth—girls calling out of the blue. Most of it was the expected prank stuff, innocent goofy calls, but it became clear that he had a girlfriend, whatever that means at age twelve. I kept finding notes wadded up in his pants pockets when I did the laundry.

"So, Eli," I'd say at dinner. "What does LOL mean?"

"LOL? Oh, it means 'laugh out loud.'"

"Uh-huh."

"Well," he'd add, "it can mean 'lots of love, too,' sometimes."

"What about WB?"

"WB? It means 'write back.' And Dad, where are you getting this stuff?"

"Maybe you should check your pockets when you put your pants in the laundry."

The girlfriend lasted a few months, until they both agreed that the hassle and abuse they got from their peers wasn't worth the grief. He met his present girlfriend on the soccer field. She goes to the other middle school in town, so they aren't distracting each other all day. They have couriers who pass notes between schools somehow, and they monopolize the phone in the evenings.

The canoes scratch across the quiet, mirrored surface. Our strokes are as steady and constant as steps. The bow waves splash gently. A somnolence settles over us. We know better than to squander this, we are thankful, but the privilege of calm doesn't blunt the drudgery.

Then, halfway across a broad bay, well out from shore, a bird falls out of the sky. Just like that. Plop. Its tail feathers stick straight up like a badminton birdie.

"Did you see that?" I point to the bird in the water.

Marypat and Eli are closest. They paddle over, but just as Eli reaches out, the bird bursts back into flight, staggers through the air, and falls again into the lake, forty feet away. This time, when they approach, Eli is able to slip his hands under the bird and cup it out of the water.

We paddle over to them. Everyone peers at the small, exhausted, half-dead bird. It looks like a longspur, we think. The bird's eyes are closed. Its breathing is rapid. Eli makes a little nest for it in the spray skirt, lets it lie there. We paddle on, whispering.

"Maybe it's just tired from crossing the lake," Ruby suggests.

"I doubt it. That's not very far," Marypat says. "I wonder if it didn't just escape from a predator and it's wounded.

"There's no blood or anything," Eli says.

The canoes stay side by side, our paddling cadence resumes. I fix on the next point of land.

"I think it's sleeping," Eli whispers, peering down at the longspur. "Its eyes are closed, but I can see it breathing."

Then Eli bends really close and looks at the bird. "No," he says. "It just died."

At the far side of the bay, Marypat and Eli paddle their canoe to shore. Eli climbs out, holding the dead bird. He looks around, then walks inland a few paces to a clump of dwarf birch, where he bends down, lifts aside some branches, and gently lays the victim under the low shrubs. He pauses there, looking at the ground.

I watch him walk back to the canoe, grab hold of the bow and shove off, hopping aboard as he does. He picks up his paddle and draws the bow away from shore. Maybe, I think, part of this business of becoming an adult, for Eli, will encompass the memory of holding a tiny bird in his hands, watching it die, and finding a suitable place to lay it down.

We paddle on, thoughtful now, into the great stillness. The lake undulates like a sheet of liquid silver. All of us ponder a death that can strike in midair, between wing beats.

Twelve

Today we found some Inuit artifacts when we were waiting for the weather to calm down. It was a hard day, just waiting. We also saw a caribou close up.

—ELI, GROUP JOURNAL

We're about to paddle into a small bay to check out a beach campsite when Marypat notices something.

"Look how that bird's flying," she says, pointing over the open water.

"It's two birds," Sawyer adds. "A big one chasing a little one."

We stop paddling, drift to a stop. A long-tailed jaeger is dueling with a sparrow-sized bird, perhaps another longspur like the one Eli laid to rest earlier in the afternoon. The birds dodge and feint above the still, shimmering water. They spiral up and down, wound tightly, one after the other, matching move for move. The small bird is fast and agile, but the jaeger mimics every move, relentless, focused. Then, so quickly we almost miss it, the jaeger spins upside down beneath its prey, reaches up with its talons, and snatches its victim out of the air.

The jaeger flies to a rock sticking above the lake surface, settles above its prey. Another jaeger, perhaps the mate, glides in and lands next to it, begins to preen as the first bird bends to the meal, tearing away feathers with hooked beak.

The pair of predatory birds, a species that spends most of its life at sea and only summers on the tundra, is still in sight when we land on the crescent of sand. A line of caribou tracks marks the beach.

"They must wait for a bird to fly just a little too far out over the lake, away from cover, and then cut it off," Marypat guesses. "I'll bet that was what happened to the bird we found, but it somehow escaped."

Marypat and I have come to relish the early mornings together. At dawn the next day, we slip out of the tent and brew up coffee. It is reminiscent of our long, solitary trips together before kids. Week after week, together in the canoe, in waterside camps, in every conceivable weather.

Those trips cemented our commitment, annealed our bond. We got so we hardly had to speak during the day. Mile after mile, the water went under the hull, our paddles hit the water, we responded to subtle nuances of body language. I have a great wealth stored away on the emulsion sheets of memory, an account full of shared fires, of washing each other's hair, of waiting out storms, of drifting along on the current, seeing wild things.

I have started to feel that same sense of depth and wealth of experience as a family; the simple accumulation of time together and shared endeavor in wild places.

The winds are back, stirring the lake, but the bay is protected and we don't discuss the weather. We settle in our chairs, the stove between us, and savor the first sip of coffee. The map is out. A wide bay lies just ahead with a large island in the center of it. Once across that, we just follow the shoreline another dozen miles to a portage across a finger-shaped peninsula that juts into the lake. Florida, we call it. The quarter-mile portage will save us six miles of paddling around the tip.

"Al!" Marypat's voice is low, but tense. "Don't move fast. Turn really slowly and look to your left." Her eyes are fixed down the beach.

I swivel my head.

AL FOLLOWS MARYPAT ACROSS A TRACKLESS PORTAGE.

What I see, thirty feet away, walking onto the sand, is a mature bull musk ox. A darkly luminous animal, in its prime, in its place, and it continues down the beach toward our camp.

The musk ox knows we're there. It emanates tension, yet it doesn't stop. He moves with deliberation, a methodical, careful approach. The breeze shifts through the shaggy coat of brown fur hanging in skirts from his sides.

We sit transfixed, coffee in hand. I notice the way his hooves articulate at the joint with each step. How the sand shifts under the bull's weight. The knurled plate of horn spreading across the forehead. I notice how constricted my chest feels, how I have to concentrate on breathing.

The musk ox stops broadside to us, directly in front of us, a dozen feet away. Then he turns to face us, takes a step forward, and we lock gazes.

I don't know how to respond, what the etiquette is. He is close enough that I can see the texture of his nostrils. The horns curl into sharp points on either side of his broad skull. His eyes are liquid brown. I see his ear twitch. The electric charge in the space between us is almost unbearable. I am doing my damnedest to radiate calm, acceptance, humility, to keep my heart quiet. It isn't fear that rises in me, or at least not a feeling I associate with fear. More a heightened awareness—ultimate, unsustainable tension.

I have never been this connected to a large wild animal, this intimate, this confronted. I sense the same crescendo of energy coming from the bull. An animal in the full of his life, who is not threatened by much, who is making his way through his territory and finds these strange visitors in his path. He seems, in his stolid way, to be weighing his options, taking our measure.

I have no idea how long this goes on. An eternity that might last a minute.

I don't turn my head, but I say to Marypat, "Do you think I should stand up?" As I speak I wave my hand slightly.

"No!" she says.

But the spell is broken. The sound of our voices, the movement, is just enough to lurch us past the unsupportable moment.

The musk ox wheels, churns up divots of sand with his hooves, pounds past our pile of gear. As he runs next to our packs, he tosses his horns at them and snorts loudly. He gallops onto the tundra, his coat blowing in the wind, the sound of his hooves muffled in the mosses. He stops, a dark outline against the dawn sky on a low ridge. He looks back at us, then canters out of sight.

"What the heck was that?" Eli calls from the tent. "It sounded like a bear!"

Marypat and I are both flat on our backs, trying to get our breath, calming our hearts.

"That was something!" Marypat breathes. Her eyes are dancing. "How often does that happen?"

In the Inuit tradition, animals are peers, kin. They are referred to as equals, other people, if you will. The divide that separates humans from the rest of the animal kingdom in the European mind-set does not exist in the Inuit reality. Many aboriginal cultures share this view. They would call the musk ox in camp "that guy" or "him."

"He was talking to you," they might well say.

It isn't only the animals that have spirits. Rocks do too. They respond to a different rhythm, to be sure, a radically different pace. The same goes for wind, or a storm. An Inuit elder might say that a blizzard is "hunting someone." Forces and objects my culture considers inanimate possess volition, intention, purpose.

When animals are our equals, when rocks have spirits, when the wind is acting according to some mission, it requires you to act differently. Fundamentally, it requires respect. Respect is what Inuit elders, and Native elders throughout North America, say is too often lacking. If we act with proper decorum, approach other life respectfully, they will give us what we need willingly. In that worldview, a hunter doesn't capture and kill his quarry so much as the animal gives itself to him.

Native people find the tagging and tranquilizing and collaring of wildlife abhorrent, precisely because it lacks respect. No matter that it is done in the interest of science and conservation. To chase down a grizzly by helicopter, shoot it with a dart, yank out a molar, and measure and weigh and tag the animal is an unforgivable affront.

Leaders from many Native traditions warn that our lack of respect is a very dangerous cultural character flaw, one that is destined to get us in trouble. They would say that earthquakes, tsunamis, hurricanes, volcanic eruptions, the unprecedented outbursts of natural forces taking place in recent history, are the earth's response to our lack of respect, to the loss of balance, and to our selfish, damaging habits. Our time to do something to rectify this is short, they say.

I don't know what was really happening with the musk ox. It isn't a thing to figure out logically. We were eight feet apart, eye to eye. Did we earn this meeting by virtue of our immersion? Were we simply in the right place at the right time? Could it have happened on Day 2?

For all I know, he was communicating something important, greeting us, inviting us in. In all likelihood it was my limitations that prevented a more profound interaction. I didn't know how to proceed.

It might have been my chance to shape-shift. I might have found a way to put on his coat. My spirit could have entered the form of that musk ox and learned things that would have changed my life.

Sure, and maybe it was just a simple confrontation, nothing more or less. A bull musk ox in its prime, an animal poised where Eli is poised, at the threshold of his physical potential, and damned if he was going to interrupt his daily beach walk because a couple of honkies were sitting on the sand right in his way.

Maybe.

I make light of it because I don't know what else to do with this experience, but I do not take it lightly. It is one of the most real things that has ever happened to me.

The kids pile out of the tent. We show them the hoofprints, the deep slashes where the musk ox galloped off the beach. They are crestfallen that they missed it. Course, if they had been outside, the musk ox never would have appeared.

After breakfast, we don't even eke out a mile before wind stops us again. At the point where the deep bay opens up, we lose the protection of land and winds howl out of the north. There is no appeal. Dark blue waves the color of night hump across the opening. Whitecaps flash everywhere. Wind-driven spume whips off the wave crests.

It's become routine, these delays. We pull the few things we require out of the canoes—tarp, reading book, journals, stove and snack food, jackets—and walk up to a flat spot below a ridge of ice-bulldozed boulders.

"Look," Sawyer calls. "The jaeger!"

Immune to the wind, the jaeger has again cut off the retreat of a small bird. Another duel ensues, another frenzied ballet played out between predator and prey. The jaeger is implacable, patient, unequivocal. When his opening comes, he takes his prey, accepts fuel, lives another day. The same as the fish we haul from the river and cook over our fires.

All day the wind blows. Occasionally I climb up to the top of the rocks, watch the lake, measure the distance to the island. We go off in search of wood, more and more a scarce commodity. I'm concerned that our stove fuel is getting low. Between the five of us searching several acres of shore, we collect a small armful of twigs, manage enough of a fire to cook our supper.

Lying on the cushion of moss under the tarp, Eli draws the jaeger, turned upside down, grabbing a longspur in its talons. We read from our third book of the summer, *City of the Beasts* by Isabel Allende. We look at maps, Ruby and Sawyer go in search of qiviut that gets shed on shrubbery. They have a small bag of the incredibly soft fur collected already.

How often do we sit still in one spot for an entire day, perhaps for several days at a time, waiting for our chance, hoping for our chance, and being together? These windbound delays alternate between prison and luxury. Nothing profound is discussed, no momentous revelations come our way. Just time in each other's company, that commodity so rare in our town lives.

Grudgingly, we give in, set up the tent, sleep through another night.

The next day, we make our move. It isn't much of an opening. The wind still blows, but the whitecaps aren't as constant. The waves are broad hills.

"Let's stay together," I say when we emerge from behind the shelter of land and the boats start bucking.

These crossings are grim and tense. The waves are always larger than they look from shore. The farther out we get, the bigger the waves are. The island is right in front of us, sharp and tangible, but a mile is a long way on a windy day in a canoe. In the event of a capsize, rescue by the second boat would be a very difficult thing. Swimming to shore in the cold water would be impossible.

I watch each wave coming toward the boat. Sets of larger ones break the rhythm. For these, I turn to quarter the wave fronts, the canoe rises and falls, water slurps past an inch below the gunwale. I look over to Marypat, stroking hard, her face turned into the wind, watching the water, the strain tensing her posture.

"How are you doing?" I shout across.

"Okay," she shouts, without looking at me. "It's not much fun, but we're making it."

After what seems like a long time, I can make out individual boulders on the shore of the island. Details come slowly into focus. I mark an orange-colored boulder to aim for, paddle and paddle, and it seems no closer. It isn't until we're past the end of the island that the waves finally relent and we can relax.

"I really don't like that at all," Marypat says.

"Let's paddle alongshore, see what the rest of the crossing looks like."

We relish the calm water, slide through it as long as we can, to the farthest edge of the island, and then stop to pee.

The remaining gap is roughly the same distance we just crossed, maybe a little longer. If we can get past it, we'll gain the protection of shoreline and be able to continue on without danger. But the waves look just as big, the water just as dangerous.

"I don't know, Al," Marypat says.

We look across to the solid land rising away from the lake. It is a moment of decision in which I am prone to let my judgment be swayed by my desire. *If we can only get past this, we're free*, I think. Marypat isn't as susceptible to the seduction. Give her a mountain peak to climb before a storm hits, and she's all for it, but this open water, this wind, handling the canoe with one of the kids, is a different matter.

We could camp here. A mile away from our last camp, which was a mile away from the one before that. We would be safe, we would wait again, go walking, look for wood, watch the lake. We wouldn't drown.

The kids don't weigh in. They don't know enough, and I think, by now, they understand that. It's our decision. They are certainly part of it, an added weight. It was the same way we felt when Marypat was pregnant with Eli. It wasn't just the two of us in the boat.

It's the same as climbing into a car on an icy day. A potentially fateful decision with objective risks. But here, with the waves rolling past, the wind tugging overhead, the awareness of our position, hundreds of miles from any resource that might remotely offer help, decisions like this can be debilitating.

We could wait days for calm. We could die in the next mile.

"I think we can do it," I say. "The last crossing was hard, but I never really felt in danger of capsizing. For this one, we'll have the buffer of the island stopping the waves for at least a while. I think we just stay together, take it easy. We'll be okay."

Marypat gives me a look. She turns back to face the lake. She is wearing her yellow rain jacket. She looks compact and solid.

"Do you think I have a very womanly body?" she asked me once.

"You have an athlete's body," I told her. "I'd take it over voluptuous curves any day."

But she is a mother, too, and right now, it's the mother, not the athlete, who is pondering the choice. She gazes across the gray, windy lake.

Then she turns, starts walking back to the canoes. We all follow her. We climb in, snug up the decks around us, tighten the life jackets, drop to our knees to lower our center of gravity. I feel the restless water under the hull.

"Ready?" I ask.

Marypat takes a very deep breath and starts paddling away from shore.

Thirteen

We came to this portage and our feet got cold and wet, but a couple of miles after the portage we had to stop because of the winds, so we got our feet warm, played games, and had dinner really late.

—SAWYER, GROUP JOURNAL

More than twenty-five years earlier, with a different partner on my first long northern expedition, I made a similar decision. We crossed a bay on a lake in northern Quebec, four days into the trip. Halfway across, my brother's boat capsized when a large wave tipped their gunwale underwater. In an instant, Craig and his partner were over, floundering in the waves, their packs floating free.

They very nearly died. By the time we rescued them, nearly capsizing ourselves in the process, they were comatose with hypothermia, their limbs stiff and rigid. When we finally managed to get to shore, we stripped down, undressed the two of them, and got into sleeping bags together, using our body heat to revive them.

It was a moment in which the impartiality of nature became vividly clear; an afternoon during which the same wilderness we came to for solace and exhilaration and spiritual refreshment didn't care whether we lived or died.

The images from that lonely, beautiful northern lake are always there when I set out on another open-water crossing in a wind. These are chances every paddler takes. To run a rapid or portage. To stay put or brave the weather. To go left or right of a midstream boulder. To strike off across open water. Calls made every day of a trip.

This time we are rewarded. The island provides enough of a wind shadow to dampen the waves. The water is rough, but the waves are regular, less choppy, more like swells. The canoes ride them well, and although the danger remains, the crossing goes easily.

"Everyone needs to pick a totem bird they want to be," Eli announces. "Then I'll draw them."

The shoreline is full of great campsites, knobs of smoothed rock covered with lichen and moss, *inuksuit* standing sentinel along the route. Our canoes coast along, sheltered from the reach of wind, sometimes at an angle that awards us a tailwind.

Periodically, as we paddle, we dip up water from the lake to drink. Filters, chemicals, iodine, boiling are unnecessary this far north. The water is clear, so cold as to be almost sterile, and we take it straight. Most towns in the northern tier of Canada do the same. They pump it out of the lakes and pipe it to houses without treatment.

This wilderness seems remote enough to be immune from contamination. To a large extent, it is. The climate is harsh, the insects daunting, the terrain difficult. Development requires a superhuman effort. There are a few diamond mines scattered throughout the tundra, some roads punched across the permafrost to the north of Yellowknife. Occasionally there is talk of developing hydroelectric power. For the most part, though, the land is forbidding enough to keep it all at bay.

That isn't to say that the environment is unsullied. Fact is, pollution is global, distributed by the jet stream, dropped in rain and snow. The organism of the planet is a dynamic web of ocean currents, winds, storm patterns, vegetative flux, water salinity, temperature gradients, thousands of factors interacting in a dance more complex than we can possibly fathom.

When the Chernobyl accident took place, in 1986, Marypat and I were spending our first winter on Lake Athabasca. We had a battery-operated radio that picked up CBC and a box full of spare batteries. We sat at the table listening to the news of the nuclear calamity by lantern light. As we heard the reports, the radioactive cloud began its migration across the globe, particularly in the high latitudes.

In the tundra North, radioactive material dropped to earth and concentrated in the moss and lichen eaten by caribou. Those same elements became further concentrated in the organs and meat of the deer.

Several years later, in 1989, at the conclusion of a trip down the George River, in Quebec, Marypat and I visited an Inuit community along Ungava Bay. We noticed that there were no dogs in town. Most northern communities are full of dogs, but in Kangiqsualujjuaq not a single one. We were told that all of the dogs had died after eating the organ meat of caribou in the years following Chernobyl.

We make camp at what looks like the last high ground before the Florida peninsula. Eli spends the evening drawing totem birds—a bufflehead for Ruby, a hovering rough-legged hawk for Sawyer, a peregrine falcon for himself, a jaeger for me, and a raven for Marypat. The winds die. Sunlight radiates the color of an oil lamp. The blackflies are enough in evidence to merit hoods, but they aren't panic inducing. I take a dip and wash up on a sloping ramp of bedrock.

The land hums, not just with bugs, but with the vibrancy of summer, the slow torrent of water running to the sea, the ceaseless urgency of growth, the inertia of life pressing forward. Our voices add an infinitesimal chord in the midst of the symphony.

When we land at the portage across Florida, the wind is back, the sky is low and gray, and the permafrost is thawing. We paddle the canoes as far up on shore as we can, but the ground is flooded for another twenty feet. Standing around, ankle-deep in stagnant water; it has been this way much of the summer. Portage trails are mucky and wet. Low-lying country is more marsh than ground. Only the bedrock is certain.

At first, I had put it down to the lateness of our stay. On previous trips, we were done by this time in August. But it's more than a few extra weeks of warmth, if the weather we've had can be called warm. There is simply more water than I remember—quite a lot more.

We take up portage mode. The kids hoist packs and dry bags, grab extraneous gear, and trudge across. Marypat and I rig the portage yokes and get the canoes set before shouldering them. Marypat has figured out how to carry the smaller canoe with her life jacket padding her shoulders.

THE KIDS UNDER HEAVY LOADS AND INSECT DURESS ON A PORTAGE.

"I'm really glad I can carry one of the boats," she says.

"Not as glad as I am."

Starting off, I avoid the deeper pools, hop from grassy tussock to grassy tussock, but it is too much effort with the boat overhead. In less than fifty feet I'm slogging through the pools in a straight line.

Much of the global warming discussion has focused on the melting ice caps, retreating glaciers, diminished pack ice. Only more recently has it become clear that the permafrost throughout the northern world is thawing at an unprecedented rate.

In Siberia, an area of permafrost the size of France and Germany combined has been steadily turning into a morass of bog and small lakes. It has been estimated that some 15 percent of the world's carbon is locked up in permafrost. As the ice melts, that carbon is being released, adding to the global warming phenomenon. Large areas of boreal forest throughout the subarctic have been collapsing into muskeg as the ground beneath the trees turns to mush.

The kids sit on packs on the far side, watching us come toward them under the canoes. Eli gets the camera out of its dry box and shoots pictures of us—red boats, gray sky, a floor of dark green peat. Then we all turn back for round two.

Thawing permafrost has a profound impact on the hydrology of a region. On the one hand, the greater supply of meltwater raises the river levels, as we have seen on the Kazan. Much of the shoreline we pass looks drowned. Even the lakes are high enough to cover low-lying vegetation, and we are here late in the season, when water levels are normally ebbing. The large amount of water certainly adds habitat for the already burgeoning populations of mosquitoes and blackflies.

While rivers have been rising, recent studies have also documented the disappearance of hundreds of tundra lakes in northern Canada and Siberia. Over a thirty-year period, and probably longer, ponds and lakes large enough to appear on satellite images have been shrinking dramatically or disappearing altogether.

A comparative study of satellite images in northern Siberia from the early 1970s to 2003 revealed that 10 percent of the lakes had shriveled significantly or vanished. What appears to be happening is that the permafrost layers under the lakes thaw, allowing the water to simply drain away into gravel soils. Similar findings have been reported by scientists in northern Canada and Alaska.

It doesn't always require deep thawing for a lake to drain away. Three or four feet, just enough to establish a drainage channel, is enough. And it can happen very quickly.

In 2005, a team of anthropologists from the University of Alaska at Fairbanks traveled with a Native family to a lake they made yearly trips to in order to hunt and fish. They were astonished to find that the lake had completely drained away in the year since their last visit.

Another Alaskan study, near Council, on the Seward Peninsula, found that fifty-one of fifty-three lakes had diminished dramatically over thirty years. The two that hadn't drained remained constant because the groundwater level was already at the surface and the water had nowhere to go.

One set of effects induced by thawing permafrost is a landscape known as thermokarst. It is the result of a cycle marked first by severe frost heave, which turns relatively level ground into a lumpy expanse. Then, as meltwater gathers, the broken ground holds hundreds of small lakes, many of which coalesce over time, forming ponds and extensive bogs. In the final stage, when deeper layers of permafrost thaw, the lake water drains off.

Water temperatures are also steadily rising—enough so that some Alaskan rivers that salmon traditionally swim up to spawn have reached near-lethal temperatures for those fish. The salmon weaken as a result, become prone to parasites and infections. Warmer rivers allow for the expanded range of some exotic fish species as well. Fish like the bream in Europe have been found in northern rivers they never inhabited before. These newcomers compete with, and in some instances prey on, native species.

The effects of climate change and shifting energy balance may be most dramatic in the high latitudes, but it is a world we all inhabit, and the ripple effects impact everyone. The lakes we paddle across, the rivers we descend in our canoes, the land bridges we cross on our portages—all of them are in play.

We only have six miles of Yathkyed Lake to go, once we've crossed Florida, but the wind is pounding down directly at us. We battle on against it for quite a while. I keep telling myself that it's all in the frame of mind. It's like the bugs. You have to rise above the onslaught, assert a kind of Zen calm. Pay no attention to that little island that has remained off my right shoulder for the last hour while we strained nonstop. Hey, we're not going backward.

Marypat and the kids are not on the same wavelength.

"This is stupid," Marypat shouts across. I am alone in my Zen-ness.

The problem is that the shore is low and wet for miles. We inch our way to a small point that looks a few inches higher than the surrounding bog and power stroke the boats as far onto ground as we can. I roll up my pants and go barefoot, hauling the loaded boats thirty feet farther inland before standing on somewhat dry ground.

We scout out a piece of higher terrain large enough for the tarp and tent and carry the essentials to it. It is cold. There is no firewood at all. The stove fuel is getting critically low. I fire it up long enough to boil water, but we can't stay warm under the tarp. Eventually we set the tent up, where we all snuggle into our down bags wearing long underwear and dry socks.

At dinnertime, or when our stomachs provoke us to declare it dinnertime, Ruby braves cold lake water up to her knees to wade out and fill the pots. I hear her singing out there, pants rolled up to her thighs, the wind whipping her hair. A hopeful band of clearing sky opens for the setting sun, but we've been suckered before. I hug Ruby hard when she comes in, still humming away.

"What do you guys say to another dawn dash?" I ask. "I really don't want to spend another day here in the swamp."

"I'm game," Sawyer says, "but look at the watch, okay, Dad? No earlier than four."

Everyone agrees.

In the predawn gloaming, I rummage around in Marypat's duffle for the neglected watch, which is still ticking, presumably keeping a semblance of accurate time. Accurate enough for our purposes. I can barely make out the hands. Three o'clock. No one stirs. The wind whispers, but seems significantly diminished.

That dark hour full of questions creeps past. When will the weather improve? Why can't we get two good days running? What have we done to our mileage average these last days? As I stew, I listen for any change in the wind.

"Time to go, guys," I say at four.

We forgo breakfast. The wind is rustling, but not yet strong. The cold comes through when we have to wade barefoot with the boats to get to deeper water. *Just give us these few miles, just get us off Yathkyed*, I think.

Eli is sleepy and not happy. "I'm hungry," he complains, a mile along. I cut him a thick slice of cheese from the lunch stores and we keep going. All the while the wind strengthens, bit by bit, until, for the last two miles, we're in pitched battle again, kneeling on the floor, stroking hard enough that our shoulders and backs ache.

Finally, the current slides under us, picks us up, helps us along. We sneak a brief rapid in a narrows, staying river left, dodging through some rocks, then come to a wide stretch. By now the kids are demanding a breakfast stop.

On a shelf of bedrock we break out the stove and a precious canister of fuel and start making pancakes. The wind, now, is shrieking. A bedraggled caribou carcass, largely consumed, lies in the willows behind us.

"We'd have never gotten off the lake if we'd waited," I say.

"Are the pancakes ready?" Eli responds.

"You know," Marypat says, looking around at the scudding cumulus, watching the cloud of her breath. "It could snow."

Fourteen

All day it was overcast and dead calm, with one small storm right before lunch. We went 28 miles all the way across Forde Lake and had some trouble finding the river again. We camped on a small, sandy beach. Lots of bugs. Today was a very long and hard day because it was almost all flatwater. All the new bannock flavors are delicious.

—ELI, GROUP JOURNAL

The waves that result from current running against an upstream wind are unique, an entirely different animal from waves on a lake or in a rapid. The two forces, wind and current, butt against each other. Each has monstrous power and magnitude. When they collide, the water humps up in a short, steep chop. Waves are closely packed together.

In the canoes, it isn't just slapping through waves that's dicey. The boat hull is fought over by the two elemental forces. The river current has hold of the canoe, bears it inexorably along in its downhill run, while the wind snatches at the hull and people, pushing and shoving upstream.

Without wind, the Kazan, here, would be a relatively flat surface, with rippling current and few waves. Under the lash of air, the river turns chaotic and our boats are little more than bits of flotsam. It is all we can do to hold a course.

Marypat and Sawyer are having a tough time. They get shoved across two-thirds of the river by the gusting wind. The boat wallows and skitters despite their efforts. Sawyer pulls for all he's worth, but he's no match. I'm not exactly controlling my canoe either, but I have more weight, more power to work with, and I can at least hold a general line.

We end up finding that seam of water against shore, out from the eddies, but slightly sheltered from the midstream forces. Without current, we'd be going nowhere. Without wind, we'd be cruising.

At the top of a long rapid we stop to scout. Sawyer immediately finds a soft bed of moss and throws himself down. Marypat has had it.

"I can't do it," she spits. "I don't care if we have current. The wind is just too much."

Ruby and Eli start collecting driftwood and dead willow while Marypat and I scout the whitewater. By the time we've discussed the run, the kids have a respectable pile that we break up and stash in the canoes. At the foot of the rapid the river fans out in a wide apron, studded with rocks, then bends into a lake section full of whitecaps that we can see clearly from a mile away.

At least we're off of Yathkyed, have a few miles under the hulls, can look ahead. I have a strange confidence that we'll get another window before the day is over. Wishful thinking or intuition, or both. Perhaps I've tuned into the patterns in some visceral way, subconsciously picked up on a sequence of wind shifts, the look of the sky, temperature change, the duration of weather patterns, enough to support this vague inclination toward hope.

Because we have wood, we go into an orgy of cooking and baking. By propping up one half of the fire pan, a partial windscreen is created, which we augment with flat rocks leaned up on either side. Even so, keeping a blaze going requires constant attention, constant feeding of the small sticks and twigs that pass for firewood.

The bannock factory kicks into action. Eli has turned into a pretty competent baker. He bends over the next mound of dough, kneads it into shape, separates the patties, slaps excess flour off of his paddle-worn hands. "More coals!" he calls. Dill bannock, bannock with sunflower seeds, cheese bannock, cinnamon-raisin bannock. Between batches we make hot drinks, cook one of our more involved meals. It doesn't matter whether it is actually dinnertime. We are fueling up, biding energy.

CAMP AND THE BANNOCK FACTORY IN FULL SWING.

The kids build a three-foot-tall barricade of rocks on a flat boulder to cut the wind. They chink the gaps with sphagnum and we huddle behind the windbreak to read and sip drinks.

"Someone's going to show up here and wonder what Inuit construction this is," I say.

"A classic reading wall," Marypat suggests.

As the day proceeds, the sky clears. By late afternoon the clouds are puffy and small. A rainbow arcs across the lake. Whitecaps still roughen the blue expanse, but the wind is going down.

It feels late when we push off again. The light has that amber quality. It's warmer than it's been in days and our departure is a liberation. Even so, near the outlet of the lake, where current picks up again, the waves are tall and steep.

"This is fun!" Eli says, reclining in the load. The boat torques and slaps through the wind and current chaos. But his exuberance dies when it keeps going and going, and when splashes of water slurp over the gunwale.

"Paddle hard," I shout to Ruby, who is my bow person. "We have to keep our momentum up in this stuff."

The river channel takes forever to reach, but finally the waves smooth out, the current takes hold, and we start to cruise. I rudder to hold our course and let the river have us. The speed is giddy, the river full of eddy and upwelling power. Shoreline whips past.

"Dad! Dad!" Ruby is urgently pointing and starts to draw the bow toward the bank. "Look!"

A small band of caribou trots along the river's edge. We paddle near. The deer are fat and sleek. Their coats are a rich chocolate brown. Their antlers are silhouetted against the evening sky.

We haven't seen the huge herds of deer, the throngs, as we call them, just these isolated bands, and this is the closest we've been to them. The animals graze along as they move, unconcerned with the bits of red color moving past.

Two main herds of caribou occupy this part of Canada: the Beverly herd and the Qamanirjuaq herd. Combined, their numbers are estimated at almost eight hundred thousand animals. The Qamanirjuaq herd calves each summer in a territory east of Yathkyed Lake, quite close to our location. The Beverly herd pushes farther north, near the Arctic Ocean, migrating some fifteen hundred miles every year.

Over the course of the summer, they pulse here and there across the tundra in accordance with food, weather, river crossings, the ancient urges of instinct. Then, some time in August, they start south again, moving toward tree line and more moderate winter conditions, as far south as Manitoba and Saskatchewan.

Along the way, calves are preyed upon by wolves and grizzly. It is common to find the small, fresh carcasses littering the migration routes. For predators, it is the time of plenty, the time to gorge and fatten young in preparation for the lean season to come.

For the Inuit, it was, and to a large extent, still is, the time to stockpile before the dark months. Traditionally, the fat deer taken in late summer and fall were the savings account against starvation. The meat was dried in strips and the fat rendered into blocks, and stores of the precious food were carefully cached away under piles of rock.

Even now, living in towns, the Native people depend on caribou for a significant portion of their yearly diet. Starvation may no longer be the certain result of an empty hunting season, but financial and nutritional hardship in northern communities clearly are. The movements of the deer are inconsistent and unpredictable. Hunting them successfully is far from assured.

When Marypat and I were here, years ago and a few weeks earlier in the summer, we saw the throngs of caribou—rivers of animals going by for hours and days at a time. We paddled our canoe among caribou swimming at crossings. We watched a wolf separate and hunt down, and then devour, a young calf.

Tonight, the caribou are lazy with plenty. They move without hurry, stop to graze and glance around. Other than the bother of insects, it may be the most relaxed and unstressed time of year for them. In the lingering glow of sunset, they look magnificent, supple, vibrant.

We slip past them. The river bears us downhill. This flow is nothing but water molecules massed together by drainage patterns and then pulled along by the impartial beckoning of gravity. Moving through lakes, past ribs of rock, rolling over gravel bars, dynamic as wind or fire. The inexorable flow is mesmerizing, hypnotic, dangerous, heady. We swing along in our boats, eating miles, watching for more caribou, while night comes on. No one talks. Ruby doesn't even sing.

It is the same day that began in the uncertainty of dawn, wading barefoot away from a mucky camp, struggling against wind, making pancakes under a sky that might snow on us. It ends on a flood-worn bench above the Kazan, where we set the tent on a smooth platform of bedrock with a view over the broad, hurrying river, and where we aren't even tempted to predict the fortunes of morning.

"I want to make it across Forde Lake today," Ruby announces at breakfast.

"I like it," I say. "That's probably thirty miles, but I like the attitude."

Every night in the tent, we study the maps. Me most of all, but the kids are well apprised of our location, our goals, what's coming up. They know what thirty miles of lake paddling would take. They also know that being windbound several days in the last week put us thirty or forty miles in the hole in terms of maintaining our average.

Forde Lake could be a major obstacle. No one has forgotten the battle to get across Ennadai Lake, or the potential for winds to stop us cold even on small pieces of exposed water. Forde Lake is wide and round, twenty miles or more from end to end. On the Barrens, no place is immune to the perils of exposure. Exposure is the given.

Our camp breakdown is an efficient process. I clean up breakfast with Ruby while Marypat and the boys stuff sleeping bags, roll pads, drop the tent. The food packs are compact and manageable now. Everything fits economically into the canoe hulls. During interludes in the packing, we wander off in search of twigs and driftwood to carry along. We all line up to brush teeth and take vitamins.

A lone caribou works its way upriver on the far bank. There is something forlorn and dejected about single caribou, like lost children in an empty park.

More river, more rapids, the hurling current, then the expanse of Forde Lake opens before us. It feels as if we've been riding a train, wind in our faces, and then are suddenly dropped off at a platform, dragging suitcases.

The lake is flat and calm. We say nothing to jinx it. A broad hill rises to the west, and far down the lake, another one shoulders against the skyline. We have to paddle down to it, past it, and on another half a dozen miles to truly make Ruby's goal.

We take it in little bites. It is too demoralizing to aim far ahead. Across a bay, to a prominent white rock, the next point, a small beach. Meantime the hill to the west slowly slides by, until, finally, I have to look back at it over my shoulder. The hill ahead is eternity. It resolves in excruciating slow motion, turns from blue-green monochrome to a landform with texture, with open patches of gravel, with boulders, with dense patches of willow. The distant horizon reels up out of the shimmering lake, dark fringes of hair in the impossible distance.

My bad arm aches, goes numb. I switch sides. The kids come up with discussion topics. School, bad teachers, what we should do for Thanksgiving, who will be the soccer coach. I keep the map on the bottom, between my feet, and maintain a chronology of points passed, bays crossed, islands in the distance, miles covered, miles to go.

Dark thunderheads tower nearby. They hardly move. There is no wind to push them anywhere. The warm air rises, forms these billowing columns of storm combustion, and they squat above the landscape, casting shadows. At the point we finally pull in for lunch, we shrug on rain gear. It spits on us. It grows suddenly cold. But the storm cloud only grazes us. The air calms. The lake remains a mirror full of sky and cloud.

"I don't know if I can do it," Marypat says, miles after lunch.

We've been creeping past points of ice-bulldozed rocks. Each one seems tangible and close but takes thousands of strokes to finally pass. I have to keep myself from pushing harder, leaving Marypat behind. At the same time, both of my arms have gone numb. I have to concentrate to hold my grip on the paddle. Ruby is adamant. The boys are game too.

"C'mon, Mom," Eli says. "We can do it."

We huddle up on the water, look at the map. The far hill is finally alongside. We have five or six miles to go, and we can save significant distance by making a beeline across the lake to the river outlet.

"That's probably a four-mile crossing," Marypat says. "Maybe five."

I take a compass bearing, aim off a bit, sight on a pimple of land along a distant ridge.

"Let's get this lake done, sweetie."

I lean over and kiss her, this woman I have passed so many watery miles with. She sighs.

I should let her take the lead and make myself stay behind, but I don't. Crossings are full of angst for me. It isn't only the potential danger, the chance that winds will suddenly come up, the urgency to make it across, the memories of that day with my brother in Quebec. That awareness drives me like a whip, but I am also driven by the need to know I've made the right calculation, that I've arrived where I hope to, that my compass and course have worked out.

There is always the chance, at these northern latitudes, that the declination has radically shifted since the map was made, that we weren't precisely where we thought we were when I took the bearing, that some iron body in the bedrock has skewed the magnetic needle. We could lose days poking around dead-end bays in search of the outlet if things go wrong.

As I paddle, holding to the distant landmark, I keep interpreting the map, looking for the defining landmarks, trying to fit things together. Marypat and Eli slip behind. The lake is restful, the sun warm. The sounds of our paddles entering the water, slinging arcs of water drops on the return, the small bow wave rippling, break the somnolence. Four or five miles is a long way in a canoe in the middle of a lake.

LINING BOATS DOWN A WHITEWATER LEDGE ON THE LOWER RIVER.

Partway across, when the land we left and the land we're aiming for seem about equidistant, I become convinced that we're heading too far north. The land doesn't jibe with my reading of the map. As long as I don't overdo it, we should be able to angle up the lakeshore and not lose much distance or get pulled off into the wrong bay.

Trust the compass, I keep saying to myself. But I'm not convinced. The land in front of me doesn't look right. I can't stand the not knowing. I push myself, say nothing, keep studying the map.

When I finally look back, Marypat's boat is a distant speck. I stop, chagrined. Ruby collapses backward on the load to rest. We sit on the open, glassy surface of the lake. It is a long time before they finally come up to us.

"Jesus, Dad!" Eli explodes.

"Why aren't you heading for that point anymore?" Marypat says. "And why wouldn't you wait?"

"I'm sorry."

We study the map together. Marypat thinks we should stick to the original bearing, but I've been stewing over this for miles now, and I'm convinced that we need to bear off higher along the shore. "Look, it doesn't hurt to come out a bit higher than the outlet. Then we just turn down to it."

"But I think the outlet might be way down there. Why don't we stick to the bearing?"

"Because I don't think the bearing is right."

"Okay." Marypat is clearly exhausted. "Where are you aiming for now?"

"See that little beach there?" I point to a white line of sand. "I was heading for that. I think the bay to the right of it might actually be the outlet."

"I'm heading for that, and then I'm stopping. I don't care if we know where we are or where the river is."

It still takes a long time, hundreds and hundreds of paddle strokes, to reach the narrow strip of gravelly beach, and when we grind into shore, we are no surer of our whereabouts. It is an agitation I can't stand.

I ignore everything while studying the map, trying to wring some bit of solid information out of it. The lake shimmers to the horizon. Long fingers of water extend away. We might follow them, find the outlet, or not. A bay dips off around the corner. I had hopes that it was the river outlet, but as we came closer, it looked more and more like a closed bay, and we didn't have the energy to paddle over and make sure.

"I don't care," Marypat says again. "We're camping here. We'll figure it out in the morning."

Fifteen

Foggy, chilly, cloudy, windy, a bit of sun. Woke up to wind and cold. We decided to go. Had to stop 8 miles down river. We decided to leave in the afternoon and go 10 miles further. We are camped at a beautiful camp site with 5 musk ox behind us. Time for bed. Bye-bye.

—RUBY, GROUP JOURNAL

Waiting for morning is not something I'm capable of. Without a word, I abandon Marypat and the kids to the chore of unpacking and strike off inland, toward a ridge, to get a vantage with a better view. The map is in my hand. I walk quickly. I know I'm shirking my duties, but I can't help myself.

The ground is hummocky, a mixture of exposed rock and mucky depressions. I have to skirt the deeper standing water but soon give up trying to keep my feet dry. Blackflies swarm my face. I pull on my head net, keep striding, brush the exposed backs of my hands from time to time.

Fourteen years earlier, we camped near the river outlet, perhaps somewhere nearby. Marypat's belly was stretched tight by then, and her face was round as a drum. Her paddle rubbed across her midsection with every stroke. When she had to pee, it meant now. Sometimes we would stop for lunch in the middle of the day and she'd nap in the sun.

The bay I still hope might be the river outlet pulls me on. I can't tell whether it ends or whether it turns to river. The closer I get, the more promising it looks, but I guard against optimism. If it is not the outlet, I'm stumped. We will have no choice but to range up and down the shore looking for clues.

Now I'm walking through pools of standing water. My legs are wet to the knees. I think, perhaps, that I see the vague texture of current, maybe. I don't let myself believe until I stand within feet of the water, where the river pulls away downhill toward a small rapid. No doubt.

Our camp is probably within a quarter mile of the place we chose when Eli was squirming around in the womb, all elbows and knees. If I hadn't kept aiming up the lakeshore, we'd be a mile or more down the coast and very confused. It's tempting to be smug, but I know better. I know it's as much luck as skill.

I turn, start back, almost trotting, full of the news.

Camp is taking shape. From a quarter mile I can see the tent going up, the pile of gear next to a cook site, everyone doing the daily chores, idly waving at blackflies as they work. Sawyer is walking the wave line, picking up sticks of firewood.

I have virtually forgotten that three of these trip members are my children. We have weeks and weeks behind us, hundreds and hundreds of miles. We've weathered everything together—the cloudbursts, the bug hatches, the days of inaction, the long slogs like today. They are only tangentially my children. Right now, they are my expedition-mates.

I find myself swearing more freely than I ever would at home. I tell bawdy jokes. Marypat and I are frank about our sexuality. Recently, at a floating rest break, Marypat reached across to my boat when I was lying back and goosed me in the crotch. Eli just shook his head.

The other day, Ruby was asking Marypat why she didn't like one of the characters in the book we're reading.

"Because she's a selfish bitch," Marypat had said.

"Jeez, Mom," Ruby said. "A little harsh, don't you think?"

"Just the truth."

From time to time they'll snipe at each other, argue over whose turn it is, fall prey to that sibling messiness. Then I remember. Oh yeah, I'm the dad here.

For weeks I waited for that protesting note to creep into the trip dynamics. I realize, now, that it isn't going to happen. They know there is no plan B. More than that, they have measured up. They know they can do it, and that knowledge makes them formidable. I don't know if they are consciously proud of themselves, but they should be.

This summer there has been no such thing as a run of good weather. It is all we can do to beat around the corner to the river outlet in the morning. Forde Lake, glass flat the day before, is nasty with waves the color of gunmetal. If we hadn't made Ruby's goal, we'd be stuck in camp. As it is, we have to quarter the canoes into the wind, battling to keep an angle and stroke forward, sideslipping until we reach current.

There is no hurry. Several wide spots, small lakes, stand in our way, interrupting the flow of river. We will only make it so far in this wind. In the first section of current, the wind comes at us from the side, so we cozy up against the bank, out of the worst of it, and coast along. Where the river widens, it turns, so the wind is not quite a tailwind.

The canoes plow through the heavy waves. In the stern, it is almost impossible to paddle forward. Keeping the boats lined up with the waves is a full-time occupation. Eli and Sawyer provide the momentum from the bow. Ruby's songs are snatched away in the gale. The land is scraped rock, erratic boulders, the ribs of the earth.

A small, domed island, the shape of a gumdrop, marks the end of the first lake section. We collect behind it in the wind eddy and climb out for a break. Ruby adds some more feathers to her collection. I see her huddled with Marypat, showing her the collection, their backs to the wind. I make a circuit and collect a handful of twigs. A small *inukshuk* stands on top, two rocks perched solidly together, gnomelike. We could see it three miles away. Sawyer builds it a companion.

I used to consider *inuksuit* inviolate. I would never even think of repairing one or building one of my own. They are the markers of another time, another reality, symbols of culture and history. Sacred.

I still think that, fundamentally, but I no longer feel so constrained around them. I would never knock one down or change it, but I've repaired a few, and I've made a few of my own. The kids feel no such compunction. They build them in the spirit of the place, to mark our passing, to say something, to keep busy. It is an impulse, I think, that the Inuit who lived here would accept.

From the island, we angle for the next river section, but pull in below a rock ridge where the current picks up. We haven't walked inland very much. There hasn't been time, the ground doesn't make for good walking, the bugs have been forbidding. Here, it is all rock, the wind keeps the bugs in the mosses, and we know we'll have to stop soon in any case.

We saunter toward the low ridge. It feels good to walk. My knee is almost back to normal. I haven't been downing medicine for a few days. I'm finally feeling healthy, in true trip shape. Caribou trails cobweb over the ridge. Ancient paths trod by thousands of hooves over thousands of years. Paths the Inuit knew all about. They are empty today, but fresh tracks are everywhere, like they were just going by this morning.

On top of the rock ridge the view opens up—more of the same in all directions. Small lakes, ribbons of streams, scraped ridges, the litter of boulders. Gray, green, blue, and the dark sky, clamped low. Nothing moves.

Nothing moves, but I know there are Barren Lands grizzly tucked away in the panorama I look across. There are herds of caribou, wolves with pups in the den, thousands of birds. Hearts beating, as full of life and ambition as mine.

The Kazan runs through it, the dominant and most dynamic feature, carving its way around bends, feeling through islands, emptying into the next small lake. And it is there, at the opening, that we get windbound again. The gusts slant sideways across the lake, piling up surf. The next river section is three miles off. If we had binoculars, we could see it clearly, but it doesn't matter.

Time has become as fluid as the river. I have forgotten how to measure it except by miles and hunger and the look of the sky. The day passes. We read. We forage alongshore for wood, kindle a fire in a patch of open gravel and make food. The boys drink coffee sweetened with brown sugar to conserve the skimpy bag of cocoa. Eli draws birds. I study the map. Nesting materials—feathers, clumps of down—are scattered around, the ephemeral remnants of season.

Much later, the wind drops several notches and we go on. My canoe gets ahead again making the crossing. I apologize again at the river outlet. I make myself follow Marypat's boat, keep my pace to hers. The winds keep dropping, the day stills. We paddle through an elongated opening in the gathering twilight that will last for hours.

A single caribou trots on shore next to us, keeping pace. It seems as curious about us as we are about it. We paddle in silence, looking at the deer. It makes its way through the rough ground, awkward and graceful looking at once, an animal made to be here.

The river makes a sharp bend where we decide to camp. A major rapid punctuates the corner. In the morning we will sneak the upper section, staying river left, then portage over a ledge lower down. The whitewater is a maze of boulders, holes, waves, ledges extending across the entire breadth of river, half a mile or more.

Five musk ox graze in the tundra directly behind our camp. They seem unconcerned by our presence. They move ponderously as they tug at vegetation. Several of them lie down, dark hills of fur.

Marypat, Sawyer, and Ruby take off with the camera on a stalk. This is the sort of thing Marypat loves. They all crouch low, run from one protecting outcrop to another, moving in for the best shot. I hear her giggle when they flop behind a boulder.

Eli is rigging a fishing pole, intent on a pool below a ledge he's identified. He watches the stalkers as he ties on the lure. This time, he can't stand being left out. He drops the pole and takes off at a fast crouch, catching up to the team.

The next morning, the musk ox are still there, even closer. While I cook breakfast, Marypat, Ruby, and Sawyer head out on another safari. Eli goes down to the fishing hole, where he lost a couple of big trout the night before. I settle in by the fire, enjoy my coffee, make notes in my journal, boil water for a hot cereal breakfast.

When Marypat and the kids get close, the musk ox circle into a protective ring, facing out. It is an instinctive strategy, designed to protect the vulnerable young who are corralled in the middle. It works pretty well against wolves, their main predator, but is decidedly ineffective against rifles.

When wolves attack musk ox, they are sometimes able to knife in and grab the nose and mouth of the prey in their jaws. They hang on, whipped back and forth, until the musk ox finally suffocates.

The musk ox move off, but several caribou with impressive racks are bouncing around, and sandhill cranes fly low over the tundra, calling. Several *inuksuit* stand out in profile against the skyline. The photo safari drops out of sight over the ridge.

When I'm on my second cup of coffee, Eli appears, striding upstream.

"Dinner is served!" He hoists up a huge lake trout. The fish is half his height.

"I bet it took me half an hour to play him in," he says. "I kept thinking the line would break! My arms are toast."

"Hey, look at that," he points inland.

A mature caribou is coming toward us at a trot. It eats the distance, right at us, and only veers off when it is twenty feet away. We can hear his leg joints clicking as he runs. Far behind, Marypat and the kids are returning alongshore, dark specks swallowed by the land.

Sixteen

In the morning we were all snuggled up in the tent and heard the wind. We got up. Cold! Then we had pancakes with berries. Yummy. The rest of the day we read, told stories, baked bread and ate.

—SAWYER, GROUP JOURNAL

Thirty Mile Lake hums with the memory of the Caribou Inuit. It is a narrow, sinuous widening, as much river as lake, and the current is discernible across much of it. Islands stud the open water. The shoreline is weathered bedrock and gravel beach. *Inuksuit* punctuate every high point, some massive and imposing, others frail and whimsical. Tent rings, graves, pieces of worked wood and bone lie on the ground. Whenever we stop, we find something of them.

Near the beginning of the lake, in a tight channel between islands, we pull in at an *inukshuk* that stands fifteen feet tall and ten feet across, made up of boulders I can't imagine moving without a forklift. Large as it is, the rocks are delicately balanced, shimmed at the corners with smaller flakes of stone. It marks an extensive graveyard.

The wind is blowing. The air is cold. It rasps against my exposed skin. Collections of rock make circles on the ground. Here and there, heaped-up piles of head-sized boulders mark the graves. Some are intact and well covered. Others are broken apart. Some are completely exposed. There are human femurs, ribs, vertebrae lying exposed to the weather, small random puzzles of bones nested together.

Alongside, in some cases, more-modern artifacts, left by some visitor, perhaps a relative—enamel cups, a teapot, a rusted pail. The kids walk soberly among the bones. They are subdued by the sight.

Eli comes around the edge of a loose pile of rocks and is ambushed by a human skull staring at him. He stumbles back several steps, can't look directly at the skull. "Bones are one thing," he says, "but that's somebody's head. I didn't expect that."

The skull has settled into the mossy ground. Dark lichen grows along the sutures of bone. The eye sockets are slightly tipped up, as if staring toward the distant horizon. A blue enamel cup rests on the ground nearby, rusty with age.

We shelter behind a low shelf of rock to eat lunch. Ruby finds a piece of caribou leg bone that has been sawed lengthwise into a thin slat. Several holes have been drilled through the bone. It must have been some kind of handle or splint.

Living here, essentially in the Stone Age, required remarkable ingenuity.

Not simply to overcome the challenges of brute survival—living through the howling winters, scraping food together, traveling across this terrain. All the little things too. How to make buttons, how to hold tiny strips of wood together to make a serving platter, what to make needles out of, how to blunt the dazzling glare of sun on snow, how to make sled runners glide, what served as an adhesive, how to mortise together the joints of a kayak frame. All of it based on technology made up of small pieces of wood, rocks, and animal parts.

When we paddle on, everyone is quiet, thinking about the people whose bones lie exposed on this lonely ground. Our route takes us through a scatter of islands. We position ourselves to take the best advantage of the wind, or to hide from it. Alongside a high island, Eli sees a set of caribou antlers poking up against the sky.

"We have to stop," he demands. "I want to get those antlers."

"We're not stopping," I say. "We couldn't carry them anyway."

I resist Eli's badgering. He is the most impulsive of the kids. When he wants something, he demands gratification, and in short order. He doesn't save his money. He hates to wait. He'll be hell on credit cards. I can see him in bankruptcy court. Sawyer, on the other hand, hoards his savings to a fault. We have to plead with him to jump on a great deal. Ruby doesn't seem to care. She loses track of her money, leaves it lying around, asks Sawyer to take care of it for her.

In the end, we pull in at the tip of the island because the wind is too strong and the lake rough. We've made our miles. As soon as we haul the boats up, Eli runs after the caribou rack. Sawyer follows.

When they return, Eli is breathless. "You know that rack?" he says. "Guess what? It was attached to the caribou! This big bull was just lying there sleeping. I walked right up to him before he jumped up and ran away."

"Probably thought he was pretty safe out here on this island," Marypat laughs.

There are berries ripening in the mosses. Blueberries and salmonberries. Small bushes, low to the ground, but loaded with fruit. Sawyer and Ruby go collecting, eating as they forage. Snatches of their chatter carry on the breeze.

This time of summer, the month of August, was the most relaxed time for the traditional Inuit. I read a quote from an elder once. "There was nothing to do in August," she remembered, wistfully. "We just walked around on the tundra, eating berries."

Considering the rest of the yearly round, full of brutal physical hardship, the day-to-day labor of survival, a month spent wandering, feeding yourself juicy nuggets of fruit, must have felt like five-star luxury.

We are windbound another day. It is the birthday of Ruby's best friend, so we christen our current prison Lizzie Island. We make salmonberry pancakes in the lee of a windbreak, then a batch of blueberry pancakes. Our hands are stained with berry juice. We read out loud from the fourth book of the summer. Whitecaps stud the view. We take turns wandering the periphery of the island. The caribou still shares it with us, but he's more wary since Eli surprised him.

The following dawn is still breezy and very cold, but paddling seems possible.

"It would be good if we made this island." Eli points to the end of the lake on the map. "We'd be right across from our next portage and done with the lake."

It's an ambitious goal, perhaps a wishful one, given the continuing wind.

RUBY, WITH A WEALTH OF BLUEBERRIES DESTINED FOR PANCAKES.

The paddling is brutal. My left arm goes numb again. I try to ignore it. Marypat is struggling too. In one or two sections the route allows us to benefit from a tailwind. It is an unspeakable relief to switch sides and let the wind help.

We stop at a prominent *inukshuk*, stretch our legs, find another isolated pile of rocks covering its scatter of human bones. Later, we stop again at a thin point to eat lunch. Late in the day, after an interminable open stretch, Thirty Mile Lake narrows down to a tight pinch with river current, then widens again for the final, three-mile slog to the island Eli marked as our goal.

The last miles on this kind of endurance day are always the worst. The end is in sight, right there, beckoning. We all know we'll make it, but the urge to be there, to end the toil, to hurry our progress, is debilitating. For the last mile I don't let myself look up. No one talks. The island is so close, yet demands so many strokes to reach. I try not to count.

Finally we slide up on a sloping shelf of banded rock, smoothed by the waves, angled just right. I stand in the canoe, arch my back, raise my arms over my head. My butt is numb, my arm hasn't had feeling for the last ten miles. I look over at Marypat. She is kneeling on the bottom of her canoe, draped forward across the packs.

"That was torture," she says. "That might have been the hardest single day of the entire trip."

On the mainland, another herd of musk ox grazes near the water. There are several calves in this group. They look comical, like masked miniatures. One of them cavorts around the adults, kicking its heels, running in circles. "Look at that little guy," Ruby giggles. This has been the summer of musk ox. They have been the trip totem animal. Twice we have been less than ten feet from them, eye to eye, staring across the divide of our universes.

Search for wood, pitch the tent, blow up pads, collect some dry grass for tinder, unpack boats, set up the kitchen, start a fire, fill the pot, gaze at the musk ox and the country they live in, face the wind to keep the bugs at bay. Day 31. Four hundred fifty miles behind us. It is all as familiar now as the details of our home in Montana. Any one of us could erect the tent blindfolded. Every one of us can efficiently build a fire. The paddles fit our hands like appendages.

Eli settles into a folding camp chair next to the fire pan, measures the day's miles with the grimy length of dental floss. His hands are chapped, dry, lined with fire soot. "Twenty," he announces. "Booyah! I thought we could make it."

"Felt like fifty," Marypat says.

After dinner we stroll around the island. The kids pick up caribou antlers. I collect wood. On a flat bench there are several tent rings. The Inuit could have camped here last week. It is a lovely spot, looking over the lake. The sky is ragged with cloud, lit red by the low sun.

Along a gravel beach, Marypat suddenly bends down, picks up a rock. "Look at this," she breathes.

She holds a short, simple pipe carved out of soapstone. It is exquisitely worked. The bowl is smooth and symmetrical. The stem has a small chip in it. Some lichen grows on the edges. A hole is drilled at the bottom of the bowl and through the stem. The pipe fits easily in her palm. You could imagine tucking it in the pocket of your coat, holding it between your fingers, putting it to your lips. We pass it around. Everyone draws air through it.

The pipe is worn smooth with use, with weather, with time. We all imagine the other lips that touched the pipe, the smoker's face squinting behind its ruddy glow.

"I don't know how I saw it in all these little rocks," Marypat says.

"Who knows how old this thing is," I say. "How long it's been lying here on the shore. You could still smoke this, no problem."

Sometimes, just getting away from camp is the biggest dilemma of the day. We're two hundred yards from the beginning of a portage that will cut off a rapid-filled bend of river, but the morning wind comes down the lake at us. Waves crash on the benign weathered rock slope we gently rode the canoes onto the night before. Trying to launch into that surf, we'd fill with water in two waves. Even the decks won't help much.

In order to leave we have to first carry everything around a point of rock where the water is calmer. Once away from the breakers, the waves aren't dangerous, but without protected water, it would have been difficult to leave at all.

The portage has three stages. First, a short carry across marshy ground to a narrow lake about half a mile long. I have a little trouble scouting out the location of the lake. I wonder if it might be one of those bodies of water that has disappeared due to the thaw of permafrost, but I eventually sight it from a low ridge.

A lone musk ox watches us as we make the carry. He approaches within twenty yards at one point before turning away. As we walk, we collect wisps of the fine qiviut and give them to Sawyer, who has a plastic bag full of fur in his wind-shirt pocket. A pair of sandhill cranes flies ponderously over the ground, legs stretched behind, long necks graceful as airborne snakes. Their burbling call is an arctic sound. Whenever I hear them in some Montana grain field, I am taken north.

Second, we heap everything loosely into the canoes and paddle down to the far end of the small lake, where we land in rocky shallows and unload again. The final carry is a quarter mile or less, down into a small gully that leads back to the bank of the Kazan below the pounding rapid. We are as much a team on the portage trail as we are in camp or in the boats. Hardly anyone speaks. We heft our loads, pick up loose odds and ends, hoist the canoes overhead, walk across the trackless land, and load up again at the end.

It is the warmest day we've had in weeks. Back on the water, we strip to T-shirts, peel off long underwear. The morning wind becomes a helping tailwind on the next lake section. We are aiming for Kazan Falls, if our luck and the weather holds.

At the next river narrows, four or five miles along, we gunwale the two canoes together, let the current pull us.

"That was the most pleasant paddling we've had in days," Marypat says. "God, what a contrast to yesterday. It felt so good to just paddle along with a wind at our backs and the warm sun on our skin. Where has this been all summer?"

"Let's read some more," Ruby suggests. Marypat takes out the book, reclines in the stern.

Lunch supplies come out in the boats. Bannock with reconstituted hummus, dried fruit, nut mix, some strips of elk jerky. It feels too sweet to stop, too heady to slip along at the pace of the river without working at it. On other trips, these good days have been if not commonplace, at least regular. This summer we've learned to savor them, rare treats followed by the next blast of nasty stuff.

A collection of *inuksuit* on a rock ridge finally entices us to land, where we wander among them. Archways made of stone, a single spall of rock in the shape of a mitten, small towers. No telling what the message is or was. Could be as simple as "I was here one day with nothing to do, so I made some art." I feel precisely as I've felt in front of rock panels of petroglyphs or by a burial mound at Troy. Someone from an unfathomably different place was declaring themselves in the same spot I now stand, where I leave the momentary impressions of my feet in the moss.

A two-mile section of rapids precedes the actual falls. We take them on river right with exquisite caution. Again and again we pull in to shore, walk downstream, assess the next bit of fast river current, talk over our plans, troop back to the boats, cinch everything up, follow each other through, then land to do it again.

It takes a long time. The kids quarry more qiviut off of some willows as we scout. The water isn't particularly difficult, but another twenty feet out the current gets pushy, the waves hump up, and the headlong rush toward the falls accelerates like a train leaving the station. At each stage, before we push off from shore for another pitch of water, I reach up to touch the stone amulet hanging against my chest.

Bit by bit, the two red boats jockey through a sequence of maneuvers. We dodge past boulders, slip around points of rock, pull back toward the bank, drop from eddy to eddy, let ourselves down the river as carefully as climbers on a rock face. Move by move, challenge by challenge. All the while the roar builds ahead. The river drops from sight. Mist rises out of the maw of the gorge.

We pull in ten feet from the brink. Another canoe length and we'd be sucked to our deaths. I yank the canoe well up, do the same for Marypat's. The Kazan jockeys past, nudging the ends of our fabric-skinned craft. We stand together in this loud place, by the bows of our boats, precisely where we stood fourteen years before, alone with our stowaway, more than four hundred days out.

Seventeen

We started with a long portage with a small lake in the middle of it. We saw ptarmigan and a musk ox during the portage. We paddled all the way to the falls. We also collected lots of musk ox fur today. The falls are the biggest I've ever seen.

—ELI, GROUP JOURNAL

The falls are irresistible, a vortex of power with a pull like gravity. We shuttle gear safely above the river, tie off the canoes, and succumb.

The Kazan funnels toward the brink, moving fast, then slides over a series of broken ledges and cliffs, frothing and pounding against the bedrock. Several sections of falls foam through ramparts and squat, resistant towers. The mist of battered water is a light drizzle. The noise is thunderous, elemental.

Below the main drop, the river channel narrows through a deep, cliff-bound vise for a mile or more. There, the water surges and piles, boils, slams around corners, spins in powerful eddies, black holes of river whirling with trapped flotsam and driftwood. Power beyond imagining.

Although I do imagine being in a boat, battling to stay upright, riding the back of this impartial, eager, wild force, it does not entice me in the least. It is sphincter tightening enough to look at it from the edge of a cliff.

A peregrine flushes out from its rocky perch halfway down the rock face. It is a profligate place, excessive in every way, throwing power around with tireless abandon. Lonely too. Quiet. Embedded in the midst of a universe of space. A nugget of sublime grandeur where hardly anyone comes. A mile or two away, you'd never know it existed.

The kids scramble through the crags along the edges, their coats bright against the gray rock. They have never been to Niagara Falls, or any other falls that approach this volume and force. All the miles, the string of camps, the thousands of paddle strokes, have brought them to this outburst, this bellowing assertion. But it doesn't feel like the middle of nowhere; it feels centered, precisely where we have been coming all this time.

A rock cairn, not an *inukshuk*, marks the beginning of the portage trail. Someone has left a single musk ox horn on the pile of rocks. It is smooth and heavy, beautifully curved, scored with ridges. Hollowed out, it would make a perfect ladle or bowl. A find the Inuit would have treasured.

A battered metal ammo box rests in the rock pile. Inside, several journals full of entries logged by people who have made their way here and stopped long enough to scribble down their stories and impressions. Notes full of hardship and triumph, wind and bugs, caribou, humor, tragedy. Underlying all of it, a reverence for place and homage to the power of an immersion in it. Everyone in every entry seems to have been altered, at least momentarily, by the experience.

We thumb our way back through the pages stained with squashed blackflies, bits of food, grimy fingerprints. Back through the years. Until we turn a page and see our names. July 24, 1991.

I remember Marypat that afternoon. She had opened the book and read a large title page dedicated to the Brotherhood of the Kazan.

"Brotherhood, my ass," she hissed. "What about the damn sisterhood!"

This night, when we retire, we bring the ammo box into the tent with us. Everyone is arranged, sprawled on sleeping bags, journals and pencils in hand. Damp, fragrant socks hang from a drying cord strung across the top of the tent. The mesh pockets bulge with antlers and sticks, bags of fur, feathers poking out at odd angles.

"Listen to this, you guys," Marypat says, and she starts to read.

To the SISTERHOOD of Kazan Falls!

I am seven months pregnant, but I am not the first pregnant woman to travel the shores of the Kazan River. The Inuit women have been doing it for centuries. It's nothing unique. Being here pregnant is not something my partner and I see as risky. If anything, there are fewer health risks here than in society. I hope my journey through this vast, open, life-giving, wild land in my condition brings out the more gentle, sensuous, female aspects of the Barrens. We who have traveled the Kazan know of its harsh weather, challenging whitewater, and insistent bug population. But the traveler is the one creating the risks and the dangers, not the land.

Being a woman adventurer comfortable within the walls of sky, I know my own limitations. No, my partner did not stern the canoe the whole way. We traded days as usual, but yes, he did carry the canoe on every portage, not that I didn't carry my share of seventy-pound packs. Our pace was more leisurely, our style more relaxed. I feel we gave up nothing and gained a lot.

I hope someday to return to this land with the life growing inside me, and show her/him the elements of earth that nurtured their unborn body. Keep the land in balance and happy travels to all.

Marypat Zitzer & "The Grebe"

As she reads I watch Eli. He lies on his side, his head propped up with his hand, looking intently at Marypat. Chills run up my back. I can tell it hits him hard, these words from the past. They hit us all. We know what it has taken to get here, what it took us with Eli in the womb. Each of us listens from the perspective of our position in the family. The words fill the space in the tent. When Marypat finishes, her eyes glisten with emotion. Everyone looks at Eli, this grown young man reckoning with his origin.

"The Grebe?" he says.

Marypat laughs. "Yeah, that's what we called you that summer. Had to call you something."

"Maybe we should go back to it, eh, grebie-boy?" I add.

I settle on my belly and add an entry to the current log book. Another chapter in the story, if anyone happens to read the sequence. Eli is thoughtful. He turns toward the wall, writes in his journal, then lies on his back, looking at the top of the tent.

I don't know what it means to come of age. I don't remember being aware of when or how it happened to me. I have milestones: getting my driver's license, opening the letter with my military draft card, living away from home for the first time, owning a first car. But that isn't it. They are only markers in my chronology.

Overcoming adversity is part of it. Accepting responsibility, being a true friend, sticking to your word, learning how to work, wrestling with values. I doubt Eli could say much coherent about coming of age. It isn't the sort of thing you can pin down or articulate, the way he could say how many paddle strokes it took to go five hundred fifty miles.

He is balanced on the cusp in so many ways. Physically, he is already there. He has taken on trip responsibilities without being asked. He vacillates between reading or going fishing and playing in the sand or running around with his siblings. At home he'll be jumping on the trampoline one minute and talking on the phone to his girlfriend the next. His judgment is still immature, prone to impulse, uninformed by experience.

I remember how stilted and contrived our ceremony felt on Day 2. Since then, the sinews of river, the roar of wind, the embrace of wilderness hundreds of miles on a side have pulled us together. It has been anything but contrived. It has been real and consequential in a way few things are in town. I don't know what it means, what it will mean to Eli, how to weigh its significance.

I do know where we are and how it feels to lie on the ground, more than a month out, in the middle of my family.

Sleep won't come for me. I leap between trips, remember our gravid summer, how cemented we felt together, how fragile and empowered we were, all at once. I have an image of Marypat, wearing the loose-fitting green overalls that served as her maternity outfit that summer, bent under the load of an equipment pack, walking slowly across a portage, tundra rolling away from her to the edges of sky.

It is late enough in the season now that it gets truly dark in the middle of the night. The falls thunder in the background. It may be my imagination, but the ground seems to tremble slightly. Ruby stirs next to me. I reach over her and feel for Marypat's face. She holds my hand against her cheek.

Later on, I have to pee. When I get out of the tent it is eerily light. A full moon hangs in the sky above the river, a cold, pale globe. Clouds wreathe through the sky. Then the clouds take on a greenish hue, shimmer like curtains. The first northern lights of the summer. The first night dark enough to reveal them, despite the moon. The lights dance over the land, above the river, fading and pulsing in the moon's glow.

"Marypat! You have to come see." I lean in the tent door.

She emerges sleepily, wearing her long underwear. We stand together looking upriver. She gets her camera, rouses the kids. They stumble out, rubbing their faces, turn to see what we're looking at. No one says a word. Ruby leans against me, warm and sleepy.

The Kazan gives voice to its innate, endless power. The moon hangs serene in the velvet night. The lights wave and dance silently. A few of the brightest stars dot the darker portion of sky.

The air feels cold, like fall is whispering its notice.

Eighteen

Woke up to sunny sunshine and a portage. Got to fast moving water—wheee!! Had some rapids—fun, fun, fun!! Then we had a little pullover at a miniature waterfall. We are camped on a beautiful island. Time to EAT!!! Mmmmmmm!!!!

—RUBY, GROUP JOURNAL

In an odd way, the cacophony of the falls is a relief. In the midst of that roar, who could listen for worrisome noises? The snap of a twig, the snuffle of a bear, the rising wind, none of it stands a chance against the constant ovation. The antennae I raise, even in sleep, are useless, so I milk it, loll around until the warmth of morning sun coaxes me out.

Even then I leave the tent quietly. Nobody moves. The tundra is still. Mist hovers above the gorge. I enjoy my morning coffee while I write in my journal. Dehydrated hash browns soak in a pan. The blackflies keep me company. We are down to our second-to-last canister of fuel, down to less than seventy miles to go, down to the final map in the bag.

Below the falls we have a good chance of running into people. Locals come up the river by powerboat to fish and hunt. Planes drone overhead, coming and going out of Baker Lake. In a few days, perhaps, we will be on one of them. That seems like an improbable reality, perched where we are. It takes a great many paddle strokes to cover seventy miles. Plenty can happen.

The last time we were at Kazan Falls, Eli's impending birth overshadowed the end of the journey. It felt, in fact, as if the adventure only changed its tone, took a geographic leap, and blended into the next chapter. Somewhere near the end of the river we made a vow to give the child, boy or girl, the middle name Kazan.

The portage cuts off a sharp turn in the river but is still more than a mile long. The start is marked with a large rock cairn built on the brow of a ridge. From there you reckon your way through the rocks and bog down to the shoreline along a wide stretch of the river. The packs are light now, relatively compact, but it's still a pretty substantial carry over rough ground, and our outfit still requires two trips, a total of roughly four and a half miles for each of us.

We string out across the portage, finding our pace. Ruby and Sawyer stop to look at things along the way. Eli makes a steady beeline at a fast stride and then sits on a pack at the end, waiting for us. Marypat and I walk together in a little cloud of blackflies. On the second carry, we shoulder the canoes. Eli snaps some pictures. The sound of the falls recedes behind us.

The Kazan drops almost two hundred feet in the last thirty miles between the falls and Baker Lake. We alternate between reclining in the boats, letting the current pull us down, and paddling across flat sections. Snow geese waddle away inland. We stop at a large *inukshuk* to look around. It is six feet tall, made up of small rocks carefully balanced together, all of the same reddish color. A small window frames the peak, with a jaunty cap rock.

The river turns a corner and the current takes over. Here, the volume is massive, the velocity like an avalanche breaking loose. Six-foot waves hump up in midchannel. Boils blister up in the blue skin. All of the accumulated lakes and ponds and tributaries, all the draining melt, a basin hundreds of miles on a side, has converged in this rockbound channel, and it's in a hurry to be done.

We ride the fringe. For much of it, our canoes are five feet from shore. The miles click by so fast I can hardly keep track on the map. A peregrine watches us from a perch in a gravel pinnacle. Several sections of sandy bank have caved in, another sign of thawing permafrost. For a second day, the temperature is warm enough for T-shirts. It is literally the first two-day stretch of nice weather we've had since Kasba Lake.

Several of the rapids are heavy enough that we stop to scout, then carefully sneak near shore. The Kazan is moving so fast, the current is so muscular, that a capsize is completely untenable. At one point, we line and drag the canoes over a series of shallow ledges to avoid a set of huge standing waves and holes.

Ruby rolls up her wind pants and wades in. This is her kind of challenge. She is ten years old, thigh-deep in the cold river, hanging onto the bow to horse the boat through rocks. The boys stand back and watch her work. She and I get both canoes through. We all climb in again.

I don't want to make it to the lake. I want a final night on the river. We stop at a high island two miles short of Baker Lake. Up a steep, rocky slope the island levels off, almost like a gravelly mesa. It affords a view of the heady river, the rolling tundra, and downstream, the open expanse of our last lake.

It is deliciously warm. The air is still. Everything is huge—the river, the sky, the land. A pair of mergansers wing upriver. Caribou antlers litter the ground. Blueberries and salmonberries weigh down the ground-hugging bushes. On impulse, I shed my clothes and wade into the river, wash up. Two feet from shore it is all I can do to hold my ground against the flow.

The sound of a motorboat intrudes. I pull on my clothes again. An aluminum boat ferries across the broad channel toward us, pulls in just below our landing. Two young Inuit men clamber out of the boat. An older man, the driver, stays seated by the motor, smoking a cigarette.

"Hello," I say.

We shake hands. The Inuit use a soft, fleeting grip.

"You want a fish?" one of the men asks. "We caught a whole box full of whitefish in ten minutes, just over there." He points across the river.

"Thanks, but we're set."

"You see a canoe, any packs?" he asks.

"No. Why?"

"Two guys capsized their canoe just up there in the last rapid," he says, pointing to the ledge we pulled over. "They lost everything."

They were just in front of us, it turns out. Two men who had paddled the entire Kazan, just as we have, and who went over in the final whitewater. There was no way they could do anything but save themselves. The river took everything.

They ran downstream for miles, looking for things, and stumbled on a women's expedition camped near the river mouth on a beach. The women had a satellite phone, and the two guys called Baker Lake. These three men came to rescue them and try to retrieve gear. If they had capsized anywhere else along the route, they would have been in deep trouble. To capsize, lose everything but the clothes they wore, and yet be picked up the same day is unbelievable good fortune.

"Well, see you," the man says, abruptly. "If you find anything, pick it up and bring it to town with you."

They climb in, pole away from shore. The motor catches. The boat swings around. It is startling how quickly they are gone, pulled away by the current, disappearing in the view.

The Inuit think of themselves as The People. They don't mean, by that, that they are in some way chosen or favored or superior. It means that they are authentic, real, of this place. The People, nothing more or less.

Most, perhaps all, traditional aboriginal cultures think this way. Each one is The People of their land. They are kin to everything that makes up their world. There is no separation between humans and wildlife and plants, even the water and rocks and weather. It is all a seamless piece.

Boundaries are fluid, merging, overlapping, layered. Everything is alive, has spirit and sentience. The boulders brought down by floods, the lichen the caribou feed on, the birds nesting in the gravel, the wind tugging at the clouds, the stories told down the tunnel of generations. Spiritual entities. Through it all, the rivers course, as real and vibrant as the arteries in our bodies, the lifeblood of the land, whispering its truth, teaching lessons, sculpting.

In that worldview, everything is bound together into a single, interacting organism. Constantly shifting, maintaining balance, informing the whole, learning from one another. The People knew how to live by looking around at the world. They paid attention. They listened.

In this sense, my own culture is, well, retarded. My culture exists within an us-and-them reality. There is a gulf, walling us away from other species. In between, often, lives fear. Fear borne of ignorance and inexperience.

My culture considers itself chosen, superior, select. My culture does its damnedest to make that separation manifest. Buffered from weather, living in artificial environments, creating distance from other species, managing the world for its benefit. Using things up. Throwing things away. Dominating.

It is possible, and more and more common, in my world, to find people who have gone through life without ever once really encountering the unfettered outdoors. Not once in a lifetime. To never have to survive a storm outdoors. To never have to build a fire to stay warm after a rain. To never feel the wind shift and know what it portends. To never encounter other species in their world, on their terms.

I have no pretension of approaching the spiritual elegance and understanding of the Inuit, their embeddedness. I am passing through, doing my best, struggling to dissolve barriers, but I am not of that universe. There is too much to overcome.

But, this day, in this place, we are partway there. We have glimpses of enlightenment, understanding, moments of grace. I look at Ruby and Sawyer. Their hands and lips are stained blue with berry juice. Eli is whittling a piece of weathered wood. Our dinner fire flickers in the rocks. Marypat is bent over a pan full of bannock dough, working it into patties. Her cheek has a smudge of flour on it where she brushed a strand of hair away. The bugs are as bad as they were on Day 1, but we ignore them, wave them off without comment.

The river courses past, the rocks left by rasping ice grow warm under the late sun. Our skin is weathered and brown. Our hands are stiff and calloused, formed to paddle grips.

We have held the artifacts of the Inuit, thought about what they mean, put them back onto the ground where they were left. We have gazed into the eye sockets of men and women and children whose spirits gave up their bodies to the open tundra, whose stories float somewhere. We have locked eyes with musk ox at ten feet. We have knelt on top of the river as it carried us, speaking to us, for many, many miles.

More and more, we know how to behave by looking around us.

Nineteen

What a marathon day! We are camped right across from Baker Lake airport after 28 miles of lake crossing. The Kazan coughed us out into the lake. We got into the rhythm of ticking off these crossings, which were 5 or 6 miles long. At lunch I suggested we stop and cook dinner but continue on so we could have a rest day tomorrow. It was a lot of hard work, both mental and physical. I could have stopped a few times. Our camp is in the dunes. We had to drag the boats into camp the last bit over shallow sandy water. What a beauty of a spot!

—MARYPAT, GROUP JOURNAL

HAULING TO CAMP THROUGH THE SHALLOWS, WITH BAKER LAKE IN THE BACKGROUND.

Emotions ambush me on the final, headlong rush of the Kazan. The river braids through gravel bars and islands, widens out, cascades down the last few feet. I aim the boat down the center of one channel. The hull slaps through waves, the current roughs up the canoe with offhanded shoves.

"Goodbye, Kazan!" I find myself shouting over the river tumult. "You great, unbelievable river. You great land. Thank you! Good-bye." I am boisterous with the energy of the water and, at the same time, almost tearful. I may never be back, not right here, and I know it. It is heartbreak and joy together.

Sawyer turns to look at me, his face quizzical. He hears the emotion in my voice. This sort of outburst is uncharacteristic. And his point of view is fundamentally different from mine; his is one of boundless potential.

Anything is possible. For him, it may not be good-bye. Even if it is, it doesn't matter. There is so much else to come.

We coast to a rest, eight feet above sea level. The energy of the river dissipates. We settle down to the familiar flatwater rhythm. Stroke, feather, stroke. Stroke, feather, stroke. Bow and stern in time, the boat furrowing the plain of water, our wake spreading skirtlike behind. It is calm, the water restful. For the third day running, an unbelievable string, the weather is with us. Nobody mentions it. We've become a superstitious bunch.

Big Hips Island is a dark shadow, like a mythical turtle's back, to the north. We spend the morning working abreast of it, moving along it, going past it. Point to point. Beaches, rocky shoals, bays. A few structures mark the shoreline, some dilapidated shacks, a picnic spot, a small complex of buildings with a Canadian flag flying out front. We are workmanlike and focused, don't talk much.

Much of the morning is spent crossing a wide bay, five or six miles of open water between points. It is hot. The air hardly stirs. Big Hips Island seems to move with us. Sweat beads up under my hat brim. My butt gets sore. My arm hurts. The endurance pace. I know we're cruising along at a nice clip, perhaps four miles an hour. It seems glacial.

We have lunch on the far side, stretch our legs, lie flat, walk around, consume fuel. The afternoon is the same. Flatwater, glassy miles, a long bay to work across. Big Hips Island finally falls behind us, becomes a low blue mound. A prominent hill on the south shore becomes the next slow-motion landform to approach and get past. The paddle strokes pile up. I picture the row of them, like threshed wheat lined out behind us.

I imagine a motorboat cruising up alongside, offering us a tow. At that moment, I'd take a ride in a heartbeat. But no motorboat comes. We reach another point, hobble out of the boats, eat a snack, look at the map. Baker Lake is visible, buildings shimmering on the far side of the lake, due north.

The most direct route involves a series of crossings connecting islands. At the end lies the main channel of the Thelon River. Across that sits the airport. The first island seems close, an easy reach, but I know better. I take a bearing to make sure of our course.

It is late in the day now. We have paddled almost nonstop all the way across Baker Lake, about thirty flatwater miles. No one says a word about stopping.

"Let's cook dinner on the first island," Marypat suggests.

"Let's cook two dinners," Eli says.

"Yeah, why not? Two dinners sound good. We have some extra food," Sawyer agrees.

We do just that when we land on a gravel point, three or four miles later. One after another we cook up a dinner, eat it, and then cook a second one. There are no complaints of being too full. We paddle into the evening.

Baker Lake slowly comes into focus. I can make out the airport, the runway lights, the larger buildings against a low hill. Occasionally a reflected glint of sunlight winks off of a vehicle on the dirt road running from town to the airport.

The day ends with a half-mile haul through two inches of water to reach a sand beach. Where the Thelon pours into Baker Lake it creates almost a delta—sand islands, channels, shallows. I climb out, splash to the bow, loop the rope over my shoulder, and trudge through ankle-deep water. Ruby pushes from behind.

Like automatons, we set up the tent, unload the canoes, cover the packs, tie the boats down, fall into sleeping bags.

"Jesus, what a day!" Marypat sighs.

"We did all of Baker," Ruby says. "You didn't think we could, did you, Dad?"

"I thought it was a long shot," I agree. "And it was, wasn't it? One helluva long shot."

The noise of a plane approaches. The evening scheduled flight. It roars right overhead, touches down, two miles away. It is a bittersweet sound, a crescendo of accomplishment and sorrow. It is always this way, these endings.

The door that closed when Cliff's plane flew away from Kasba Lake is opening again. It will pull us in, out of this dimension, this place full of water, walled by sky, rampant with wind; this life both simple and profound, this existence both meek and empowered.

My body is numb with the day. I lie on my back, opening and closing my stiff hands. I fall to sleep thinking about my partners.

Baker Lake is the only major Inuit settlement in the interior of the Barrens. All the rest—Chesterfield Inlet, Rankin Inlet, Arviat, Gjoa Haven—are located on the coasts. In the early 1900s, trappers, missionaries, and explorers made inroads here, set up missions and trading posts. The economy changed, disease was introduced, the population was decimated by smallpox, the people were seduced away from subsistence hunting and gathering, from following the *tuktu*.

There were starving years. Bit by bit, by attrition and enticement and propaganda, fueled by desperation, The People were relocated, taken off the land, pulled into communities and the bureaucracy that runs them. On Baker Lake, it didn't completely run its course until 1960 or so.

The residents of Baker Lake are descended from several bands of Caribou Inuit. Some came from the Back River drainage, others from the country of the Kazan, still more from the Thelon. Most traditional bands comprised loosely-affiliated family groups who lived and hunted together. They straggled in, remnants of a people once intact and robust and numerous, people who knew how to live in a demanding land, but who had been inflicted with unprecedented, unfathomable hardship. Not a bit of their misfortune was their doing.

Some of the elders in Baker Lake, people who watch television and drive snowmobiles and eat Tater Tots, some who still tell stories and carve soapstone and hunt the deer, remember childhoods in the Stone Age.

By morning, the wind is howling. Sand spatters against the tent fabric, drifts into everything. The lake is wild and gray. The runway may be two miles away, but it might as well be in South America.

"Guys," I say. "There's something I want to tell you. I've been thinking a lot about what it's been like to be together here. There were days at the start when I wondered what we were doing, how we were going to pull this trip off. Mom and I had our doubts. To be honest, this was a bigger challenge than we thought it would be.

"But then, right about two weeks in, it started to come together. We didn't have to make rules or demand that you do chores, it just started happening. Everyone pulled their weight. You guys knew what had to be done, and you did it.

"We've been on a lot of trips like this. We've traveled with a lot of partners. What I want to say is that you three are right there with the best of them. In some ways, better than the best of them. I wouldn't trade you for anyone I've ever done trips with, and I totally mean that."

"Ditto," says Marypat. "And another thing. We'll go back home. We'll be with friends, go to school, play sports. All this will fade in our memories. But no one can take away what we have shared this summer as a family. Who knows how it will help us, what it might mean years from now. We share this time, this land, this adventure. It is something to cherish."

The day passes in the wind. I am reminded why I mistrust sandy camps, what a gritty pain living in a sandstorm is, where zippers fail, food is crunchy, sand insinuates itself into sleeping bags, clothes, toothbrushes, bodily orifices.

I open a collection of poetry I've brought along for reading material. It is the first time I've cracked a book the entire trip. We've read books out loud, but not once have I opened my own. It's typical, and it's a mark of the transition that I succumb now.

Eli stretches out in the wind shadow of one of the canoes and reads his book. He exudes comfort and contentment in the midst of the wild day. A caribou antler rests in the sand next to him. We take baths in the shallow water. Marypat walks a circuit of the island, reports quite a lot of trash strewn around.

At one point Ruby strips naked and takes off running in the watery flats. Her hair blows behind her. She is tall and lithe. Her body is starting to curve like a woman's. She runs long, looping circles, the water splashing behind her. Out to a sandbar, around it, back again. She runs and runs for nothing but the joy of it, like a filly in a spring pasture. The windy sky and storm-tossed lake frame the scene.

It is twilight when the wind finally tapers off. We are ready to go. What we hoped would be a repeat of the drag into camp out to a deeper channel turns into a much longer slog. Hardly any of the water is deep enough to paddle through efficiently. It's easier just to slosh along, hauling the boats by their ropes.

Ruby bends to the task, pulls with a will, takes it as a fun diversion. Besides, it's more time in the water, always a plus in her mind. Marypat and the boys lag behind. Finally we come to the river channel of the Thelon. Finally the sand bottom drops away and we can climb into the boats.

Motorboats roar past, making the last trips of the day. Our two red canoes slice across this new current, a river with a different personality. We make its acquaintance, briefly, and come to rest at the end of the airport runway, just as a set of strobe-light markers starts flashing.

"I'll walk around the corner to look for a place to put the tent up," Marypat says.

The rest of us sit in the pulsating stabs of platinum light, waiting for whatever it signals. Marypat is gone for a while. Eventually the distant drone of an approaching plane is audible. The night flight approaches. The big plane cruises just over our heads. The noise is tremendous. The wheels touch down, the plane taxis, turns, comes around to the small terminal building. The strobes stop.

"We can camp down the shore a bit," Marypat says. "It isn't much, but there's room for the tent and then we can figure things out in the morning."

Back in the boats, we take up our paddles. Ruby pushes us off. We stroke around the corner in the twilight, come to rest on a skinny beach less than one hundred feet from the edge of the runway.

The tent goes up, the boats are emptied. The sleeping bags and pads are organized. Inside it is gray with the fading day. Nearly the end of August now. The long night is coming, inexorable as tide.

I see Eli sitting up in the gray light. He holds his counting stick in his hands, whittles a final notch all the way around, near the bottom, looks at it. I wonder what he thinks, gazing at the symbol of our time in the Barrens. The stick is crowded with whittled rings, stacked with days. Barely an inch of unmarked wood remains.

I see, watching him study the pile of days lying in his hands, then carefully placing it in his clothes duffel, that it is not the tally of a sentence at all. Perhaps it never was.

PART II SAWYER
THE YELLOWSTONE RIVER

SAWYER CONTEMPLATES THE VIEW FROM MARSTON PASS, WITHIN STRIKING DISTANCE OF THE HEADWATERS OF THE YELLOWSTONE RIVER.

Twenty

I am a week away from the due date and have feelings of fear and anxiety, yet excitement and surprise are also close to the surface. We never thought we could get pregnant again, so this was a total shock. Eli is still so little and nursing full time. These kids will be so very close together.

—MARYPAT, BIRTH JOURNAL

Sawyer came to us in the dead of night, after one o'clock. The street outside was quiet. Our bedroom was dark and stuffy, dim as a cave. Eli, sixteen months old, slept in the next room in his crib. He hadn't made a peep since Marypat had nursed him and put him down earlier in the evening, before her labor grew intense. Marypat gave birth on her hands and knees, centered on our bed, a stance she chose for hours.

Contractions had begun on the morning of March 6. Marypat spent the day monitoring them. During the afternoon, she swam three-quarters of a mile with Ursula at the university pool and rode her bike home. By dinner, the contractions were strong enough to call Vicki, the midwife. She suggested that we take a walk.

The moon was nearly full. It was also at its closest approach to earth, close enough to look us in the eye.

We strolled through moon shadows and pools, as if wading through light, up to a local ridge in town. It was cool and still, not yet spring. The lights spread away into the whitewashed distance. The mountain ranges were black cutouts, serrating the night. We held hands, stopped every time a contraction came, looked at the watch, felt the luminous pull of the moon.

Back home, I started making calls. Ursula, Nancy (Marypat's sister), our friend Sue, and, on impulse, another Nancy, who hadn't been able to have children and who had just gone through the ordeal of her mother's death. By nine o'clock everyone but Vicki was at our house. Marypat sat in a rocking chair in the living room, taking part in the conversation, which paused every time she had another contraction. She put her head back on the chair, moaned softly, then breathed deeply when it was over. I wrote down the time and duration in the birth book we'd started.

Vicki and her assistant arrived around ten. She took some notes, brought in some equipment, settled in calmly to wait. By eleven, Marypat waddled to the bathroom and threw up dinner.

"God, that's a relief," she said.

"You're already seven centimeters," Vicki told her, after checking her cervix.

"Seven. Yes!" Marypat said. "I was hoping for four."

Labor has that bated quality, tense but patient, strained and expectant, punctuated by trips to the bathroom to pee, water breaking, checking the fetal heartbeat, changing positions. I wasn't as anxious as I had been during Eli's birth, and Marypat had gained veteran status. At various points she tried standing, leaning over the bed, holding on to our hands. During contractions, her legs would shake and tremble. She straddled a birthing stool, but kept ending up on the bed on hands and knees, sweaty head resting on pillows.

"My knees hurt, but it's the most comfortable way to be," she said.

For a time we were in the bathroom, Marypat trying to pee, enduring intense contractions. I sat on the edge of the bathtub, facing her. She gripped my arms, dug in her nails at the peak of pain. We rested the tops of our heads together. Vicki stood nearby. Everyone else huddled outside the door, listening.

"Something's coming," Marypat said, suddenly.

Vicki moved in to check. "Yes, it is," she said. "The head's right there."

Back on the bed, Marypat breathed, pushed, held back, groaned, cried out. Vicki massaged her with oil. The impossible stretch began. The top of the head filled the space, pushed against the band of tissue, worked slowly, insistently past.

"Just breathe it out," Vicki coached. "Easy now. Don't push too hard. It's coming fine."

"But I want to push!" Marypat wailed.

For the second time in my life, I put a hand under the emerging head of my child. First touch—virgin skin, the tiny ball of life, warm and wet from the womb. Another contraction, another breath, another push. First an arm, a tiny fist raised, then the body slithered free. I caught it with my other hand, a gush of elbows and belly and knees still plugged in by umbilical cord.

A remarkably short umbilical cord. So short that Marypat had no choice but to stay on her knees, touch the baby awkwardly while resting on her head. She cooed at it, this new life, made those noises of unbelievable relief and unutterable emotion, feeling the body, talking to it, making contact.

"Hi, sweetie. It's your mom," she said.

Finally, Vicki cut the cord so Marypat could nurse.

"I like to wait for the placenta," she said, "but this cord needs an extension!"

"Look at that, MP," I whispered. "It's a boy."

We had assumed all along that this baby was a girl. We had had no ultrasound, no evidence but our intuition, but we were sure enough that we hadn't even bothered considering boy's names.

"It is," she said, looking into the tiny face. "Look at him."

In fact, Sawyer was red faced and had his eyes squeezed shut. He seemed very sensitive to light and touch.

"Those long fingernails are a sign of being a bit overdue," Vicki said.

But Sawyer looked to me as if he was not at all ready, much less overdue. When we drew Marypat an herbal bath and tried to put Sawyer in the water with her, he wanted no part of it. He nursed readily enough, but his eyes never opened. Everything about his body language said, "I'm not ready yet!"

Ursula brought in a birth cake with one candle on it. We popped the cork on a bottle of champagne. Outside, the moon threw shadows of winter trees across the sidewalk.

Everyone headed home. We slept for a few hours with our new, nameless boy between us. The Baby.

When Eli woke, we brought him in with us. He was not happy about sharing the bed, and his solitary cuddling time, with a brother. In fact, he was cranky as hell. I thought about baby birds pushing siblings out of nests.

Marypat picked up Eli, snuggled him close, held him to her breast. He kept glancing over at the new, unexpected, not entirely welcome addition on my side of the bed.

For more than a day, the baby remained nameless. He was, briefly, August, Grady, Singer, Keegan. I remembered the advice of a friend on the subject of kids' names.

"Go to the front porch and yell it at the top of your lungs three or four times, like you're calling the kid home for dinner. See how you like it after that."

Then, buried in a name book we checked out from the library, Sawyer—A Woodsman.

Twenty-One

South of Yellowstone National Park, in what's known as the Thorofare region, the wilderness lies farther from a road than anywhere else in the continental United States. Exhilarating wilderness, and a depressing reality. Exhilarating because this country is truly wild and isolated. Depressing because 25 miles is not that far from a road. I can't decide whether to be more impressed by our road-building proliferation, or by the depth of wilderness.

—AL, PERSONAL JOURNAL

At the end of the dirt road up the South Fork of the Shoshone River in northern Wyoming, we pull into a large, nearly empty parking lot, presumably near the trailhead. Road dust settles. Cabin Creek tinkles through an apron of outwash. It is after six in the evening. The trail is nowhere in sight.

An SUV rolls up nearby and two women get out.

"Do you happen to know where the trail starts?" I ask.

"No idea," they shrug. Then they look at the five of us and our backpacks. "You goin' up there?" one of them points up the valley.

"Yeah."

"You're spending the night out? Camping?"

"Yes, we'll be in there for a week."

She shakes her head, a local knowledge shake, a schoolmarm shake. "You be careful," she warns. "The Griz is out."

"The Griz?"

She nods, takes a long look upriver, then back at us. She turns back to the safety of her vehicle.

"Well, that was pretty helpful, eh?" I say.

First day. First days are always half-baked, neither here nor there. Half in a car, half on a trail. Slipping away from the grasp of town life, not yet in the embrace of trail life.

This day has been particularly tortured. It started yesterday, in town, when I came home in midafternoon to a lake in the kitchen, water gushing from under the sink. I ran downstairs to turn off the main valve. Water poured out of the basement light fixtures, dripped through the ceiling plaster onto the pile of backpacking gear we had been amassing.

I used every towel in the house, then carried the soggy mess outside to hang on the clothesline and drape across the trampoline. For the next two hours, I mopped up the lake, wrung water into a five-gallon bucket, carried the bucket outside and watered trees, moved the stove and refrigerator and cabinets, mopped some more. I unhooked the water filter that had sprung a gasket and tossed it in the garage, reconnected the water line to the faucet, turned the water back on, shut down the electrical circuit in the still-dripping basement, mopped the basement by headlamp, then hung out our sopping gear—tent, backpacks, sleeping pads, rain coats.

Remarkably, the next day we managed to drive away from the mess around midmorning, damned sure the water was turned off in the house. Not the dawn departure we had planned. Normally it's a three- or four-hour drive from Bozeman, Montana, to Cody, Wyoming, but it took us more than five, punctuated with a lunch stop, pee stops, gas stops. It took another hour to drive up the rough road to the trailhead, where we changed clothes and started organizing our packs.

"Hey, where's my other boot?" Eli asked.

"It's got to be there," I said. "Look around."

"I have. It isn't there." His tone is accusing. It's a tone teenage boys are prone to.

I rummage around in the back of the car, toss things out, search the cartop rack, check under seats. He's right. No boot.

"Jesus!" I explode. "You'll just have to wear your tennies."

"No way," Marypat says. "It's a fifty-mile hike. We're climbing a twelve-thousand-foot peak. He can't hike in those flimsy things. We'll have to go back to Cody and find some shoes."

"What? It's already three-thirty. It's Sunday. We're going to drive an extra two hours on the off chance we can find cheap boots in town?"

It is precisely what we do. Load back in, rocket down the road to town, screech into the parking lot of the outdoor store at four-thirty. It happens to be open. In half an hour we buy a forty-dollar pair of hiking shoes in the bargain basement, stop at a deli to buy dinner, and careen back up the road.

Now it's past six, the Griz is out, and we can't locate the trail.

It is late summer, mid-August. We have already spent the better part of July paddling the entire navigable Yellowstone River to its confluence with the Missouri in North Dakota. This hike is phase two of Sawyer's coming-of-age expedition, a quest for the headwaters of the Yellowstone, deep in the alpine terrain of the Washakie Wilderness of northern Wyoming, just south of Yellowstone National Park. We thought about coming earlier, before the float, but snow persists above ten thousand feet well into July. So the river is still fresh in our minds, still alive in the paddling calluses on our palms. Somewhere twenty-five miles away from the parking lot, thousands of feet uphill, the first thread of the river we came to know rolls off on its journey.

This summer has been a perfect illustration of the insanity of modern-day family life. Immediately after school let out, Sawyer joined a group of eighth-grade language students on a trip to Europe. For almost two weeks they traveled Spain, France, and Germany. Eli took the same trip the previous year.

Both of them earned half of their trip costs by fund-raising. When I was a kid, you could actually hold a job. These days, kids fund-raise. When could they possibly work a job in a daily schedule that starts at 6 AM and often goes full bore to dinnertime, crammed with sports practices, workouts, music lessons, club meetings? Homework gets sandwiched in between dinner and bed.

What happened to coming home from school, shooting baskets in the driveway, playing football in the park or Ping-Pong in the basement, ramming around with friends? What happened is that parents aren't home. Terror alerts and sexual predator advisories have everyone locking doors and driving kids to appointments. Ride a bike. Go play in the park. Walk to school. How quaint. How dangerous. Organized activities fill the calendar, replace family time, and drain bank accounts.

Our lifestyle doesn't have to conform, and it often doesn't, but the kids' friends are on the treadmill. Nobody wants to be left behind. Fundamentally, it is completely nuts. I know this. Marypat and I talk about it at night. Parents roll their eyes on the sidelines. But we're still doing it.

It is all we can do to get in the trip down the Yellowstone after Sawyer's jaunt to Europe. Immediately after we got off the river, Eli took off for a soccer tournament in Minnesota. Ruby and Sawyer joined family friends for a raft trip down the Salmon River.

Within a day of our return from this hike, fall sports practice will start for both boys. In between it all we gardened, managed chores, saw friends, and made the money it takes to support the enterprise.

No wonder it takes a few days to make the shift.

The first evening, we set camp barely two miles from the car, just across the Washakie Wilderness boundary, almost in sight of the ranch buildings near the end of the road. Our tent perches on a bench of ground above the wide outwash plain of the South Fork of the Shoshone River. The trail, once you find its source, is a horse-packing highway. It isn't obvious from the parking lot, but once on it, the dusty, beaten path is as blatant as a trail gets. In the first mile, we ford the South Fork twice.

Each time, we shuck boots and socks, change to water shoes, and navigate the slippery, rolling cobbles in surging current. Two-thirds of the way across the second ford, I lose my footing and fall hard, dunking the binoculars and topping off the day's chemistry.

In camp, the Griz is on my mind. The Griz is on everyone's mind.

This country is renowned bear habitat. South of Yellowstone Lake, in the Thorofare region of Yellowstone Park, and on into the mountainous wilderness of northern Wyoming, a massive block of truly remote country sprawls from the Tetons to the Wind River Range. In the center of it, you are farther from a road than anywhere else in the Lower 48. It is also prime bear country—unpopulated, full of game, dense with forests and meadows and tundra—wilderness the way Lewis and Clark encountered wilderness, and replete with more grizzly than anywhere outside of Alaska and Canada.

When Eli walks a quarter mile across the flats below camp to wash his face in the river, I watch him the way a parent watches their child disappear through a school door the first day of kindergarten. I scan the valley for movement, scrutinize the clumps of willow and aspen for the dark, languid shape of bear.

Sawyer, Ruby, and I initiate the first installment of the evening comedy routine, hanging food from a tree. We try slinging the rope, weighted with a carabiner, over a high branch, but it gets tangled in dense lower branches. Sawyer scrambles up the trunk, the cord comes back down. It takes both of them heaving under the bags while I haul away to get the mass off the ground. As usual, the food hangs too close to the tree and a little lower than we'd like. Any ambitious griz on its hind legs could have our food in no time and a little piñata sport in the bargain.

Twenty-Two

The Greater Yellowstone Ecosystem is billed as the largest nearly intact northern temperate zone ecosystem on earth, with Yellowstone National Park at its core. It encompasses roughly 20 million acres and includes three states, two national parks, and five national forests.

Less than half a mile from camp, after breakfast, the first bear tracks appear on the trail. Fresh that morning, sharp and clear in the fine yellow dust—that print so much like ours. Beans, the family dog along for this phase of the expedition, sniffs at them, then drops into the middle of the pack. Usually he ranges out front, scouting, busy with smells.

"Okay," Ruby says. "Let's sing a song."

The night before, I felt foolish being paranoid so close to the road. Now, not so much. My hand feels for the bear spray canister on my hip. We hike on in tighter formation, making more noise, singing songs.

Generally, I feel pretty safe in a group. Bears are rarely aggressive when confronted by more than two people. Still dangerous, still unpredictable, but less likely to attack. Of course, that's a mental calculation, a cerebral rationale, and it has no effect on the emotional pulse that picks up when I step across fresh bear sign. The tracks stay with us, leading the way into the canyon.

The trail climbs steadily. The fast, milky green river becomes a ribbon far below, the rapids faintly audible. Tributary creeks careen in a series of white waterfalls down the sides of the valley. Our pace is steady. The kids are all fit. They are carrying respectable packs, thirty to forty pounds each, but they keep up a two-mile-an-hour pace even uphill.

The first horses of the day catch us, two riders moving fast, perhaps going ahead to prepare camp for the dudes who will follow. We stand to the side, stay still while the horses pass. The dust subsides, the smell of horse sweat lingers. The path contours across a broad skirt of boulders. We pause now and then to look down at the river or across at waterfalls. We adjust the fit of packs, pulling on straps, tightening waist belts, shifting the loads.

"I say lunch at Needle Creek," Eli suggests, looking at the map.

Our goal is the first trickle of the Yellowstone River, twenty-five miles up the trail, somewhere around eleven thousand feet in the alpine terrain of the Absaroka Range. Treks to the sources of major rivers are a grand tradition. For one thing, the literal founts of drainages tend to be mysterious, difficult to precisely nail down, remote by definition. Think of the White Nile, the Congo, the Amazon—watersheds that support the better parts of continents. Their sources were shrouded in mystery for centuries, secreted in the mists of jungle mountains in the most remote heart of Africa, deep in unexplored wilderness, territory inhabited by aboriginal peoples and undocumented species of wildlife.

Not unlike the quest for the poles, the conquest of Everest, or the race to navigate the Northwest Passage, expeditions were mounted to seek the very beginnings of the rivers of the world. Expeditions supported by dozens of porters, financed by royal families, led by the exploring elite of the day.

STRUNG OUT ALONG THE TRAIL, WITH BEANS, AND VIEWS OF THE HIGH PEAKS.

Even the Mississippi's source was a matter of debate as late as 1890. Expeditions penetrated to the Lake Itasca basin in northern Minnesota, searching for the literal source of flow in the boggy lowlands and swamps surrounding the lake. Competing books substantiating rival claims were written, historical societies were pulled into the fray, fanciful maps drawn, reputations won and lost before the geographic snit was put to rest.

SAWYER PERFORMS ANOTHER IN A SERIES OF PROTRACTED DANCES, TRYING TO KEEP FEET DRY AND NOT CHANGE SHOES.

The Yellowstone's source is subtle and elusive in its own right. Even the people who live within the Greater Yellowstone Ecosystem have a very sketchy grasp of its location. Most would guess that the river begins somewhere in Yellowstone National Park. The more informed would narrow it down to Yellowstone Lake. Fewer still would be able to name the Thorofare region, south of the lake. Maybe one in one hundred would know that, in fact, the source lies south of the park. That the river winds quietly through the unpeopled meadows past the arms of Yellowstone Lake, ascends up narrowing valleys, crosses the arbitrary park border, and that, near the end, the river splits into two forks, the south and north, making a necklace around Younts Peak. Younts Peak, which we hope to climb, forms the literal head of the flow, overlooking the high valleys from better than twelve thousand feet.

Before our hike, I couldn't have pinpointed the Yellowstone's source within twenty miles either, and I've paddled the river for decades.

We reach Needle Creek, rushing toward the South Fork of the Shoshone, after a morning of hiking and a mile of trudging through powdery trail dust four inches deep. Dust that coats our boots, our legs, our faces. Dust that clogs our nostrils and rises in hazy, cloying clouds around our heads. Horses may be romantic and redolent of western tradition, but they can beat the hell out of a trail.

I bend and splash cold water on my face, dunk my head. Sawyer succumbs to the temptation of a narrow, slippery log sticking over the river to see if he can balance his way across without taking his boots off. Ruby and Eli follow his lead. They spend a good ten minutes experimenting, throwing stepping stones in the creek, and clambering around on the slippery log before they give in, sit down, take off their boots, put on sandals, and slosh across.

At every river crossing, the same scenario repeats itself. There is always a spot that just might work, where we mess around for ten minutes, teetering on rocks, arranging logs, getting wet feet, before finally giving in to the shoe-changing routine. Once in a while the experiment works, which encourages the folly.

"If we just immediately sat down and changed shoes and walked across, we'd probably save hours a day," I say at the fourth or fifth crossing.

"Yeah, but what fun would that be?" asks Sawyer.

Late in the day, almost ten miles along, clouds move in. Light drizzle falls. We consider rain gear but decide against. It's better to get a little damp than to sweat inside the coats and pants. The final mile is always the longest. We keep trudging toward the spot on the map we've picked for the day's goal. The kids are ready to stop. I'm ready to stop. Our feet are sore. Our shoulders are sore.

At another stream crossing, a long string of horses with riders, pack mules, and several dogs clop past us. There is at least one pack mule for every rider, heavily loaded with canvas panniers carrying wall tents, cots, cast iron Dutch ovens, mess kits, bedding, fishing paraphernalia, lanterns, stoves. Horses and mules, twenty or thirty of them, swing past, the loads swaying. Their hooves churn the loose river gravel. The stream runs muddy in their wake. They shit and piss in the water.

The wranglers, in slickers, look slightly bored. Every week another trip heads upriver to backcountry fishing camps. Every week they meet another batch of clients who have paid good money for the western experience, to be waited on, cooked for, shown the prime fishing holes, catered to. It's a job. Better, perhaps, than slapping plywood in new subdivisions or holding a sign for road construction, but a job nonetheless.

The dudes look uncomfortable on the horses in the drizzle and sheepish about their luxury, all in the name of catching and releasing a few trout somewhere upriver. We're only slightly envious of their comfort. We stand there, wearing a coat of trail dust, our legs muddy and scratched, while the caravan creaks past. The dudes avert their eyes as if they exist in a different dimension, which they do. The dogs come over and sniff Beans's butt.

Twenty-Three

Sawyer is changing every day, but he continues to be our most compassionate child. One who can really take in the whole picture and see when another is in distress or needs comfort and attention. Sawyer still prefers to be with his family or parents over being with friends. He wants to live with us forever, or at least next door.

—MARYPAT, SAWYER'S BIRTH BOOK, NOVEMBER 2000

Sawyer wasn't an easy infant. Some deep-seated discomfort seemed to afflict him. It was a period, for me, marked by helplessness, frustration, the sorrow of impotence. Babies are capable of communicating a great deal. They are really good at telling you when they want to eat, sleep, move, go to someone. In the case of Sawyer's trouble, even if he knew, he couldn't tell us. It could have been anything—a food allergy, a hidden physical malady, a brain tumor, emotional angst, a developmental stage he needed to endure.

We held him. Marypat nursed him. Eli played with him. Friends held him. I have no idea how many miles I walked, doing laps with him on my shoulder in the living room. It's best not to know. I sang and hummed. I was quiet. I walked fast and slow, held him different ways, played music, let him suck on my little finger, patted his back. Once or twice the mention of colic came up.

When it came to changing his diaper, Sawyer was a two-person job. He thrashed and screamed and kicked out, writhing around on the changing pad. It was a full-time job to pin him down while the second person wrestled through his windmilling legs to get the diaper in place. Something unfathomable and mysterious had hold of him and neither he nor his parents had a clue how to get free.

But it wasn't all difficult. Sawyer spent afternoons lying contentedly on a sheepskin in a spot of sun on the living room floor. He napped in Marypat's arms after nursing, laughed when Eli tickled him, let strangers hold him, sat quietly in the stroller on walks around town.

We took him on his first canoe trip at one month, a short float on a local river. He lay on the bottom of the boat in a soft cradle, tethered to Marypat by a length of webbing, feeling the current through the boat hull. In June, at three months, Sawyer joined his first canoe expedition, a weeklong float with friends, including several toddlers, through Labyrinth and Stillwater Canyons on the Green River in Utah. Later that June, he was the only male, albeit tied securely to his mom, on a women's canoe trip down a section of the Yellowstone River.

After about six months, he started sleeping more soundly, grew more relaxed when we changed him, smiled more. By September he was crawling.

He took his first wobbly steps in mid-December, at nine months. He watched Eli closely, saw him jump off steps or climb on things, and was determined to follow.

Then, as a young toddler, maybe two or three, Sawyer went through repeated bouts of inconsolableness. I don't know what else to call them. Not tantrums, exactly, although they had some of that quality. Again, as when he was a newborn, the sense I got was of some possession, a force that took hold of him in an unbearable way.

The outbursts would erupt out of nowhere—at a Thanksgiving dinner with relatives, in the midst of playing in the backyard, alone in his room. He would throw himself down, wail, refuse people, run off, scream. Nothing we tried worked. Finally, Marypat took to holding him fiercely, just hanging on to his hot, struggling body through the storm of his cries, saying nothing, loving him, refusing to be outlasted.

In the midst of the outbursts, desperation took hold. This was true wilderness, this navigation of mystery, this encounter with the unknown and terrifying. Looking into the face of my son, trying to read his eyes, to come up with some response, figure out what the hell to do. A blank map and no compass.

We tried changing diet, administering homeopathic tinctures and flower therapy, going to doctors, changing his sleep schedule, getting chiropractic adjustments. There was no apparent malady, nothing identifiable to treat. Marypat heard about a local medical practice that claimed to read and interpret auras. Someone she trusted recommended it. We made an appointment.

They laid Sawyer on an examination table. The doctor, if he was a doctor, came in with a woman who was wearing a white lab coat. She was the channel through which aural energy passed to him. She laid hands on Sawyer. The doctor held onto her shoulder. It was quiet. Sawyer had on tiny blue shorts and a T-shirt. He lay still on his back, watching the woman. He looked very small, a little boy, mine. The woman closed her eyes. Traffic passed by outside. Whatever happened, happened, between the three of them. The doctor moved in and performed some gentle manipulations on Sawyer's head, talked about adjusting his energy fields.

We wrote a check, held Sawyer's hand on the walk back to the car. He looked out the window as we drove home. And, like everything else we tried through that period, the visit had no discernible effect.

One afternoon, Sawyer descended into another bout of whatever ailed him. Something Eli did had provoked him. He ran past us, wouldn't let us touch him, slammed the door to his room.

I gave it a minute, then pushed the door open. Sawyer had thrown himself onto his small bed. He lay on his stomach, his head turned to the wall, his body tight and hot. He wouldn't look at me. I had no idea what to say, what move to make. I felt as exhausted as Sawyer was wound up.

I started to rub his back. I said nothing, just took the rigid body of my son in my hands and rubbed. The wings of his shoulder blades, the tiny knots of vertebrae, the cords of muscle in his neck, the dowels of his ribs. I watched my hands cover the small space of his back, kneading, saying whatever it is hands have to say.

Sawyer started to relax. His muscles softened, the stiffness went out of him. Whatever it was began to seep off, steaming away like poisonous smoke. The rest of the house was quiet. Marypat had taken Eli outside to play—my turn to deal. I kept gently working Sawyer's back. He fell slack under my hands. Relief, both of our relief, filled the room. Tears burned in my eyes.

Twenty-Four

The second morning, it happens again. We're not ten minutes from camp when we cut bear tracks. Large bear tracks vivid in the dust. Marypat crouches to take a picture with Ruby's open hand for scale. A little further along, a thick smear of bear shit steams on the trail. Beans whines, sticks close. We all peer up the slope and into the sparse forest, listen for sound. The bear could be watching us, could be five minutes ahead, might right now be waiting around the corner.

"Do you think we should stop and let it get ahead?" Marypat asks.

"It's tempting, but we'd be stopping and waiting every couple of hours, at the rate we're seeing bear sign," I say.

"These bears have to be so used to people and how to avoid us," I start to rationalize. "Horse packers come up here every week all summer long. Bears totally know where we are and how to move out of the way. They know where we camp. I mean, look at these tracks, hardly out of sight from where we had our tent pitched. Just because we hang food doesn't mean the bears don't have us pegged."

"I know," Marypat says. "It just makes me nervous to be so close behind. That poop looked like it was about five minutes old!"

"Yeah," Eli says. "I keep thinking of that Indian saying, 'It's a good day to die.' Only, it doesn't feel at all like a good day to die. Actually, I've been realizing how much it would really suck."

"Okay, let's just keep moving, stay together, watch Beans, make some noise. No bear with half an ear is gonna stay in range of our singing."

When Lewis and Clark came up the Missouri, they found grizzly bear everywhere on the Great Plains, as far east as the Dakotas and Nebraska. Bear, elk, bison, wolves were plains animals. Why would they brave the rugged terrain and difficult climate of the mountains? It was only with the encroachment of agriculture, roads, and towns that large species were pushed higher, corralled within shrinking wilderness preserves, and have ever since been forced to adapt to deep snows, limited food resources, and narrowing or blocked migration corridors.

Historically, the Greater Yellowstone Ecosystem and Yellowstone National Park were relatively devoid of wildlife. When mountain man John Colter first explored the Yellowstone Plateau, in the years immediately following his employment with Lewis and Clark, he found it an area sparsely populated by man or beast. It is a very recent development, during the last century, that Yellowstone has garnered its reputation as the Serengeti of North America, and only because wildlife has been forced to make the best of that rigorous environment.

Avoiding humans is the first commandment of survival for most species, particularly for bears. Messing with people and their possessions is a death sentence. They quickly figure that out or they die young.

Nevertheless, seeing bear sign fresh on the trail, that great track, the easy gait of an animal potent with power and armed with acute sensory capabilities, is chilling. Eli is right. It doesn't feel like a good day to die. Our hope and blithe assumption is that the bear feels the same.

Having bear around, and not being at the peak of the food chain, is also exhilarating. Hiking along, I am very awake, very attentive, very alive, the way I should be all the time. The way all other animals have to be, if they want to make it through the day. We assume we can go anywhere, do anything, and that nothing stands in our way. It's good for us to cower once in a while, to consider our vulnerability, to pay humble attention. Ultimately, it's a matter of respect. Too bad it takes an animal that can maim and kill us to slap us awake.

Fine sentiment to spout around the backyard barbecue; quite another thing to remain sanguine and philosophical in the face of eight-inch footprints made a few minutes earlier, leading us deeper into the wilds.

The Griz is out, somewhere ahead on the trail, swinging along, scenting us, hearing us, distracted by our clatter. We advance in tight formation, belting out our repertoire of six songs over and over. If we only had some sensory acuity, and more time in the wilds, we'd be better able to act with the same decorum wildlife accords us. Instead we thunder down the trail, hoping for the best, trusting that bears will cover for our lack of manners and stay clear.

A mile or two along, another stream crossing confronts us. We dillydally, dropping logs across the current and chucking in stepping stones as much to let the bear stay ahead as to avoid changing shoes, and on the far side, the broad tracks are still wet. The forest is shadowed and still, the air heavy. A woodpecker drums in the distance.

The tracks finally veer away into the trees. We pick up the pace, glance around. I feel the gaze of bear on us, the quiet breathing, the great heart beating its rhythm. I imagine the bear distinguishing each of us by scent and sound, factoring in Beans, letting our noise recede, and the relief of silence that washes back in our wake. In a way, having the tracks ahead was reassuring. Now, who knows where the animal is, or what prompted it to leave the path, or what else is coming our way.

Beans moves ahead, scents through the grasses in a meadow. I watch him for clues. At the same time, I don't really want to know everything he's picking up. A little ignorance is just fine. Mountains lift against the sky above the valley. Early thunderheads build up. The morning is already hot by the time we turn right onto the Marston Pass Trail and start to climb.

It has only been a year since the Kazan. Ruby is still in elementary school. Yet, the epic experience in the Barrens allowed the three of them to break through a barrier when it comes to hitching up to expedition expectations. Only a year, but they take on full packs, hike with a will, and have absolute confidence in their abilities. It feels like a leap has been made, a chasm of experience and attitude crossed. It is also a striking geographic contrast, from the austere, glacial tundra of the Far North to the rugged heart of the Rockies. From the vantage of this trail, our summer on the Kazan feels like a different lifetime.

"Where can we have lunch?" Ruby asks.

Benchmarks are important. The kids are good hikers, but they need to pin their progress down, have goals to look forward to. I'm the same way.

"What about this little tributary creek," I suggest, pointing at an intermittent stream on the map several miles away. "Hopefully there's water, and it's at least halfway to where we want to camp."

She looks at the map, eyeballs the distance against what we've already walked, turns and hikes on, popping a piece of gum from her personal treat bag into her mouth.

When the kids were little, we used to hand out periodic food diversions during the day to keep them occupied and distracted. These days, they each get their bag of goods—gum, hard candy, licorice—and do their own math. Amazing what you can tell about a person by how they go through their treat bag. You can identify the bingers, the hoarders, the compulsive schedulers, the savorers. Who needs personality inventories when you could just administer the goody-bag survey?

In the case of our three, they are very peer conscious. They watch each other like hawks. The worst fate is to run out when your siblings still have some left in their stash.

The pace settles. Each of us watches the boots ahead. In a hiking day there is the serious middle, the belly of the day, a period of steady pace, eating miles, getting it done. The trail angles uphill. Our conversation dies away. We all hope that little tributary has water.

It does, but not much. When we pull up next to it, an anemic flow oozes through a steep, muddy talus slope, barely three inches deep. Good enough. The bottoms of our feet ache, and it's past time for a break. Each of us finds a perch along the trickle, a place with enough of a pool to soak our feet. The cold water numbs our bruised soles. After eating, we lie back against our packs, let the cold seep up from our feet.

All afternoon the grind uphill continues, switchbacking through mature, silent forest, encountering no one. At every stream crossing we dunk our sweaty heads, drink up, before moving on. Near the top of the grade, Marston Creek disappears. It goes abruptly from a healthy, chattering flow to dry streambed.

The trail levels out in a wide meadow, glossy with grass, rimmed by snowclad cliffs. The stream isn't running, but there are pools of water.

"We should camp," Eli says.

It does look inviting. We've finally arrived in the high country, leaving the dust and dudes behind. We've worked really hard to get here, almost ten miles and two thousand feet of elevation this day alone. Marypat and I look at each other.

"We still have lots of daylight," Marypat starts. "The next meadow is only another mile or so, then we'll be close enough to get to the headwaters easily tomorrow."

"But look how beautiful this is," Eli says. He puts his arms out, a salesman inviting us to take in the view.

"I know, but the next spot will be beautiful too. Let's just do one more mile."

To their credit, the kids are game. We line out along the trail, skirt the edge of the meadow to a final set of switchbacks leading over a low ridge. Two turns up, Sawyer stops at an opening in the forest. "What's that big brown thing?" he asks, pointing down at the meadow.

The brown thing is a glaring contrast to the emerald grass—large, animal-like, not moving. I grab the binoculars, focus in. Everyone waits.

"It's a dead horse," I pronounce.

They all look. The horse is laid out like it's sleeping, glowing in the sun, but it's obviously dead. Also untouched, fresh, the hide intact. A very large and irresistible cache of meat that, five minutes earlier, we strolled blissfully past.

Sawyer lowers the binos. "Suddenly," he says, "I'm not so tempted to camp. Maybe we should go a couple of miles!"

The next meadow is dry. Thunderheads are threatening. From here the trail climbs one thousand feet to Marston Pass. We drop packs and fan out, looking for water and tent sites. Old bear scat litters the ground, along with sign of elk and deer. There are good tent spots but no water.

I take Ruby and Sawyer with me, carrying all of our water containers, to a meltwater stream gushing out of a snowfield that we passed about half a mile back. Beans trots along. Eli and Marypat stay to set up the tent. The waning day suddenly feels gloomy. Faint menace hangs in the air. I do my best to hide my unease, but my bear antennae, such as they are, are powered up.

It is a spooky night. Beans is restless. After dinner, he paces up the meadow and stands, peering intently into the forest above, as if monitoring something moving through the fringe of trees. His body quivers with tension. His ears perk forward. He stands there for a long time, watching and listening.

I wake often during the night, listen to my family breathing next to me. Through the hours I hear Beans stirring outside. A couple of times he runs off somewhere. Once he barks. I keep thinking of the horsemeat a mile away, how it will attract animals large and small—ravens, foxes, coyotes, wolves, grizzly. They will come, inevitably, naturally. How could they not?

They will establish their hierarchy, feed by turns, plunder the wealth lying in the pretty meadow. Along the way, some of them will skirt our camp, moving past using the protection of forest beyond the range of our senses. Only Beans knows how active it has been through the dark hours, how close creatures came to the five of us packed inside the thin shell of nylon.

Twenty-Five

Good it's quiet I'm first up—couldn't stand the hard ground and my shitty pad any more. Besides, the sun was on the tent I've got a cup of coffee next to me. The stove is off. The sun is warm. The sky cloudless. The wind still Way in the distance I can hear what might be water tumbling down a steep slope Maybe it's simply the vacuum of silence.

—AL, PERSONAL JOURNAL

Every trip has barriers to break through, levels of being there to achieve. When I get up after my fitful night, it is cold enough for a coat. I boil water for coffee. The grass shimmers with frost, but then the sun booms over the ridge into a clear, deep blue sky.

None of our outfit was touched during the night. Beans was curled up outside the tent door when I got out. The morning is brilliant enough to hurt.

Whatever went on around the horse carcass, whatever might still be going on there, no longer dominates my mental radar. In bear country, you never forget. When a twig snaps during the night, it's a griz. When a shadow moves in the forest, before you identify it as a bird, it's a bear. When one of the kids walks off somewhere, I think about ursine ambush.

You never forget, but it's possible to gain equanimity. I remember a Native man I met in Fort McPherson, Northwest Territories, on the eve of a canoe trip in the Far North. When we asked him about dealing with bears, he told us to hang a bright coat on a tree where we camp, make ourselves known. They won't bother you, he said. On one level his response was simplistic. There is no end of what-if scenarios you could come up with for which hanging a coat wouldn't be much help. But it revealed a level of comfort with sharing space with an animal that can kill you without breathing hard. It's not at all that he took bears lightly, but on a basic level, all he was saying was to respect their space while announcing your own. Taken that way, it is pretty simple. Bears don't want trouble any more than we do.

I can't pin down why I feel at peace this morning. The pretty day full of promise, the prospect of alpine country just up the trail, the accumulation of time and miles and effort logged to reach this spot. Whatever it is, I'm across a threshold, eager to move deeper.

I feel strong physically too. It's not a thing I assume anymore. I'm fit enough aerobically, but ever since about age forty-five, I've realized that I can't take robust health and general immunity from pain for granted. This hike has felt good, though. It's reassuring to carry a pack loaded with a week's provisions, hike ten miles a day with a healthy dollop of elevation thrown in, and still feel strong.

"Breakfast's on!" I call out.

The trail angles up the shadowed side of a ridge, through conifers. It's still early. Our pace is steady, efficient. I'm behind Sawyer. He has the build of a cross-country runner, lean and lanky, still only a few pounds over one hundred. In fact, he is a cross-country runner. At ten, he was the youngest participant in the local John Colter Run, a seven-mile trail race that follows grassy ridges, has some steep climbs and descents, and ends by splashing across the Gallatin River. He has run it every year since. He has the head for solitary endurance, the mental resilience to find a pace, persevere through side-aches, push past pain.

"When you're up on those ridges, just running and looking around, it was so cool. I forgot that I was running. It was like I was flying," he said after his first race.

A Clark's nutcracker flashes into a dead bristlecone pine, calls down at us, a harsh cry. Beans sticks largely to the trail, his energy for chasing chipmunks and squirrels damped down by the pack of dog food he carries. Whenever we stop, he lies right down and catches a nap.

Trees fall away behind us. We keep climbing up rocky slopes. Tundra ridges and craggy peaks bracket the view. Still not a cloud in the sky. At Marston Pass, a weathered sign less than three feet tall reads 10,300 feet. Just around the corner a small lake fills a depression. A lingering snowfield hangs above it. From the right vantage, the Grand Tetons shimmer in the hazy distance. Higher ridges loom above us. Green valleys that will eventually become deep canyons start their journeys at this divide. They sweep gently away, wide, shallow basins with trickles of water and fields of wilting elephant head flowers.

"Let's camp here." I drop my pack. "We can hike on to the headwaters, see about climbing Younts Peak, and come back tonight."

"I'll make some lunch," Marypat says. "We'll empty the smallest pack and use it for our daypack."

The day holds. This is the payoff for the miles of dust and heat, the thousands of feet climbed. Without packs, we feel buoyant and fast. The view is panoramic, wild, endless. South to the Wind Rivers, north to Yellowstone Park, west to the Tetons, east out over the plains. In the foreground, small lakes, snowfields, rolling tundra, bands of cliff, mountain summits.

I hike with Eli. "I like to get there," he says when we take a break and look back at Marypat, Ruby, and Sawyer meandering through the wildflowers, taking their time. Eli and I are similar in our point-to-point focus. We skirt the edge of boggy meadow to a trail that switchbacks up a ridge, toil steadily up it, crossing some old snow, and round a corner where Younts Peak shoulders in front of us, dominating the view.

It's an imposing peak, pyramid shaped, with one sloping side and two steep, cliffy ridgelines. Below us, the South Fork of the Yellowstone River arcs away in a gentle curve. If we contour and stay high, it looks as if we can bushwhack around the head of the valley, cross the stream near the source, and continue to the pass at the base of Younts Peak. From that saddle we will look down at the North Fork of the Yellowstone.

"Wow! Isn't this cool?" Marypat exudes that glow that comes over her in wild places. Her blue eyes crackle with intensity. "You guys, there's the Yellowstone, the very beginning of the river we paddled all the way to North Dakota. This is where it's born."

Marypat embodies adventurous spontaneity. It was one of the qualities that attracted me to her when we first met. That, and her joy on the dance floor. Some people doubt the wisdom of adventure at first suggestion. They find reasons it can't be done. Marypat rises to possibility, takes on how to make it happen. This is where she comes alive, where her laugh slips out, where the engine of desire visibly kicks in. It's an energy she has passed on to her children, and to Sawyer in particular.

She is as fit a woman as I know. Her legs are pistons. I am very accustomed to the rear view of my partner as she pulls away from me going uphill. Never mind that she is at the cusp of fifty. Marypat is buff. People regularly ask her if she is a bodybuilder. More than that, joy pumps out her pores on an alpine hike the way sweat pumps out of mine. One of my abiding fears is that Marypat will come to a point in life where this sort of activity becomes impossible. If that happens, the sorrow and loss might be unbearable.

"So that's Younts?" she points at the blocky mountain.

"Looks like a walk-up on the one side," I say, "but it would add a couple of miles to get to it. We might be able to go straight up the ridge, too, but it looks gnarly near the top."

She looks through the binoculars at the approach. The route leads up a snowfield, then a steep, somewhat exposed ridge, and culminates in a broken, cliffy band near the summit that might be a showstopper.

"Hmmm," is all she says. "Let's go check out the river."

The trail peters out. Each of us follows a line through the hummocky tundra grasses and across rubbly slopes, trying not to lose elevation, aiming for the head of the valley. The kids are ranging out in front, three abreast, almost running. Beans trots alongside, stopping to sniff and explore as he goes. Marypat and I stride together watching the kids. We don't say anything, but I know she is reveling in their energy, in their physical confidence. They have evolved from those early days when we had to cajole and distract them down the trail, enduring endless rounds of "When will we get there?" Now they wait for us. Now they think nothing of hoisting a pack, taking on a ten-mile day or a peak climb. They are not daunted in the slightest.

Ruby is the first to get there. Around a final corner, a long tongue of snow appears, pasted against a steep rock slope. The snow melts into a shallow pool, just inches deep, and then funnels into a trickle. The flow speeds up, runs over a band of bedrock. The Yellowstone is only a foot or two across. We can easily straddle it. Right at the start, the river erodes a miniature canyon through the layer of rock, then threads away down the valley, a thin, glittering promise picking up speed, heeding gravity, fed by the snows of last winter. One hundred yards uphill, a gently sloping ridge divides the Yellowstone from Younts Creek, which flows back off toward the Shoshone drainage.

Ruby lies on her belly, puts her face right in the water, drinks deep. I lie next to her. The water is pure, fifty feet from its source, cold and icy as it goes down. We still have paddling calluses on our palms from three weeks of working boats across the state of Montana. We have grains of sand lodged in our shoes and clothes from campsites. We might well have silt and sand still imbedded in the roots of our hair.

First water of the Yellowstone, Ruby drinks deep.

The Yellowstone is sharp in our visceral memory. Every mile of the great flow—scribing through mountain valleys, across the plains, picking up tributaries, used by towns and industry and agriculture. Its sunsets, its heat, its throaty rapids, its storms and gravel bars and quiet backwaters and side canyons. The Yellowstone became part of us. Now we lie down and drink it straight, pure and unfiltered. It becomes us, entering through our cell walls, refreshing muscles, carrying away wastes, fueling our metabolic engines.

When I stand up again, the river burning cold in my belly, I am confronted by the steep ramparts of Younts Peak.

Twenty-Six

Me and Mom were the only ones to make it to the top of Younts Peak. We had lunch there. On the way down we all went glissading which was awesome. It was an amazing day. When we got back to camp I went glissading naked into a pond, then saw some bighorn sheep.

—SAWYER, GROUP JOURNAL

The spring Sawyer was five, we paddled the Marias River, in northern Montana. My parents came along. Eli was six and Ruby was barely three. We had just graduated from the five-people-in-one-canoe phase of our family paddling evolution.

In the new configuration, Marypat and I each paddled a canoe turned backward, so we could position ourselves to paddle solo. One of the boys would sit backward in the stern seat, as if it was the bow, and paddle when they were motivated. Ruby ended up somewhere in the load on one of the canoes or perched on the tip of the boat like a hood ornament, chubby legs dangling above the water. After years of cramming five people, gear, and food into a single hull, it was an unbelievable luxury of space.

It poured rain throughout the drive to the put-in at a rural highway bridge, but late in the day, as we got under way, the sky cleared. We camped near some cottonwood trees three miles down the small, winding river.

While Marypat and I got camp set and dinner started, the kids went off on an explore with their grandmother. We could hear them shouting and playing in the grove of trees. Sunset fired the retreating rain clouds above the arid buttes. Dinner simmered on the stove.

Then, rending the placid camp scene, one of those piercing screams that make a parent drop the stirring spoon and start sprinting. The kids were coming toward us from the cottonwoods. Sawyer was wailing in pain and fear. My mom hovered over him, doing her best to calm the situation.

Marypat swooped in, gathered Sawyer up in her arms, and started running toward camp, stooped over like an infantry soldier carrying wounded toward the throbbing safety of a helicopter.

Sawyer was bleeding from the neck. When we were able to tip his head back, the mouth of a wound gaped wide, less than an inch from his windpipe and deep enough to see muscle.

If this had happened in town, we would be speeding toward the emergency room. Here, none of our options for help were good, if doable at all. We were more than three miles from the nearest road, across sagebrush and deep draws and over fences. It would be dark in an hour. To get back in the boat and paddle three miles upstream would be physically exhausting and time consuming. Our shuttle drivers had already taken the vehicles. Once we reached the road we'd have to hitchhike, but where? The nearest town of any size, Fort Benton, might or might not have medical facilities where we could get help. We might end up having to travel to Great Falls.

Sawyer was suffering from shock and trauma as well as pain. He wasn't pulsing blood, so he hadn't cut any major blood vessel. His breathing was fine. The wound was a clean slit, one to two inches long, deep but apparently without complications.

Marypat cradled him, sitting in a camp chair. The rest of us hovered around in the gloaming. The limited options kept running through my mind. We'd have real trouble trying to get help. We had to handle this on our own.

Sawyer kept crying hard, didn't want us to examine the injury, fought our attempts to look him over. Eventually the story came out. Sawyer had followed Eli up the sloping trunk of a cottonwood tree. Eli reached a flat spot on the rough bark to rest and waited for Sawyer to reach him. Just as he was getting close, a dead branch broke off and he fell more than ten feet, landing on the sharp stick that punctured his neck.

Finally Sawyer was quiet enough to allow us to work on him, now by headlamp. The wound was alarming, but clean. We gently swabbed it out with a cotton swab and Betadine, closed the cut with Steri-Strips as best we could, covered it with a large gauze bandage. Sawyer was still very fitful and traumatized. He kept moaning and crying, squirming in Marypat's embrace.

All night, we slept next to him in the tent. He turned and cried out through the hours. I thought about how we might evacuate in the morning, retracing our steps, retrieving the vehicles, getting home. By then it would be too late for stitches. Marypat and I took turns cuddling Sawyer, holding him close.

At dawn we rose. Sawyer came out with us. We held him, tried to get him to eat something, checked the wound. Eli came over with a picture book. He sat down next to his brother and started turning pages, pointing to things, making up stories. Sawyer slowly responded, still shaken, but distracted and entertained. We took the opportunity to change his bandage. The wound looked good, no sign of infection, no further bleeding, the cut knitting together in a thin line.

Within twenty minutes, Sawyer had squirmed off of Marypat's lap and was turning pages with Eli. Then the boys got up and went down by the boats, started chucking rocks in the river. By the time we had breakfast ready, we had to call them back from their play.

"Do you think you can go on, sweetie?" Marypat asked him.

He nodded.

"You won't be able to swim. No rough playing, either. And you'll have to let us keep changing the bandage to keep it clean, okay?"

Another nod between spoonfuls of hot cereal.

Sawyer is the kid who tries things first. Part of it stems from his drive to keep up with Eli, do what his brother can do. But it is also his personality to go all out, to the point that he endangers himself.

"Sawyer, you go," his siblings say, teetering on the brink of an iffy enterprise. More often than not, he will. He'll be the one to jump from the branch, dive into the river off of a cliff, slam into a tree trying to ski through thick forest.

The result has been an accident legacy that includes stitches, a split nose, chipped teeth, black eyes, and various wounds. Ruby and Eli both have a healthy sense of self-preservation that I wish Sawyer would cultivate. They get their share of bumps and scrapes, are pretty game when it comes to taking risks, but they hold back from the ultimate commitment enough to avoid the truly gruesome wrecks.

The other consequence, however, is that Sawyer is up for just about anything. He's the one who takes up Telemark skiing, mountain biking, whitewater kayaking without hesitation. Big trip, new sport, a year in a wilderness cabin…sure, when do we start? When you ask him if he's up for a peak climb, he says yes and doesn't worry about details. With the other two, more often than not, it's how long, how hard, can I go to a friend's house instead?

Several times, Marypat has brought up the idea of spending a year in another country, going to school there, doing some traveling, swapping houses with another family, somehow making it work. Eli and Ruby groan. They want no part of separating from their friends and peers, adjusting to a new school, new friends, new sports teams, foreign cultures. Sawyer would pack up tomorrow. In fact, he reminds us of the plan regularly.

Twenty-Seven

Hiked hard and fast through the cool hours. Didn't have hot sun until Needle Creek. Kept going all the way to the car, finding a killer swimming hole near the end, where we all dove in and rinsed the dust off. M P took a hard fall, tripping over a rock. Forest fires just over the ridge.

—AL, GROUP JOURNAL

The option to circle down the valley and hike up the sloping ramp to Younts Peak never comes up again. No one really wants to grunt the extra miles, and the challenge of the ridge is seductive. Cresting the pass at the base of the peak, we pause to look down at the North Fork of the Yellowstone River— wild country, cliff walls, a sketchy trail very few people use—another place to come back to someday. Then Marypat leads sharply uphill, aiming for the

KICK-STEPPING UP A SNOWFIELD ON THE ASCENT OF YOUNTS PEAK, WITH THE VALLEY OF THE SOUTH FORK YELLOWSTONE RIVER BELOW.

bottom of a long snowfield we glassed. The rest of us fall in behind. If there are doubts, no one voices them.

The snow is soft enough to kick steps into. The kids haven't done any real alpine snow travel, but they drop into the cadence. Marypat leads. I bring up the rear. The angle is moderate and the texture of the snow is consistent. We methodically kick each step, placing our boots one after another into the divots, back and forth across the face of snow. Above it, the ridge continues at a steep angle through sparse vegetation and loose rocks. Conversation stops. We labor toward twelve thousand feet. Marypat and Sawyer start to pull away.

Younts Peak, and the final band of cliff, looms against the blue sky. The ridge narrows. It becomes a sharp edge of rock, loose and exposed. Ruby is right in front of me. Her boots skitter on the gravel, she leans into the slope, making her footing even less stable. Below, the cliffs fall away into space. She starts to lose her nerve.

"Daddy, I really don't like this," she says.

"It isn't that bad, sweetie. You can do it," I reassure her. "Slow and steady, one step at a time."

She is not reassured. She keeps leaning against the slope, not putting her weight firmly over her feet, fear in her movements.

"I don't want to be here," she says, her voice shaky.

The ridge drops steeply away below us. The rocks are like ball bearings. The really steep section rises ahead of us.

Ruby slips again. She sits down. "Dad!" There is real fear in her voice. No matter that the approach is quite safe, her emotions have the better of her.

Marypat, Eli, and Sawyer stop to wait on a flat platform about the size of a double bed. Ruby and I struggle toward them.

"I don't want to do this," Ruby says, slumping against a rock.

"The final pitch looks pretty sketchy," I say, looking uphill. It's only a few hundred feet to the actual summit, but Ruby is in no shape to go on.

"Whatever we do, I think we should decide as a family and stick together," I say.

"No way," Marypat says. "I want to get to the top. Who else wants to go?"

"Okay, be that. way," I respond, squelching the anger that rises in response to Marypat's predictable appetite for the summit. She is unwaveringly honest about her desire, but to me, it seems pretty selfish. Fact is, gaining the absolute summit doesn't matter much to me, but Marypat can't countenance not standing on the peak.

"I'd go," Sawyer says.

"Doesn't matter to me," Eli says.

"I don't want to leave Ruby alone," I say. "I'll stay put."

"I'll stay too," Eli agrees.

Marypat and Sawyer stand up, start moving into the steep, loose rocks, carefully finding their way through the cliffy layers toward the peak. Beans goes with them. It is slow going, but it is quickly apparent that they will make it.

The three of us recline on our airy perch. I hand out some snacks. A boiling plume of forest fire smoke rises in the southeast like a dark cumulus cloud. I walk to the edge of the platform. The cliff falls sheer into the upper reaches of the North Fork. More valleys and ridges rumple the land, beckoning and mysterious. When I turn, the Tetons serrate the horizon and the high plateaus of the southern Absaroka Range swoop away. You could wander for days following ridges, summiting peaks, roaming the open plateaus, discovering pockets of beauty. I check off possibilities—there, and there, and over there.

A shout from above. Sawyer and Marypat stand against the skyline at the peak, wave their arms at us. We wave back. They savor the peak for a few minutes, take pictures, before starting down, gingerly testing each step, weaving back and forth for the best route through the layers.

"It was great," Marypat says, when they get back. She has that exultant grin on her face. "What a view!"

Her joy almost heals up the irritation I felt with her.

"You could still go," Marypat suggests. "We'd wait. It isn't that bad."

"That's okay," I say. "It'll be pretty late in the day by the time we get back to camp. I don't care about the actual summit. Not like I used to, anyway. And certainly not like you do."

We start down, Ruby a bit more game, but still whimpering with nerves until we get off the exposed ridge.

Then we introduce them all to the fine tradition of glissading. At the top of the snowfield we start skiing down on our boots, making sharp turns to slow the descent, sliding and turning through the corn snow, picking up speed, making hockey stops.

"This is the best," Eli whoops. "I just found my favorite outdoor activity!"

The slope is over too soon. The kids race off in search of another pocket of snow to slide down, and all the way back around the head of the valley, they strike off after snow patches. At the head of the South Fork, they climb up the steep face of snow that melts to create the Yellowstone. All the way up to the rock cliff at the highest tongue of snow, and then they careen down, schussing and shouting and falling, right to the edge of the shallow pool, where Marypat takes a picture of them all lined up making snow angels.

Back in camp, Beans is limping badly. The pads of his paws are sore and tender. We coax an ibuprofen down him. He curls up in a camp chair and won't move. Marypat and I down a dose of vitamin I to keep him company. The kids, still hungry for snow sports, strip down to underwear and sandals, race around the lake to a patch of snow, where they ski down on their feet right into the shallow, icy water.

After dinner, the full moon breaks the horizon along a ridge, plump and serene and cool. *What would life be without the moon*, I think, watching it rise. What would life be without mountains to be in, wild places to inhabit, snowfields to descend, storms to cower before, rivers to run? At this moment, in this camp, I could imagine staying put for a month, strolling through the upper valleys, traipsing free of trails or any agenda, drifting

MOONRISE AND TENT GLOW ABOVE TREE LINE IN THE WASHAKIE WILDERNESS.

loose from the moorings of clocks and meetings and manic clutter that I come to consider normal.

Marypat and Sawyer head up to a ridge above camp and sit together. They are savoring each other, their time together on the summit, the knowledge of how matched their climbing appetites are. A band of bighorn sheep dots a distant ridge. Beans doesn't even raise his head. I put the dinner things away as moonlight washes in, a tide of light pooling into the valleys, hitting our camp, bathing everything in pale luminosity.

Except for the hum of space, it is absolutely silent. Silent enough to feel the inexorable lift and grain-by-grain erosion of mountains, the fractional growth of summer flowers, the turning of the planet. Also, how heroically small we are in it. The birds are still, the wind is calm, only the lapping noise of light drowning everything in its grace.

Turning away from the high country the next morning feels like packing up and leaving home. *To hell with soccer tryouts*, I think, heading down toward the trees, toward the end of the trail where our car waits. I keep glancing around at the ridges and peaks, the craggy outbursts of rock, the patches of snow, the places to explore. And I think ahead to the meadow with the dead horse lying in it, a few miles away.

Beans walks tenderly, still limping. The rest of us are in good shape. The packs feel light. My family strings out, spots of color and life, each of us thinking our thoughts. I'm guessing that the dead horse is a prominent theme we share.

I have looked at the map carefully. If the meadow with the horse seems too dangerous to approach, there's a bushwhack route down a steep ridge to a lower section of the trail that might be possible. Difficult and time consuming, but better than confronting a grizzly on a carcass.

"We need to come in quietly and stick together," I say. "We can glass the meadow from the trail above, still in the forest, and see what's happening." I try to sound matter-of-fact.

"What if there's a bear there?" Ruby asks.

"We'll figure that out once we see what's up."

The closer we get, the quieter we all become. The forest is still, full of shadows, the morning coolness lingers. We pass our old camp. Bits of the sunny meadow come into view. It is a stellar day, full of tension.

"Let's have a look," I whisper.

Through the binoculars the green grass is brilliant. I glass around the border of the open valley. Nothing moves. Slowly, I sweep back and forth across the meadow, stopping at every dark spot, waiting for some raised head, something lying satiated in the grass. Finally I come to the horse. It lies in the same spot, but it's as if the carcass has been deflated.

In the past day and a half, the same day and a half we camped and glissaded and climbed through, the horse has been consumed. The body is a collapsed shell of hide.

"It's been eaten," I say. "It's a bag of bones."

Everyone looks through the binoculars. We wait and watch for a long time. Nothing stirs in the grass.

"Okay," Marypat says. "Everyone gets their bear spray out. Let's keep quiet and keep moving. No stopping."

I pause once more before we emerge from the forest, take a final look. Still nothing. The five of us bunch together. Everyone has bear spray out like cops sneaking up on a stakeout. Beans sticks close. The trail is completely trampled with animal tracks. Bear and wolf prints overlap, intermingle, going both ways, a highway to dinner. We place our bootprints over the top, walk as fast as we can, just short of running.

"Keep up the pace, Soy," Ruby hisses at Sawyer's back.

"Don't get your undies in a bundle, girlie," Sawyer says, glancing over his shoulder.

The car waiting fifteen miles away, and what it might transport us to, sits in another dimension, an inaccessible dimension. Right now it is the sunlight, the grass moving in the breeze, the consumed kill and our furtive, tense passage that define our universe.

Half a mile downhill, I'm still thinking about the risks we share with our kids. They trust us implicitly, have absolute faith in us, follow without question. It is their lot to do what we do, to believe what we tell them. We put them in cars, trust them to babysitters, tell them to walk home from a movie, put them in the way of myriad environmental threats—from weather to pesticides. Here, we encourage them to slide down steep slopes, slosh across rushing streams, scramble along exposed ridgelines, and tiptoe past a fresh kill in the heart of a wilderness brimming with large predators.

I wouldn't change it. I do believe that the benefits and the joy of wild life outweigh the hazards. But there are moments when risk tingles in the air like the electricity of a lightning strike, and when the enormity of the trust my children grant me weighs heavy.

Twenty-Eight

Certainly got our water legs by starting at Gardiner (without Eli), and rollicking down the river at high water. Big standing waves, holes, strong eddies. Had to stop repeatedly to bail, but lots of fun. Bill did us the great favor of watching Eli while we made the four-hour run and meeting us below Yankee Jim Canyon.

—AL, PERSONAL JOURNAL, 1992

July Fourth weekend, 1992, at the lower end of Yankee Jim Canyon on the Yellowstone River. Eli is eight months old and unhappy. He squalls as I hand him, zipped into a quilted carrying bag, to Marypat. She lays him in the hull of the canoe in front of her feet. She coos at him to no effect. Perhaps he has picked up on the fact that his parents are winging it. Perhaps he has some intuitive sense that once we leave shore, we've committed to a month on the river with a teething, diaper-clad, completely dependent and defenseless infant.

The river is high, dirty with runoff. Current jostles the end of the boat. Eli's caterwauling is getting to me.

"Are you ready?" I ask.

Before Marypat answers I shove off. The Yellowstone pulls us quickly away from the boat ramp. It sounds gritty as sandpaper against the canoe hull. I take my first strokes toward North Dakota and the confluence with the Missouri River, five hundred fifty miles and twenty-five days away.

We'll be damned if having a kid is going to change our lifestyle, we had said to each other, planning the Yellowstone trip less than a year after our return from the Far North and well ahead of Eli's first birthday. People take their infants on road trips, put them in the hands of nannies. Babies have gone to the wilds before, or have been born in the wilds, or have had to survive earthquakes and warfare and prolonged incubation in hospitals. The traditional Inuit had their babies on the tundra.

What's a month on the water? Of course we can do it.

Our families, and many of our friends, especially veteran parents, were dubious. What about diapers? What about food? What about sunburn and mosquitoes? How are you going to keep him contained in the boat, not to mention around campfires and snakes and current? What happens if you capsize? What about hailstorms and hundred-degree heat?

Good questions, ones that had cropped up in our minds too. We thought we had a few answers—a hand-crank food mill for processing leftovers into baby gruel, a sun hat with neck flap, an electronic device sent by my parents that supposedly emitted a mosquito-deterring sound approximating dragonfly wings, a backcountry harness/tether system adapted from the mall harnesses you see parents using in town. We had a few experiments to try out—cloth diapers in favor of disposables, a baby backpack we hoped would serve as a high chair at meal times, dried bananas for teething distraction.

We figured we'd adapt as we went. There hadn't been the opportunity for a test run. Coping with an infant at home and gearing up for a month on the river had been more than a full-time occupation. We'd allotted ourselves plenty of time, enough so that, at high water, we could almost drift the length of the river. Ultimately, if it became unworkable or dangerous, we could quit the trip. The Yellowstone isn't the Barren Lands. It is a river bordered by roads, punctuated by towns. We could call a friend and be home in a day.

Of course, having a road two miles away doesn't help if you capsize in a rapid, but if you start entertaining what-if scenarios, you're doomed. Besides, there is no end to what-ifs we encounter in town and at home. What if the baby falls against a table corner or down a flight of stairs? What if we get in a car accident? What if they suffocate with a plastic bag or crawl off the back porch or get into the cleaning supplies under the sink? Like that. Can't go there.

All of those sensible questions come back, however, before we round the first river bend and while Eli continues to complain. Marypat finally gives in, unzips the carrying bag, and hoists him up to nurse.

Eli wears a tiny life jacket. Most of the infant models we tried he will have no part of. They have more in common with cervical collars than flotation devices. Because his life jacket favors wearability and comfort over bombproof buoyancy, we've added a harness to the system and a webbing tether tied around Marypat's waist. That way, if we go over, she can reel him in and get to safety. The only counterargument we've heard is that the tether might get tangled in deadfall and entrap the swimmers, including Eli. Given the choice, though, we're both more comfortable being connected to him than watching him bob off like a cork on the current.

I paddle solo. I have the feeling that, for whoever is in the stern, solo paddling will loom large on this trip. The day before, we had had our fling with paddling together, like old times. We may be risk takers, we may include our infant son in the bargain, but we aren't stupid enough to take him through the first-day whitewater of the Yellowstone, from the park boundary to below Yankee Jim.

It is far and away the biggest water of the entire trip, all packed into the first day and no place for a baby. We girded the boat with a spray deck, took on the sets of huge standing waves and holes near the town of Gardiner, and then the boat-swallowing rapids of Yankee Jim Canyon. The river was full of power, snarling and thick, lathered with curling waves. Great fun in an empty, decked boat, indulging the dance of our paddling partnership in a way we hadn't in many months.

Eli's godfather, Bill, agreed to tend to the boy while we had our fun. He met us at the take-out, more than ready to hand off his charge and head back to town and leave us to face the reality of our life-won't-change-because-we-have-a-kid bluster.

We had been told, once we succeeded in having Eli, that becoming pregnant again was a complete long shot. For one thing, we were older. I turned forty days after Eli was born, and Marypat was thirty-seven. For another thing, Marypat was full-on nursing. Getting pregnant is even less likely for nursing mothers. Finally, we were told that the notion that once you have a kid, you've primed the pump and more will come is a complete myth.

It took you that long to have your first, doctors told us. Don't expect to get pregnant again any sooner, if at all.

So what? We had Eli. Another kid was way down the to-do list. Marypat would love to have more than one, but she certainly wasn't planning on it. I was profoundly grateful to have survived the infertility phase of life, fully occupied with the demands of one child, and quite happy to let things ride.

We didn't take precautions. Why bother? And besides, we were really out of that habit. More to the point, we were so jaundiced by the fertility quagmire, and so overwhelmed with the reality of this very alive offspring we'd managed to conjure, that the possibility never came up. To go there felt like quicksand, a place we tiptoed around.

When Marypat missed her period in June, it didn't even register on our radar. Periods were irregular by definition after a birth.

What we don't know, now that Eli is aboard and our trip plans are being put to the test, is that the word never got to Sawyer. He is along for the ride as well—a fetal bud busy doing cell division, a quiet ambush growing in Marypat's womb, about to enter our lives.

Twenty-Nine

It's been frantic in the weeks leading up to this departure. Ruby's soccer tournament finished yesterday, which was also Marypat's birthday. We had cake and ice cream in the backyard with friends. We had to farm Beans out to Sue. Up at six AM to a big to-do list MP tended the garden while I ticked things off. At 8 AM the send-off flotilla started arriving—a dozen or so folks in rafts, canoes, and inflatable kayaks. As expected, a ponderous put in, not on the river 'til nearly noon.

—AL, PERSONAL JOURNAL

Fast-forward to this day, toward the end of June 2006, in which Sawyer is strapping on a blue helmet and settling into an inflatable kayak on the Yellowstone River just upstream of Gardiner, Montana, and at the border of Yellowstone National Park. The river is roaring with spring runoff, dirty brown, boisterous, and cold.

Unlike our foray down the river with Eli, fourteen years earlier, or our lonely departure from Kasba Lake the previous summer, our launch is crowded with friends. There are several rafts and a bevy of inflatable canoes and kayaks. Paddles, pumps, boats, dry bags, life jackets, and colorful clothing are strewn across the rocky shore. A mob of kids, friends, godparents have joined up to see us off by spending the first, rapid-filled day alongside. Several of the kids are friends Sawyer has grown up with on adventures. A number of them, including Sawyer, are competent paddlers, eager for whitewater.

Sawyer is the first to shove off. On this stretch of the Yellowstone, there is no warm-up, no chance to find a rhythm. Immediately the dance is on. He strokes toward midriver and the first set of waves. The red boat bounces over the crests, disappears in the troughs, only his helmet visible. His paddle glints wet in the sunlight. The rest of us sort ourselves out, hop into boats, follow his lead.

The day is warm and clear, the water frigid. Within minutes a kayak flips. One of the kids swims alongside hanging onto the paddle, but then rights the boat, clambers back in, and is immediately swallowed by the next hole. The rafts lumber behind, mother ships full of whoops and laughter.

Where the Yellowstone emerges from Yellowstone Park, it is arguably as fresh as any river in North America. It has already come more than one hundred miles from the first drips off of the snout of snowfield where we will lie on our bellies to drink, six weeks after this launch. It slips down from the alpine valleys into the meadows of the Thorofare, past Two Ocean Pass, gathering strength and volume before spilling into Yellowstone Lake, that thermally restless, massive body of freshwater.

Yellowstone Lake is the largest lake above seven thousand feet in North America, with 110 miles of shoreline and depths to four hundred feet. It fills a portion of the gigantic caldera created by the last epic volcanic eruption, an explosion that rocked North America some 640,000 years ago. That eruption was six thousand times larger than the one at Mount Saint Helens, and scientists suggest that Yellowstone is overdue for the next big one. Swarms of small earthquakes, several thousand each year, keep seismologists employed, and geologists follow the slow breathing of the lake floor as it domes up and settles back in response to pressures from the magma chamber simmering below.

The largest of some fifty tributaries to the lake, the Yellowstone pools there before pouring out again, pounding over Upper and Lower Falls in the Grand Canyon of the Yellowstone, a mist-cloaked tumult, a spectacular chasm adorned with perpetual rainbows, where osprey perch on volcanic spires and the ground steams with geothermal heat. The Grand Canyon may well be the most photographed, painted, and sketched view in all the West. On past Tower Junction and the Lamar Valley, into the Black Canyon of the Yellowstone, over more falls and rapids, where the current carves out contours of relatively temperate wintering ground for elk and bison. Then, finally, charging across the arbitrary boundary we have drawn on maps, into Montana, where it is immediately sullied.

Right in Gardiner, raw sewage regularly leaks into the river. The antiquated town sewage system has failed repeatedly, spilling untreated human waste by the thousands of gallons directly into the Yellowstone. There is nothing malicious about it. Everyone feels badly. There is simply not enough money in the town budget to fix the problem.

Where the current roils under the first highway bridge the tone is set. For the rest of its run, the Yellowstone pays the price of human occupation. From the moment it rushes out of the park, and all the way to the confluence with the Missouri, more than five hundred miles away, its fate is to be valued and used and assaulted—by irrigators, cities, factories, towns, anglers, recreators, Jet-Skiers, livestock.

All of us nurse from the river. We use its power, value its wealth, sap its strength. We love to live on its banks, fish its waters, run its rapids, hear it whisper past under winter ice, know it is there. Without it we literally couldn't survive. For the most part we don't give back. What we return, more often than not, is polluted and depleted.

In this way, the Yellowstone is a microcosm of our relationship with Mother Earth. A case study of what happens everywhere, from Greenland to China.

Ruby finds an arrowhead where we stop for lunch. She comes up to me, wearing her soaked life vest and bathing suit, teeth chattering, still drenched from the antics in the rapids. "Look at this, Dad." And she hands me the point. There on the riverbank, in the gravel, Ruby spied a perfectly preserved point chipped out of chert. The worked stone feels warm.

The Yellowstone is a rock hound's dream. Its gravel is full of agate and petrified wood. The arrowhead is a surprise, but finding treasure is not. Since the kids were tiny, they have hunted rocks on the gravel bars. It is a matter of pride to come back from the Yellowstone heavier than we start. We feed the stones into a rock tumbler in the garage, wait a month or more, and gather the glistening gems. We give them away as presents, fill bowls with them, set them around the garden.

Our habit is to walk around river camps with our heads bowed, as if strolling in prayerful contemplation, looking for keepers. The dull translucence of agate, the telltale grain of wood. The kids have developed their eyes to the point where I hardly have to look anymore. I just wait for them to bring rocks back by the fistful. I have announced that my goal in life is to find a Yellowstone agate the size of my head.

CULLING THE ROCK PILE FOR KEEPERS, A DAILY ROUTINE.

Agate forms in the pockets of volcanic rock left by escaped gas. Water percolates through the porous strata, carrying minerals, including chalcedony, a microscopic quartz in the same family as jasper, flint, and chert. The chalcedony is left behind, lining cavities, when the water evaporates. Over time, repeated deposits fill the holes, sometimes leaving a banded agate, other times clear.

Yellowstone agates are known for the "moss" in them, feathery growths made of dark mineral mixed in with the chalcedony that look very much like moss. It can create delicate designs that appear as miniature forests or landscapes.

As the volcanic layers erode, the harder quartz endures, falls free, and eventually slides down into drainages, where it is dispersed along the waterway, moving in floods, deposited on gravel bars, migrating with gravity. The same process creates the petrified wood made from trees buried in volcanic ash and lava during massive eruptions. Sometimes the mineral that makes up petrified wood happens to be chalcedony, in which case you find pieces of agatized petrified wood.

The Yellowstone is very rewarding. Almost any gravel bar yields up keepers. As a trip goes on, we become more and more discriminating. Even so, we end up with bulging, weighty sacks of river stone that make up ballast in the boats and that we heave around from camp to camp.

Our boat brigade sails on, past Church Universal and Triumphant land, famous for a brief period because their leader Elizabeth Clare Prophet predicted the end of the world and set off a round of bunker building and weapons procurement within her following in preparation for Armageddon. The predicted day came and went, Prophet was subsequently cast out of the church, and things have quieted down ever since. CUT remains one of the largest property owners in Park County.

Yankee Jim Canyon is the crescendo of the float. The rocky defile has three significant rapids—Revenge, Big Rock, and Boxcar. The whitewater is only four miles long, so it lends itself to yo-yo cycles of repeated runs. Every year or two someone drowns, and even seasoned paddlers regularly flip rafts. The hole below Big Rock is particularly renown for upending rafts. Locals refer to it as Boat Eater. The canyon itself is named for a frontier entrepreneur who ran a toll road through it.

Ruby is in a tandem kayak with her friend Natalie when we enter. In the first rapid, they flip in a side-curling wave that turns them over with smooth inevitability. They come up sputtering. People help them right the boat and they climb back in, shivering, but determined to prove themselves.

Everyone makes it by Big Rock safely, skirting the dangerous snarling hole downstream. Boxcar Rapid is one of the most conflicted pieces of water I've ever known. The river is black and deep there. The rapid doesn't look like much from a distance, just some choppy waves, but the current is chaotic and squirrely. Upwellings surge to the surface in powerful blisters. The eddy line is strong enough to suck down the tube of a raft, and it is deceptive. Water churns past sheer cliff walls. Waves slap at boats from every direction.

But our parade makes it through. Ruby and Natalie triumph. They hold their paddles over their heads in celebration. Soon after, all the kids pull off at an old trestle bridge to jump into the river. The rest of us proceed to the take-out, where our solitary expedition will begin.

Within an hour we've switched inflatables for traditional canoes, keeping one solo inflatable kayak along for the fifth paddler. On the Kazan River we had opted against a third, solo boat. The trip was too remote and difficult to put one of the kids on their own. The Yellowstone is a different story, a perfect river for the rubber-ducky class of vessel.

Three weeks' supplies fill the canoe hulls: dried food, tents, cook gear, five-gallon water jugs. The boats settle in the water under the load. Friends take pictures. We pose for the before shot in clean clothes, smiling at our neighbors and comrades. Then we climb in for the first time, take our seats, let the river slide us off toward North Dakota. In the initial moments, I experience one of those time lapses. The memory of taking off with infant Eli squalling in the bow, and of our shaky bravado as new parents, flashes back sharp and vivid.

Our first camp is less than a mile downstream. We pull the boats up on a gravel beach at the upstream end of an island. Montana river-access law allows camping below the high water mark, so beaches and gravel bars are fair game. The unpacking is a well-rehearsed drill, despite the nine-month school-year intermission. The tent goes up, the fireplace is located, all the gear gets dropped in place. Sawyer heads off to collect driftwood for a cook fire. Ruby paces down the center of the gravel bar, head bent, looking for agate.

Cars flash past on the road, half a mile away. The river, full of summer volume, grates by with its load of sediment. After the day full of people and rollicking water, the mood is subdued, a little deflated.

"No bugs!" Sawyer says when he drops wood by the fire pan. "Pretty cushy compared to last summer I'd say, eh, Pops?"

Thirty

Mule deer, pelicans, bald eagles, blue heron, osprey, nighthawks. Thunderheads built during the day, but never hit us. Clear night. No bugs.

—Group journal

I sleep in as long as I can stand it. It's been light for hours by the time I slip out of the tent. No dawn dashes this summer, we hope. No lakes to cross, no clouds of blackflies, no winter weather expected. Our only deadline is Eli's Minnesota soccer tournament. In order to make it, we have to average about twenty-five miles a day, which, with the helpful current, shouldn't be difficult.

Even so, I want to make it a big day. If I get my way, we'll paddle some thirty-five miles, all the way through Paradise Valley, and camp in the yard of friends on the outskirts of Livingston. They've offered us a barbecue dinner, and my ulterior motive is to put "paradise" in our wake.

The Yellowstone flows north through a scenic valley from the park boundary to Livingston, where it makes a sweeping turn to the east and heads for the high plains. Paradise Valley is rimmed by the Gallatin mountains on the west and the Absaroka Range to the east. The peaks shine with snow, run in jagged lines of ridges and crags against the blue sky. Many of those mountains we have climbed—Cowen, Electric, Ramshorn, Black— they beckon in every direction.

Seeing this valley fresh must have been a heart-constricting experience. The heady river looping down it, the nodding grasses, the gauntlet of mountain ranges. To see it new and unsettled would have been worth a lot. From a distance, it is still stunning—sleek horses grazing in pastures, bald eagles and osprey perching in cottonwoods, views up the sweeping curves of river, the timeless peaks rising pure and evocative above the valley.

Problem is, Paradise Valley is a poster child for what's happening in The Last Best Place. Everyone wants a piece of it, no one wants to be hassled by zoning or planning guidelines, and the geography is being smothered by its admirers. Drift boats full of anglers flail the waters, catching and releasing the same tired fish over and over. Five or six months out of the year, every access is jammed with rigs and trailers. Second homes built on an obscene scale festoon the banks, crowding to the edge, cluttering up what were once open vistas with vain ostentation. Busy US Route 89 buzzes with traffic on the periphery.

When back-to-back hundred-year floods roared through the valley in 1996 and 1997, it put the fear of nature into everyone. The river eroded its banks in gigantic bites. Homes toppled into the flood or had to be burned before they tipped over the edge. Islands and gravel bars migrated, disappeared, or were made new. Logjams piled against bridge abutments. Even the interstate highway bridge was threatened. Pasture land and valuable real estate succumbed to the hungry meanders of the Yellowstone, water humping by at better than thirty-five thousand cubic feet per second, well above flood stage.

Those flood years set off a frenzy of riprapping, levee-building, dredging, and diversions, all in an attempt to control the river. Never mind that the river was only acting as a river does, which is to periodically flood, to writhe back and forth across the valley floor, to build up and tear down banks in its inexorable migration. Never mind that just because homeowners tally their land as if the river is a static and predictable presence, it doesn't mean that the river accepts that assumption.

The upshot is that the upper Yellowstone has largely become an armored channel, lined with boulders and rock barbs and iron walls and levees, in spite of the studies and planning initiatives that were designed to understand and adapt to the dictates of nature. Pretentious new homes destined to be occupied a couple of weeks every year continue to sprout on the banks, degrade the view, and pollute paradise.

That is what I want to hurry through. Once the river bends east and leaves Livingston behind, it is increasingly quiet and sane. The sooner the better.

I start the morning fire. It feels like cheating. Everything on the Kazan was challenging, every day, from finding wood to paddling against headwinds. This morning is clear and calm, already warm. We didn't even bother to put a rain fly on the tent overnight. The driftwood lights with one match. I set a pot of river water on to boil for coffee, sit nearby with journal open on my knee, facing the boats turned over near the water.

I'm also anxious to leave home behind. Paradise Valley is only twenty-five miles, and over Bozeman Pass, from our house. Enjoyable as it is to start off in the company of friends, to reclaim comfortable landmarks, to see country I have seen dozens of times from the hulls of boats, it doesn't feel like a trip until the familiar fades away and river time asserts itself. The first days out always have that edge to them, the stalled period of transition.

By the boats, Ruby left me a pile of rocks for consideration. I stroll over with my second cup of coffee and settle in the gravel next to them. The ritual is to wash the rocks in the river, scrub them clean, and hold them up, still wet, for inspection. The agates are translucent and gray. With the help of sunlight, hints of banding and moss reveal themselves. I throw a few into the keeper sack, leave the rest. Sometimes the kids lobby for reconsideration on behalf of a particular favorite, but for the most part they accept my choices. Early in the trip, I'm easily swayed.

Ruby comes up behind me, drapes herself over my shoulders, snuggles close, still sleepy and warm. If there were an Olympic event in hugging, Ruby would sweep the gold, no question. You have to brace yourself for her embrace. If she catches you unawares, rib injury is a real danger.

She looks over the rocks I've culled, picks one up as if to protest, but sets it back.

"Mornin', sweetie," I say. "Want some hot chocolate?"

We walk back toward the fire, holding hands. Ruby stops once to pick up a rock, tosses it aside.

Eventually the rest of the crew emerges from the tent. We cook our hash brown breakfast, one of half a dozen morning options, and take our time breaking camp. The funneling winds Paradise Valley is famous for are quiet when we slip onto the water.

Stints of paddling alternate with lazy floating interludes, during which we raft up and visit. Choppy water rouses us to action. The boats break away from each other, we choose our lines, pick up speed, jostle through waves. For long periods we paddle steadily, bend after bend curling away like liquid smoke behind us. Whitetail deer bound away into the cottonwoods. Bald eagles watch us pass. Because the water is thick with sediment, the drift boat traffic is light.

At one point, Ruby takes off down a side channel in the inflatable. I watch her bob away out of sight. The island is a long one. I think about deadfall trapping her. We stop at the downstream tip to wait. It feels, for a time, like waiting for someone who is late coming home from a trip, conjuring scenarios, tempted to call somebody. But then she appears around the bend, paddling hard toward us.

"Peetree!" Sawyer sings out Ruby's latest nickname. "What took you so long?"

After lunch, a dark thunderhead builds over the valley. On one bend it looks imminent and threatening, on the next like it will sail past upstream. Gusty winds buffet the boats, shove us around. All of us bend to the work, paddle hard, trying to outrun it. Ruby falls behind in the ducky. We wait for her to catch up, watching the brooding storm.

Paradise Valley ends at a constriction of cliff walls known locally as the Wineglass. I can see it for miles, tantalizing but elusive. It is the one spot on the river narrow enough for a dam to be considered. Back in the mid-1900s, that period when no major river was safe from the drawing boards of the US Army Corps of Engineers, when the Colorado and Missouri and Columbia and dozens of other rivers were being stoppered at will with plugs of concrete, the Yellowstone, right at this spot, came under scrutiny.

Plans were made, the usual arguments trotted out—flood control, power, irrigation, recreation, blah, blah, blah. More than thirty miles of the valley would have been drowned by a dam standing nearly four hundred feet tall. The residents of Paradise Valley wanted none of it. Even then, in the face of the highway-building, rocket-launching, dam-building technological juggernaut that marked that period of American history, local residents knew better than to inundate this special place under a lake.

The outcry was enough to delay, and finally defeat, the engineers with their spiffy plans and statistics. Yellowstone remains technically undammed, the longest major river in the Lower 48 to claim that honor. Paradise Valley may now be under siege from unfettered development and landowners messing around with the fluvial dynamics, but at least it isn't underwater.

There are, however, diversion dams. On the upper river the dams are small, located in side channels. Between Billings and North Dakota, six major low-head structures span the main channel, siphoning off irrigation water in canals and impeding the flow.

Just above our friend's house, we stay far left and come up on one of the smaller dams. At high water there is enough flow to run over it on tongues that break through the smooth recirculation wave, but it remains deceptively dangerous. Even small low-head dams can entrap a boat and swimmers. They look like nothing, a wave you could easily punch through, but if the boat gets sideways and tips in the recirculating currents, getting out is immediately a desperate life-and-death struggle. Even a small volume of water is startlingly powerful.

The most reliable escape tactic is counterintuitive. What traps a person is the constantly recirculating wave. The only way to get free is to dive for the bottom, where filaments of current move on downstream against the riverbed. Diving for the bottom, however, is the last thing that occurs to people who are struggling for breath and going around and around, fighting the buffeting water.

I'm in the lead, paddling with Eli. Above the dam, Eli grabs a fistful of willow stalks and holds the boat while I scramble down the bank for a look. Right against shore the river runs smoothly over the dam, missing the wave. It's thin, but doable. Ruby wants no part of it.

"You can do it, Rubes!" I say. "No biggie. Just keep your boat straight, right against shore, and you'll shoot through."

"I'm scared," she whimpers.

"We'll put you in the middle," Marypat tells her. "Sawyer and I will go first because I want to take some pictures. Dad and Eli will follow you over."

Ruby has a tendency to freak herself out, make her mind up to balk. I have to keep reminding myself that she's eleven. She's tall and strong for her age, able to beat everyone in her grade at arm wrestling, but she can dissolve into tears when something like this diversion passage comes along.

It takes a few minutes of cajoling, and Sawyer humoring her, before she inches forward in line. Marypat's boat dives over, smooth and straight. Eli pulls Ruby into position. She's shaky, but committed. He lines her up, lets go. The little red boat fishtails over the ledge. Ruby strokes hard. Eli and I follow her down, a silky bump over the concrete step, then on to the swimming hole at our friend's house where we like to refresh on hot summer days.

Thirty-One

I'm an agate rolling down the Yellowstone River in a flood. When I rolled down the river I got bumped and bruised. I just got stuck on a gravel bar. It's almost dark I see a weird thing It stopped where I was. They almost stepped on me. I see them get in a weird bag When it was light a weird alien picked me up. Aaaah! He put me in a weird leather thing! I needed to take a nap, and when I woke up I saw tons of aliens holding me! I got dropped in a pile of rocks that was in a boat I started moving down the river. I got scared of falling out I held onto a rock's head. The rock said, "Stop holding onto my head!"

—SAWYER, THIRD GRADE STORY

On our first trip down the Yellowstone, Eli was on the verge of walking. He could hold himself up by the boat gunwale, bounce up and down on his stout, bowed legs and exhort pelicans as we floated past. In camp, we hauled the canoe up on shore, threw a ball and a few toys inside, and called it his playpen, as much to give us a break as to let him play. The tent was his other option, where he could spend the better part of the afternoon crawling around in the fluffy pile of sleeping bags.

Containment was the challenge. Eli may not have been walking, but he was a robust crawler. We brought a picnic blanket to keep him on, but he'd ramble off and start stuffing everything from gravel to goose turds into his mouth, an indiscriminate examination of the world by mouth.

Textures also fascinated him. He'd sit in the warm sand, running his hands through it, feeling the fine grains drain through his fingers. Everything was new and worth investigating. One hot afternoon we stopped at a tiny tributary. Eli parked himself in front of a small waterfall where a sheet of clear water dropped over a foot-high ledge. Repeatedly and with great concentration, he put his hand through the water and pulled it back out, trying to make sense of what seemed solid, but also yielding and transparent.

Swimming, before children, was an occasional part of river trips. Every few days we'd take baths or escape the heat with a dip in the currents. After kids, swimming became a regular daily feature of the routine. Even as toddlers, they would take our hands and we'd edge out together into the channel, wearing nothing but life jackets and river shoes. Slowly we'd work into the river, sidling out against the strong flow. Within a few steps, the kids were swept off of their feet and hung downstream, gripping our hands, surfing on top of the river. Then we'd lift our feet, let the flow take us through small waves or over a bump of ledge.

"Again!" they'd demand, as soon as we floundered to shore, and we'd slosh back up for another trip.

By the time they were five or six, they were swimming small rapids, shaking loose of our hands to line up for the biggest waves. Now, on rivers like the Salmon in Idaho, swimming has evolved into a more and more daunting daily recreation. Anymore, they're the ones daring us to swim with them, taking on turbulent wave trains, Class III rapids, and cliff jumping from twenty or thirty feet into deep pools.

On the Yellowstone, in the heat of July, swimming is as prominent an activity as paddling. The kids plop over the sides a dozen times every day, refresh themselves, try to overcome the buoyancy of life vests to dive to the bottom, drift along with the current for miles, until the cold drives them back into the hull of the canoe. Their skin takes on a dusty, gray hue, the sediment layer.

When they see a big set of standing waves coming up, they drop paddles and leap out of the canoes. Marypat and I hitch the inflatable onto the stern of one of the boats like a trailer and paddle solo, coasting along, watching the three heads rise and fall over steep, cresting waves.

One of Eli's main trip goals is to work on his tan. Ruby and Sawyer are less driven, but we have to prompt them repeatedly to put their life vests on for rapids or swims. For the most part, Marypat and I keep our clothes on, more preoccupied with melanoma than with tan lines.

At least once a day early in the trip, the kids coax us out to swim through a bigger set of rapids. First we run the turbulence in the canoes, but that's an appetizer. As soon as possible, we angle for shore, where all five of us shed clothes in a pile, cinch up life vests, and make our way upriver to a point well above the whitewater.

Holding hands, we string out in a line, moving together into the deeper and faster current, feeling our way over boulders, supporting and unbalancing each other in equal measure, angling for the best ride. Then, when we are barely able to stand, we flop onto our backs, lift our feet in front of us to fend off rocks, and backstroke for position.

The river mauls us, pulls us under, slaps water in our faces. On top of the waves, we catch glimpses of each other, grin like fools. Then we slide into the trough and disappear. The bulges of boulders go under us, sometimes bumping our butts. The current momentarily keeps us in the backwash of holes, twisting and pulling. Through with the thrill ride, we stroke hard to regain the boats.

"Again," they yell, and we jog back up through the uneven river cobbles.

The best campsites are those with a wave train going by and an eddy just below. Campsites like the one at the end of Day 3, not far below Springdale. We have already come eighty-five miles. Home and friends are fading. Clock time loosens its hold. The highway hums in the distance, trains moan as they pass, farms spread away from the banks, but the river has us. It is a different dimension altogether.

The fluvial world is made up of muscular threads of water, cormorant rookeries in cottonwood trees, the slap of waves against boat hull, the dull glint of agate in the sun, driftwood fires, and warm sand under our beds. The people cruising past at seventy-five miles an hour on the highway, listening to the radio, on their way somewhere, move in a different reality.

We notice them. They may glance over at us. Ruby idly counts semitrucks to pass time. But we have, at the moment, nothing in common with them.

At this camp, the waves heave up in a lengthy, vigorous line. The approach requires wading over slippery rocks across fast shallows at the tip of the island we're camped on. The ride is long and pushy, just the way we like. Before the tent is even up we all head for a run. And then another one. Marypat and I lose interest after three circuits, but the kids keep going, exclaiming over the great beatings they take and strategizing for the next ride.

Usually the kids help with camp chores, but we let them keep swimming while we set up the tent, spread out bags and pads, organize the kitchen. It doesn't take long. The river dimension doesn't require a lot of maintenance. When we're done, we share some trail mix and watch the parade of heads ride past. Ruby waves as she slides by.

"I like how they get on trips," Marypat says.

"Adults talk about how relaxing it is to be on a trip," I say. "But they forget that kids relax too. All the stuff they have going on at home just slips away. They start to play like they always have on trips."

We watch them come slopping out of the shallows. "I didn't know if I would make it back in that time," Ruby is breathless. "I waited too long to start swimming back."

"This time let's hold hands all the way through," Eli suggests. They troop back up, leaving a wet trail across the gravel.

"I think it's time," Marypat says.

She heads for a smooth, flat patch of sand behind the tent, picks up a piece of driftwood, and draws a large, rough circle.

"Last run," she calls after the trio. "We're doing Sawyer's ceremony."

Thirty-Two

The mother of us all,
the oldest of all,
hard,
splendid as rock
Whatever there is that is of the land
it is she
who nourishes it,
it is the Earth
that I sing.
    —HOMER, "HYMN TO THE EARTH"

Sawyer stands in the center of the circle. The four of us take up rough compass directions, just inside the ring. I hold a rock, representing earth. Ruby has an eagle feather in her hand, for air. Eli holds a candle, shielding the flame with his free hand. Marypat holds a container of water. Sawyer stands self-consciously, fidgeting a little, looking back at us. The sand is warm and yielding underfoot. The river mutters in the background. A slight downriver breeze ruffles the feather in Ruby's grasp.

This time around, I feel less awkward about the ceremony. It seems less contrived, more authentic. After our epic tundra immersion the year before, and the first days of this journey, it feels very right to honor the elements, pay respect to the living entity of the earth, and to recognize the power these experiences have in our lives. The formality of it feels clumsy, but also serious. I know that the expedition is the ceremony that truly matters, the string of days together on the water, the slow erosion of barriers between us and our surroundings. But this is also necessary, even if we have to make it up. Without it, the enterprise has less intention, less weight.

"By the earth that is her body," I say, feeling the smooth weight of stone in my hand.

"By the air that is her breath," Ruby adds, looking down at the feather.

"By the fire that is her bright spirit," Eli intones.

"By the waters of her living womb," Marypat says, looking right at Sawyer.

"The circle is cast," we chorus together.

We stand silently, focused on Sawyer, then I drop my rock at my feet. Ruby bends to plant the feather upright. Eli puts the candle down. Marypat stains the sand with water. We all look at Sawyer. He stands with his hands at his side, smiling back at us.

Marypat steps forward. She pulls a silver bracelet out of her pocket. It has a wave pattern on the outside. Inside, it's engraved with Sawyer Kesselheim—Yellowstone River '06. Sawyer holds out his wrist. Marypat slips the shiny bracelet onto his brown arm. It gleams in the sun. She holds his face in her hands, looks at him intently, kisses her boy. He is several inches taller than she is.

I see, watching them, that this business of coming of age has as much to do with our accepting change as Sawyer. We have to acknowledge our son for who he is busy becoming, growing inexorably away from us. As much as we welcomed him as our child, held him and nourished him and worried about him as our baby, the product of our marriage, it is now our challenge to appreciate his singularity and let him be—something undeniably of us, but also irrefutably his own.

Sure. Easy enough to say. Almost cliché. But hard to do. All of that— the acceptance, the warmth, the history, the sweet pain, the leaving—is in Marypat's face, in her glistening eyes.

We all move in. Our arms grapple into a messy, sensuous knot of embrace. Warm skin, smiling faces, blue eyes, sand shifting under our bare feet. We linger there, a constellation loosely held together by the gravitational forces of birth and history.

"Let's go swim," Sawyer says.

The spell breaks, we walk out of the circle, leaving our symbols there, the ephemeral marks of our gathering. The next wind will groom it smooth.

A shadow passes over us. We all stop to look up. There, less than twenty feet overhead, flies a mature bald eagle. Its wings are set, six feet across. The white head is cocked. A yellow eye stares down at us. The eagle flies directly over the circle drawn in the sand, then over us, gliding silently. The bird continues upriver, diminishing in the distance.

"That was cool," Sawyer says.

"That was auspicious as all hell," I say.

"Or just coincidence," Eli adds.

I think of the musk ox that approached us that tundra morning on Yath-kyed Lake the summer before, the charge of connection in the air between us, the confrontation, and, also, the feeling amongst the adrenaline-laced jumble that somehow we had earned the honor of its recognition.

You could make too much of a thing like that, or of this eagle flying overhead. You could read deeper meaning into it, make it more portentous than necessary. But it would be worse to not make enough of it.

Later, the kids cook dinner: chili and mashed potatoes. After dishes, they take up a new game, sandbar baseball. Driftwood sticks for bats, small rocks for the ball. A lot of ducking out of the way of line drives. A lot of giggling and razzing. I resist the temptation to stop them, resist the fear of injury, let them play.

We sleep without a rain fly again. All night the river runs by. Trains rumble past. Strange, but I don't mind waking to the sound of train whistles.

At dawn I'm wakened by another sound, the guttural, watery call of a sandhill crane, very close. I get up on my knees, look through the screening on the back door of the tent. The light is still gray, the morning cool. The three-foot-tall long-beaked bird is standing in the middle of the circle still marked on the sand a few feet away.

I wake Marypat. She turns sleepily, rises on her knees to join me at the window. The bird calls again, then lifts into the air. The heavy wings beat past, a sound like flapping sailcloth. The crane melts into the new day.

Thirty-Three

At noon the two canoes were finished. They are 28 feet long, 16 to 18 inches deep, and from 16 to 24 inches wide. Being lashed together, everything was prepared for setting out to-morrow.

—WILLIAM CLARK, JOURNAL, JULY 23, 1806

The weather stays warm and clear. The river bears us steadily east, miles clipping away under our hulls. When the wind is at our backs, Marypat's sarong becomes a sail. The two bow paddlers tie the sarong around their paddles and hold it up. The colorful yellow wrap bellies out, pulling the boats downriver, while we recline with one foot hooked over the other canoe's gunwale and read out loud or sing oldies. "Do You Believe in Magic" is this trip's pick, because we can at least get through a few verses before starting to hum.

SAILING UNDER SARONG POWER ON A DAY WITH A TAILWIND.

It feels like Huck Finn travel, as if we stole away from civilization in the night, loosed the boats from the willows, and lit out for the Territories. Montana goes past in twenty-five-mile daily hunks. The Crazy Mountains float before us, snowy and isolated, then drop behind. Sheep Mountain and the Absaroka Range slide past. The Beartooths rise to the south. Along the river, yellow cliffs soar up from the water's edge, bald eagles hunch in snags, cormorants and white pelicans fish the currents, deer bound into the cotton-woods. Ranches spread away, quilted landscapes of irrigated crops and pasture.

Every night, we find a new camp on an island or gravel bar or section of riverbank. We cook with driftwood on a fire pan, set our tent in the sand. Although civilization surrounds us, traffic zooms by on the highway, we coast along unnoticed, directly encountering no one for days at a time.

In 1806, Captain Clark explored the Yellowstone watershed on the way back to Saint Louis from the Pacific. Clark traveled with a party of ten, including Sacagawea and her infant son, Pomp. Along this stretch of the river, Clark and his group rode horses, naming creeks and landforms as they went, drawing maps, and searching for cottonwood trees of an adequate size to carve dugout canoes. They planned to rejoin Captain Lewis and the rest of the expedition at the confluence with the Missouri.

Not far upstream of present-day Billings, an Indian raiding party stole most of Clark's horses under cover of darkness. Fortunately, they were camped in a grove of large cottonwood trees, and Clark ordered the men to start carving canoes. They spent several days hewing out two twenty-eight-foot hulls. They lashed the dugouts together, outrigger-style, loaded up, and proceeded downstream.

By that point in the expedition, the men were old hands at carving and paddling dugout canoes, having navigated much of the Missouri and Columbia Rivers, including some daunting rapids, in similar boats. They tore downriver at a breakneck pace, paddling from dawn to dusk, covering as many as eighty miles in a single day.

After two years in the wilderness, the men's clothing was in tatters, the tents had succumbed to mildew and rot, the party was utterly exposed to weather and mosquitoes, and the motivation to return to civilization was building. Clark wrote in his journals about rainy nights spent huddling together, and of mosquitoes so thick that he couldn't sight down a rifle barrel to shoot game.

Our Corps of Discovery lands at a city park in Columbus, just below a highway bridge. Every few days, we have to resupply our drinking water. River water serves for cooking and washing, as long as we boil it, but we carry three five-gallon jugs of fresh water for drinking. Eli and I take the plastic containers across the campground and trudge back with the load.

"Makes you think of all the people in the world who have to haul their water every day, sometimes from miles away," I say, when we stop for a break.

On the river, we get by using a couple of gallons of water per day for a family of five. The average American household uses 150–200 gallons a day. I read once about a Bedouin tribesman who traveled to Europe from his home in the desert. During his visit he was taken to view a waterfall. He stood there for a long time, watching the endless flow, waiting for the profligacy to stop. He said afterward that he would never have the heart to tell his people that such a thing as a waterfall existed.

During our descent when Eli was a baby, one of our biggest challenges was washing dirty diapers. We had decided to go with cloth diapers rather than disposables. Places to dump trash are infrequent along the river, and we couldn't bear the thought of that burgeoning toxic bag. It's one thing to throw diapers away one at a time, but quite another to watch them accumulate, day after day, growing more rank and unwieldy by the hour.

Instead, we took twenty-five or thirty cloth diapers. If they were just wet, we'd rinse them in the river and lay them out on the boat to dry during the day. The canoe was always festooned like a gypsy wagon, with three or four diapers draped over our packs and hung from thwarts. Rinsed and dried, we could reuse them two or three times. With poopy diapers, we disposed of the waste in a cathole (much as we did for our own waste), rinsed the diapers out, and stored them in a plastic bag. At several points in our trip, roughly a week apart, we pulled in at a riverside town like Columbus or Miles City, found our way to the local Laundromat with our bulging, fragrant plastic sack, and threw in a load of wash.

This trip, there is no need to linger in the hot campground, no laundry to take care of. The jugs of water are strapped back in the boats. In less than five minutes, we slide out from the shade of the highway bridge and leave the noise of town behind.

Towns, ranches, the highway, trains, irrigation motors, powerboats. Some mornings I can lie in the warm, sunny tent and listen to a schizophrenic medley of the river schussing past, a red-tailed hawk's scream, and the distant hum of rubber on pavement.

Yet, because the river is undammed, our camps are much as Clark would have found them. The same gravel bars full of petrified wood and agate, the same piles of driftwood brought down by floods, the same sandstone cliffs and sets of waves. But then I turn and look upstream, and a ranch house squats in the middle of the view or a semitrailer cruises past, heading for California.

"This isn't the Kazan, is it, Dad?" Ruby says one night.

"Do you miss it?" I ask her.

She nods.

"The Yellowstone is what it is," I say. "It's a great, powerful river with people using it all along. It's just as wild as the Kazan, but it's saddled with a different fate because of where it is."

"I feel bad for it," she says.

"I know what you mean. It's tough to feel how it gets abused, and it's nothing like the wilderness up north," I agree. "On the other hand, it'll outlast us. Eventually it will reassert its hold. In the big picture, our occupation is a fleeting moment."

There are stretches along which you can fool yourself, where the ancient river the Indians knew and Lewis and Clark encountered holds sway. The piece between Columbus and Laurel is like that. The river bends away from the highway and train tracks. Sheer cliffs tower above. Sparse forests of ponderosa pine clothe the slopes. Great blue herons flap up from the shallows.

The river is fast and powerful, rapids punctuate the flow. We stop for lunch in a sandstone alcove carved by the river, a curve as smooth as a racetrack, held in the echoing din of water.

A day later, the smokestacks of the oil refinery in Laurel come into view, the stench wafts upstream. At a boat launch ramp on the outskirts of town, we park the canoes. We've told our friend Sue that we would call her. She wants to meet us at Pompeys Pillar, a few days down. I walk up to the busy highway in the afternoon heat. Downtown Laurel is a mile away, but a casino and bar sit nearby. I head that way.

It is like walking into a dark movie theater. The air-conditioned cold feels brittle and artificial. My eyes adjust to the gloom. Video poker machines gleam neon in the darkness. People hunch in front of them, rounded backs, faces intent on the screens, drinks in reach. It's midday. The machines beep back at them as they punch buttons, cards appear and vanish.

I walk through the cold toward a bar. A heavy woman with bad teeth comes around the corner, looks me over. I'm wearing river shorts and sandals, a grubby T-shirt, week-old beard stubble. She gestures toward the bathroom sign, assuming, I guess, that from all indications I must need to wash up.

"Could I use your phone?" I ask. "I need to make a credit card call."

"We only have our business phone," she says curtly. "We can't tie it up."

"It wouldn't take long," I say. "We're on a river trip and we need to call someone who's going to meet us."

My explanation does nothing to redirect the conversation. She shakes her head.

"You get that many calls?" I push her a little, but she glares back.

Back outside, I see a Sweetheart Bakery store next door. It's busy with people when I walk in, but the woman at the counter just hands me the phone and says sure, go ahead.

It's an older phone with a long cord. The clerk and I dance around each other while I dial and she bags up loaves of bread and rings up sales. It takes a few minutes to connect and arrange a possible rendezvous.

"Sue, I'm really in the way here, so I can't tie up the phone, but we'll try to be there at noon, two days from now. If you can make it, we'll catch up then."

"Thanks," I say, to the clerk. "I really appreciate it."

"No problem," she says, like she means it.

I jog back to the canoes. "Weird juju," I say. "Let's get out of here."

Thirty-Four

Weather: Cool, misty morning. Cloudy most of the day with a few hours of hot sun in the afternoon. Thunderstorms brewing in the early evening.

Wildlife: Beaver, pelicans, herons, young eagles, osprey, fawns with spots, catfish, cormorants, swallows, yellow-breasted chat, white-throated swifts.

—GROUP JOURNAL

The river skirts most of Billings, the largest city in the watershed. A few bridges cross, some dry hills scarred with dirt bike trails sit to the south, but most of the city hulks to the north, screened off by cottonwood groves.

Our canoes round a long bend under the shadow of Sacrifice Cliff, a tall yellow escarpment famous for being the site from which Crow Indians threw themselves to their deaths in a desperate, poignant gesture to appease the gods and thwart the scourge of smallpox that was decimating their people back when Billings was little more than a frontier outpost. In 1837, scores of Crow people died of smallpox in a camp on the outskirts of town.

Directly across the river from the cliffs squats a coal-fired power plant. A concrete intake tower sits square in the current, white smoke billows from the stacks. Downstream, Interstate 90 angles over the flow, four lanes of concrete ramping up to the level of the cliffs.

Billings was the upstream end of navigation by steamboats in the 1800s. The steamship *Josephine* probed to the end of the navigable channel in 1875, where the crew notched a cottonwood trunk to mark the spot. For several decades, steamboats offloaded their goods on the riverbank, and wagons or stagecoaches continued west to the Bozeman Trail.

Just past the interstate, I hear the unmistakable sound of a Jet Ski. Weekend, I realize. They come into view. Several sleek plastic personal watercraft doing doughnuts in the river, raising rooster tails behind them, poisoning the air for a mile radius with their incessant recreation-gone-mad whine.

Give me blackflies as thick as fur, howling headwinds, maddening mosquitoes, a week of rain, anything but these exhaust-belching, fuel-spewing, noise-polluting water pigs. They have no use but momentary thrill for the rider. They desecrate the water with their inefficient engines. They wreck the day for anyone within earshot. They force wildlife to run for their lives.

We paddle on. They do circles around us, figure eight the bridge abutments. Our canoes rock in their wakes. Oil and gas fumes hang blue in the air. Jet Skis are one of the few things that might provoke me to violence.

One man stands up as he drives. A cigarette dangles from his mouth.

He wears a neoprene wet suit. He seems to think we enjoy his company, keeps dogging us as we continue downriver, zooming ahead and zipping back past us. I conjure vivid scenes featuring crashes and spectacular fireball explosions. On the south side of the river, a refinery full of smokestacks and fuel tanks fills the view. It is a long time before the distant wheedling drone finally dissipates, Billings recedes upstream, and the sounds of the river reassert themselves.

Finally we can raft up, lean back, let the river take us on at the speed of gravity. I realize I've been clenching my teeth.

"Jesus," I sigh. "Jet Skis are the epitome of what's wrong with our culture."

"Yeah, but they also look kind of fun," Eli adds.

"Fun for one person while everyone else for miles suffers," Marypat responds.

A freight train rumbles past, gives us a toot. A hand waves from the engine cab.

"I'll bet the same engineers drive these routes day after day," I say. "I wonder if they keep seeing us along the river, marking our progress. I'm guessing we're a topic of conversation along the tracks."

About a mile above the Huntley Diversion Dam, late afternoon squalls move in. We paddle up on a nondescript bit of shoreline. A great blue heron watches us land. The storm cell grazes past, pummeling us with wind while we grapple with the tent. We dive inside, as much to hold the tent down as to escape the pattering shower.

I have a splinter of something in my index finger. It's been bothering me for days, growing more and more inflamed. I work at it while Marypat reads out loud. It's a tiny bit of wood or metal, nothing I even thought much about, but now it's an angry red swelling, and it's difficult to bend my finger.

"Geez, Al," Marypat says when she sees it. "Why don't you do something about that?"

"I didn't think it was anything to worry about."

"Yeah, well it looks pretty bad now. You should put some antibiotic cream on it and a Band-Aid."

The rain and wind quiet down. The kids get in a few innings of baseball while we cook dinner. Eli smashes a drive that whistles past Sawyer's ear. I take up a position in the cobble outfield. Ruby is up and abruptly hits a ground ball that knocks over my cup.

"What are the chances of that?" I mutter.

Then she hits a pop fly that I run under. I catch the rock just as I hit the slippery wet edge of the river. My feet go out from under me and I fall hard, banging my knee.

"Got it!" I call, holding up the ball. "But I think that's about enough." I pick myself up out of the slick shallows and hobble off the field. "Two hits and I lose my drink and smash my knee, for crying out loud."

"Dad," Sawyer observes later. "You keep saying how dangerous it is when we play baseball, but you're the only one that has gone down so far."

In the morning, we pull off a rare early start. For the first time, I use a stove to boil a quick pot of water. Mist is still rising when we start paddling. We're scheduled to meet Sue around noon, more than twenty miles downstream.

The Huntley diversion comes up first thing. A large sign warns us of the danger, advises us to portage. The concussion of falling water wafts upstream. At the tip of a gravel bar we land to take a look. All of us clamber up the concrete structure, stand over the cascading sheet of river going over a ten-foot drop, our hands tucked into the sides of our life jackets. It is an impressive unbroken wave, a quantum leap from the side channel diversion Ruby was nervous about. There is no way you'd want to go down any part of this drop.

Across the river, a canal leads irrigation water away to be distributed amongst water users, spread over fields, nursing crops. For us, the good news is that the river is still high enough to fill an overflow channel around an island along the left bank. We sneak down slow current, slipping around snags, and come out well below the dam, escaping the rigors of a portage.

Eli and Sawyer take turns paddling together, switching bow and stern. They both suffer from overcorrection syndrome, like new drivers, and they don't have an instinctive feel for the right strokes in the stern, but they manage to head downstream and miss the important obstacles.

Few activities highlight the flaws in relationships like sharing a canoe hull. Couples who seem perfectly in harmony in town transform into red-faced antagonists in a canoe, screaming at each other, blaming their partners for every mistake, each struggling for control. Five minutes into an outing and it's "What are you doing?" "Why didn't you miss that rock?" "Where are you taking us?" All at an embarrassing decibel level. I knew a couple who dropped thousands of dollars on a boat and gear— and who sold the entire outfit at garage sale prices after one outing. That or divorce court, they told me. We're thinking maybe solo boats, when we can afford them again, the husband said.

Plunk two adolescent brothers less than two years apart into a canoe and the fun really starts. *Harmony* is a word that rarely comes to mind in the best of times. Horsing a canoe down moving current together, an enterprise that depends wholly on cooperation and synchrony, harmony disappears from the radar.

I remember a family vacation on which my parents rented a tandem bicycle and mounted up my brother and me, roughly the same ages as Eli and Sawyer are now. I remember looking back after a block and seeing my parents doubled over in hysterics watching us battle for control, wobbling down the road and shouting death threats at each other.

Eli and Sawyer have been in boats enough and know how to read water well enough to escape the elementary pitfalls, but there is still quite a lot of strident conversation—What the hell are you doing? Paddle harder! You're going to hit that log! I see them battling each other around the bends the same way I remember my brother and I each trying to control the destiny of that tandem bike.

I take a turn in the inflatable ducky. Paddling steadily I pull in front, lose the sound of the boys yammering at each other. The highway and train tracks are far away. The Yellowstone winds through sets of forested islands. Bald eagles coast overhead, hunch on overhangs, flap off of nests. There are dozens of them, both adult and immature.

SAWYER ASSESSES A PRECARIOUS-LOOKING TREE OVERHANGING THE RIVER.

The valley is dense with cottonwood groves. Dangerous snags protrude from dirt banks. Submerged logs lurk on corners. The current is deceptively fast, rolling through the quiet bottoms full of trees and birds and water. The air smells of damp earth. Warblers call from the underbrush. The sky is overcast, the air cool, a relief after the string of hot, cloudless weather. It is good to be self-contained, in my own boat, settled into a rhythm, letting thoughts roam.

Pompeys Pillar sneaks up on us, a wart of sandstone rising 150 feet above the river. It bulks abruptly over the cottonwood canopy. Clark stopped here in July 1806. He was a devoted and skilled mapmaker, and he used the elevation of the landform to give him the lay of the surroundings. Clark etched his name and the date, in neat cursive, on the river side of the formation, where it is now protected under a glass case.

Just as we are getting out of the boats and stretching, Beans comes racing around the corner to greet us, and Sue saunters down to the river.

"I just pulled up," she says.

"Talk about timing. Driving from three hours away and paddling from twenty miles upstream and we arrive at the same second!"

Ruby is busy reuniting with Beans, who has been staying with Sue. "Hi, buddy!" she keeps saying, patting his back. He makes the rounds of the family, whining in excitement, rolling over for belly rubs, jumping on Marypat.

Sue has brought a cooler full of fresh fruit, ice cream, cold beers, and pop. We sit in the parking lot, swilling frosted drinks, spooning ice cream right out of the containers, gorging on chilled fruit. She fills us in on town news, updates on friends.

Cars come and go, tourists who pull off the interstate long enough to take in the national landmark, then speed on. One man climbs out of his pickup truck, ranting to no one in particular about news headlines taken out of context while he sprays down his toddler with bug dope. It doesn't seem to matter that there are no bugs out.

We all stroll up the boardwalk steps to the summit. From the top, the Yellowstone arcs away, marked by a ribbon of trees. I think of Clark standing just here, his focus downriver, toward Saint Louis. Across the river, a broad valley sweeps north, grasses yellow in the sun. It doesn't take much to imagine bison moving through the summer heat. But turn around and the highway buzzes with traffic.

It is late afternoon by the time we finish visiting and talk the park employees into letting us fill our water jugs at the sink in the headquarters. We hug Sue, give Beans a final round of loving up, but it is good to slide away on the pulse of current. Ruby and Sawyer ignore the canoes. They wade right in to the river and start swimming. The day has turned hot. We laze along for another ten miles, swimming much of it, stopping to dive off of a boulder.

Our camp is set along a side channel, below a yellow cliff, a secluded spot with a breeze whispering through cottonwood leaves and a pleasant swimming hole. Ruby and Sawyer are busy planning for a Salmon River trip

Sue told them they'd been invited on that will leave shortly after our return.

This is one of the ways we know to live. We also have our town lives, full of school reports and sports programs and volunteer causes and library fines. But here, the tent sits on a smooth bed of sand, oriented for the view of cliff, our evening driftwood fire flickers under a pot, the boats are turned over and tied to willows. We move through the easy chores, sit and write in journals, read out loud, munch some snack food.

This evening, in the easing heat, Eli takes on making bannock for the next day's lunch. His hands are sticky with dough. Oil sizzles on the griddle. His strong, bare back is dark bronze.

Tent-door view of a typical gravel bar camp.

Thirty-Five

Went 33 miles today. When we got to camp we went swimming. It felt good. Then Sawyer and I tried to make a boat, but it didn't work. We ate dinner and went swimming again and got back and set off fire crackers.

—RUBY, GROUP JOURNAL

I come awake in the dark to the muffled rippling sound of the river and the terror of being suffocated. Sawyer has his legs draped across my face so that I'm sucking in nylon when I breathe. I shove his sleeping bag off, push him roughly back onto his pad. He grunts but doesn't wake.

You have to be on your guard sleeping next to Sawyer. He has a very active night life that can erupt into full gallop at any moment. It isn't simply a matter of migrating, sliding here and there in the tent, lying across people, ending up in various contortions. That's just how he sleeps.

More alarming, Sawyer will take off on missions known only to him. Several times every trip, he'll jerk into action from his sleeping bag, muttering to himself about saving Katie or needing to tell Dylan something or making sure he gets on the plane, and head blindly for the tent door. Only by tackling him can we stop him.

"Sawyer!" I'll call to him.

"What?" he'll say, annoyed.

"Are you awake?"

"Yes."

But he is not awake.

"Sawyer! What are you doing?"

"What the heck? I'm going to get my green shoes and bring back the beer," he'll answer, frustrated at the delay.

"Sawyer!" By this time I have him by the shoulders, yelling in his face. "There are no green shoes, no beer. Lie down and go to sleep."

"What the heck!" he says again, trying to shake free, still working toward the tent door.

Eventually he'll lie back down, go to sleep, thoroughly disgruntled, but succumbing. By that time, he's the only one actually still asleep.

"Just tell him very sternly to lie down and go to bed," Marypat will say. "It's the only thing that works, and even that sometimes doesn't, but there's no use trying to reason with him."

"And he's never awake," adds Eli. "Don't even ask him that."

At home, we've woken to lights in the living room and found Sawyer curled up in his boxers on the couch, or sitting in the kitchen sound asleep.

On his way back from Europe, his group spent one night in a New York City hotel. Sawyer roomed with a couple of his classmates. In the middle of the night he got up, walked out of the room and down the hallway. The door locked behind him. Eventually he woke up. Fortunately, he remembered where he was and what room he was in. He went back and knocked. Nobody answered. He knocked louder. He kicked the door. He called their names. No one woke up.

Wearing only his underwear, he had to go down to the lobby and into the bar to get someone's attention so he could get another room key and return to bed.

When he leaves to go on a trip with a friend's family, we have to give the parents a little training session to prepare them for Sawyer at night.

"Okay, sure," they'll say. "We'll keep an eye on him."

"We're serious," we stress. "You never know where he'll end up."

"Yeah, yeah. Got it."

Sometimes things go fine. More often, the parents come back nodding their heads. "I see what you mean about Sawyer at night," and they launch into another chapter in the annals of Sawyer's sleepwalking exploits.

Sawyer's nighttime peregrinations are alarming and often annoying, but it's impossible to stay angry because his awake personality is so loving and humorous and giving.

He likes to plop into my lap and cuddle. He is completely unabashed about kissing me on the lips in front of his school friends. He says "Love you" every single time he goes out the door, even if it's only to walk the dog.

The morning after my near suffocation, Sawyer saunters up to the fire.

"Mornin,' Daddio," he greets me. "Sleep okay?"

"Other than being mauled most of the night, half suffocated, and bruised, I can't complain."

"Oh, yeah, well, I wouldn't know anything about that, would I? So, whaddayasay we have some hot chocolate?"

River time is a dimension that keeps deepening. During the first stage, the ticking schedule of our workaday world evaporates—that eat-dinner-at-six, get-to-work-at-eight, drive-to-soccer-practice-at-four-thirty, walk-the-dog-before-school compulsion. Within a week, watch time is irrelevant. It is replaced by the dictates of headwinds, rapids, hunger, daylight, the need for a refreshing dip. In a way, the reality tethered to clocks is the most superficial layer to lose.

After that, the pulse of place starts to insinuate itself. On the Kazan, it became a spiritual influence, powered by the vast spaces, the unfettered weather, the weeks without human contact, the interactions with wildlife, the eerie and undeniable presence of the Inuit.

The Yellowstone is less pure. Reminders of the overlay of civilization keep intruding. Buildings, smokestacks, dams, bridges, the rubbery buzz of tires, herds of cattle, irrigation pumps, rusted heaps of old garbage tipped over the riverbank. Even so, the cadence of the river won't be drowned out. Its rhythm is timeless. It was here before us. It will still be here when our infrastructure is long gone. It becomes the beat of our days.

It carries us on its back, speaking to us through the boat hulls, responding to our paddles, pulling us around long bends, over shoals, through channels cut between islands. It is a fluid language that whispers through the night, finds its way into my dreams.

More and more, the cacophony of our mechanized culture becomes a backdrop. We drift much of every day, sometimes all day. The kids slip into the river and swim, their bodies lithe and brown. They plummet for the bottom, arms stretched over their heads.

Ruby's head breaks the surface. "I couldn't touch," she splutters.

Sawyer gulps a huge breath, goes down. After a long time he surges up for air. "I couldn't either," he says. "It's really deep here."

Marypat and I relax in the canoes, watch the kids. The quiet, summer-held prairie surrounds us under the bowl of sky. Low yellow cliffs line the bank. Swallows bomb through the air, coming and going from their mud-daubed nests. Eventually, the kids come aboard with great splashes of water, glistening like otters, teeth chattering. Marypat and I take a turn.

(LEFT TO RIGHT) ELI, SAWYER, RUBY—THREE OTTERS.

Cooled off, we pull out a book, read aloud from *Al Capone Does My Shirts*. Miles slip away in our wake. We paddle only to avoid deadfall or stay clear of eddies. Cattle watch us from islands of shade. A pair of immature bald eagles shift as we pass their perch on a river-worn cottonwood log. We can afford to be cavalier about reading the maps. Bridges and prominent landmarks are frequent enough to keep track of our progress.

A dozen miles below Pompeys Pillar, we are careful to hug the left bank and take the overflow channel that bypasses Waco Diversion Dam. There are no warning signs above the dam. We know we have gotten by when we look back up and see the smooth line of whitewater, the break in the river horizon where another slice of volume runs off into fields.

On the yearlong trips Marypat and I took before Eli was born, river time never stopped deepening. On Day 400, it was clearer and more profound than on Day 399. We went miles without saying a word. In camp, I could sit still, watching the water go past and the clouds move in the sky. Doing nothing. Being there. I was a speck of color in the vault of space, unaware of the niggling passage of time.

Our dawdling, savoring pace on the Yellowstone reminds me of our summer with baby Eli. Much of that trip was spent at the pace of the river. Eli watched Montana go by, hanging on with his chubby hands to the gunwale. Or he slept on the bottom of the canoe, feeling the current tickle against his back. Or he nursed at Marypat's breast and slept in her arms under the summer sun.

In camps, we carried Eli in an infant backpack so our hands could be free to set up the tent or collect firewood. The backpack, set on the ground, doubled as his high chair at meal times. At night, we spread our sleeping bags out like quilts and Eli slept between us on our sand bed. His ever-present diapers hung from canoe thwarts, driftwood branches, tent poles.

There were challenges—nights he cried through, a time when he singed his hand in the fire, a pelting hailstorm we cowered under, days when nothing would console him. It was not always idyllic and serene, but the challenges were no different in intensity than the ones we faced at home.

The Bighorn River flows into the Yellowstone not far below the town of Custer, Montana. It is a long, significant river rising in the Bighorn Mountains of northern Wyoming and winding hundreds of miles to the confluence. It is as good a spot as any to mark the shift in the Yellowstone drainage from mountain to prairie river, from fast, cold-water habitat to warmer, slower-paced flow. Also, from a river renowned for its blue-ribbon trout fishery to a drainage that is home to that less glamorous class of fish—channel catfish, carp, stickleback chub, pallid sturgeon, paddlefish—bottom-feeding, whiskery species you snag with forbidding treble hooks or fish for with worms and spinners and strange congealed balls of bait.

At least the Bighorn used to mark that shift in fluvial habitat, that is, until several dams were built along it, transforming it into a cold-water, trout-stocked fishing destination. Dams have changed the temperature and turbidity and flow dynamics not only in that drainage, but also downstream, in the Yellowstone.

We may be a species capable of seeing the big picture, but when it comes to dam-building, our view is decidedly anthropocentric. The rationale rests on human-based arguments—flood control, irrigation, power generation, recreation, and tourism. Some research goes into impacts on fisheries and habitat and stream characteristics, but it's a sideshow, and everyone knows it.

In the pre-dam era, the spring surge of meltwater triggered the spawning urge in warm-water fish species. Sturgeon, paddlefish, burbot, and dozens more species came nosing upriver, swimming high up the tributaries to spawn and lay eggs. The lower Yellowstone was a reach hundreds of miles long, extending down to the main stem of the Missouri River and encompassing major tributaries like the Bighorn, Tongue, and Powder for habitat. All of that is gone on the Bighorn.

Since the dams, the watershed has been thrown into flux, adapting itself to new conditions, silting up the impoundments, changing the temperature regime, affecting everything from how the river erodes to how fish populations interact. Not the least of the impacts is that fish can no longer migrate up and down the drainage of the Bighorn as they once did. Even if they could overcome the altered living conditions, the dams are as real a barrier as a chain of mountains for the warm-water fish that once thrived here.

Now the Bighorn is a trout-fishing mecca, thronged with boats and anglers, punctuated by a series of lakes, outfitted with boat ramps and marinas and the rest of the tourism and recreation juggernaut. Its spectacular canyon is now a cliff-walled pool. For what?

The confluence with the Bighorn is also historically significant. In 1807, Manuel Lisa built a fur-trading outpost here. It was the first in a series of trading forts built and abandoned on the site until 1876, when the last, Fort Pease, was finally abandoned.

Lisa employed John Colter, of the Lewis and Clark expedition, to explore the surrounding region and report back on the character of the land, its potential for fur trapping, and the demographics of its inhabitants. Colter was, by all evidence, the most intrepid wilderness adventurer in the Corps of Discovery.

In 1806, as the corps was descending the Missouri after more than two years in the wilds, they came upon two men who were heading upstream for the Yellowstone and a season of trapping. They asked Colter if he might want to partner up and act as guide. Colter negotiated a release from the expedition and turned back into the wilderness.

A year later, following his trapping sojourn, Colter was yet again headed toward Saint Louis on the Missouri when he ran into Manuel Lisa. Lisa cajoled Colter into his employ, and back upriver he went. Colter spent the following winter exploring hundreds of miles by snowshoe across a vast, rugged region of what is now southwestern Montana and northern Wyoming. His discoveries included Jackson Hole and sections of what would become Yellowstone National Park.

Colter's tales of steaming ground, erupting fountains of hot water, and bubbling mud pots were so fantastic that for years people assumed that the explorer had gone daffy. They referred to the region as Colter's Hell.

Colter's most famous exploit took place with another trapper near the three forks of the Missouri. He and his trapping partner were ambushed by a band of Blackfoot Indians. The Indians summarily executed Colter's companion but decided to have some sport with Colter.

They told him to strip naked and barefoot, then gave him a running head start. Colter took off at a sprint through the sagebrush and prickly pear cactus, heading for the banks of the Jefferson River. The warriors soon took up the cry and came pelting after him. Colter was fast. He outran all his pursuers but one, who was steadily gaining. Colter waited until his antagonist was almost on him, then whirled and so surprised the Blackfoot warrior that the man tripped and fell, whereupon Colter grabbed his spear and ran him through.

Colter reached the Jefferson, where he waded in and concealed himself in the water under a pile of driftwood. Meanwhile, the Indians searched the banks upstream and down until dark. Much later, shivering with cold and under cover of darkness, Colter slipped soundlessly downstream and away from danger.

Although he'd escaped the immediate threat of death, Colter was stark naked, without moccasins, and three hundred miles from his home fort at the mouth of the Bighorn. Over the next weeks, Colter managed to make his way back, where everyone had given him up for dead.

In 1810, Colter finally returned to civilization. He settled in Missouri, took up farming, and married. By all signs, civilized life didn't suit Colter. After a career spent surviving grizzly attacks, Indian skirmishes, rapids, blizzards, and starvation, Colter quietly succumbed to jaundice in 1813, at the age of thirty-nine.

Every fall at Missouri Headwaters State Park, not far from our home, where the Jefferson, Gallatin, and Madison Rivers join up to make the Missouri, Sawyer's favorite cross-country race is held in honor of Colter's famous escape. Most races have bagels and fruit and energy drinks waiting at the end. The John Colter Run boasts tapped kegs of beer.

Thirty-Six

We go on, looking for a camp. First, we pin hopes on an island, but it turns out to be muddy and uninviting. Then a gravel bar, but it's full of cow shit and has few tent spots. A sandbar that looks good from a distance is backed up by a stagnant slough buzzing with mosquitoes. Finally, a toe of gravel on a point, with a sand bench for our tent and some shade. We plant the flag.

—Al, PERSONAL JOURNAL

On July Fourth, we stroke past the mouth of the Bighorn. It is our habit to ride the line where two currents mix together at a river confluence. The Bighorn is slow and silty butting up against the greener, faster Yellowstone. Ruby dips in her hand and pronounces the Bighorn colder, another indication of an upstream dam. Where they meet, the rivers froth and swirl, resisting each other, then blending.

Another hot, cloudless day with a slight headwind. But for a few threatening clouds and a couple of light showers, we could have done this whole trip wearing shorts, a T-shirt, river shoes, and a hat. A few fishing boats are on the water, trolling for catfish or walleye. Above Billings, the angling is dominated by drift boats and fly-fishing. On the Lower Yellowstone, it's decidedly blue-collar, marked by aluminum powerboats and bait casting.

Within a mile, another diversion dam blocks the flow. No signs mark the danger, but we hug the left bank along a steep bluff and sneak up to the irrigation canal. A concrete ledge about ten feet across funnels a slice of the Yellowstone off into fields. The main current tumbles through a rocky barrier that checks the flow.

A couple and their young boy are set up on the sidewalklike structure, fishing. They have a little barbecue grill, lawn chairs, and picnic supplies. The noise of the river sounds like wind. The family watches us unpack and carry our outfit across the concrete to the eddying water below.

The boy comes up to Sawyer. "Hey, you want to go fishing?" he asks, eagerly. "C'mon, let's go. I know a good place."

"I don't have a pole," Sawyer says.

"That's okay," the youngster pleads. "You can use mine. C'mon."

"I have to do my chores," Sawyer says, grabbing a dry box.

"Well, as soon as you're done then, okay?"

He watches us paddle away, waves forlornly.

It's been a long day, but campsites elude us. Likely islands are muddy and low. A gravel bar turns out to be full of cow shit. A sandy beach that looks promising is backed by a stagnant lagoon humming with mosquitoes.

We finally make do on a toe of gravel on a sharp bend, backed by a grove of cottonwood and directly across from the railroad tracks. The flat space is about the size of a modest living room. We scrounge for driftwood, set up the tent, strip down for a dip.

The kids swim across the river, scramble out on the rocks below the train tracks, balance along the rails in the orange light of sunset. They are lean and bronzed, glistening from their swim. A big log comes drifting around the bend. Sawyer leaps down through the rocks and strikes out after it, nudging the log into shore. He and Ruby climb aboard for a wobbly, giggling ride.

We brought along a small bag of fireworks for the holiday occasion.

"This is hardly anything," Eli protests when he returns.

"Hey, what do you expect?" I say. "This is a river trip, dude. You're lucky you have anything."

At twilight we light them off. They pop and flare colors and spin on the ground. It feels subdued, perfunctory, kind of weird. Then it falls quiet. Cicadas buzz in the trees, an irrigation motor hums in the distance, the first bright planet pierces the coming darkness. The moon is half-full and waxing.

I work on my swollen finger, still oozing pus, still red and painful.

We are floating along midriver the next day, in the midst of an animated discussion of house remodeling plans in order to give Sawyer and Ruby separate rooms, when we see the first bona fide paddlers of the trip. Several kayakers come stroking toward us from upstream. At first I feel like a slacker, caught lazing along in Huck Finn mode. It must be my puritan work ethic kicking in. Then I relax, let them catch us.

We have come more than halfway down the river, almost three hundred miles, but have encountered no other travelers. It is a strange fact that almost no one camps on the Yellowstone. On the Wild and Scenic portion of the Missouri River in central Montana, which is a plodding, pedestrian piece of water if there ever was one, the river is packed with campers, a parade of rafts and canoes and kayaks. The Yellowstone is far more interesting. The camping is much better. Yet no one spends the night.

Perhaps it's due to the lack of public land along the river. Maybe it's the proximity of roads and railroad tracks. Whatever the case, I think it's a pretty good bet that my kids have spent more days paddling and more nights camping on this river than any children in history.

These kayakers are no exception to the camping rule. They are paddling from Livingston to Sidney, the better part of the navigable flow, but they are using the sag-wagon approach, staying at motels every night and meeting a van every day for lunch. They take turns paddling and driving.

We chat briefly with them. They show us their customized maps, blown-up pages featuring the ribbon of river flowing through white, empty background.

By contrast, ours are tattered, 1:250,000 scale topographic quads, the same set we used in 1992, when Eli was a baby. I penciled in little notations about campsites, rapids, places we stopped, diversion dams. On our map, each sheet exposes a respectable chunk of Montana. On theirs, the river is the one and only feature.

These guys are making miles. I can't tell if they envy us our reclined style, or if they think we're quaint and boring. After a few minutes of conversation, they head over to a bridge access where their lunch awaits. We keep sliding downstream, rafted up together.

I pull out the bag of maps. I love the names, and the stories they suggest. Froze-to-Death Creek, Valentine's Flat, Starved-to-Death Creek, Buffalo Rapids, Lost Boy Creek, Rosebud, Louie and Scottie Creek, Poverty Flat, Sunday Creek, Belle Prairie, Bad Route Creek. They provoke a mental slide-show of sod homes, winter blizzards, wrenching drought, romance, hard-bitten couples held together as much by stubbornness as affection, horses in fields of belly-high grass, waking in the dark marrow of winter to the stun of silence, being stuck for a week because of mud.

A map with only the bending blue stripe of river through it and all the rest stripped away is an impoverished snippet of the story.

In 1992, with Eli aboard, it never crossed our minds to run the diversion dam at Forsyth. We clung to a narrow channel along the inside of a long, thin island, stopped well above the turbulence, and portaged around, carrying Eli in his quilted fabric bed. In my memory, he was asleep in the bow. He lay there sleeping while we took the first load around. I think the mosquitoes were out.

This time we take the same channel, but slide right up to the brink, hanging on to some willow branches while we take a look. I stand in the boat, crane my neck to see around the corner. It is cool there in the shade. A few mosquitoes rise out of the vegetation.

A canoe-width tongue of river hugs the edge, right against the concrete abutment.

"Follow me," I say.

Sawyer is paddling bow. We edge out, straighten the boat, let the current inch us along. The bow cleaves the sloping drop, we speed up, cruise over the ledge, and come cleanly into the eddy below near a boat launch and picnic site. The other two boats follow, bobbing through the fast water, swinging into slack water.

"I love cheating a portage," I gloat.

The campground is muggy, full of stately cottonwoods, somnolent. We fill our water jugs from a spigot, sit at a picnic table full of carved initials and ketchup stains. A few cars wheel up to the boat launch. People look our boats over, look at us, drive off.

"We must be on the Forsyth cruise route," I say.

Nearby, a man is busy with a dip net along the edge of the dam. We see him pull up batches of silver, glittering minnows and dump them into a coffee can. The kids can't resist. They walk over to watch.

"What are you doing?" Ruby asks.

"Catching bait," he says. "Want to try?"

She steps up, takes hold of the net handle. The boys crowd in.

"Right there." The man points to a small aerated pool among the rocks. "Put the net in there, wait a few seconds, and then scoop it up."

She does, her focus intent. A batch of flopping silver comes up, flashing like coins in the sunlight. She drops them in the can.

The boys have a try.

Marypat and I walk over.

"I've known of at least five people to drown in that water," the man points out into the current. "Mostly they try to go up it in boats or water skis and get sideways, then can't escape. Just two weeks ago, people were still Jet-Skiing up the dam."

He watches the kids' technique with the net. They are our social ambassadors. If it were just Marypat and me, we never would have made contact. The man seems kindly, grandfatherlike, relaxed. He has lived in Forsyth all his life.

"It's been windy here lately," he says. "Used to be that an east wind always meant rain. Not anymore. In fact, it's been hot and dry the last six years. Feels to me like things are changing."

Thirty-Seven

Most prized river-trip technology:
Bent-shaft paddles; hooded wind shirts; inflatable sleeping pads; good topo maps; waterproof box for personal treasures; bomber river sandals; self-standing tent; press coffee pot

Technology we leave behind:
Watches; cell phones; computers; video games; iPods; television; anything that goes beep.

—GROUP JOURNAL

God, this is such an easy, loafing, meandering life. It feels like we're getting away with something faintly illegal, playing hooky. We should be working at something, or at least overcoming some actual hardship.

I remember talking to a friend after our 1992 trip down the Yellowstone with Eli.

"Yeah, we just put the canoe in fifty miles from home and went down the river. We took our time; we were out almost a month," I told him.

He got such a wistful, faraway look. I could see how simple it sounded to him, how anyone might do it. Why didn't he do something like that? Just pack up and go. And he was right. It is simple. Way easier than most family vacations. Even without much preparation, you could pick up supplies in towns and mosey downstream, taking it as it comes. You can do the whole thing for a couple hundred dollars. And yet, how many people have paddled the entire Yellowstone River? Thousands of Americans have taken cruises to Antarctica, tens of thousands every year spend their vacation wad going to Disneyland or Las Vegas, but I doubt that one hundred have paddled the Yellowstone.

We live in the age of technology, the age of labor-saving devices, time-saving efficiency, an era of leisure and luxury. What a load of bunk! This is luxury. Right here on the water; this is ease and comfort and relaxation. There is nothing onerous or even mildly difficult about it. Even the worst times are a piece of cake. The hardest thing is carving out a block of time bigger than a week or two to escape the rat race.

This day we stop on a whim on an island that looks good for prospecting, scatter, wander aimlessly in that downcast posture, searching for agate, and gather back up with our T-shirts sagging under the load. Together we circle around the mound of treasure, do some culling, add the rest to our bulging sacks.

Sometime later we stop again for lunch and a refreshing swim, more rock hunting. We siesta under the warm sun, sprawled out with the river murmuring past, until someone stirs and provokes us back into the boats, where we pick up the cadence of the flow.

River life is the absolute antithesis of the frantic, errand-filled, taxi-driving, task-juggling, bill-paying, chore-doing, moneymaking life in town, and we're less frantic than most. Back there, the temptations to plug in and tune out are legion, inescapable. The distractions are overwhelming, the work never-ending, the fraying of connection with the environment insidious. Weeks at a time I forget to notice what phase the moon is in, where the wind is coming from, what the clouds look like.

We have one television that gets two channels if you fiddle with the antenna just right. Eli is the only one in the family with a cell phone, and he pays for it. The kids have iPods, but that's as far as the technology intrudes. To their credit, the kids would rather jump on the trampoline or go for a run than watch TV. They rarely play video games. While Eli does his share of text messaging, none of the kids know their way around the world of Facebook and instant messaging and chat rooms, not to mention the strange, atavistic escapism of virtual reality.

It is a matter of no little pride that they play in the traditional sense, the way I used to play as a kid. They explore thickets, mess around in creeks, catch snakes, find secret hollows in the woods, climb trees, ride double on bikes, invent games, come home muddy and wet, dragging treasures.

I have a friend in Bozeman who told me that his wife gets nervous leaving her two young children alone in the car for the few seconds it takes her to return library books to the book drop, a journey of roughly forty feet. In Bozeman, Montana! You just never know where a pedophile or terrorist might be lurking, ready to pounce and snatch your kids.

I suggested that maybe his wife watches too many television shows. Maybe she takes George W. Bush and his terror alerts much, much too seriously.

Along the Yellowstone in the evenings, after the chores are dispatched and we've indulged a cool-down dip, the kids wander off.

"We're taking an adventure," they announce, and troop off toward the willow thickets.

From time to time, we hear them crashing through the underbrush, whacking away with sticks, or shouting to each other. Sometimes it's very quiet. I imagine them stooped over a frog pond or playing a version of hide-and-seek, stalking each other.

"I was following Sawyer," Ruby says one night. "He rammed right through this bush so I went after him, but I tripped on a branch and fell right in the mud."

"Next time you can lead, Peetree," Sawyer tells her. They head for the river, stripping clothes as they go.

Eli joins them sometimes, but not always. He talks about his upcoming soccer tournament, wonders how his girlfriend is doing, works on his tan, hangs out by the fire.

Later, in the tent, Ruby bends close over Sawyer's armpit. "Sawyer, is that a hair?" she asks.

"Of course," Sawyer says. " I have lots of 'em."

"Nope," she concludes, pulling away. "Just dirt."

Both Eli and Ruby hit full-on puberty by sixth grade. Eli is already shaving periodically. But Sawyer isn't on the early hormone program. He is growing incrementally taller. In the end, he may be the tallest of the bunch, but puberty is taking its time. Luckily he's good-natured about the nightly hair-watch ritual.

If it isn't Sawyer's lack of armpit hair, it's my "whale breathing" that comes in for ridicule.

We're all lined out in the tent like enchiladas in a pan. Marypat will start to read out loud. I'm lying on my back and invariably fall asleep within two pages. I'm told that, under these circumstances, I have a habit of letting out soft, explosive breaths, little puffs of air. Usually I wake up to the sound of laughter and my family mimicking me.

"Don't you guys have anything better to do?" I say, turning over.

"It's cute, Dad," Ruby cuddles up to me. "I like your whale breaths."

"This family tent business has its limits," I grumble. "Where's a person's privacy?"

"I agree, Pops," Sawyer says. "You can't lift an arm around here without somebody inspecting."

Most mornings I'm first up. I like emerging at dawn, looking around, drinking in the bated quality at the opening of day. I throw together a fire, an easy matter, bring water to a boil, sip the first cup of coffee. Sometimes I write in my journal, but for long periods I might just sit, feeding driftwood into the flames. A raven croaks from the cottonwood across the river. The Yellowstone ripples along, supple and seamless. The morning sky warms. Brown hills step away into the blue distance. Swallows come and go from their mud-daubed nests, knowing exactly which apartment is theirs. My bare feet burrow in the cool sand.

One morning our camp is set on a low gravel bar directly across from an irrigation motor and power pole. The farther downstream we go, the more difficult it is to avoid the noise of water being pumped out of the Yellowstone and into fields. Every mile or two another rig hums or roars away, sucking water. A few of the motors are muffled, but most are not. At least this one hasn't been running, which might explain why a ranch truck comes jouncing down the dirt track and backs up next to the pole.

The man who emerges stops momentarily to gaze across at our camp— the canoes turned over, the blue-and-white tent, the fire. He doesn't stare, doesn't wave. His look is little more than a hesitation in his errand. He grabs some tools and a part from the bed of the pickup, strides over to the motor, loosens a couple of bolts. It is quiet. I hear the clank of tools, the loose gravel under his feet.

It doesn't take him long. He finishes up, throws the tools back into the truck bed, and swings into the cab. The battered truck heaves over the top of the riverbank, disappears. The sound of the engine fades. I think about him having coffee with his wife later in the day, how he would mention our canoe camp and how, together, they would wonder what we were up to.

I hear the tent zipper open. I know without looking that it's Ruby, my morning companion. She carries her journal over by the fire, unfolds a camp seat.

"Hi, Daddy," she says.

I grab her cup and lean in for the pot of water, still simmering on the corner of the soot-blackened grill.

Thirty-Eight

We passed into another environment today. We left the huge cottonwood groves behind, the hills have risen up in gray desert buttes with junipers and big open spaces. The current still clips us along, some fast water after Miles City to Kinsey Bridge. The train is behind us, the river in front of us, and the full moon rising above.

—MARYPAT, PERSONAL JOURNAL

It is Saturday when we approach Miles City, another town named for a military man of the Indian Wars era, General Nelson Miles. Once, it was the bustling end of the cattle trail that extended south to Texas. It is a rail town, a stock town, a rodeo town. It's claim to fame, still, is the bucking-horse sale held here every spring.

I know it's a weekend because there are boats on the water, aluminum power boats with people flaying the water for fish. The Tongue River presents itself, river right, an anemic muddy trickle made more so by the diversion of irrigation water at upstream dams. Strange, but what crosses my mind is that I feel sorry for the Tongue, that it must be embarrassing to show up to a confluence so depleted and flaccid.

If I didn't know to look for it, I would have missed it altogether, and it is one of the major prairie rivers of eastern Montana. It heads in the Bighorn Mountains of Wyoming and has a run of three hundred miles before it arrives here. Along the way it feeds towns, ranches, coal mines, and power stations. It survives one major dam and a handful of minor ones. What's left at the end, in midsummer on a hot year like this, would hardly put out a campfire.

An abandoned iron bridge spans the Yellowstone. Swallows flurry from the girders when we coast through the shadow. We are an oddity, our trio of red boats, our habit of self-propulsion, our lack of fishing poles. The motors roar around us, the smell of gas permeates the morning. One very large human, shirtless and hairy, heavily tattooed, waves as he throttles upstream. We slap through the chop in his wake.

"Wow, there's a dude who needs a big boat," Sawyer says.

We have to stop in town to fill water jugs and make a phone call. We're about a week from the end and we need to alert our shuttle-driving friend, Bill, who has agreed to drive our car across the state to meet us where the Yellowstone merges with the Missouri, 185 river miles downstream and just over the line into North Dakota. Barring surprise, we have a good estimate of our arrival day.

Just past the Highway 59 bridge, a fishing access boat ramp comes up. A garish pink hotel-like building perches on the opposite hillside. Downtown

Miles City is some distance north of the river, through blocks of residential housing. Just because the river flows through a town on the map doesn't mean things are actually convenient. Montana towns, even if they were once poised on the riverbank, have migrated toward the railroad and highway, which is fine, unless you need to find a phone.

Lewis and Clark were in the habit of leaving handwritten notes to each other, skewered on a pole and set prominently on a sandbar. Once, up the Jefferson River, a beaver chewed down the stick and the missed communication meant one party continued on upriver the wrong direction several miles. Where Clark and Lewis rendezvoused at the confluence of the Missouri and Yellowstone, in 1806, Clark waited several days before the mosquitoes drove him mad enough that he posted a note for Lewis and sauntered downstream toward Saint Louis, where the parties reunited some days later.

On August 4, 1806, Clark noted that "the face of the Indian child is considerably puffed up and swollen with their bites; the men could procure scarcely any sleep during the night."

They had separated ways weeks earlier. While Clark and his splinter party navigated the Yellowstone, Lewis traveled overland into northern Montana, exploring the upper reaches of the Missouri's tributaries and getting into a scrape with some Blackfeet, after which he made haste for the Missouri and escaped downstream. Clark's scrap of a note fluttered in the breeze, waiting for Lewis, in the middle of unexplored country the size of Australia. Yet, Lewis found it without difficulty, and the Corps of Discovery managed to coordinate their logistics despite predating cell phones and satellite communications by several centuries.

Much as I'd like to leave a note on a pole for Bill to find and carry on downriver without stopping, we're going to have to find a phone. Marypat and the boys haul the water jugs up the ramp and go looking for a refill. Ruby and I wander the nearest street in search of a likely house to knock at the door.

We walk up to one that looks well kept. The car is in the driveway. The curtains are pulled shut. We knock. An overweight middle-aged woman answers. She's in sweats and a T-shirt. A large television, airing the sixth inning of a baseball game, drones behind her facing an empty power lounger.

"We're on the river," I say, explaining our weathered appearance. "Is there any chance we could use your phone to call the person who's meeting us at the end? We'd call on our phone card."

"Honey!" she yells toward the shadowed back rooms. At the same time, she beckons us inside. We step across the shag-carpeted living room to a counter-topped island by the kitchen. We haven't been inside a structure, other than during my casino adventure, in two weeks. It feels stagnant, stale, airless. I catch a whiff of rum and coke from a tall glass under my nose on the counter.

A man appears from the back hallway, carrying a drink and smoking a cigarette. He looks me over. I'm wearing shorts and river shoes, the same shirt I've worn for the last week. He leers at Ruby.

"They want to use the phone," the woman says.

"Sure, whatever." He is still looking Ruby over as he makes his way to the faux-leather lounger and settles in.

"Thanks." I punch the numbers, listen to it ring, wait for the answering machine. I leave Bill the message, tell him we'll call to confirm from Glendive, a few days downriver.

"What'd you say you were doing, little sister?" the man questions Ruby.

"We're paddling the Yellowstone," she says.

"The whole thing?"

She nods.

The air is too close, and the lecherous drunk is pushing my buttons.

"Hey, thanks for the phone," I say. "Gotta keep going." I drag Ruby out the door.

Ruby takes my arm as we walk. "I didn't like that guy," she says.

"Good call, babe," I say. "Pay attention to your instincts with people like that. I didn't like him either. We got our call made, though."

Down the street, Marypat and the boys are standing outside a fenced yard. Two kids are inside the closed gate. They have a garden hose draped over the top, and it's filling the last of the jugs.

"Thanks, kids," Marypat says when it bubbles over.

The youngsters solemnly pull the hose back to their side, watch us lug the heavy plastic containers across the street.

"They wouldn't let us in the yard," Eli says.

"I'm sure their parents aren't home, and they told them never to let a stranger in. At least they turned on the hose for us," Marypat answers.

Water in the boats feels like money in the bank. We're good for another four or five days. The five-gallon jugs slide into their spots in the load, are lashed down. We use two or three gallons a day, tops.

Miles City drops behind us. The sounds of town fade. The anglers are concentrated upstream. We see no one the rest of the afternoon. The Yellowstone pulls us back in. Weekend warriors, Saturday drunks shuttered in their houses, kids who won't open the gate, all slip into that dimension we recognize less and less as having much to do with us.

A few pleasant riffles pop up instead, helping us focus again. Twelve miles along, we camp on shore near a grove of cottonwoods. Many of the rocks are rich with iron, heavy metallic nuggets burnished to a dull shine by the river, gleaming in the sand. Through the lingering evening, the kids swim and play in some ledges, contriving games and competitions. They are lithe and playful water animals.

I take the inflatable and nose around the ledges, surfing little waves, dancing with the filaments of current. The river is a ready partner.

A full moon floats above the dry hills at twilight. All night it is bright as a streetlight on our tent. When I wake, several times, I see my sleeping family bathed in the blue, holy light. At dawn, three rangy horses are grazing around the tent.

Thirty-Nine

Pallid sturgeon have been called one of the ugliest fish in North America. Essentially unchanged over the past 70 million years, these huge, ancient bottom-feeders reach 3-5 feet in length, 85 pounds in weight, and can live as long as a century. They are an endangered species along the Yellowstone and Missouri Rivers.

The pair of half-wild horses nosing around our tent at dawn might belong to Roger Muggli. If not, he is certain to know the owner. Muggli lives near here, downstream of Miles City, a third-generation rancher and unlikely conservationist who is neck-deep in water issues.

I've heard Muggli called the busiest man in eastern Montana. Besides running the family farm and pellet-feed factory, he serves as the elected supervisor of the Tongue and Yellowstone Irrigation District, as did his father and grandfather before him. He is active on a handful of boards and committees and is a spokesperson on water issues ranging from coal-bed methane drilling to fish passages around dams.

Muggli has spent his life along the Yellowstone. He confesses that the longest he's been away from his farm in almost sixty years is two weeks. He grew up before the Clean Water Act, an era when the Yellowstone shared the plight of most rivers in America. Towns and farms used rivers as dumping grounds for garbage, sewage, and junk vehicles. Industrial runoff, pesticides, and farm waste ran into the water unchecked, and the demands of irrigators ruled the day.

Muggli admits that he was born both Republican and Catholic—and that he's followed one hell of a detour to become an environmentalist. During his childhood, after chores, his mother would let Roger and his siblings out to play. Invariably, they'd head for the river. He remembers that his mother always confiscated shoes before she let the kids roam, either to save on footwear or to limit the range of exploration.

At the root of his conversion to environmentalism were his childhood experiences along the irrigation canals and rivers. Although Muggli has no formal training in natural science, he has spent his life observing his surroundings and asking questions. Water that irrigates his fields comes from a diversion at Twelve Mile Dam, constructed by Miles City businessmen in 1886 on the Tongue River. Since then, fish by the thousands have been entrained in the irrigation canal and dumped into ditches that water crops. He remembers watching them struggle and die in the fields. Carp, catfish, chub, whitefish, sturgeon, bass, and many other species ended up as fertilizer along with the irrigation water.

Muggli, from a young age, couldn't stand watching the gasping fish with mud working through their gills. He'd scoop them into buckets and run like hell for the Yellowstone, which ran past the fields, where he'd release them. Later, he tried to put homemade screening over the diversion, but it would clog with vegetation and his father pulled it out again.

Decades later, when Muggli was elected to supervise the irrigation district, he made it a priority to effectively screen the canal and to work to create a fish passage channel so that the fifty-some species of warm-water fish could once again, for the first time in 120 years, swim upstream on the Tongue.

Much to Muggli's surprise, the project took twenty years to complete. At several points he got so frustrated with bureaucratic quicksand that he collected buckets of floundering fish from the fields, took them into government offices, and dumped them on the floor to make his point. In the end, it still required countless meetings with stakeholders and the donation of his own time and equipment to get the job done.

By the same token, Muggli may have been the only person who could have accomplished the task. If some pointy-headed environmental organization had showed up with a proposal, local opposition would have been predictable and fierce. Muggli is as local and authentic as they come, in addition to being stubbornly passionate about the cause.

During the summer of 2006, construction got under way. Using Muggli's backhoe and the donated time of a heavy-equipment operator, the fish passage was dug to grade and readied to hook up with the main channel of the Tongue.

Midsummer, with the passage largely complete, an ill-timed thunderstorm front moved across southeastern Montana. Muggli was working in the fields, busy shifting irrigation water, when he felt the air change. Then the rain came, sheets of it, and it kept up, pounding onto a landscape that rarely sees rain, much less a monsoon.

Muggli dropped what he was doing and hopped into his truck to drive the canal. While lightning flashed and stabbed around him, he struggled with the huge metal wheels at the irrigation gates, opening up ditches to cope with the slug of water he knew was coming. He got to the fish passage just as water broke through at an oxbow bend of the Tongue just upstream. A torrent of muddy river rushed across the field, straight for the vulnerable, unfinished channel.

The flood tide ripped across the field and plunged into the passage, filling it to the brim with churning current. Muggli stood in his hip waders watching, knowing that the whole project was in danger of washing away like so much sand. He gingerly felt his way toward the edge of the channel and found himself slipping right into the bottom, suddenly up to his chest in the whirling torrent.

Then, to his surprise, he felt fish bumping past him, heading upstream. It was as if he'd just stepped into a can of sardines, he reported. There were fish hitting his boots, pushing past his legs, running into his chest. The river was thick with them. Muggli started shoveling them out by hand to see what species were swimming past—channel catfish, carp, bass...

Muggli described it as a majestic moment. Despite the fear that his project might be ruined, at that moment he knew that it would work. Here were these fish, in the midst of a flood, eagerly pushing upstream past the barrier that had held them back for more than a century.

As it turned out, the flood did serious damage to the passage and added several weeks to the work schedule, but the fish channel was completed early that fall and more than fifty species of warm-water fish were again allowed access to ancient spawning grounds and habitat that had been cut off by agricultural thirst for irrigation water since shortly after Custer's Last Stand.

One fish passage at a minor dam on a tributary of the Yellowstone is significant, but only one piece of a much larger vision shared by folks like Roger Muggli. That it required the better part of one man's life and energy to complete is a testimony to the magnitude of the challenge. Still, Muggli's success is fueling momentum. Upstream diversions on the Tongue are slated to be breached to allow fish access to almost two hundred miles of river habitat. The diversion dam on the Yellowstone at Forsyth is targeted for a fish passage, and most significant of all, the diversion at Intake Dam on the lower Yellowstone, downstream of Glendive, is scheduled for a fish ramp and irrigation canal screening to the tune of $40 million. The project is being completed by the US Army Corps of Engineers (USACE) to facilitate the upriver migration and successful spawning of warm-water fish, including paddlefish and the endangered pallid sturgeon.

If and when all those pieces fall into place, the entire Yellowstone River valley, from a fish's perspective, will be transformed. A watershed covering much of eastern Montana would be restored, or at least reopened, as habitat for the fish that have traditionally spawned and lived there. Beyond that, the Yellowstone might serve as an example for the kind of restoration possibilities that could be applied to the entire Missouri basin and other rivers throughout North America.

The cumulative effects study undertaken by USACE along the lower Yellowstone drainage has been an unprecedented approach to river management, one which treats the river corridor as a dynamic, shifting territory encompassing vegetation, erosion channels, island migration, and fish and wildlife species, as well as human interests. For more than a decade, a working consortium of scientists, ranchers, environmentalists, and agency representatives have cooperated to find holistic strategies to manage the river.

One such strategy is the creation of sloughing easements, which acknowledge the meandering nature of a river channel and allow farmers to put riverside property into easements that leave the river free to erode and move and alleviate the temptation to armor and riprap large sections of vulnerable channel.

The Clean Water Act of 1972 was a huge step toward mitigating the unchecked pollution and careless misuse of rivers. Broadly conceived strategies like those being considered along the lower Yellowstone, especially those that incorporate the input of local interests, are the next step in restoring watersheds to something akin to their original state, insofar as that is possible.

THE YELLOWSTONE RIVER RUNS THE GAUNTLET OF HUMAN CIVILIZATION ACROSS MONTANA.

The farther we paddle down the Yellowstone, the more personal the toll on the river becomes. This is a hot, dry summer again. In the distance, to the west, the smudge of fire smoke hangs against the horizon. Summer fires have become part of reality in the West, a factor as real and inevitable as weather. Along the lower river, the raids on its water are constant.

Every mile or two, another irrigation motor thumps away, siphoning river water up to the fields. It becomes more and more difficult to find campsites out of earshot. In addition, each diversion canal takes its slice of water, hundreds of cubic feet per second, and dispenses it over fields, where it soaks in or evaporates, making agriculture possible, but depleting the river already waning in the dry summer. Oil refineries, beet factories, power plants suck up more river water to lubricate industry. Towns and cities pull off their share.

In turn, what comes back is treated sewage, industrial wastewater, agricultural runoff. The Yellowstone is drained and insulted by the mile. It is impossible for us not to take it personally. Riding the back of current, we feel the raids on its vitality like a weakening pulse. Thousands of times a day, we pull paddles through the silty river, communicate with it, and sense the toll of our demands on it.

All of us are guilty. It's easy to point at refineries and pesticides, but we drive cars fueled by refined oil, we eat the grains and beef grown on farms and ranches, we flush our toilets and fill our sinks and wash our clothes. Only, day after day on the river, seeing the depletion and the pollution, watching eagles and swallows, the swirls of fish, the flash of whitetail, the truth of what we do is visceral, sensual, wrenching.

It feels like visiting a friend with cancer. A friend whose head is bald, whose body is emaciated, and whose reserves are low. And yet they go on, they keep living. What else would they do? More and more, paddling the Yellowstone feels like that bedside visit, like we are attending to a friend in dire straits, a friend whom we have seen in the full bloom of health, but with whom, now, there is little to say and only our companionship to offer.

Forty

Went 30 miles. Had eggs for breakfast. Paddled and floated and swam all day. Camped on a rocky ledge on the left side of the river. There we saw a rattlesnake in the river.

—Eli, GROUP JOURNAL

The morning wind has shifted 180 degrees, which I adapt to by turning the fire pan and windscreen before lighting the tinder. Marypat reads out loud in the tent until hot drinks are ready. A stand of corn rises in an unnatural green crew cut across from our camp. Sawyer wanted to cross over and pick some for dinner last night.

A white pelican coasts upriver through cool morning air. A killdeer scolds along the shore. The highway is barely audible, a distant thrum. The river rose an inch or two overnight. I know because the tub of margarine I left cooling in the shallows is bobbing around, bumping against the corral of rocks I built.

Much of the morning, paddling with Eli, we talk about my father's family. It takes some doing to cover the issues of immigration, stepbrothers, a half sister, and my grandfather's habit of trading in his Lincoln Continental every two years for a new one. Then, somehow, we get onto the subject of life insurance, which I try to explain as a gambling proposition with your life as the stakes. Eli shakes his head, waves his paddle at the engineer of a long coal train steaming upriver. An arm waves back from the engine cab. Swallows scythe through the air over our heads.

Fifteen miles into the day, the turbulence of Buffalo Rapids appears ahead. It is the first whitewater of any significance at all in almost two hundred miles, and it rouses us. The river pours over a sandstone ledge that juts more than halfway across the channel. As rapids go, nothing much, but we're hungry for variety and stop for lunch on an island of rock in the midst of the watery din.

It might not be much to us, but during the steamboat era in the later half of the nineteenth century, it was one of the most daunting obstacles to navigation. In 1879, the steamboat *Yellowstone* foundered on the rocks and wrecked here, dealing a blow to business interests in the state and throwing into question the always problematic viability of steamboat transportation.

"At this place they were obliged to let the canoes down by hand, for fear of their splitting on a concealed rock; though when the shoals are known a large canoe could with safety pass through the worst of them. This is the most difficult part of the whole Yellowstone River," wrote William Clark near the end of July 1806.

BUFFALO RAPIDS, ON THE LOWER YELLOWSTONE RIVER.

Lunch is reconstituted hummus spread on bannock baked by Eli over driftwood flames the previous night. Lunch is also a sideshow to the main event, which is frolicking in the current. Ruby strikes off across a waist-deep channel to another island of bedrock. The boys follow. The three of them bodysurf the wave below a smaller ledge. Marypat and I wade in to refresh, to feel the surge of river around us, sensual and certain.

When we leave, the boys each stern a canoe through the rapid. Sawyer sets up more sideways than I'd prefer, but he pulls it straight in time to slap through the waves and stay dry. We have never taken a formal approach to paddling instruction. All three kids have been in boats since birth. They know what an eddy feels like, that a V of water indicates the deepest channel in a rapid, how a curling wave can hold a boat stationary, surfing, while the river flows past. In some cases they don't know the terminology, but they know how water acts and what it will do to a boat.

From the time they were toddlers, they've held paddles in their hands, tried things. Again, they haven't always known the names of strokes or techniques. They simply figured out what worked. Much as they learned to walk and run and ride bikes by trial and error and synaptic feedback, they have learned to guide boats, respond to waves, aim for deeper water, stay clear of snags, shift their weight.

The Powder River comes in a few miles below Buffalo Rapid. Too thick to drink, too thin to plow is the saying about the Powder. It is a long river, winding through austere ranch country far into Wyoming and watering agriculture all the way, but it isn't much to look at.

From the perspective of spawning fish, however, it's a big deal. During spring melt, the Powder is an important spawning ground for a number of prairie species. Fish swim hundreds of miles to reach the Powder in a year when the flows are adequate.

The banks of the Yellowstone rise in sheer bluffs. Rough-legged hawks perch on the overlooks. Deer cut trails that angle across the steep, loose gravel. We probe a few bends up Lost Boy Creek, a deep coulee that I remember exploring in 1992, when Eli was an infant. On that trip, by the time we reached the lower river, Marypat suspected that she was pregnant again, that the medical advice had all been wrong, and that we had another fetal stowaway on a river journey. She was always tired and didn't have much appetite, and she still hadn't gotten her period. She didn't talk about it, but it was a gathering certainty.

There was more water on that first trip, but otherwise nothing looks changed. Sediments in badland pastels, coal seams, the truncated horizon. The air is hushed and stagnant in the clamp of the side valley. We turn back and reenter the broad stage of the Yellowstone, paddling into an upriver breeze as the day wanes.

Camps run together. An island on the outskirts of Terry with better than average rock hunting and a small band of bum lambs, which the kids chase around in the twilight. Sawyer gets up early there, saying he wants to read. By the time I emerge, he has a fire going and water simmering.

Then, the next night, a narrow bench of sand near a jumble of angular boulders where we stop late in the day to swim and then decide to make camp. There are fossils in the bedrock, ancient reeds and other plant impressions between layers. There are some rich fossil beds along the lower Yellowstone, full of shark's teeth, ammonites, fern impressions—reminders of the slow pulses of change and the reality that we, too, will be simply another layer in the record, all the hubbub of our civilization rendered flat. I am about to strike off toward an outcrop to look for more when I hear Ruby yell.

"Rattlesnake! Come look." She beckons me over. The kids are gathered together, a shifting, nervous knot around a rock in the water.

The first rattlesnake of the trip is swimming among the same rocks we found so attractive. It seems quite comfortable in the cool water, crosses from rock to rock, climbs up into the sun, appears generally unconcerned about the gallery of onlookers. We watch it for some time, decide that we've had enough swimming for now, and I think better of my trip to the outcrop.

Next morning, as I start the fire, a man walks upriver toward our camp. I recognize his agate-hunting posture at fifty yards. He wields a walking stick, which he probes ahead with, alerting snakes. Although civilization surrounds us, we have had little face-to-face interaction. I find myself shy.

"Breakfast ready?" he asks when he comes near.

"Workin' on it," I say.

He looks around at our outfit, at the rest of the family getting dressed in the tent. Sawyer and Ruby step out. Each of them finds a rock to sit on and opens a book.

"I'm just out walking, looking for agate," he explains.

"I'd offer you coffee, but haven't got it going yet," I say.

"No bother," he says. "I like to walk while it's cool anyway. Been too hot this summer."

"Yeah, we've been in shorts for two weeks solid. And we swim almost as much as we paddle," I agree.

Turns out he lives in a riverside house we passed a day earlier. It was his band of bum lambs the kids chased around the island a few nights back. "My son is taking care of them," he says. "They were such a pain in the ass around the house. It's easier just to put them on the island."

He waves, continues upstream.

"Keep studying," he says, when he passes Sawyer. "Keep studying."

I stoop to feed wood into the fire, watch him pick his way through the sage and boulders, head down, pausing now and then.

- -

Glendive is the last town of any size the river passes close to before the Missouri. We need a few supplies and want to call Bill to confirm our pickup. Less than a week remains.

It is another hot day. Three bridges span the river as we pull our way through town. The air is still, the town silent. At one bridge with a fishing access, I walk up to the nearest street, but it's a residential area. I don't feel like knocking on doors and I'm hoping for a convenience store for some treats.

Below an old railroad bridge the kids find some large fish lounging in the gravel shallows. Sawyer gets out of the boat and sloshes after them. The fish are ancient looking, with spiny fins. They flail away, flashing in the sun. Sauger, perhaps, another of the unsexy, warm-water species, but we can't be sure. Spines or not, Sawyer would pick them up if he could catch them.

Nothing looks promising before the huge Interstate 90 highway bridge. Here we will lose the traffic hum that has been our companion since Livingston, close to four hundred miles upstream. We park in its shade. The bank is steep, the sun hot, the mud at the river's edge cloying. But we have no choice.

Sawyer and Ruby keep me company. We take one empty jug to fill with water, I rummage around in my clothing bag to find my wallet, and we start up through the grasses. I'm sweating within one hundred yards. Truck traffic washes past. The sun beats down. The grass is dry and brittle. Grasshoppers clack away in the heat.

The nearest gas station and store is a solid half mile away. Even Sawyer and Ruby, usually energetic and playful, are bludgeoned to a trudge by the heat. We walk single file along a narrow path through the grass in our river garb. Cans and bags and six-pack holders litter the ground. The gas station shimmers ahead, a questionable oasis.

As I step inside, into the mechanical chill of air-conditioning, I immediately feel that I need a shower and a washing machine. Something about the enclosed store, wafts of chemical scents, antiseptic hints of cleanser that provokes that shower-a-day mentality.

"Pay phone's outside on the wall." The obese cashier points back out at the heat shimmer. Ruby and Sawyer idly peruse the aisles of junk food while I go to make the call. Sweat runs down my sides under my T-shirt as I dial Bill's number.

This time, he answers. We exchange news for a bit, I give him our estimated arrival time. He promises to be there. Besides the fact that I'm standing in the direct glare of sun and that the receiver is slippery with sweat against my ear, I hate these impositions to trip rhythm. The call is necessary, but I want nothing more than to get back to the boats.

We fill the water jug at an outside spigot, pick up a bag of chips, some ice cream bars for immediate consumption, and cold drinks. I grab a six-pack of beer from the cooler, the cans sweating with cold, and pop one open as we head toward the river. We take turns lugging the five-gallon jug.

Marypat and Eli are reclining in the shade, dodging swallow poop from the girders far overhead. They gobble their dripping ice cream bars. I hand Marypat a beer. We push off, back into the dazzle of heat. The river picks us up, pulls us away from the exhaust and roar and litter. I open another beer.

Across from the island camp where we stop for the day, a small trailer sits in the shade of cottonwoods. It is obviously someone's getaway. A bench overlooks the river. The trees rustle in the breeze. A magpie lands in the branches. The river gurgles past, green and tired in the sunset light.

Marypat goes into pizzeria mode. She makes a quick dough and a tomato sauce, while the rest of us get busy finding wood and building up enough coals to bake with. The first Dutch oven pizza is gone in thirty seconds.

"More!" Eli shouts.

She makes another one. We gather more wood. I drink the last beer, tepid by now. The second pizza disappears almost as quickly. Marypat makes a third, then a fourth. We scour the sand for bits of driftwood. We could eat another, but no one wants to make the effort. It is gray twilight by the time we clean up.

Forty-One

In a three-year study conducted from 1996 to 1998, between 382,000 and 809,000 fish per year were entrained in the canal at Intake Diversion Dam. While there is a theoretical possibility that some of these fish might survive and return to the main channel, Montana Fish, Wildlife and Parks reports that not one tagged fish that has gone into a diversion channel has been known to survive.

—MATT JAEGER, MONTANA FISH, WILDLIFE AND PARKS BIOLOGIST

When people tout the Yellowstone as the last free-flowing, undammed river of consequence in the continental United States, they ignore Intake Dam, to say nothing of the other five major diversions upstream, which stand as a significant asterisk on the statement. Whether you define it as a bona fide dam or not, it is unquestionably a portage for us.

We hear the concussion half a mile off and sidle up hugging the right shore, landing just above the concrete abutment. The bows of our canoes knife into the mud. Ruby hops out into ankle-deep clay and hauls one boat up to firmer ground. Just ahead, the river piles through the chaos of rock. As I do at any rapid, runnable or not, I study the whitewater for a navigable line. At Intake, the drop lacks the passages of a natural rapid. It is a chaos of unbroken froth from bank to bank. White pelicans rest in the churning currents. Two teenage boys fish from a gravel beach below.

To create the Intake Diversion Dam, a barrier of boulders was dumped into the river. A set of wooden cribs contains the rocks, and some concrete work reinforces the structure, but the basic design is little more than a very large pile of rocks. A thick metal cable crosses above the river. Periodically, floods or ice dams shove boulders downstream. From time to time, replacement rock is sent across in a metal scoop suspended from the cable and dropped into the cribs.

Intake was constructed by the Bureau of Reclamation between 1905 and 1909 to provide irrigation water to farms across the northeastern quadrant of the state. An ice jam summarily blew out the structure in 1910, after which it was rebuilt. Ice remains the single biggest threat to the dam's integrity, along with rare major floods.

The barrier pools the river enough to allow for a diversion of twelve hundred cubic feet per second to be pulled off, river left. The Intake Canal is a river in its own right, with more volume than any regional watercourse except for the Yellowstone and the Missouri. It courses parallel to the Yellowstone and irrigates some sixty thousand acres, mostly sugar beet fields, all the way north to the Missouri River.

Twelve hundred cubic feet per second constitutes more than half of the entire river volume in a dry year, like this one. It is the single most precious commodity for agriculture, a commodity upon which economic survival rests, and when it comes up for debate, the talk is instantly hot. Squabbles over water are nothing new. The story goes that the first official murder in Montana Territory was the result of an argument over water claims.

Even now, in the era of global positioning systems and computer-programmed combines, water distribution is based on an archaic and labyrinthine system founded on the nineteenth-century first-in-time, first-in-right doctrine and administered by a far-flung cadre of ditch riders and a completely overwhelmed water court.

To say that water adjudication in the West is an exact, tightly-enforced science is like claiming that abstinence-only sex education is an ironclad guarantee of chaste teenagers. In the case of water rights, allocations are adjusted by lifting boards in and out of ditches, and farmers are largely trusted to do the right thing by their neighbors. And the whole enterprise is based on the hodgepodge of ancestor's claims to water going back to the homestead era.

The portage is the length of a football field, along the concrete wall and down to the beach below. Everyone takes a couple of trips and the work is quickly done, despite three or four hundred pounds of agate and petrified wood stuffed into bags and packs. For the last few days, we've been pestered by tiny, gnatlike, biting insects. They crawl in our ears and nostrils, get in our hair, ping off our faces. Nothing like the blackfly hordes of the Far North, but a nuisance. We plunge into the river to escape them, soak bandanas and wear them, bandit-style, over our faces.

We ferry the boats across the river in the turbulent current below the dam and land at the fishing access ramp. We've heard that there is water in the camping area and want to fill another jug to tide us over. The camp is empty. Cicadas sing through the heat in the cottonwoods. We pump up water, but it stinks of sulfur, a reminder that this is petroleum country.

"Yuck!" Ruby summarizes, making a face. "I'm not drinking that!" We fill the jug anyway, for backup reserves, and lug it down to the canoe. Our last water stop. The trip's end looms a few days away.

There is nothing worth lingering over below the dam. It smells vaguely of fish guts. We pile into the boats, paddle away with the shock of pounding water beating against our backs.

The Bureau of Reclamation engineers in the early twentieth century didn't give much thought to the effect a dam might have on fish populations. It was an anthropocentric enterprise, typical of that era, focused on irrigation water and little else. Besides, there were plenty of fish.

Nevertheless, the effect was profound. For thousands of years, perhaps millions, fish like the pallid sturgeon and paddlefish—ancient, whiskered, armored species—responded to the thick, heady flows of spring floods by migrating up the Missouri and Yellowstone Rivers to their spawning grounds. Up they came to tributaries like the Powder and Tongue and Bighorn, nosing against the current, spreading their eggs, feeling along routes mapped by primordial instincts, following cues unfathomable to us, but as unerring as the migrations of monarch butterflies or arctic terns.

Intake put an end to all that. As effective as a cork in a bottle, it blocked the upstream travel of many warm-water fish. Only rarely, at exceptionally high flows, do paddlefish fight their way upstream of the rocky dam. Sturgeon never make it. These are not leaping fish, like salmon or trout. They need gentle inclines and laminar flows with eddies to rest in. A climb like Intake might as well be Glen Canyon Dam.

So what? Well, the barrier to migration cuts out thousands of miles of habitat in the watershed, and, in the case of pallid sturgeon, it is literally a matter of survival. This unintended consequence is another reminder of our inability to account for all the fallout of our meddling with Mother Nature.

Here's what we now understand. It turns out that pallid sturgeon, when they hatch, are incapable of swimming. They drift downstream at the whim of the river current. About all they can control is their buoyancy, so they can adjust the level of their existence in the water column, but that's it for mobility. For the first two weeks of life, they literally go with the flow, and they require that flow to feed and survive.

In the case of the lower Yellowstone, pallid sturgeon need roughly 180 miles of moving current to accommodate that two-week window of immobility. The problem is that between Intake Dam and the slack water impounded above Garrison Dam on the Missouri there is less than a hundred miles of current; the baby sturgeon drift into that stagnant pool and perish.

The population of pallid sturgeon in the upper Missouri and lower Yellowstone is trapped. The adults, which can grow to five feet and weigh eighty pounds, are becoming elderly. Many are fifty years old or more. The only juvenile fish in the reach are raised in hatcheries and released artificially. The entire population of naturally occurring pallid sturgeon is down to less than 150 individuals. Many of them have been tagged and are monitored. They have been known to mate and spawn, but the cycle never completes.

Then there's the paddlefish, a prehistoric-looking species if there ever was one, who occupy a bizarre sport-fishing niche. Intake Dam is the epicenter of the sport, if you can call it that. During a frantic season every spring, the paddlefish come up against the Intake Dam and collect there, following instincts that served them well for millennia, but which, for the last century, have been blocked.

I hesitate to call paddlefish angling a sport because there is very little about it that qualifies as sporting. Paddlefish don't go for lures or bait. They snuffle around in the bottom sediment for their food. The only way to catch them is by snagging the fish with huge treble hooks and dragging them, like recovering a dead body, out of the river. So the fish are concentrated at this one spot, milling around in their confused attempt to move forward, and they fall prey to "sportsmen" dragging the river with heavy tackle.

At the campground, there are fish-cleaning huts. Paddlefish caviar has become a delicacy and a quirky local economy. Folks drag the bottoms until the seasonal quota is met, then everyone goes home, some with paddlefish steaks for the freezer.

Strange, the stuff we do in the name of recreation.

When I slip out of the canoe and swim, I think of the inhabitants my pale legs go past in the underwater gloom. Fish that might weigh as much as my children and be older than me. Species with armored plating covering their bodies and skeletons made of cartilage. And the prehistoric web of intelligence we mess with in our self-centered drive to live as we wish. I think of respect, and the lack of it. And the forbearance of our neighbors.

The good news is that we are, slowly and haltingly, getting the message. A coalition of stakeholders with interests along the Yellowstone has been meeting for years in an attempt to fashion strategies that take into account the needs of irrigators, government agencies, environmental groups, and municipalities. Although fish did not figure prominently in the initial scope of work, they have moved onto the radar.

Efforts like Roger Muggli's fish passage on the Tongue River have gotten people's attention. The plight of species like the pallid sturgeon have come to light. Proposals have been floated.

At Intake, USACE is building a $40 million fish ramp and screening the irrigation headgate in a response that will continue to provide for irrigation demands, but which will also create the gentle laminar flows that warmwater fish require to continue upstream. The ramp designed to incorporate a variety of flows will run off of a new sill and extend roughly sixteen hundred feet downstream at an average grade of 1 percent. USACE began construction in 2010, and the hope is that the upstream migration of fish will begin the process of restoration of natural conditions on the lower Yellowstone.

From the point of view of pallid sturgeon and dozens of other species, it would be money well spent and it can't happen soon enough. For the sturgeon, and to a lesser extent, all fish, a viable way past Intake and perhaps on upstream past the diversion at Forsyth would mean literal survival and a return to ancient reaches of habitat.

Intake recedes in our wake, river bends coil behind us, stretching, now, some five hundred miles back to the border of Yellowstone. The river is noticeably shrunken, and the miles come harder. There are stretches where we actually run aground on sandbars if we aren't careful. Herds of cattle slosh across in front of us. We paddle through Black Angus and Herefords. On one stretch, gusty winds slam upriver and we bend to the grueling work. On the next, the same winds shove us along and we read out loud. In calm periods, the gnats descend.

The river valley widens, braids through clusters of large islands. Huge cottonwood groves rustle in the heat. Dense flocks of terns rise up from sandbars as we pass, like schools of shining fish against the pale blue sky. Badland colors paint the hills and side valleys, pink and brown and red pastels, dry, eroded prairie.

Devil's Canyon leads evocatively into colorful, etched terrain just downstream of our camp on a sandy beach. As we start to cook dinner, the winds build. Towering cumulus thunderheads cruise ponderously through the sky. Whenever one passes near, the winds are terrific. We guy down the tent, weight the boats to hold them in place, do our best to keep sand out of the dinner pot. Grit swirls into everything, drifting behind the canoes and packs, stinging our skin. We eat standing up, above the worst of the sandy ground blizzard.

To distract myself from the onslaught, I stroll across the flats looking for more rock. The kids head into the thicket of willows on another evening adventure. I hear them thwacking through the brush. Then I see an amazing fossilized slab of rock, a tapestry of leaves and plant matter, that, on closer inspection, reveals itself as the mud-soaked surface of a sofa cushion.

"Jesus, you idiot," I mutter, straightening up.

Near dark, we all herd into the tent, as much to hold it down as to go to sleep. Wind half collapses one side in spite of guylines reinforced with the weight of rock-filled sacks. Sawyer is the anchor holding down that side of the tent. It is hot and close inside. We strip naked and lie on top of our sleeping bags, but sweat just the same. Sand as fine as dust drifts through the netting, settles in a layer on our damp skin. Wind pummels and flaps the fabric. Slowly it grows dark.

I keep expecting one of the gargantuan thunderheads to let loose above us. I wish for it. Anything to nail down the drifts of sand, to stop the blizzard of grit. It grows very dark. Distant pops of lightning flare momentarily, low rumbles of thunder. But no rain, only the mist of sand falling on our eyelids, filling our nylon sleeping bags, drifting onto the piles of clothes. We all lie as still as we can, strive for the Zen of acceptance, wait for it to pass, for calm, for rain, for morning.

Suddenly the wind shifts and collapses the other wall of the tent, above Eli. I have to pee anyway, so I slide out under the flap to weight down the stakes and check on things. It is cooler outside, but howling. A patch of stars glimmers through a break of clouds. A monstrous, majestic cloud fills the horizon up Devil's Canyon, flickering with lightning, creeping past with its cell of hurricane winds. I stand in the black night, naked, with the island of stars serene overhead and sand rivering through my legs like dry current.

Forty-Two

The bears, which gave so much trouble on the head of the Missouri, are equally fierce in this quarter. This morning one of them, which was on a sand-bar as the boat passed, raised himself on his hind feet; and after looking at the party, plunged in and swam toward them. He was received with three balls in the body, and he turned around and made for the shore.

—WILLIAM CLARK, JOURNAL, AUGUST 2, 1806

The biggest chore of the morning is ridding our camp and ourselves of sand. Every sleeping bag, every piece of clothing, every shoe gets a thorough beating. All of us walk around slapping clouds of sand off of bags and packs, shaking out the boats, unearthing cook pots, rinsing things. Sleeping bag zippers and the doors of the tent are clogged with grains of sand. The tent is barely sealable. All but one of the door zippers separates. Marypat spends a chunk of time babying zippers closed and rinsing sand out of the nylon teeth.

"Only use this door," she cautions, when she finishes. "Don't even touch any of the others."

"If we get hit by a storm, we're gonna be wet," Sawyer says.

"I'll take a storm over another night of wind," I say. "I have sand in quite a few places where the sun doesn't shine."

The finish of the trip looms before us. The river braids through Elk Island and Seven Sisters Island, moves sluggishly, depleted and thick. In 1992, I remember much more vigorous current right up to the confluence with the Missouri. I remember, in fact, what a feeling of deceleration it was when we hit the current of the Missouri. Not this summer. The Yellowstone is turgid and shallow. The currents we clipped along with, drifting for much of the day, have been bled dry. We have to paddle steadily to make any mileage.

Along a narrow channel past an island, an elderly couple with sacks walks bent over, picking for agate. Their aluminum motorboat is pulled up in the shallows. They straighten to watch us go by, but don't wave.

We drift past the backyards of Savage and Crane, tiny towns facing the two-lane highway, past Burns Creek and the Brazeau's Houses, ruins of a trading post active during the 1820s, then the Seven Sisters Recreation Area. Wind rustles through the dry cottonwoods. Irrigation motors thump through the hot air, the vague smell of diesel, more of the river pulled off to spread over parched ground.

Another camp, within earshot of Sidney, Montana, and within a couple of miles of North Dakota. I hide from the sun in the narrow eve of shade thrown by a flood-smoothed cottonwood trunk to write in my journal. The distant thrum of cars and air conditioners and crop dusters hovers.

Sawyer discovers a full-body mud wallow just up the shoreline. Exactly his sort of thing. When I look up, he is stripped naked and immersed to his neck. He raises a glistening black arm in a wave. Ruby and Marypat can't resist. They go to investigate, and before long they, too, are butt naked and wriggling in up to their necks.

SAWYER MAKES THE MOST OF A RIVERSIDE MUDBATH.

"C'mon, Dad," Sawyer calls.

"I think I'll pass," I say, "but I'll take pictures." Eli opts out too. These antics, more and more, are out of his comfort zone.

"People spend a lot of money for a clay bath like this," Marypat says.

"Yeah, you guys could open up shop. Pretty soon you'd have all the sugar beet farmers down here getting their rejuvenation treatments," I say.

"Good idea, Pops." Sawyer rolls onto his stomach. Mud laps up on his chin.

The three of them squirm around, giggling and slippery, in the deep wallow. They troop off in a line of Claymation figures into the river, leaving a muddy trail of footprints across the rocks.

The last full day on the river, the little gnatlike insects are a torment. The winds are still, the sun hot, the river slow. We soak bandanas and drape them over our faces. The bugs crawl into our ears.

A blocky sugar beet plant hunkers on the riverbank, spewing exhaust from a tall stack and piping water, or at least liquid, back into the river. Later, the Highway 200 bridge spans the valley, sloping upward from west to east. A slow pulse of traffic cruises overhead.

Just upstream, the old iron railroad bridge crosses the valley. The lift section, set on massive pulleys, designed to let steamboats pass underneath, sits over a side channel. Chunks of concrete weights the size of train cars hang suspended, ready to pull up the iron girders and sections of tracks.

"I wonder if it still works," Marypat says.

Slowly the bridges recede behind us. We paddle methodically. The bugs attack. The valley is broad, bordered by shale and mud escarpments, banded in pastel colors. Cicadas buzz loudly in the heat.

This final night, we elect not to eat dinner. Wood is scarce. Camp is a muddy sandbar a foot or two above the river. We snack on some bannock, make enough of a fire for tea, and call it good. An irrigation motor rumbles from across the channel. Finally, at twilight, a kid on a dirt bike roars down and shuts it off. Silence swoops into the vacuum. The air is still. The river glides by, green, molten, a whisper. The insects finally vanish, triggered by temperature, darkness, some cue known only to them. We are grateful.

We don't use a fly on the tent. Given the state of the zippers, it wouldn't provide much protection in any case. Everyone lies naked, waiting for whatever coolness night will bring. Ruby conducts a listless hair watch on the nearest of Sawyer's armpits, but the humor is tired.

Forty-Three

My eyes open in the cool, gray light. I pull the sleeping bag around my shoulders, relish the chill. Sawyer lies next to me, his head buried deep, a lump under nylon. On the other side, Ruby lies half out of her bag, disheveled hair across her face. The day stirs. A pheasant calls from the woods, a harsh, metallic screech.

We're done, I think. Mentally I tick back upstream, counting camps. It is a memory exercise I indulge, summoning the litany of camps, each with its salient image—the cliff across the channel, the blue heron in the mist, the complex of swallow nests pasted into rock face, the spectacular agate in the gravel, the swimming hole, the train light burning through the black night. I reel them in, up past Glendive, past Forsyth and Custer and Hysham and Billings, back onto the upper river. Columbus, Reed Point, Big Timber, Livingston, Emigrant. All the way up to the gushing torrent at the border of Yellowstone National Park, and the colorful outburst of boats and friends seeing us off.

It has only been three weeks, but it seems long ago and distant. Equally unfathomable, the fact that Bill is driving to meet us with our car. That, in a matter of hours, we will hug on a boat ramp, dismantle the folding boats, cram everything in our car. More, that within a day, we will drive back across much of our route, past all those camps, back to our house, our garden, our town. That Eli will be heading off for soccer camp. That we will be paying bills, answering mail, confronting a few hundred messages, reentering. It feels like preparing for the atmospheric buffeting in the leap between worlds.

Jet lag is nothing compared to river lag.

After our first trip across Canada, more than two decades ago—before children, before my first book, before our marriage—it was a year before we were really and truly back. It took that long to readjust, to leave the long, wild immersion behind and truly be part of town life. For months, our senses were overwhelmed by the sheer volume and intensity of the cacophony—sounds, colors, billboards, the speed of cars, the clatter of civilization.

More wrenching, the change in daily rhythm, from one dictated by the flow of water, shifts in weather, a routine of moving fifteen miles forward, setting up camp, feeding ourselves, reacting to the world, to one of sensory bombardment and confusion. For a long time it felt like mourning, accepting a kind of death. Half a year later, I was still ambushed by vivid moments in which I would find myself back on the tundra, in that rolling, verdant, austere wilderness. I would feel the raw wind tugging past, hear the slap of wave against land, turn toward the *inukshuk* standing sentinel on the gray ridge behind me.

This transition will be nothing like that. In a matter of days we will be up to speed. To be honest, I am ready to return. But it doesn't lessen the urge to resist, to stay, to remain on river time. I am ready to leave what the Yellowstone has become, but I am in no hurry to lose my river life.

I hear some wild turkeys behind the tent, their guttural conversation. A yellow-breasted chat, the largest and most vocal North American warbler, runs through its playlist of raucous calls. Everyone starts to rouse in the tent.

We eschew breakfast. Funny, but we aren't hungry. We haven't eaten a real meal since lunch the day before. It feels like part of the ending, this lack of interest. Marypat sets up a final group photo, lined up by the loaded boats that lie half in the water. We rub bare shoulders, jostle against each other, put on smiles.

Sawyer is in the bow of my canoe. He is gregarious this morning. He wants me to teach him the lyrics of an old Peter, Paul and Mary song. We work at that for a while. He is a pretty terrible singer, but has plenty of feeling.

"So, Dad," he says after he gives up the song. "If a meteor hits an ozone hole in the atmosphere, will it still burn up?"

"Jesus, Sawyer. Where do you come up with this stuff?"

Then he asks me what made me pick the college I did, and if I had gone for a scholarship, what would it have been in.

I keep looking for the confluence, the meeting of the Missouri and Yellowstone, where Clark waited several days for Lewis to show up. When Marypat and Eli and I pulled in at the same spot, in 1992, after our month on the river, we found the mosquitoes just as troublesome.

Finally, Sawyer stops gabbing. We fall into a cadence together. I love watching his stroke. It is strong, smooth, unhurried, one of the sweetest paddling motions I've ever seen. It is a joy to work with. I'd love to take credit, but it's all his. I time my strokes to match. The canoe planes through the water, the day still young. The only sound is the slight splash of our bow wave, and the swirl of paddle through river.

This place—the mantra of my strokes, the canoe tearing through the satin tension of river, the wordless rhythm with a partner—is as close to meditation as I ever get. The other boats recede. The life I will return to recedes. My sorrow for the river fades away. We hum downstream together, strong and sleek and practiced.

Then, around a bend, just when I have stopped expecting it, the confluence. We both quit paddling. The canoe drifts toward the meeting of great rivers, a timeless junction. Still, we say nothing, just look ahead, riding our momentum.

Suddenly, Sawyer stands up. He pulls off his hat, tugs his T-shirt over his shoulders, steps out of his shorts, stands naked in the bow. Looking at him, I don't think, *There's my baby*, or *There's my boy*. I think, *There's my son*. Right there.

He stoops to grab the gunwale and vaults lightly out of the boat, into the river we have lived with for nearly a month and ridden on for more than five hundred miles. The river we have literally immersed in much of every day. It is absolutely the right thing to do, swim with it to the end.

I stand up, strip out of my clothes, jump into the Yellowstone. The canoe rocks, empty, next to us. Behind us, Ruby and Marypat are doing the same. Eli, in the inflatable, simply tips over. We all feel the river, the last of it, sullied and anemic as it has become. It caresses our skin, slips around and past us.

Some of the very molecules rubbing against my chest, slipping past my legs, may have dripped off the snout of a snowfield high in the Absaroka mountain wilderness of northern Wyoming, pure enough to drink, glistening briefly in the summer sun before joining the small trickle of clear water rolling downhill over the first lip of bedrock, picking up speed, purling into the lush, flower-studded alpine meadows under the shadow of Younts Peak.

PART III · RUBY
THE SEAL RIVER AND THE RIO GRANDE

RUBY—BALANCING WOMAN—IN THE MIDST OF DESERT SCENERY.

Forty-Four

I lie in bed and feel my body rhythms. I wonder at the meeting of this small, new person. Knowing this is the last time I'll be pregnant and carry life is sad, yet the birth momentum is so overwhelming. The emotions are hard to stay with.

—MARYPAT, RUBY'S BIRTH BOOK

"Okay," Marypat snuggled against me in bed. It was very late. We hadn't seen each other in five days. "I'm ready. You can make the appointment."

She was just back from her annual women's trip, a loosely organized event that usually takes place in September, but sometimes June, and that, despite the fluid and sporadic logistics, had been happening every year for more than a decade. The only constant was that it was a women-only jaunt and that Marypat and Ursula were the unfailing, steady participants. They had floated the Yellowstone, hiked in Glacier, explored Idaho's Sawtooth Range. Groups ranged in size from four to fifteen. Marypat usually managed to get all participants to disrobe for a photo session in some spectacular scenery. Sawyer was the only boy ever to go along, because that year he was a nubile three months old and still nursing.

This year, five women hiked up onto the West Boulder Plateau of the Beartooth Mountains, in Montana. I was home with the two boys, getting a taste of single-parent reality. For the better part of a week, the women roamed the alpine plateaus above tree line, and Marypat spent a good deal of time off by herself, an escape from the demands of our two toddling boys, a time to pause, just her, with her thoughts and the luxury of space, a commodity she hadn't enjoyed in years.

On the final day, they descended into a tributary valley of the Boulder River, following a trail marked on the map. Only, as they got into the trees, the trail disappeared. They were too far along and the day too gone to turn back, so they bushwhacked ahead, casting about for the elusive path, clambering over blowdown, fighting through thickets, following the stream as best they could. Bear sign was thick—impressive grizzly tracks, mounds of fresh scat.

While there may once have been a maintained trail deserving a dotted line when the topographic map was produced, the valley had reverted to wild habitat, one, apparently, popular with bears. What should have been half an afternoon's walk turned into an eight-hour marathon. The group staggered, triumphant, scratched, and bruised, back onto the road as twilight settled in.

Meantime, I was home with the boys preparing dinner for Mom. And then waiting. Eventually we ate. Still later I put the boys to bed. It grew gray with twilight, then full dark. I thought about the accidents that might have delayed them. I conjured car wrecks, rock slides, bear encounters; I both feared and longed for the inevitable phone call. Finally, around ten, the phone rang.

"We're at the Road Kill Café," she said. "It was a nightmare getting out. I'm sorry we're so late, but we had to bushwhack for miles." I could hear a jukebox in the background, the babble of conversations. I pictured the scene at the funky café on the county road south of Big Timber. I swallowed my worry and frustration, gave in to relief.

"Come soon," I said.

By the time Marypat got home, looked at her boys, took a shower, and went to bed, it was the next day. The bedroom window was open. Summer breeze washed in. A train rumbled through town. We held each other.

"I really thought it over on this trip," she said. "I spent a lot of time just sitting on rocks or hiking up some knoll by myself. I needed head space. And I'm okay with you getting a vasectomy. I really am. It's time."

After Eli's birth, I had brought up the option of a vasectomy. One kid, after all we had gone through, was a terrific gift, perfectly adequate, to my way of thinking. Marypat was not so inclined.

After Sawyer, I called for an appointment. The doctor insisted that we both come in to discuss the operation.

"Vasectomies are very difficult to reverse," he told us. "It is something you both need to be wholehearted about. Believe me, it can lead to real issues in your relationship if you're not together on this."

I was happy with two children. I also struggled with the ethics of adding more people to the population juggernaut.

"I'm comfortable with it," I said.

"I can't say that," Marypat said.

"You need to think about this some more," the doctor told us.

Months went by. A year.

When it came up, Marypat remained ambivalent.

"I understand," she would say. "And I agree, but I can't get myself to block that possibility. What if we lost one of the boys?"

Marypat was nursing Sawyer. She took to motherhood like she takes a mountain, with joy and pride and certitude. She liked being pregnant, nurturing life in her womb, feeling it through the months. Later, she reveled in the contact, in her role as the provider of nourishment, even in working on Eli's potty training. And she was a natural mother. She read no parenting guides, didn't pay attention to the latest fad in child rearing. She responded instinctively, surely, firmly and with love.

I remained a peripheral figure, at least from my perspective, much as I had during the pregnancy. I did my part, but as long as nursing continued, the biological connection was hers. Motherhood was her ambition, her career, and very little distracted her.

The morning after Marypat's midnight announcement, I called and made an appointment.

Less than a week later, Marypat realized that she was pregnant.

And the week after that, I went through with the vasectomy.

So Ruby's was not a planned arrival. Then again, in our case, none of our children were expected.

Eli erupted out of despair after years of failure, and after we had given up hope. Sawyer ambushed us—quickly, subtly, and completely counter to conventional wisdom. Ruby only reinforced our tradition.

Now that I know Ruby, it's hard not to suspect that she willed herself into being through sheer force of character.

"This little soul really wanted to be here," Marypat said when her contractions started during the early morning of May 8, 1995. Once again, she had relished the pregnancy; the fact that it was her last lent it special significance. The boys were in the loop, but pretty confused. They kept patting Marypat's belly, feeling the kicks, demanding attention.

By our third time, we were veterans of home births. We couldn't imagine why people would subject themselves to a hospital for a normal delivery. Marypat invited a gaggle of friends and relatives to attend. Her contractions intensified during the morning.

All day, Marypat loomed around the house, hands cradling her heavy belly. She was a warm globe of expectant energy, finishing the flurry of household chores she'd taken on over the final week, succumbing to that nesting, gathering, putting-in-order impulse. People came and went. The boys rammed around in the background.

By late afternoon, the contractions intensified. The party moved to the bedroom. From my point of view, the crowd and festive atmosphere were distracting, almost inappropriate. The boys' births had been intimate and hushed, private. This felt like a festival. All of these friends were appreciative and sensitive, but the room was a hubbub of side conversations.

I kept leaning in next to Marypat, trying to make contact. Every so often the heart-rate monitor issued that fast, gushing pulse, life poised at the brink, biding its time, lingering in the murky darkness. Marypat lay on her back, propped up with pillows.

"I want to feel the head come this time," she said. "It isn't the best position, but I want to see it all."

The head did come. Marypat felt for the emerging crown of skull. She grinned, sighed, pushed. Sweat beaded her face. I put my hand out, supporting the head. Marypat pushed again, tore a little, and the baby slithered out in a rush of wet skin.

"Oh, it's a girl!" Marypat's mother cried.

A girl, but her face was deep blue, the color of Concord grapes. The cries of emotion and celebration died away. The midwife cut the umbilical cord, wrapped around the baby's neck. Silence. We watched this blue face, a strangled face. Then she breathed. She cried. The blue faded away, replaced by pink rising like a thermometer. Everyone in the room started breathing again.

Ruby. We'd known all along if it was a girl, it would be Ruby. Eli would have been Ruby. Sawyer would have been Ruby. I had accused Marypat of holding out for a girl and for the chance to finally use her favorite name.

For years, Marypat taught a water aerobics class for seniors. The classes were full of archaic names—Rose, Ione, Hilda, Wilma—names of our grandparents' generation. And Ruby. Marypat loved that name. It had gone out of favor and was saddled with the taint of the "Ruby, don't take your love to town" song lyrics, but all along, it was going to be our daughter's name, if she ever arrived.

Ruby took to Marypat's breast, started to nurse, eyes wide open, staring into her mother's face. Her brothers leaned in close, bumping against each other to see their sister.

Marypat and I had made a pact destined to confuse school systems for years. Boys got my last name, girls got hers. So Ruby became a Zitzer, but I won the contest over middle names—Sage.

Forty-Five

While Marypat and I start organizing the bomb debris, the boys work on their own agendas, the dialog from which goes something like this.

"I gotta go pee."

"Where's my bear?"

"Can I have a sucker?"

"I gotta go pee, now!"

"Just a second, Eli."

"I wanna take all these books."

"Don't touch that, Sawyer! It's a cactus. Remember, we talked about that"

"Dad, I want new pants."

"Why?"

"Cause I peed in these ones."

—AL, PERSONAL JOURNAL

Picture this: the Subaru, laden like a gypsy wagon, comes to a stop in front of the muddy river. Doors fly open as if a grenade has gone off inside, exploding children's books, garbage, toys, packs, paddles, and people—several quite short and exhibiting the frenzied energies stored up over the twenty-five hundred miles between Montana and Mexico.

Ruby's official birth river is the Rio Grande, along the Mexico border and Big Bend National Park. In February of 1995, Marypat, seven months huge with Ruby, and I gathered ourselves in an appalling leap of parental faith and drove a Subaru station wagon topped by a red canoe and crammed with our outfit, along with our two toddler sons, ages two and three, from Montana to Mexico.

Four days later, on the riverbank near Lajitas, Texas, we shoehorned everything from the car into a single seventeen-foot canoe, abandoned the vehicle, and spent two weeks navigating the canyons along the border, riding the meager shallows of a drought-stricken river that hadn't seen rain amounting to more than a sprinkle in a decade.

Fourteen years later, when we pull out of our Montana driveway in our Honda van with 210,000 miles on the odometer, it has been twenty below zero for a week. The kids are skipping school to augment the Christmas holiday. The car is packed to the roof with our gear. The canoe doubles as a roof rack, with five river bags stuffed inside, but, even so, we can't see out the rearview mirror. The bow line of the canoe is a frozen clump of rope I had to chip free of the ground with a shovel. It won't thaw until somewhere around Cheyenne, Wyoming, more than five hundred miles south.

I have had my doubts about this. Every expedition requires overcoming the urge to stay home. Every trip means building momentum, starting the tasks. There is always the temptation to let it slide.

This time it was especially difficult. We had to wrestle the itinerary into Christmas vacation and take extra time away from school. We couldn't afford it. My freelance work had come to a standstill in the tanking economy. We hadn't gotten a Christmas tree. We sent no holiday cards. The house stood uncharacteristically dark and undecorated.

"We can't very well not do a trip for Rubes," I said to Marypat in November, when the odds didn't look good.

"I know," she said, "but it's going to be really challenging to pull it off."

We started dehydrating food eight days before leaving. It was all we could do to pull our resources together, empty the bank accounts, prepare food, and overcome the grief of missing the holiday at home. The night before, we were up until midnight, still packing, digging the canoe out of the snow in the dark, finding river shoes, checking the food list, nagging the kids to bring their extra homework, writing a note for the house sitter. I felt, even late on the eve of departure, that it might not happen.

Next morning, in the dark, frigid December predawn, we piled into the car, backed out of the driveway, and creaked out of Bozeman.

"I'm already exhausted," Marypat said.

I reached across and squeezed her leg. "Denver, here we come," I said, and my words sounded as lame as they felt.

But the Rio Grande was not Ruby's first coming-of-age trip. The first took place the previous July, and it was all her doing.

Ever since our summer on the Kazan, Ruby had mourned the northern tundra and the deep wilderness we dove into there. Despite the difficulties we had faced on that journey—the bugs, the torment of headwinds, the grueling miles across lakes—the spell of that northern fastness had latched hold. I recognized the condition. It is one I share.

On the Yellowstone, she had pinpointed the contrast between true wilderness and a wild river subjected to the gauntlet of civilization. I watched her look around at the vehicles passing, the houses sprinkled across the landscape, and the towns we coasted through, and make her comparisons. It had made me want to defend the Yellowstone, but I knew exactly what she was feeling.

On our other backcountry excursions, even in the most untamed country in Montana, you could see her assessing, and you could see that Montana didn't measure up. Not when you'd paddled hundreds of miles without sign of humans. Not when you'd been surrounded by the ghosts of the Inuit. Not when you'd walked up to musk ox. Not when you'd lived week on week within endless rolling space, and the exultation of it roared in you like fire.

Hers was the same mourning Marypat and I had experienced after returning from our long expeditions in the North. It had taken us months to regain our footing in civilization, to stop cringing before the sensory bombardment, to put away our loss and cope with the business of life in society. We recognized Ruby's grief. We loved her for it.

"I want to go back north," she kept saying. "I miss the tundra."

"I know, sweetie," we would say. "I know. But it's a hard thing to pull off."

"I'll help," she said. And she meant it.

Back in 1982, Marypat and I took our first canoe expedition together on the North Seal River in Manitoba. I had just moved to Montana to be with Marypat and try my hand at a freelance writing career. Before we even found a house to rent, we hopped on her BMW 750 and took off across country on a motorcycle tour. In Wisconsin, we met four friends, parked the bike, and headed north.

It was the trip that began our passion for Canadian wilderness and for extended canoe journeys. Marypat was already an accomplished outdoorswoman and athlete. She picked up canoeing skills quickly, thrived on river life. The Seal was the inaugural journey in a decade of trips that led to our yearlong immersions and to the beginning of our family.

When Ruby lobbied for a return north, I knew we couldn't manage another tundra expedition, but I started looking at the boreal wilderness just south of the Barrens. If we could put it together right, we might avoid the expense of plane flights and still travel through pristine wilderness, even if it wouldn't be pure tundra. I started looking at Manitoba.

I had always been curious about the southern branch of the Seal, and when I studied the maps I realized that it might just be possible to put together a sweet logistical package that would allow us to drive to the put-in, leave our car, and take the train back to our van from Churchill, Manitoba, at the other end. We'd have to portage across the height of land between the Churchill River system and the drainage of the South Seal. It would entail forty miles of ocean paddling on Hudson Bay from the mouth of the Seal to the town of Churchill, through densely populated polar bear habitat.

But it looked doable and financially in reach. And it would take Marypat and me back to country we hadn't seen in twenty-five years.

"Ruby, it won't be tundra, at least not until we get close to Hudson Bay," we said. "We won't see musk ox and probably not caribou. But it is a remote, beautiful, really wild place. It will feel like coming back north."

"Bomb-diggity," she said. "Let's go."

"I'm in," Sawyer echoed.

"A whole month on the river?" Eli said. "All of July? I don't think so."

Forty-Six

We all complain about sore butts and backs. We got lucky tonight with a sandy beach covered in dead trees, with enough room to pitch the tent. We talk of Eli and miss him. The kids swim every night. Dragonflies are abundant and there are lots of tracks in the sand—moose, wolf, otter.

—MARYPAT, GROUP JOURNAL

On July Fourth we celebrate by slogging fourteen miles in a pestering wind on Southern Indian Lake. At lunch, Marypat complains of a muscle strain in her side. Southern Indian Lake is part of the Churchill River system, in northern Manitoba, a vast body of water, dammed at the outlet as part of an extensive hydropower project along the drainage. The dams have raised the lake enough to drown trees along the shores and change the topography significantly from what our maps show. Navigation is a fuzzy process, and most of the shoreline is littered with dead trees, piled like pick-up sticks.

I had imagined beaches and sloping bedrock, beautiful camps around every corner. Instead, most of the shore is bouldery and dense with vegetation or jammed up with dead trees, inhospitable as porcupine quills. Near the end of the long day, a narrow strip of beach pulls us in at the base of a sandy cliff. It is the first manageable camp we've found in miles. Even at that, we have to jockey space for the tent between the wave line and a barrier of dead trees.

By the time we camp, Marypat is stiff with pain. Sawyer and Ruby organize the tent while she stretches and I comfort her. She turns to me and I hug her, rubbing her back.

"I miss him," she says abruptly. "He's my first baby. I thought I was prepared for this. I didn't think I'd miss him so much." She cries in my arms.

Eli, this same day, is water-skiing with friends and watching fireworks from a lakeshore in Montana. His absence is a hole in our family, evident in the empty space in the car, the lack of his voice in our conversations, the loss of his paddle stroke during the day and his picture drawing in the tent at night. For Marypat, it is the severing of a biological tether, as visceral as umbilical cord.

For months, I had assumed we'd overcome his resistance, talk him into our plans the way we always had. He has always come around before, and even when his capitulation has been grudging, he never held it against us, always participated wholeheartedly. Not this time.

"If it was two weeks, no problem," he kept telling us. "But it's a whole month, right in the middle of summer. I want to be with my friends. I want to work and make some money. Most of all, I want to go to a soccer camp."

Eli is now sixteen years old. He has his driver's license. Many weekends we hardly see him between Friday afternoon and Sunday at dinner. He is staying at friends' houses, going to parties, dancing, attending football and basketball games. He isn't sullen or rebellious. He hasn't rejected us. His priorities are simply elsewhere. When this trip came up, it was nowhere on his horizon. After weeks of negotiations, it became clear that this summer, while we could force him to go, he would not join us willingly.

His ambition has always revolved around soccer, a game he has played well since kindergarten. During his freshman season, playing with the varsity high school team, he made a cut going for the ball against a defender and his knee buckled under him. I was on the sideline. I watched him try to get up, only to collapse again. While I jogged around the end of the field, he crawled to the bench. Over the next few days, we confirmed that he'd torn the ACL in his left knee, a common sports injury and a season-ending one.

Within weeks he had surgery to repair the ligament. He spent the winter in physical therapy and at the gym. The following spring, he played club soccer on his repaired knee and seemed fine. In the fall, during the first game of the high school season, he went up for a header and came down funny. He heard his knee pop.

After what seemed to me a pretty cursory exam, the surgeon proclaimed that he'd retorn the same ACL and would need another surgical repair.

"No way." Eli was adamant and angry. "And even if I do have surgery, I'm not going to him."

Both the diagnosis and the leap to a surgical conclusion seemed flippant. To subject the knee of a fifteen-year-old to that level of surgical trauma twice in less than a year, without considering other opinions...we shook hands and walked out of the office.

On impulse, I called a physical therapist I knew whose daughters both played soccer. One of his girls had torn her ACL, and he had overseen her successful rehabilitation. She had gone on to play at college.

"I want to see that knee," he said. "Bring him in at five tonight."

He spent two hours with Eli. Marypat and I might as well have not been there. For the first time, a doctor spoke directly to Eli, spoke plainly. He took Eli's MRI results and broke them down meticulously, testing the knee to confirm his own findings. He looked at how Eli stood, checked his muscular development, asked him to walk, climb stairs, stand from a sitting position.

"The ACL is certainly damaged," he concluded, "but I don't think it's completely torn. I want to give him exercises and a regimen to follow. The worst-case scenario, if he eventually needs surgery, is that his knee will be in better shape. In the best case, we can rehab the knee, address the muscle imbalance that brought this injury on in the first place, and see about playing with a brace."

He gave Eli strengthening exercises and stretches. He instructed him on how to properly go up and down stairs, how to sit in a chair, how to stand up. He confronted him about his responsibility, his future, his hopes. For the first time, a doctor gave him power over his body. For the first time in a year of rehabilitation and surgery, a doctor tried to figure out why this injury had happened in the first place and set about to correct it.

Eli emerged from that visit transformed. He had gone in depressed, angry, envious of his healthy friends; but when he came out, he had a plan. He had determination and hope and specific things he could do.

Our son became a gym rat, and by the final weeks of the fall season, he was practicing again, wearing a brace, and playing a few minutes in games.

When we found a summer soccer camp in Chicago, and Marypat's sister offered Eli a place to stay, we gave in.

But it didn't prepare us to hug him in the driveway early that July morning and then drive away. All of us were stricken with emotion. Eli looked both forlorn and eager, being left behind for the first time but also looking forward to a month of independence.

"Don't forget. We'll try to call you with the satellite phone on July 10," I reminded him. Marypat and I didn't trust ourselves to talk for the first ten miles out of town, heading east toward Bozeman Pass, into the sunrise.

It is twelve hundred miles from Bozeman to Thompson, Manitoba. We covered seven hundred of them the first day, through the July heat, the browning plains of eastern Montana, north into the Canadian prairies, around the city of Regina, into the cleared brush and fields, trending north. Much of the day we paralleled the Yellowstone River. I recognized campsites on gravel bars, wave trains we'd swum together holding hands, bald eagles roosting in cottonwoods, the diversion dam at Intake, the irrigation canals brimming with water destined for sugar beet fields.

"Remember that windstorm?" Sawyer said, north of Glendive, Montana. "I had sand where the sun don't shine."

"Thanks for that, buddy," Ruby said.

Gas started out at four dollars a gallon and went up from there. The farther north we drove, the more expensive it became. The Canadian dollar, in July, was worth a bit more than the American, and I got so I couldn't watch the gas gauge. Sixty, seventy, eight dollars a pop, in a Honda van. By the time we hit the north woods, on the second day, around The Pas and Thompson, gas must have been seven dollars a gallon. I'd swipe the credit card and walk away.

"I wonder what Eli's doing," one of us would say a couple of times each day.

We'd arranged to leave our car at a campground in Thompson and pay for a driver to accompany us to our put-in on the Churchill River. At the end of our trip, we'd catch the train known as the Tundra Express south from Churchill to Thompson, and the same driver would meet us at the station.

Thompson has the feel of a staging point. Its economy is based on a vast nickel mine, but it has a floatplane base and airport full of bush planes and ancient DC-3 freighters supplying fishing lodges and northern mines. Right out of town, the roads deteriorate, soon turn to dirt.

The drive to the put-in at the small Indian village of Southern Indian Lake consumes the better part of a day and another whopping tank of gas. Our driver lingers at the launch, talking to the local Natural Resources officer and watching us assemble our two folding canoes. It is sunny and warm. The mosquitoes are light. A short-tailed weasel whisks around the edges of our commotion. We confront the fact that we've forgotten our folding camp chairs.

"Damn," I say. "I hate it when that happens."

"Well, we managed for years without them," Marypat adds. "We can do it again."

Between the winding road and a complicated shoreline, I'm not sure which way to paddle when we start. I bend over the map, check the sun. The Resources officer points the way.

Within a mile, we pass a ferry dock where the dirt road makes a bridgeless crossing of a narrows. Three or four young men stride to the end of the metal boat deck to watch us pass. The currents swirl through the pinch of land. We have to paddle hard to make headway.

"Where are you going?" one of them calls across the water.

"Churchill," I say.

A long silence while we keep stroking forward.

"How far is that?" another one asks.

"Four hundred miles," I answer.

The ferry slowly recedes, with the gallery of young men who live in the boreal North but for whom, I imagine, Churchill might as well be Paris. The horizon of lake opens before us. Islands punctuate the blue view. Four hundred miles seems a long distance, one stroke at a time. The hundreds of miles we drove, the country we crossed, the worn interior of our cluttered van, the people back home who are going on with summer plans—all of it recedes. And Eli, severed from us, on his own.

Forty-Seven

At the north end of Little Sand Lake, a shallow stream leads to a small lake, paddle to extreme end of this pond, then portage over esker (height of land) 200 and some paces... Portage trail starts in bay at the N.W. corner of this lake, the loonshit shoreline makes it difficult to land and unload, trail is wet but passable.

—TRAPPER'S NOTES ON OLD MAP OF THE LAND OF LITTLE STICKS, WHICH COVERS MUCH OF
NORTHERN MANITOBA

A week in, we face the climb out of the Churchill River system toward the divide of land separating it from the South Seal River, the first real crux of the expedition. The drowned lake funnels down to a set of narrows and constricted channels, until it finally pinches off to Big Sand River, a robust title for what amounts to a winding creek. Side by side, the canoes enter the mouth, the underwater weeds streaming out against us. We begin our ascent, stroke by stroke.

From the comfort of home, and with the luxury of distance, Big Sand River looked like a tiny portion of a long itinerary, one twisting link in a chain looping across hundreds of miles. How bad could it be?

At the start, the alley-wide focus, the bends full of lily pads, the shift from days of open water and long crossings and windbound camps is refreshing. Sawyer spots northern pike flicking away into weed beds. Ruby reaches for lilies. Bends fall away, the horizon narrows down to the wooded valley and the next turn. Breezes blow in the treetops, but at the water level it is still, the sun warm, glinting with dragonfly wings. A kingfisher bolts from an overhanging branch, calls harshly.

The upstream rhythm settles in, reeling the canoes up past sandbanks, quiet backwaters, beaver slides, stirring forest. I picture the aerial view, the spread of lake we leave behind, the long hump of land we are starting across, and ahead, several days away, winding its own steady course full of unknowns on its way to Hudson Bay, the Seal.

The banks close in, the creek bends back on itself in tight coils. Here and there trees topple across the stream. We duck under where we can, slip past the tips of branches, occasionally have to get out and jockey the canoes through debris. One or two shallow, rocky riffles force us into the water to haul our way past. The mosquitoes swarm thick enough to force us into our bug shirts and head nets for the first time.

I spot one or two openings where a camp might be possible, but the forest is dense, the ground lumpy, the banks steep and muddy. I enjoy the intimacy of the stream, the opportunity to peer into the woods, see game trails, smell the dirt. But what began as a sun-dappled change of pace becomes increasingly like work.

Logjams become more frequent. Every bend has a litter of dead trees to work past. More shallow riffles force us to wade, hauling boats. Now and then, fallen trees completely barricade the channel. We have brought a cheap army-surplus saw to cut up small driftwood for fires, but we have nothing to deal with these full-size trees. At every blockage, we have to shove the boats either under or over the trees. The bark is slippery. We fall in. The fabric boat hulls are vulnerable. We saw off tree branches and sharp stubs to limit the damage, but the abuse is unavoidable.

Another obstacle on the way up Big Sand River.

For a while the challenge is fun. Sawyer and Ruby rise to it the way they do to a bushwhack around a waterfall on a hiking trail. We work our way around, under, over, between the debris, lose ourselves in the diversion. But it goes on and on. The mosquitoes swarm around our heads. The thickets of logs come around every bend. The shallows become more numerous. We lose count of the logs we heave the loaded canoes over—forty, fifty, one hundred?

On one bend, the jam of trees is so huge there is no way to negotiate it. The banks are sheer ten-foot walls of mud. I clamber up into the forest, scout to the upstream bend of river, and we start to portage. The hard part is getting everything up the bank through knee-deep mud and then back down on the other side.

By this time, the novelty is a distant memory. I'm wondering if the creek might wall us off altogether and thinking about what plan B might be if we can't continue. What looked like a minor wrinkle in our itinerary on the map goes on and on. Bend after bend, logjam after logjam. In and out of the boats, bugs clouding our heads, feet slipping on sharp rocks.

It is not without comedy. On one tree, Sawyer and I perch above the boat and prepare to wrestle it over once again. The log is slippery, the bark loose. I slip off on the upstream side, get wet to the waist, get back up, then slide off on the downstream side, dunk again.

"Jeez, Dad," Sawyer says, helping me up. Marypat and Ruby are convulsing in their boat, waiting their turn, doubled over at my muddy antics. I narrowly avoid going in a third time before the canoe is across.

"I must be tired," I confess. "I'm certainly not that uncoordinated, eh, Sawyer?"

"Whatever you say, Daddio," he agrees.

At one point I think I hear voices. "Did you hear that, Sawyer? It sounds like someone yelling in the distance."

"I hear it, but I don't know what it is." We stop to listen.

Then Sawyer points to the bank. "Wolves," he whispers.

We were hearing wolves howling, and here on the bank two wolf pups pop out to have a look at us. One has the coloring of a German shepherd. The other is tawny white. They are twenty feet away. They scamper off into the tall grass. Ruby and Marypat come around the bend behind us.

"Wolf pups!" Sawyer says. "Right there."

"Are they gone?" Ruby laments.

Just then they appear again on the bank, looking at us, heads cocked, ears perked, fuzzy puppies. "Oh my god," Ruby says. "They are so cute."

They keep coming out, looking us over, then dashing off. We continue, rejuvenated, but weary. More bends.

The canoes are full of sticks and moss and mud. Our packs are grimy. We are all soaked to the waist, dead tired, but the creek won't end.

"I don't know how much longer we can go," I say at one point.

"I know," Marypat agrees. "If we see a camp we should stop."

But there are no camps. We slog up more shallows. I notice lily pads again. Perhaps that's a good sign. I'm not banking on anything. In the distance I hear a loon calling. I picture it on a lake. It has to be on a lake. But it could also be flying overhead, on its way anywhere. The creek keeps bending its tortuous way. At each turn, I anticipate relief, an open vista, the spreading water of Little Sand Lake. At each bend, I am disappointed.

It is very late. The summer light is gray. We have probably gone twenty tortured miles. I am getting sloppy and careless. I don't care. I feel every one of my fifty-five years.

And then it dawns on me that we have arrived. The shallow creek has widened into a lily-skirted bay. We paddle into the twilight calm of lake. We paddle directly across to a densely wooded point. We will camp here. We don't care if we have to sleep on boulders.

The tent just squeezes into a tiny alcove between spruce trees. It is all we can do to boil water and cook a simple pot of food. I don't taste it. We topple into the lumpy beds. They feel exquisite, five-star; I've never felt better mattresses. I will not think about tomorrow.

But tomorrow comes.

When it does, I wake in the frail light of new day and wait, listening. There is something satisfying about a camp in a thicket of forest, something camouflaged and secret, a place someone might pass right by without noticing. That primordial impulse to be hidden, watching, assessing. But I wait for the loon.

The call of loons has become my talisman, my touchstone. After a windbound rainy day early on, I woke at dawn, just as I have this day. It was utterly still. Then I heard a splash in front of camp, followed by the clear, close yodel of a loon. I took it as a benediction. I gave thanks. It reminded me of the need to be grateful, each day, in a conscious way.

Each day since, at dawn, I have heard a loon. Each day, we have made our way successfully forward. It hasn't always been easy, but we have managed. More than that, we have found good camps, reached our goals, made our crossings, been blessed by conditions.

I have no idea if it means anything or whether I am indulging my superstitious side. Being grateful feels absolutely right. And the loon calls have been eerily consistent. I don't know whether these are signs that always hover in the air and that I only occasionally tune in to receive, or whether it is personal.

The fact is, when I hear the loons, it gives me peace and comfort and a sense of well-being. The how and why of it doesn't matter.

I have come, more and more, to believe that the way we are in the world actually has an impact on the world. When we are respectful, joyous, grateful, engaged, the world responds to that in concrete ways. When we are angry and resentful, or selfish or bitter, things sour around us.

This day I lie in the lumpy moss, sheltered in the shadowed forest, half a continent from home, and listen. I want to get up, but I wait. I think back across the days, fixing camps in my memory. I drift, hearing my family breathe and stir. And then two loons fly over, calling to each other. In the stillness I can hear their wings beating through the air above the trees.

At the end of Little Sand Lake, the next challenge lies across our path, a short blue squiggle on the map linking up to the next lake. The connection is no more than half a mile, but as we paddle into the green reeds at the tip of a finger of lake, there is no sign of it. We probe here and there in the boats and finally find a trickle of current oozing through the mud.

Our canoes enter the dubious filament, push forward. Fifty yards in, it becomes too shallow to paddle, so we step out—and immediately sink to our crotches. The mud sucks at our shoes, lets off a sulfur stench.

"Wow," Ruby says. "This is interesting."

"Hold on," Marypat pauses. "I gotta get a picture of this."

It gets worse. Across the patch of mud, the channel enters a morass of swampy woods.

"Short of dynamite and machetes, there is no way," I say, peering ahead.

A low rise of drier land sits to our right. "Wait here for a sec," I say, climbing out of the water, "I'm going to take a look."

Keeping the alder-thick drainage in sight, I work my way forward through swampy ground. Moose tracks pock the mud. Game trails come and go. In a few minutes, I find my way to the next lake. It isn't far, but the route is mucky and indirect. On the return, I move logs out of the way and recon the most direct, unobstructed path.

"We can portage," I announce when I get back.

"Good," Marypat says, swatting bugs in front of her face, "because there is no way we're getting up this thing."

The day proceeds in this stuttering pattern, dead-ends followed by reprieves.

The actual height of land is a high, sandy esker ridge with a snowmobile trail over it. We hump the canoes and gear steeply up to the top and steeply back down. It is that quarter mile, a thin line of sandy high ground, that separates two major drainages. Presumably, from here, the water flows with us.

But when we search for the outlet stream we hope to follow out of the first lake, there is nothing, no break in the shore, not even a faint trickle slipping downhill.

We munch our lunch in the canoes, feeling the spread of country, trackless country, extending hundreds of miles on a side. We bend our heads in a close huddle over the map.

"What about this spot here?" Sawyer points at a narrow land bridge separating the lake we're on from the next in the chain we need to follow.

"I was looking at that too," I agree. "We've been following this winter snowmobile route. If it keeps going, that's the obvious spot."

And it is there, precisely where we guessed, a vague but obvious worn trail across a marshy section of land. We portage.

Initially, I had assumed we'd go to the stream outlet from this lake to Trout Lake, but the winter trail is making me reassess. That and our luck with finding drainages with any water in them. If we follow a narrow finger of lake to its tip, another half-mile portage would bring us to the end of a bay on Trout Lake. If no trail exists, we'll have to backtrack and try the stream, losing half a day in the process, but we all agree it's worth a shot.

The passage is beautiful. The day is warm and calm. Our canoes work along narrow channels bobbing with lilies, their hefty yellow flowers wide to the sun. Be in the moment, I keep reminding myself. Don't worry about the portage. Just be right here, stroking across this mirrored, pure, unvisited space with its hum of summer life.

"God, this is beautiful!" Marypat gushes. She has no problem being in the moment. Never has.

At the end of the lake, we park along a beach. Sawyer steps out. "Bear tracks," he says, looking at the sand. "Fresh ones."

More to the point, there is no obvious trail. No obscure trail. No sign of any trail at all. We range up and down the shore, looking for a break in the mossy woods.

More map study. The distance between lakes isn't far, but the forest is dense. If we're off by a couple of degrees in a compass bearing and have to wind our way through, we could miss the bay completely. The possibility of getting badly lost is very high.

I take a bearing. We spread out and walk in a line, casting about for signs. There are some promising game trails, but they peter out or head off in the wrong direction. The trees are dense enough that horsing a canoe through would be really difficult. We keep calling to each other.

At another spot down the lakeshore we do the same thing, heading in, looking for some sign of a path. I break twigs off of trees to mark my way back. The idea of blindly following a compass bearing that may or may not be accurate spooks the hell out of me.

"Damn," I say when we regroup at the canoes. "I would have sworn the snowmobile trail would go this way."

"Well, if we have to retrace, we have to," Marypat says. "Let's paddle all the way around the end of this bay. If we can't find a trail, we'll have to head back."

Sawyer and I take the lead. We coast past the wooded shore, fifteen feet out, looking for anything. Along the far side of the bay, a mucky wide spot entices us in. It doesn't look promising, but we land anyway. Ruby and Marypat hover offshore.

"Hey," Sawyer stoops over. "A hatchet." He holds up a rusted tool, the broken wooden handle wrapped with black electrical tape.

I scramble over the load to shore. We start searching in earnest. Then we find some small logs lined in a ramp across the mud. It leads into the woods, where a path picks up. The trail widens. Marypat and Ruby join us. Energized, we hike over the rise. The rusted carcass of a snowmobile rests off to one side. Bear scat steams on the trail. Half a mile later, Trout Lake greets us.

"Yes!" I shout, triumphant. We all high-five. The day has been long, but we almost trot the loads across, making noise to warn bears.

Again, it is late by the time we paddle the shores of Trout Lake, but we are exuberant. It has been a very good day. One more day and the descent of Trout Creek will bring us to the Seal.

I have already studied the map ahead. Trout Creek looks like an encore of Big Sand Creek. Winding, shallow, full of trees, if it has water at all. However, down the shore of Trout Lake, at the back of a shallow bay, I've found what appears to me to be the obvious route a snowmobile trail would follow. It involves a mile-long portage to a small, round lake. Across that lake, another portage, perhaps a mile, connects to the Seal. It is so obvious that I could be convinced to go right there and not even bother checking out Trout Creek. But that's tomorrow.

This evening, a pair of otters cavort in some rocks as we stroke past. Around a point, a crescent sand beach screams camp. No team of engineers could make a more exquisite, smooth, perfect curve of sand. We are tired, but not as tired as the day before. There is energy to swim and wash. The site is about as ideal and picturesque as a person could ask for.

"What about cinnamon rolls?" Ruby asks.

"Why not?" Marypat agrees. "We've certainly earned them."

MARYPAT'S FAMOUS CINNAMON ROLLS.

Forty-Eight

Wildlife: Yellowlegs, big northern pike, 2 cow/calf moose pairs, black wolf, muskrat

Weather: Broken clouds early, becoming completely overcast. Strong, gusty east wind. Cool temps. Spitting rain in the evening.

—GROUP JOURNAL

The next morning, no loon calls.

I stay in bed a long time, listening. I am thankful, but the dawn is silent. Eventually I get up, start the fire, put coffee water on. All through breakfast I wait for it. Even a far-off wail would do.

I bring up the option of the portage but get outvoted.

"We should give the river a chance," Marypat insists. "Don't be so pessimistic. We're on the other side of the divide."

Later, I look across to the far shore as we paddle to the outlet, trying to pick out the spot we might explore if the creek isn't viable. Several miles slip away. I forget about the loon, focus ahead, keep an eye on the map. Trout Creek leads out of a shallow bay. I search for the gap of river, but the rocky, willowy shoreline looks unbroken. Trout Creek doesn't reveal itself until we are on top of it. It bends sharply off into the vegetation, a narrow gap mined with boulders.

I am paddling with Ruby and still thinking about the portage. My worry is that we'll probe our way down, committing to the creek, and then get blocked. Marypat and Sawyer stroke toward us. We hover in the first flicker of current.

At that moment, a loon flies over us, calling. The bird swoops low over our canoes, its call ringing, and flies down the lake.

"I guess we're good, Rubes," I say. "Let's go."

Right around the first bend, we startle a cow moose with a large calf. They thrash out of the water, high-stepping into the brush, then vanish. The willows close behind them like a door shutting.

Trout Creek is never generous. The flow is shallow and gentle, coasting down through marshy grasses, barely covering rocks. But it remains doable. The canoes nose along the deepest channels, gliding between rocks, finding the way. The banks are not heavily forested, so the downed trees I expected never materialize. We only rarely have to step out to free ourselves from rocks.

There is no way of telling where we are on the map. The morning passes. Another moose crashes away into the brush. Yellowlegs scold from the mudflats.

Trout Creek widens out dramatically. In every direction marsh leads away, fields of waving reeds and mucky ground. The creek becomes a sheet of water two inches deep with a barely perceptible deeper channel winding across the monotonous topography. No end in sight.

First, Ruby and I lead the way. Eventually we get hung up and have to slog through knee-deep muck back to the deeper water, while Marypat and Sawyer go by. They lead for a while, until they bottom out and we trade places. We've come too far to turn back, but this does not look good, and it seems endless.

At one point, I look behind us. Flat marsh forever. I look ahead. The same. We push on, poling against the muddy bottom as much as paddling.

Suddenly, the water gets deeper. There is something different about it. The marsh still surrounds us, but the current widens. It dawns on me, finally, that we have reached the Seal and that the marshy outlet of Trout Creek blended seamlessly into the marshy banks of the South Seal River.

We have arrived. Maybe it isn't as dramatic as Lewis and Clark crossing the Rockies or wagon trains breasting South Pass, but it feels pretty damn good. As soon as we find firm ground, we stop for lunch. It is windy and gray.

Sawyer naps in a rock "beanbag" chair.

"Let's have a fire," Ruby says. She gives me a hug.

"Don't hurt me," I plead.

She is taller than Marypat by several inches and weighs almost as much as Sawyer. You need to be ready for one of Ruby's hugs or you risk neck injury.

For most of Ruby's life, my most commonly employed adjective to describe my daughter has been *robust*. Not just physically, but in every way. In seventh grade, her gym teacher offered a Coke to anyone, boy or girl, who could beat Ruby at arm wrestling. No one ever won the bet.

She has always been a hugger, and she prefers men. Once, before she was a year old, when she was just learning to walk, Marypat and I took her with us to a lecture in town. We sat in a row of amphitheater-style chairs. There were probably thirty people in the same curved row. At one point, Ruby got fidgety and Marypat put her down. She started navigating her way along the aisle, hanging onto the seat backs.

Every time she came to a man, she stopped and put her arms up. Every woman she passed right by. She went all the way down the row, sitting happily on every man's lap for a few minutes, then continuing, and pointedly avoiding every woman.

Even now, men come up to me in town and tell me how Ruby gave them such a great hug at some recent event. They think they have a special bond with her. What I don't tell them is that half the male population of Bozeman, including the UPS driver and the mail carrier, share that bond.

The winds build all afternoon. Gusts blast the canoes. To me, whatever distance we make is gravy; I had given the day to finishing the crossing and reaching the Seal. Late afternoon, clouds scudding overhead, Sawyer points out a black shape on the far shore.

"Can't tell if it's a bear or a wolf," Marypat says.

The animal works slowly upstream along the muddy riverbank. It is black as night, large, solitary. A bear, I assume, but then it sits on its haunches and stares across at us. Unmistakably a wolf. It is not spooked. It watches us and then pads along, finally turning into the woods and slipping away like a dark wisp of smoke.

Winds howl into the next day. From camp, we battle half a mile across a bay to a sand point, where the waves pile in. To continue is folly. We remain satisfied to have made the Seal, to have the height of land behind us. Besides, it is a beautiful place.

Wild roses bloom in the sand, pink blossoms nodding in the wind. A grove of aspen offers shelter. The leaves shake and laugh overhead. White trunks contrast against gray sky and white-flecked lake. We layer on clothing, build a fire behind a windbreak, make hot drinks and eat snacks. Sawyer and Ruby each carry a stash of birchbark fire starter in a plastic bag. They carry birchbark the way people carry the key to their safe-deposit box, and they are right to do so.

The day flies past on the wind, in this sublime place where we recline and spend time together, reading, chatting, writing in journals, looking into the distance. Some families barely manage to share meals a couple of nights a week. What luxury to stall in a place of beauty and power with nothing on the agenda but being together for the day.

The next morning, before dawn, the air is still, the tent heavy and wet with dew. Mist steams up from the lake. On the water before breakfast, before sunrise, our canoes cleave the stillness. Water shimmers in dark skirts behind us.

Marypat stops and points with her paddle. A pack of five more wolves jog along the lakeshore through the mist. The sun breasts the horizon, blinding us, warming the day, sucking up the fog. The South Seal leaves the lake. Current picks up. Miles stack up, satisfying as cordwood put up against winter. Before lunch, yet another wolf, a solitary animal the color of dirty snow, watches us pass.

"This is the summer of wolves," Ruby declares.

"We get to call Eli tonight," Marypat says.

The Seal is a broad flow of water. The current bears us along. We lunch at a series of minor ledge rapids, take dips. I nap on the warm rocks. There is nothing so restorative as a twenty-minute snooze in the open air with river running past your toes.

Later, a hailstorm pummels us. We pull on full rain suits, hunch in the canoes. Pellets of ice bounce off of our heads, collect in piles on our packs. The river is beaten to a lather.

The dark storm cloud moves on, replaced by dazzling sun. I strip off layers. We paddle on. After a short rapid, the Seal widens into a wide, slow section, and a sand esker shimmers like snow ahead, where we land to camp. Another cloudburst approaches. We set up the tarp in the brooding air and dive under as the first drops wallop the fabric. Later, we climb through glistening vegetation to the crest of the esker ridge. I carry the satellite phone.

We had told Eli we would try to call him on this day. We had also been told that satellite coverage for this area was spotty. At the top of the ridge, which commands a sweeping view over the wide flats of river, the snaking esker trending into the distance, the dark mat of forest, I turn the phone on. White cumulus clouds roll overhead, casting dynamic shadows, moving fast.

For several minutes, the phone seeks a satellite. Nothing happens. Finally it locks onto one. I start to dial. Before I finish, the phone loses the connection. I keep trying. Five or six times I latch on and then lose the signal. Once or twice it lasts long enough for Eli's phone to ring on the other end, then goes dead again.

"Damn thing," I explode. I hadn't realized how much I was counting on hearing Eli's voice.

I try again. It goes dead. And again. Nothing. A third time. It rings. Rings again.

"Hello."

"Eli! It's me, Dad."

"I know it's you, Dad." I hear him chuckle.

"Listen, the phone keeps losing the signal. Eli, I love you. You have no idea how much we miss you. We hope you're having a great time, but we really, really miss you."

I stop babbling. The connection is gone again.

"Dammit!"

I turn to Marypat. "At least I got to hear his voice," I say. "He sounded fine. I just wanted to tell him we miss him and love him. Hopefully he got that much."

Ruby and Sawyer start up some antics on the sheer slope of the esker where it drops into the river. Marypat takes videos of the two of them stripping to the buff, screaming downhill, arms windmilling, and plunging into the shallow water.

Sawyer has had a recent growth spurt. He's taller than me now, can't fit into my shoes anymore. Ruby may be thirteen, but she has a woman's body. She and Eli hit puberty the same way, early and fast. Sawyer has been more incremental, but looks destined to be the tallest of the family. He may not be shaving yet, and he is skinny as a pole, but he is a man.

Back in camp, I start the dinner fire. Marypat retreats to the tent with the phone, keeps trying Eli. I hear her muttering, punching buttons. It reminds me why I hate bringing electronic intrusions with us. She snaps the box closed, takes up her book to read. But in a few minutes I hear her get the phone out again.

"Eli!" she says, suddenly. "Hi, sweetie. How are you?"

I want to rush to the tent, but resist. Instead, I listen in. It doesn't last long, but long enough for Marypat to share some trip details, tell Eli that we're on schedule and having fun, and to hear from him how his camp is going and what it's like being in Chicago.

"Oh, there he goes," she says.

It isn't much, but it's contact, it's reassurance. The phone gets put away, that maddening, tantalizing gadget. Where we are seeps back around us, the sound of his voice, the image of his face, fades again. We ache for him and try to take care of it by hugging each other.

"He sounds good," Marypat says. "He told me he lost eleven pounds in one day at the camp because it's so hot and humid. And that he had to be the designated driver one night at Janet's after a birthday party celebration."

"Great," I say. "Driving around in downtown Chicago with a bunch of drunk people. How long has he had his license?"

"Cool," Sawyer says.

"I lost my necklace," Ruby interrupts.

Apparently, in all the clothes-flinging, bug-swatting, and running-around frenzy on the face of the esker, Ruby's necklace got misplaced.

She is desolate about it. It is a necklace she was given at a special evening ceremony Marypat had for her. Her grandmother came, her aunt, a cousin, her best friends, women friends. They acknowledged Ruby, shared stories about her, talked about what being a woman meant. Everyone brought some token to signify her passage. The necklace was one of those gifts.

She and Sawyer go back and scour the sand while we finish cooking dinner. No luck. She searches again before we head to the tent, comes back crestfallen, and when we pack up the next morning she still hasn't found it.

"I'm going one more time" she says before we push off. She runs down the sand shore. We paddle slowly to the point. The day is warm and sunny. Ruby climbs halfway up the steep slope of sand, bends over near an aspen tree, roots around in some leaves and vines.

"Got it!" she sings out. "I thought it might be there." I can feel the lift in her mood from a hundred yards. She comes jogging down the sand, grinning and light. The day floods with her happiness.

For some reason, watching her, I remember the first day she got her period. I was on my way to teach a writing class in Yellowstone National Park. I had stopped at a friend's house on the way, and the phone rang.

"It's Ruby," my friend said. "She sounds upset."

"Hi, babe," I said. "What's going on?"

"Daddy," she sobbed. "I think I got my period. Mom's not home. I have to go to school. I don't know what to do."

Marypat had prepped Ruby well. This was no dark secret mystery, no spontaneous, terrifying bleeding without explanation. Ruby knew precisely what had happened, but it was still a daunting event and one she was facing alone.

"Forget the bus," I said. "Mom will be home in a little bit. Wait for her. She'll figure things out and get you to school."

"I wish you were here, Dad," she said.

"Me, too, Ruby, but hang tight. Mom will be there in a while."

I went on to my class, thinking of my little girl. Meantime, Marypat did come home. She dropped what she had planned and tended to Ruby. They went to the store for supplies. Marypat bought Ruby flowers to mark the event. They had tea together. By the time Ruby went to school, she had it under control.

Since then, the monthly trial has been anything but a mystery. "Too much information!" the boys keep protesting when Ruby and Marypat discuss their "moon blood" issues.

Forty-Nine

An idyllic day on the river. The miles came easily, the scenery was beautiful, and the weather perfect. We drifted much of the day, swam off of the boats, saw our first seals. Found a sweet camp with rapids on either side of a rocky island. Fantastic swimming. Maybe the best camp yet

—AL, GROUP JOURNAL

SAWYER FINDS A MOOSE ANTLER ON AN ESKER HIKE.

The belly of the expedition. One hundred fifty miles in, where we join the northern branch of the Seal, regaining the river Marypat and I paddled with friends a quarter of a century earlier, in the first months of our relationship. We tilt east toward Hudson Bay, entering the space in a trip that seems, for a time, completely divorced from any other life, unconnected from both past and future. A time wholly made up of this northern place and the thread of our ephemeral energy running through it. Days run together in a collage of water and sun and cloud and camps, that seamless fabric both between things and smack in the midst of things—immediate and all consuming.

Ropey weeds resisting the hulls of our canoes in the predawn shallows of Tadoule Lake…a campsite that appears after twenty miles of boulders and brush, like a gem—sand beach, smooth rock points, open forest…Marypat and I sneaking to the tent to make love while Ruby and Sawyer explore a beach…a fisher loping across the ridge of an esker we walk along, like an elongated, humpback cat…

In our bedroom at home, we have a picture taken on Shethanei Lake in 1982. I am shirtless and tanned and sport a full head of hair, and the lake is flat calm to the horizon. Twenty-six years later, we get a similar day on the same lake. Marypat has everyone pose shirtless, making muscles, with the placid lake all around.

We are using the same topographic maps we used in 1982. They still have the penciled notes from that journey, identifying camps, noting rapids, portages, with sparse descriptions. "Scouted from left, ran right of center… beautiful tundra camp, heard wolves howling…portaged on right shore, lined canoes through rapids…"

"Can you believe what whitewater wimps we were back then?" Marypat exclaims.

"I remember the water being higher on that trip, so the rapids might have been more intense, but even so, most of the rapids are pieces of cake," I agree.

Rapids that we stopped to scout, held protracted councils over how best to run, and often either portaged or lined back in 1982, we barely pause for today. The bow paddler stands up, looks it over, and down we go, making moves on the fly, easily passing through. One turbulent section in particular, known as Nine-Mark Rapid for the number of hash marks on the topo map, we took the better part of a full day to navigate the first time. This trip we stop to look a couple of times, but mostly read and run from the boats, following each other through the miles of rock garden.

"We've seen a lot of river since then," I say at the bottom. "It's pretty amazing now to see what we were intimidated by."

Islands of tundra dot the boreal forest, more of it as we approach Hudson Bay…long sets of fast water—five miles at a whack of cantering flow—the canoes nod down the miles—mesmerizing, hypnotic…a day full of forest-fire smoke, thick as twilight, later swept away by a wind shift…thirty or forty seals basking on rocks at the bottom of a wide, fast section—flipping into the river at our approach, porpoising around the canoes, black heads glistening and curious…walking the ridges of sand eskers, miles of them gleaming in the sun, beckoning us to the crests…fifteen miles, twenty-four miles, thirty miles a day, chewing our way across Manitoba…a camp on a ridge of bedrock so sharp we have to lash the canoes into some willows on the spine for the night…canyon stretch full of whitewater, sheer rock, scolding terns.

The energy of the kids lends this trip a completely different feel from our first descent, in the early days of our love affair. Then, the expedition was a serious effort, fraught through with an awareness of the depth of wilderness and the consequences of any mishap. It was exhilarating and joyous, too, but it never escaped the overlay of that what-if mentality.

The kids change that. Of course, we take our endeavor seriously, but on a hot day they think nothing of stripping down and diving out of the canoes, floating for a mile in the current. At lunch they surf in the ledges, arms stretched out, river beating against them, their smiles white in the sun. We pick camps purely for the swimming potential, stop early, frolic in a froth of whitewater for an afternoon. The kids wander off to pick cloudberries for morning pancakes. They cavort in the river shallows like the seals we see almost daily as we approach Hudson Bay.

RUBY AND SAWYER IN A WHITEWATER JACUZZI.

Setting up the tent, Ruby bends and breaks one of the tent poles. We have to splint it with a metal stake and duct tape…morning fire in a drizzle started with birchbark…a sudden cloudburst we don't have time to dress for and get drenched to the skin by, then dry in the hot sun…a cow moose reclined on the bank that lumbers up at our approach, lingers for a moment, reluctant, then trots off into the tundra mosses...agonizing day in winds, beating our way downhill...

Then, where we stop for lunch in some muddy, gravel shallows at the end of a long rapid, the abrupt end of the trip looms up when Ruby bends over a large divot in the mud. "Is that a bear track?"

It is an old one, if it is, but huge. Polar bear size, as big as a platter, sunk into the soft ground. We all bend over it, try to dismiss it. We are more than twenty miles from the ocean. It could be a dislodged rock. We can't make out any other sign of a bear nearby. I stand and look around the expanse of rock and mud and rolling tundra, miles of it lying silent and motionless. We discount it, but I can't think what else it could be.

Fifty

In 1717 the Hudson's Bay Company established the first permanent settlement at the mouth of the Churchill River to capitalize on the lucrative fur trade in interior Canada. More recently, Churchill has operated as a northern grain shipping port, serviced by slow-moving freight trains. The town is known as the Polar Bear Capital of the World and depends on tourism for much of its economy. Paddlers navigating rivers draining into Hudson Bay can take the train back south to Winnipeg.

"I want to paddle Hudson Bay," Ruby says. It has been her refrain for days.

"We'll see," I keep saying.

Ruby wants it all. The boys accuse her of being like Marypat, only worse. They both suffer from the cram-it-all-in syndrome, which makes for a full, spontaneous existence, but also leads to a frenetic, harried pace. That tension is probably the single biggest stress in my relationship with Marypat, and I feel the same rise of reaction when Ruby lobbies for options A, B, C, and D.

One day last September, Ruby and Sawyer returned from a hiking trip with some friends. They had hiked out seven miles through slush that morning. Later on, Ruby decided she wanted to go for a run on a mountain trail, but there was no one around to drive her to the trailhead. She hopped on a bike and rode eight miles, ran for six, and then rode home again.

"Jesus, Ruby," Eli exclaimed. "You're such a freak!"

Hudson Bay is the second crux of the expedition. From the mouth of the Seal to the town of Churchill, where we will catch the Tundra Express back to our car in Thompson, is forty miles. It is shallow, ocean coastline renown for shipwrecks, for sudden storms, and for tidal flats that can extend out five miles. It is also home to one of the largest concentrations of polar bears anywhere in the world. During the summer, bears lounge along the shores, and they tend to concentrate at river deltas.

A major denning area lies just south of Churchill. Female polar bears den up there in the fall, give birth to one-pound babies in midwinter, and reemerge late in winter with their cubs. Young polar bears stay with their mothers for two years or more. During their spectacular growth spurt, cubs nurse on milk that is 50 percent fat. Meantime, the rest of the population waits on land for the ice, where they escape into the frozen world. There bears subsist almost wholly on seals, which provide the body fat to keep them warm through the winter and last them through the lean summer months.

Polar bears are known to swim as much as sixty miles of open ocean to reach ice. They are also capable of sprinting at twenty-five miles an hour on land. An adult male can weigh fifteen hundred pounds and measure more than eight feet from nose to tail. It goes without saying that they sit at the pinnacle of the food chain.

When we paddled the Seal in 1982, we were confronted by a bear at the delta. What started as a picture-taking opportunity turned into a tense standoff. The bear swam toward us, cutting off our route. Our canoes were pinned on the shore while the bear swam lazily back and forth in front of us. We shouted, pounded pots, tried to look formidable, to no effect. The bear finally let us pass, and we went on to paddle successfully to town, but polar bears are a very real danger. They have no rivals besides well-armed humans and show no signs of fear. The bear that investigated us on our first trip exhibited none of the tentativeness a black bear might. It was curious about what we were, and, by God, it was going to check us out for as long as it felt like it.

We had heard that the polar bears were particularly numerous and aggressive this summer in the Churchill area. No one knew why, but according to local sources, there were a large number of bears around, and they were more confrontational than normal. No conclusions had been reached for the high numbers of cantankerous bears, but neither did anyone suggest that it was a sign of a healthy species. In fact, the general consensus was that it was more likely a sign of ecological stress.

"Maybe they're just pissed off," I had said to Marypat earlier. "Who could blame them?"

Marypat, usually game for the most challenging option, has been surprisingly vague about her commitment to paddle the ocean. While our first experience had been good, she isn't as sanguine this time around. Sawyer is as up for adventure as anyone, but he's picked up our vibes and straddles the fence.

Before leaving Bozeman, we had made contact with a man in Churchill who has a summer sideline of picking up canoe parties at the mouths of several area rivers and taxiing them in to town by boat. He was expensive. His fee alone would double the cost of our trip, but if it seemed like the safe and prudent course, we were prepared to bite the financial bullet.

"Give me a call on the sat phone when you decide," he had told me.

Our final night on the river, I angle for a balance between staying inland enough to avoid coastal bear habitat and being within striking distance of the bay. We settle on a marginal site of riverbank about a dozen miles from the ocean. The weather is cold, windy, with a driving drizzle. The following day brings more of the same.

"I think we should lay over," Marypat says in the morning. "If we go on, there's no chance we'll paddle the ocean. I know we're burning a day of our cushion, but by tomorrow it could improve and we'll have more options."

The next day it has improved somewhat but remains gray and gusty. The river has risen significantly, or the tide is in and affects the river level this far up. In either case, our fireplace is six inches under water and the door of our tent is only a few feet from the river.

"This is no weather to be on the ocean in a canoe," I say to Ruby when she repeats her desire to paddle all the way to town.

The last dozen miles of river wind through bouldery shallows, braided channels, widening delta. I keep looking for the white of bear, and I notice everyone else is especially vigilant. The coast is low and flat, covered in scrubby willows.

The most significant whitewater of the entire month, Deaf Rapid, punctuates the main channel a mile or two from the end. It isn't even marked on our maps, but when we arrive, the huge holes and waves make us pull over. The main turbulence would swallow a big raft in one gulp.

"You would not want to be out there in a canoe," Sawyer says with feeling.

We watch a seal make its way up the rapid. It barely advances against the flow. Repeatedly it flings itself out of the water, arcing forward, making its way in slow increments past the strongest current, finally gaining the slower water.

A sneak route offers itself along the near shore, skirting the dangerous water. Back at the top, we cinch into our life vests and kneel in the canoes. Ruby looks back at me, worry in her face.

"We're good, babe," I say. "Just follow the shore, stay out from the shallows, and we'll be fine."

Marypat and Sawyer follow us down. It is uneventful, even anticlimactic. I look over at the massive waves as we ride past, and then the loud rapid fades behind us.

"You can see the cabin from the last rapid," our contact had told us.

Sure enough, when our red canoes schuss down the last riffle, the plywood shack appears, river left, hunkered on a clay bench above the tidal zone. Hudson Bay opens to the east, gray water to the skyline. We pull in. I step barefoot onto the wet surface. The ground feels like a spongy rubber mat, yielding but firm.

A short aluminum ladder lies on the ground next to the building. It dawns on me that the ladder is there as an escape route. Doors are no impediment to polar bears; if they sense something interesting inside, they simply rear up, place their front paws on the door, and give a shove. The only reliable refuge is on the roof.

Decision time. The tide is in. If we are going to paddle the shoreline to Churchill, we need to take advantage of the high water. We had given ourselves enough time, but is it the right choice?

If we decide on a pickup, we might have to wait a day or so, but he would eventually come for us and we could avoid the dangers of paddling on the ocean. We scope out the cabin, which is standard bush decor—unfinished particle board, a wood-burning stove, a collection of frying pans and pots, a couple of chairs, some bunks. The windows are boarded up, and it is dark and stale inside.

A journal lies on the table, and we find several accounts that highlight adventures with bears. I find myself leaning toward a pickup, although my resolve is weakened by the drab cabin, the vulnerability represented by the aluminum ladder, and the prospect of waiting, perhaps several days, for our ride.

"Let's call in and see what he says," Marypat suggests. "Maybe he can give us a weather report or at least let us know how long it would be."

We trundle back to the canoes. The tide is easing out a little. The clock is ticking. I get out the satellite phone and power up. It takes a few minutes, but when I dial, I get our contact right away, loud and clear.

"Okay," he says after I explain our position. "There are ten paddlers from a camp in Minnesota coming to the cabin tonight. They have priority. You have to give them the cabin. I can't pick them up for two days, and they make a full load. You'll have to wait at least another day. Also," he adds, "the wind is supposed to go down tonight."

As he talks, I'm imagining this place full of adolescent boys. I imagine pitching a tent somewhere. I imagine spending four days with bears nosing around.

"We're going," I say when I hang up. Ruby whoops. I stride for the canoe, which I start hauling toward the water's edge. Marypat and Sawyer scramble to catch up.

Then we're paddling.

Fifty-One

We think of polar bears as white, but their skin is deep black to absorb warmth. They never drink water, but instead, get all the liquid they require from the food they eat.

Our mood is ebullient. Stroking into the open expanse, leaving the river, it feels like all of us wanted this outcome. The canoes sing through the waves. Ruby has evolved into a solid, strong, steady paddler. On the Kazan, and at ten years old, she was a pretty spotty partner. On the Seal, she paddles all day long. She handles herself well in rapids. She slogs for hours against a head-wind. She takes on collecting wood or pitching the tent without being asked.

All of us have spent nearly a month getting in shape, working across some 350 miles of northern Manitoba. I can't imagine better trip mates.

As if to mark the final threshold, several pods of beluga whales swim nearby. Four of them surf ahead of Marypat's bow, porpoiselike. They are pure white, not quite the length of our boats. We hear them surface and breathe—soft, airy explosions. Ruby and Sawyer grin with delight.

The shoreline is low and nondescript. I taste the water now and again to know when we've left the freshwater delta and several miles along to see when we are near the mouth of the southern branch of the Seal. The maps aren't much help in this featureless terrain. The sky improves, and a slight tailwind pushes us on at a good pace. After six miles, we ease out around Point of the Woods. The tidal shallows get tougher to thread through.

A floatplane drones low overhead. We wave our paddles at the pilot. He buzzes down over our canoes, waggles his wings.

Eventually there are more rocks than water. Passages drain away as we watch, and we get let down by the tide at a slightly elevated mound of rubble. I'm guessing we've made ten miles. The tidal flats continue east out of sight, blending with distant ocean.

Our strategy is to paddle only at high tide, keeping close to shore and making twice daily leaps of six to ten miles. It is the approach that worked well for us in 1982. By staying close to shore, we avoid the possibility of getting caught miles out when the tides return and the weather changes.

Between tides we will nap, eat, hang out. Our days will be twelve hours long, a schedule dictated by the lunar pull, and we will paddle whenever the water is in, day or night.

We leave the boats packed, removing only dinner supplies and sleeping bags. In every direction, the intertidal zone extends for miles. Inland, the coast is a vaguely defined haze of green. The watch that has been stowed all month comes out, along with the tide charts. High tide is due at 2:37 AM.

We eat dinner. The sun slides toward its brief night below the horizon. The sky continues to clear.

"I'm really excited," Ruby says, "but I'm also a little scared."

"Let's get up around one," Marypat says. "We'll pack and be ready when the water comes."

The bugs are light. We set up a quick tarp and roll out our bags on the rocky ground. Another floatplane flies up the coastline in the paling light. We watch it make a low circle just south of us, then continue. My eyes meet Marypat's. We are both thinking the same thing: it was checking out a polar bear. We say nothing.

By nine-thirty we are laid out in our bags, minds busy with the day and with the coming night. Way too jazzed to sleep.

After what seems a long time, I lift the edge of the tarp, peek out. The waning moon is rising over the ocean. I nudge Marypat and she exclaims at the sight. Later still, Marypat asks me to lift the tarp again. I think she wants to gaze at the moon. Instead she says, "Look at the water!"

Sure enough, the water is pulsing in, coming fast, and it's only eleven-thirty. We all shake awake, start stuffing bags, rolling pads, striking the tarp. We have less than five minutes. The boats bump in the rocks by the time we have everything packed and hop in.

No sleep. Back in the boats. All night ahead of us.

It is soon dark enough that if we get separated by more than a couple of canoe lengths, we can't see each other. We blink headlamps to reconnect. Rocks mine the way. We repeatedly get hung up and have to work our canoes off, losing each other with each delay.

The lights at the Port of Churchill glimmer in the distance, thirty miles off. The moon rises in the east, the following breeze is off my left shoulder. It is enough to maintain a general bearing, but more immediately, we feel our way blind. When we aren't hitting rocks, we know we're veering out to sea and bend back west. When the rocks are a continuous frustration, we angle east.

The novelty of night paddling wears off, supplanted by fatigue and rock-snagging annoyance. At some point, I know we're passing the Knife River delta, because I taste the freshwater. We stop long enough to fill a collapsible five-gallon water container. Ducks wing past in the darkness, whistling softly. Eider ducks, I think, although I have no idea. Once or twice we rouse flocks of geese that honk and stir. Looking behind, I see a faint haze of northern lights, green curtains in the stars.

Although it is very dark, the hint of sunset never completely fades from the eastern horizon. Sometime around three in the morning, light begins to return, at least enough to make out shore. The eastern sky fires up in reds and pinks. We straighten our course. Low tide will be coming, with its chance to nap and recharge. I start looking for landmarks, still vague in the dawn light. We are paddling along a sandy shore, and I assume that we are somewhere past the Knife River delta.

Ruby points. "There's a polar bear," she says, fear in her voice.

She's right. The fuzzy shape of bear, a cream-colored contrast against dawn-lit sand. We stop paddling.

The bear looks at us. It walks directly to the water's edge, then into the water. Then it starts swimming toward us. "It's swimming!" Ruby wails. Her face is chalk white, rigid with fear. We all start paddling, hard. Marypat and I scrabble for the bear spray canisters between strokes.

Ruby and Sawyer keep craning their necks, looking for the implacable white head. I have no illusion of outracing a determined bear, and I have no idea whether bear spray will be an effective defense. Nonetheless, we all paddle like hell, heading for deeper water, fatigue replaced with the caffeine of adrenaline.

"Funny," Sawyer says, "I hardly feel tired at all anymore."

"It stopped," Ruby says. The bear is standing in the shallow water, huge looking, head weaving. We keep right on paddling. Damned if I'm going to get dropped by the tides.

"We should have stayed at the cabin," Ruby laments.

"It's back on shore," Sawyer says, looking over a minute later. "But it's following us."

The bear lopes along, easily keeping pace. The swells build, deepwater swells. Marypat is notorious for motion sickness, even in a canoe. She retches over the side of her boat. Ruby is still ashen, her usual song-singing cheer and bring-it-on fortitude swallowed by anxiety. Miles go by. The bear parallels our progress, a shape so fluid and languid and beautiful, and also so powerful and terrifying.

We are approaching Button Bay, a broad, deepwater dip in the shoreline before the long peninsula that ends with Eskimo Point and the turn into the mouth of the Churchill River, where town and the end of our trip waits. Conventional wisdom, which I agree with wholeheartedly, holds that you do not cross Button Bay. It is a tempting mile-saving prospect. The far shore seems tangible and in reach. In fact, it is a six-mile crossing known for huge waves and sudden weather shifts.

In 1981, the summer before our first Seal River expedition, a canoe party paddling for town crossed Button Bay. They were behind schedule, out of food, desperate to finish. Partway across, the winds rose. Thirteen-foot waves crested over their boats. All rescuers recovered were a few fragments of gear, including poignant pages from their journals.

Just the day before, I had cautioned the kids about Button Bay. "It's tempting," I had said, "but it's stupid."

Now we are cruising along with that slight following breeze. The polar bear is keeping pace. The far side of Button Bay beckons. Crossing would shake the bear for good, and, more important, it would get us to a deep shoreline free of extensive tidal flats. I'm thinking it might not be such a bad idea.

We take a breather, the two canoes gunwale to gunwale. Everyone looks drawn and tense, faces tight. I outline my plan, to cross to a dip in the far shore called Seahorse Gully. I figure the distance at five miles. I take a compass bearing to be sure of landmarks.

Everyone knows the gravity of this. Everyone looks over at the bear. We have paddled, essentially nonstop, almost twenty-four hours, covering more than forty miles, most of it on the ocean and through the night. Fatigue, hunger, fear sit with us like another paddler. But everyone agrees.

We snap our spray decks tight over the canoes. Marypat gets out a bag of energy bars. We gulp them down, simple fuel.

"Okay, guys. We don't need to push," I say. "Just paddle steadily, stay together. We'll be across in less than two hours."

It isn't long before the deepwater cadence takes up its beat. The waves are broad-backed, rolling under the canoes. We paddle side by side, but between waves, Ruby and Marypat disappear in the trough. I don't ever feel that capsize is imminent. The waves only rarely crest, but the water becomes huge, mesmerizing.

Shore and the bear slowly drop behind. We are grim and focused. Sawyer bends to his strokes. Marypat stops to puke bile. Ruby moves mechanically, her face forward, enduring. Halfway there, I calculate.

"Al, you have to talk to Ruby," Marypat says, waking me from my trance.

"Ruby!" I say. "Sweetie! You are an amazing girl. You are strong and happy and full of energy. We are almost there. You just have to hang in a little longer."

She says nothing, cries quietly. I see her wobble in her seat. I start singing her songs, any songs. "You Are My Sunshine, "Yesterday," "Tom Dooley"—lullabies, gospel, old folk tunes, beer commercials. She looks over at me, face pleading.

"C'mon, babe," I say. "Almost there. Keep focused. Help your mom."

When we do finally land, after two hours in the waves, surf bashes us against rocks. Sawyer stumbles out of the bow and falls down. A wave fills my spray skirt, drenches my back, pours into the boat. I stagger over the side into the water, crawl to shore. We haul the canoe bodily out of the waves, heavy with water. Just down the shore, Marypat and Ruby are doing the same. Solid ground is precious.

When I can walk, I go to Marypat and hold her. She leans against me.

"That might be the most dangerous thing we've ever done," she says.

I hold her tight. "We're here" is all I can think to say.

Sawyer and I carry the boats and gear above the seaweed-strewn high-tide line. Marypat and Ruby find an acceptable camp, a nice patch of flower-dotted tundra, and immediately start setting up the electric bear fence we got for just this purpose. When the tent is up and everything stowed, Marypat and the kids dive in to sleep.

My nerves are still jangling. I want to write. I need a cup of coffee. I start water to boil, get out my journal. The ocean sparkles in the sunlight. Belugas surface in the distance, sentient whitecaps. I can hear the reassuring pulse of electricity in the corral of wire surrounding camp.

For weeks we have lived and traveled in unsettled country, seeing no one, in the company of wolf, black bear, moose, seal, loon. I have slept soundly every night; I have never felt a hint of threat. But here, tension hums in the air like the electricity in our fence. I keep glancing over my shoulder, checking the horizon. To be honest, right now I would give a great deal for a gun.

The day slides by. I stoke the fire, nap fitfully, sip hot drinks, watch the tide start to inch in. Around midday, my family stirs and emerges from the tent, revived and hungry. Our last meal was twenty miles up the coast.

"The polar bears have no fear of us," I say while we cook breakfast. I'm trying to voice…what? Some framework to fit our fears on, to reckon with the vulnerability that erupted when the bear came at us at dawn, and that lingers like brooding weather. "Who knows what that bear was doing. He could have just been bored."

Just then, and I'm not joking, I look down the shore and see another polar bear, one hundred feet off, moving toward the water.

Fifty-Two

Beluga whales are sometimes referred to as sea canaries for their high-pitched, twittering vocalizations. They summer by the thousands at the mouths of major rivers and spend winters under the Arctic ice pack, where they have an uncanny ability to locate small open leads of water to surface and breathe.

"Damn, there's a bear!" I say.

Everyone looks at me like I'm kidding. When they see my face, they turn and see for themselves. Fear singes the air. We stand, clustered in the center of the enclosure like penned sheep. I grab the bear spray.

"What do we do?" Ruby asks, as if we have options.

The fence that gave me such comfort through the morning now seems as frail as a spider web. The posts are tentatively anchored in the rocky ground. If a bear brushes against the wires, the whole thing might collapse.

The bear moves down through the rocks, in no hurry, nosing here and there. Then it catches wind of our fire and stops. The white head turns toward us, long neck stretched. The bear climbs to the top of a boulder, scents our way. Marypat takes a picture. Time stalls. What happens next is up to the bear.

POLAR BEAR NUMBER TWO CATCHES OUR SCENT.

What happens is that the bear turns and shambles away, covering ground the way water flows, smooth and seamless. The white shape slips though the rocks, around a corner, gone.

"Thank you, bear!" I say.

"Good bear," Marypat adds. "Good bear."

Relief floods through us like sunlight. At the same time, whatever budding security we had been nurturing evaporates. No more rationalizing about bear behavior.

We eat breakfast, glancing around between bites, and when I suggest that the tide is coming in, the waves have calmed, and that Churchill is only eight miles away, everyone nods. The decision to repack and paddle to the end is made without a word.

When we launch, the swells are still huge, but smooth and unruffled. Long stems of seaweed undulate in the glass-green depths. Every white boulder in the distance stirs a momentary surge of anxiety. The miles whisper in our wakes. I think of all the country we have seen, the rapids with seals sunning on rocks at the bottom, the twilight I watched Sawyer and Ruby come into camp with huge bundles of firewood sticks, the cloudberry pancakes we ate during a drizzle two days earlier.

The Port of Churchill sidles into view midafternoon, twenty-four hours and forty miles of ocean after the phone call from the cabin. Town squats on low, glaciated bedrock. The Churchill River empties into the sea, ending its sinuous run across the continent. Much as I pride myself on being at home in the wilds, and much as I find sustenance in that immersion, the sight of this drab northern town provokes a gush of relief.

And here, the belugas welcome us. That is the only way to put it. At first they appear at a distance, white blinks in the waves. Sawyer pulls the bow toward them, but it is not necessary. The white whales come to us.

Several surface just behind our stern. I turn at the sudden blow of air in time to see the sleek white backs hump and dive. A cow and calf rise together, parallel to the canoe, almost in reach. A lone adult slides under the hull, turns on its side, and hangs there, looking up at us. Another takes its place, flips on its back, regards us through the window of green from a world as foreign as Neptune.

The whales are serene, benign, composed. They keep coming, pod after pod, approaching behind us, sliding under, looking up, permanent smiles on their blunt heads. Several times they are within inches of touching the canoes. They surface so close I catch fishy whiffs of breath. I think about touching them, but don't try. Several return repeatedly. I recognize the distinctive scarred patterns on their backs, the result of yearly sloughing and shedding of skin.

We stop in their midst. "Sawyer," Ruby whispers. "I almost touched one."

Neither of the kids wants to move, but Marypat is still seasick. Despite the magic, we are all drained, numbed by exertion and lack of sleep. We

COW AND CALF BELUGA WHALES NEXT TO OUR CANOE GUNWALE.

paddle slowly in, stopping to savor the contact, the palpable sense of being greeted, escorted to the end of our journey.

The white whales take us almost to shore. In the slow heave of swells, to be held in the attention of these marine creatures, here each summer to give birth and raise young, takes on a momentous quality. Their attention matters a great deal. Also, that we return that regard with equal decorum, equal weight.

When we turn, finally, into the sand beach below the town, I have a momentary foreshadowing: I will encounter these white shapes, these serene gazes, in dreams. I know, too, that I will dream the fluid dread of white bear on the endless, textured plain of tidal flat. Side by side, shades of white, menace and embrace.

Fifty-Three

Hoped to pull out around 6 AM, but between wrestling packs under the canoe and stuffing the car, Ruby losing Beans, going to get bagels, refinding Beans, it's more like 7:30. The cold has let up some. After a week of −20, the temp is up around 0.

—AL, PERSONAL JOURNAL

It is a mark of our world that in the space of a few months, our family can go from the shores of Hudson Bay, where we landed, trembling from exhaustion and jacked-up with manic pulses of emotion, to the frigid departure for Ruby's next phase, half a continent away, along the border with Mexico.

"It's a good thing you guys stopped having kids," Sawyer observed during the frantic days of packing. "We'd be heading for South America for the next one."

This time, the geographic leap is the least of the transitions. Over those same months, the trapdoor to our world opened and we dropped through along with everyone else in our capitalist system. What had seemed solid and substantial evaporated. The bastions of our economy, firms too big to fail, had been revealed as illusions. Or they revealed themselves to be outright crooks.

Billion became an everyday number—hundreds of billions—billions to bail out banks, billions to stimulate the economy, billions to back up bankrupt companies. Investment products sold by trained and intelligent analysts and fortified by fancy charts and portfolio statements were exposed as so much smoke and mirrors. Simple greed, it turned out, overwhelmed training and common sense and experience. Greed was a drug that fueled madness. The security most of us had come to count on, in the form of painstakingly accrued investments and employment expectations, disappeared altogether or withered by half in a matter of weeks.

"You're actually pretty recession-proof," a neighbor had commented to me a month earlier. What he meant was that we carried no debt. Our modest home had been paid off years before. We don't have car payments, credit card debt, outstanding loans of any kind.

He was right, but we also live close to the bone. Marypat and I don't have health insurance. Our income is variable, based largely on my freelance work, which, in an economic crash, shrinks dramatically. It is a choice we have made—independence and flexibility over a steady paycheck and benefits. I like to think that I've been taking my retirement all along, and that my work, often, doesn't feel much like a grind. Good thing, because I'll probably have to keep right on going through retirement years. But what that means, now, is that our shallow pockets are the extent of our safety net. We may not have far to fall, but when we hit bottom, it is still bottom.

It makes the world gray. All the glitter and shimmer of industry, the bustle of commerce, the new clothes and indulgences, travel, the luxuries of dining out, going to movies, buying what we desire, accumulating stuff, goes drab. Ultimately, it is a mirage. Held up close, there is nothing behind the neon flash.

A few weeks earlier, I had ridden my bike out to the offices of the insurance company where we have what counts for our retirement plan. I had avoided taking stock of our situation, but I needed to reckon with reality. When I reached the office building, the parking lot was deserted. The building was locked tight. I peered through the windows.

The company logo was still on the door, but from what I could tell, everything inside had vanished. The desks were gone, the phones unplugged, the pictures taken off the walls. Doors stood ajar. I wondered if I'd come to the wrong building, but there was the logo. I looked around for someone, rode my bike around the block. The office had evaporated. I rode back home into the teeth of a bitter headwind feeling bleak beyond words.

It turned out that the company had recently moved. With a few phone calls, my financial world was resurrected, diminished but tangible. Still, that moment in the empty parking lot with the abandoned building and the blustery wind served as an apt metaphor. For many people, the empty shell of building, and everything it symbolizes, is not a metaphor, but painful truth.

It feels more fundamental than an economic interruption, a downturn. Politicians and policy wonks talk in terms of tweaking and stimulating the system, as if what we've been doing all along simply needs some rejiggering, like tuning up a car. But to me, it feels like the paradigm is in question. What's worse, whatever replaces that structure remains unclear. The way forward is a murky wilderness we fumble toward, hanging on to the old while feeling into the void for the new.

December sunrise comes up over the Beartooth Mountains. The winter night fades to day. Jagged lines of rock ridges limned in snow. Brown fields of wheat stubble. The Yellowstone River bending east, chattering over a gravel bar through icy banks. A raven hunched on a post. The kids nap as best they can in the backseat.

Our economic underpinning may be insubstantial as quicksand, but the natural world goes on untouched. The decline in stocks, the fate of General Motors, the victims of Bernie Madoff matter not. Here, the sun rises as expected, water slides on at the will of gravity, pronghorn antelope paw for forage, the raven contemplates dawn.

I find reassurance in that. On some level, the thing we call real life isn't very real at all. It's our day-to-day version of reality television. The cold wind, the snow writhing across the pavement, the flock of sparrows lifting out of a skeletal tree—that's real, and there's comfort in that recognition.

We turn south toward Wyoming, into Crow Indian country along the Little Bighorn. Lodge Grass. Crow Agency. The Custer battlefield. Wind whips across the highway, sculpting the crusted snow. A rough-legged hawk veers across a field, the same species that soars over the arctic tundra every summer.

Ruby opens her bulging backpack, full of homework assignments, and works through a math sheet. She is a solid student, but it doesn't come easily. Almost weekly, she goes to school early to retake a test or get extra help. Sawyer bends over to explain what x means in her algebra equation.

Over the past year, Ruby has become a poet. My computer desktop is littered with her saved poems. Her teachers encourage her. I encourage her. Poems help her express the burgeoning passions and emotions that swell inside her. It is the same urge I felt as a teen when I wrote reams of awful, sentimental poetry. It was the emotional faucet I could turn on, my release valve. It is a comfort to know that Ruby has it too.

At one point, she e-mailed my father one of her poems, along with a challenge to write one of his own back. He is always prompting her to take up musical duets or prepare a piece to play on saxophone during a visit, so she figured it was fair game to set the bar for him. He managed a poetic response, and it began a lyrical back-and-forth through cyberspace.

"Grandpa Donn," she'd write. "Here's my new poem. It's about our red canoe and writing poetry. Write me one back! Love you. Ruby Sage."

WHERE POETRY HIDES
It can happen any time.
When I wake at midnight, or in the middle of math class,
or flying on skis through deep powder—
Memories flash of the red canoe.

I travel with paddle in hand, and images take over.
The smell of a campfire on a brisk morning, hot chocolate waiting.
The sun shines through the tent, waking me from my dreams.
The flow of the river tangled with destinations the red
canoe has taken me, relaxing and challenging.

I feel the polar bear's dark eyes cut into my heart
stopping it cold, as he stalks us in ocean waves;
or the misty lake at first light on a "dawn dash";
and dipping the water bottle in the clean, cool northern lake,
drinking it straight.

I look at the green world through a bug net.
I hear the lash of rain and howl of wind, and know there will
be no paddling today—a relief to keep snuggling in my bag,
but also the weight of extra miles to make up.

Caribou at sunset,
Tarantula in the desert,
Seals basking on rocks,
White pelicans fishing on the Yellowstone.

At sunset I hunt for pretty rocks on gravel bars.
The red canoe takes me to poetry.

I could hear my dad groan on the other end. "I'm supposed to compete with that?!" he'd say.

If there is a silver lining to the desperate economy, it is that gas prices have plummeted since our summer trip. In Casper, after fighting through a fierce headwind with the low-fuel indicator light on, we pay $1.25 per gallon. I figure that our entire first day, from Montana to Denver, some 750 miles, will cost us less than a single tank of gas did in northern Manitoba in July.

Every time we pass a gas refinery or town, the buildings appear decayed, in decline, almost visibly slumping. Part of it is the gray winter grit, but more of it is the revelation that the entire enterprise is so shaky and vulnerable. Douglas, Cheyenne, Fort Collins, the sprawling paved sea of Denver.

I check the time of sunset, hoping for more daylight as we travel south, thinking about short days on the river, the opposite of twenty-hour days in the North. Yucca plants sprout on the landscape. The plains roll east into the coming night. The western peaks are tinged with red. Full dark by the time we navigate the metropolitan labyrinth and arrive at Marypat's sister's home in Denver.

Although we leave before six the next morning to avoid rush hour, we still creep through the city in a river of red brake lights. Invesco Field, the high-rise buildings off of Colfax Avenue, layers of highway stacked and coiled on top of each other, warehouses, gritty neighborhoods, amusement parks. I think of Roman ruins.

South of the city, at dawn, a coyote lopes through a field of crusted snow parallel to the busy highway, ears perked for the sounds of mice, paying no mind to the steady crescendo of traffic. The Front Range is shrouded in cloud. Eli takes a turn behind the wheel.

Part of my pretrip reticence had to do with my memory of our first marathon from Bozeman to the Mexico border. Trapped in a small station wagon with two potty-training toddlers, Marypat uncomfortably pregnant, saddled with frequent stops for one thing and the next, that trip felt endless, grueling, one of Dante's rings of hell. We took it in small bites. It consumed four days. By the time we got to the launch at the river, we were fried.

This drive is nothing like that. Eli can help with the labor. The kids are veteran road warriors, used to all-day stints. We transect the West in

750-mile gulps. Denver the first night, El Paso the next. It isn't exactly jet lag, but it still feels abrupt.

The landscape incrementally shifts from the snowclad peaks and frozen rivers of Montana to the windy plains of northern Colorado. Dawn in Denver is forty degrees warmer than dawn was in Bozeman. Layers of sandstone jut out of the earth. Piñon pine, ponderosa, yucca, prickly pear, the Arkansas River.

Passing Colorado Springs, I look east toward the plains, where I spent a year after college working on a ranch. Over Raton Pass, into New Mexico— mesas and buttes, cholla cactus, the land yellow and dry, adobe churches, landforms that seem to float against the sky. Las Vegas, Wagon Mound, the Rio Pecos, the turn to Taos, driving through a snow squall into Santa Fe, another place I lived for a time. I remember shaking piñon nuts out of trees onto a sheet. Where we step out at a gas station in Albuquerque it is T-shirt weather. A burrito shop sits across the street. The cashier talks to a friend in Spanish. Eli takes his shirt off.

Just south of town, Interstate 25 crosses the Rio Grande. At seventy miles an hour, it's a glimpse, nothing more—a sandy and shallow channel, a braided sheet of river coursing through cottonwoods. Ruby looks dubious. "That's my river?" she says. "You sure there's enough water?"

"This water never makes it to Big Bend," I tell her. "It goes dry somewhere around El Paso. We use it all up. We have a habit of using up all the water in rivers before they get to the border. The Colorado River doesn't make it either. The water we'll paddle all comes from Mexico, mostly from the Rio Conchos. In fact, down there the river should be called the Rio Conchos if we were being fair about it, or at least the Rio Bravo, which is what Mexicans call it."

Fifty-Four

If you sit here and look out right over there; look at that. The rocks: the way they are. The trees and the hills all around you. Right where you're on, it's water...You're just like that rock. You're the same as the water, this water. You are the ridge, that ridge. You were here in the beginning. You're as strong as they are. As long as you believe in that...that's who you are. That's your mother, and that's you. Don't forget.

INDIAN ELDER SPEAKING TO A YOUNG MAN

A few months earlier, in September, I took Ruby with me to Flathead Lake, in northern Montana, to hang out with Indians. For three days, we camped in a tipi overlooking the lake and listened to traditional elders talk about their world.

Much of the time was spent sitting and listening. I worried about Ruby's stamina for sedentary time, but she remained engaged and intent. Each day began with a fire circle, with everyone ringed around a blaze started at dawn, blessing the day, giving thanks. Men and women, elders from the Six Nations, the Hopi and Navajo, Kootenai and Salish, people who had been at Wounded Knee, men and women whose life force centers on carrying on traditional ways of being in the world and combating the threats to that continuum.

Every day, people spoke of those traditions, of their ceremonies and histories, of their ancestors and the inclusion of all life in the circle. Above all, they stressed the role of respect and gratitude in a balanced life. Young people, including Ruby, served the elders first at meals. One evening we ate dinner at the community hall in Saint Ignatius, Montana, a reservation town with all the problems of modern day Indian culture side by side the heartbeat of ancestral traditions.

The food had been harvested and collected locally. It had taken weeks to gather and prepare the roots, berries, venison, wild greens. Afterward, a group of singers performed in the hall, beating a drum the size of our dining room table at home, singing. The noise was overpowering, primal, surging. The singers were men and women of all ages, several young people. The songs and pounding drumbeats were exultant, impenetrable, terribly powerful. I rode back to the camp on the bus, through the night, through the lights of towns, with the elemental beat still firing in my chest.

Ruby's favorite memory of the weekend was a short video we watched about a woman named Pauline Whitesinger. Whitesinger is a Navajo elder in her late seventies. She lives alone on Big Mountain, Arizona, Navajo country, miles from the nearest neighbor. By our standards, her life is impoverished. She lives in a tiny block home the size of one bedroom in my house. She has

68 LET THEM PADDLE

no electricity, no running water, no telephone, certainly no computer. Family and friends look in on her from time to time, bring her water and supplies.

The movie consists of her speaking Navajo. Her nephew interprets her words. The camera cuts to scenes of the surroundings, her sheep, her garden, the sagebrush and piñon landscape, the dome of arid sky. She is simple. She is profound.

She talks about who she is, where she comes from. She thanks the sun each day, she pays attention to the plants, to the clouds and storms, her animals—more than that, she understands what they tell her. She lives according to natural law, which overrides years of governmental attempts to relocate her according to their laws.

Once, when a government agent arrived at her home with a ream of paper that documented the case against her, she asked if that law was more powerful than natural law. He told her that, yes, it was a powerful law, the law of the federal government. Then, she said, it should be more powerful than this, and she threw it into her woodstove.

She has stubbornly and steadfastly refused to move. This land is me, she says, in so many words. How could I abandon it? Watching her, it is evident that she has a connection to place most of us are incapable of understanding. She speaks to that land, and to the plants and animals and weather and stars and water that are her company. To say that Pauline Whitesinger is of that land is not hyperbole or sentimentality; it is as real as saying who your grandmother is.

The movie has no plot, no tension, no graphic gymnastics. It is real. A real person talking about real things. The room of more than fifty people watching it was as still as midnight.

The Flathead conference was a continuation for me. The year before, I had attended a similar gathering in Haida Gwaii, the Haida homeland that we know as Queen Charlotte Islands, well off the coast of British Columbia. I was asked to attend as a journalist. As such, I considered myself an observer as much as a participant.

Haida Gwaii is powerful beyond words. It rises out of the ocean, vast, rugged, and thickly wooded. Ocean currents ripple through the islands like liquid wind. Traditionally, the Haida were powerful and numerous, and the island was home to some ten thousand people who traveled in massive cedar canoes, carved totem poles, traded extensively, made war, held gatherings, lived off of the bounty of the sea and rain forest, and who had evolved complex cultural traditions.

Then the Europeans arrived. In a matter of a few short generations, between warfare and disease, the Haida were reduced to some fifty individuals. Their villages were pillaged for anthropological artifacts. Human bones, artwork, totem poles were shipped off to museums around the world. The songs were forgotten, the language fell into disuse, no one carved canoes. The remote villages lay deserted and decaying. Bit by bit the population grew, but the culture continued to wither against the onslaught of western influence.

Only in the past generation have the Haida begun their revival. Since the mid-1980s, and with the encouragement of traditional elders from throughout North America, the Haida have begun singing their ancient songs again, speaking their native tongue, teaching children the dances, holding ceremonies, repatriating the bones of their ancestors from museums, carving canoes the size of small ships.

It is not easy, nor is it assured. At the same time that people honor the long-standing currents of culture, young people play video games, drugs and alcohol erode the fabric of family, violence and despair rot the foundations of community. That the rebirth of culture is happening at all, given the history, is staggering. That it is as robust, loving, joyful, and absolutely serious as it is is something to behold.

For me, it was a bedrock reordering of my understanding of Indian reality. Some things stand out, still, from those days spent on the coast in the shadow of the cedars, with the sea sighing against rocky beach, bald eagles coasting past, ravens perching on totem poles.

I remember sitting in a conference room in a circle of perhaps a dozen people. A woman from Colorado was talking about her distress and her inability to find a clear way forward in life. One of the women elders, an Oneida, said matter-of-factly, "It sounds like maybe you should talk to some trees."

To my discredit, I almost chuckled. I caught myself, because it was clear that she was quite serious. She was trying to help. Her suggestion was as straightforward and commonsensical as if she had suggested seeing a psychiatrist.

"Not all trees are good," she went on. "Some are better than others. But in general, trees are really helpful."

Another day, after lunch, I was speaking with an elder from Greenland. He is a man who performs ceremonies and makes presentations around the world. His message is that the ice is melting in the North. He is what you might call a runner for his people, telling humans everywhere what is happening.

He mentioned that he had recently been in New York. It had been very hot during his visit. One afternoon, after a discussion, he suggested that they all go cool off in the Hudson River. He began to jog toward the nearby riverbank to take a dip. People called him back.

"You can't swim there!" they told him. "The water is polluted."

He stopped, turned in astonishment. "I just read a news story this morning that claimed that New York was the most highly educated city in the world," he said. "Are you telling me that you are the most educated people on earth, and yet your river is too polluted to swim in? I don't understand."

On the third morning of the conference, we held a dawn fire circle on the beach. Each day had begun this way. Sometimes half of the morning would be spent sharing in this circle. This morning, the fire had been built well before dawn and tended properly. A food offering had been made to the flames. The directions had been recognized, prayers spoken in Mohawk.

The Haida had brought a young man to introduce. He stood outside the circle, waiting. A bald eagle coasted by over the restless bay. An island hovered in the view. He was patient.

Finally, after all the offerings had been made, one of the Haida elders introduced him as a person who was responsible for bringing back a number of the ancient Haida songs. He had also introduced new songs to the people.

When he stepped forward, he broke into tears. He said that he was very moved by the ceremony around the fire, that it meant a great deal to hear real emotions being expressed and an authentic reverence being shared. He went on, crying openly. He talked about how very hard it was to stay on the path. How every day his resolve is tested. Seductions were everywhere, relentless; drugs, alcohol, video games, television, money, all of it. It is really, really hard, he said, to stay true.

He composed himself. No one spoke. He sang one of his songs, a song of the ocean, of the ancestors, of the people and land in the middle of the Pacific.

It was at that moment, watching him, listening to his words, hearing him sing, that I realized I was no longer a journalistic observer. I understood that he was not simply speaking of his condition, but of the human condition. He confessed his trials, but they are trials we all endure. They are my trials, everyone's trials. It struck me like a wave of heat. This was not an Indian struggle. It was my struggle too.

Now, I did not go to Haida Gwaii with any intention of quitting drinking. I made no vow after hearing this man's testimony. But I simply stopped, and I haven't touched a drink since.

Months later, when I mentioned this to the founder of the institute that sponsored the conference, he said that ripple effects like that happen all the time. "We keep getting reports of life-changing events," he said. "We are stimulating this energy, and it has a way of spreading."

At the end of the conference, everyone had a chance to say whatever moved them. A number of people made statements about the state of the world. Some shared their despair, others, their sense of hope.

Right at the last, a man got up and introduced himself. "I am the direct descendent of General Sherman, of Civil War fame, who said many times that the only good Indian is a dead Indian. He was intimately involved in the massacre of Indian villages at places like Sand Creek, in Colorado. Defenseless men, women, and children shot down in their tipis or hunted and murdered as they fled."

He turned to the Haida elders. He asked one of them to join him. The Haida man stepped forward, stood in front of him. This descendent of a general from the Indian Wars knelt before the Haida elder, took his hand in his.

"I love the Haida," he said. "I love you. It is my great honor to know you."

He rose. The two men embraced. Both were crying. Most of us were crying.

The conference on the Flathead, for me, felt less profound, less elemental, less personal. Haida Gwaii hit me like a wave. It moved my world. At Flathead, the energy was different, less remote and wild, more political.

For Ruby, though, it was an entry point. She began by staying close to me, but within a day she was on her own, visiting, helping people, going to listen to someone speak, paddling a canoe. People recognized her, acknowledged her. One morning, across the fire circle through drizzle, I noticed Wilma Mankiller, a powerful elder, watching Ruby, a wistful smile playing across her face. And if any group of humanity rivals Ruby for sheer hugging energy, it is the Indians. By the end, Ruby was in hugging nirvana.

Fifty-Five

The Rio Grande has a long history of providing irrigation, extending back through many generations of traditional Pueblo people. Currently, it irrigates more than 2 million acres of cropland along its course, to say nothing of the additional demands of mining, industry, and urban centers that deplete its flow.

Driving east out of El Paso is a tour of decrepit capitalism. The sky is the color of soot. For miles the clutter of marginal businesses lines the highway. Tire shops, junkyards, abandoned warehouses, appliance repair bays. Scraps of plastic and paper cartwheel like so much tumbleweed or flutter from skeletal trees. It smells of fuel and rubber and asphalt.

I know El Paso has its historic district, a cultural legacy going back to the 1500s. It has residential neighborhoods, old Spanish architecture, but along the interstate it is a wasteland, a testimony to the barren fruits of a throwaway culture. Driving through has the same desperate, exposed feeling as walking the aisles of one of those dollar stores, where things are rendered to their true status. Clothes and dishes and appliances that once sat on the shelves of Kmarts and Costcos and Targets, that have sifted to the bottom of the consumer ladder and landed where they are worth a buck. It is materialism laid bare, consumerism reduced to its ghetto, obsolescence reeking from the shelves.

Somewhere to the south, across the sandy, littered expanse and demarcating that contested, overwrought border, lies the dry streambed of the Rio Grande. It is a river exhausted, quite literally.

Beginning six hundred miles north and west, across New Mexico and southern Colorado, the Rio Grande trickles out of the deep snowfields of the San Juan Mountains in the southwestern corner of Colorado. There, the fourth longest river system in the United States begins its run. I have stood on those alpine divides, in the thin air where shooting stars and elephant head flowers nod in the breezes and peaks razor through the skyline, craggy gray ridges thrust into the blue horizon. Water seeps through the tussocky meadows, pauses in small lakes perched above tree line, picks up speed down the flanks of the forested hillsides, gathering and coalescing into a frothing, noisy flow; a river, a burgeoning force uncoiling its energy across the broad high valleys of southern Colorado.

Near Alamosa, in the San Luis Valley, the Rio Grande slows and widens through a swampy section full of ponds and channels. It is a staging spot along the central bird migration route where snow geese and sandhill cranes and myriad ducks and waterfowl collect to rest or feed in grain fields before moving on. Hawks and eagles whirl overhead. Phalarope and coot and swans coast on the surfaces of ponds. Avocets and willets and yellowlegs probe the shallows.

Near the Great Sand Dunes, where prevailing wind eddies deposit a restless quadrant of sand hills worthy of the Sahara, the Rio Grande shunts south toward New Mexico along the western rampart of the Sangre de Cristo Mountains. The rivercourse is defined geologically by the Rio Grande Rift, a series of basins separated by resistant bedrock strata where the river has eroded its canyons. In the basins rest the marshes and bosks where waterfowl find sanctuary.

From the start, farmers raid the river for irrigation, towns siphon water for drinking and industry. Tributaries aren't sufficient to replenish the main stem. While the Rio Grande is a long watershed, it is never much for volume. It has one-twentieth the volume of the Colorado River, which also has to withstand the raids of desert evaporation and human thirst, and which also never reaches the sea.

The great river dwindles, at first imperceptibly, but as it winds south, carving canyons, watering fields, filling reservoirs where evaporation takes another toll, the diminishment becomes inescapable.

It remains wild enough in spots, charging through the rapids of the Taos Box, in northern New Mexico, vertical volcanic canyons rising above dramatic whitewater drops where rafters dot the river like so many party balloons. On past the dry basalts and ash deposits of Bandelier National Monument, whispering under the dark energy of Los Alamos, the pueblos and corn festivals, braiding through Albuquerque where people collect wild asparagus along the canals each spring.

On it flows, failing by the mile, through the Bosque del Apache, where snow geese collect each winter by the tens of thousands, rising at dawn like schools of white airborne fish and roosting again at nightfall, landing in whistling flurries to spend the dark winter hours. On to the cotton fields, the pecan orchards, the chili gardens, the towns—Las Cruces, Truth or Consequences, Socorro, Hatch.

Delayed in the reservoirs, losing more to the sun—Caballo Dam, Elephant Butte Reservoir—out-of-place lakes glinting in the desert heat. Finally, into the draining thirst of El Paso and Juarez, more irrigation, the last metropolitan slaking of appetite—going down the toilets, lubricating industry, filling water tanks.

Thereabouts, most of the time, the last depleted, sullied, overworked dregs die into the sands. Driving south, paralleling the watershed, I think of the river as a thinning thread, literally a pulsing, affirming, life-sustaining artery that finally bleeds away to nothing, a wet stain in the sand, victim of our thirsts.

El Paso winks out of sight in the rearview mirror. The dry riverbed angles southeast, away from the highway. Traffic stops at an immigration station, creeps along through a checkpoint where a Hispanic soldier asks if we are all US citizens.

Creosote flats spread away to the skyline. Black rock outcrops, little towns with adobe churches and sun-faded water towers, miles of parched earth. We leave the interstate at Van Horn, lose an hour to the time zone, angle toward Big Bend. A pecan orchard lines the state highway for miles, rows of pruned trees, irrigation lines, barrackslike housing units. Yucca plants taller than me, agave plants, mesquite trees, acacia, cholla, turnoffs down dirt roads to distant ranches.

The border is a tension in the air, like electricity. Near Marfa, a tethered drone hovers above a security installation, surveilling the desert expanse, wasting taxpayer money, hanging above the road like some gizmo on a low-budget sci-fi movie set. Perhaps the placement has to do with the persistent UFO activity around Marfa. People regularly head out to the flats east of town around twilight to check out "the lights of Marfa," which appear around dusk, dance above the horizon, and which no one seems able to explain.

At Alpine, we turn due south toward the river. We have driven more than fifteen hundred miles from our frosty driveway, packed in among our river gear like riders on a second-class bus in Mexico. Big Bend is decidedly out of the way, hundreds of miles out of the way. Visitors make a point of coming to this park, as we have.

It is seventy degrees outside. We wear T-shirts, leave the windows open. Homework has been forgotten since Wyoming. We are in a different universe.

A Native legend has it that when the earth was created, there was a pile of leftover stuff that had to go somewhere; the Creator decided to dump it in what we call Big Bend. The land begins to look that way. Tusks of dark rock jut out of the ground, rock layers twist and fault against each other, heaps of volcanic rubble lie around, geomorphology runs rampant.

"Hey, there's a warthog!" Sawyer calls out, pointing at a scrubby fence line.

"Javelina!" I say, turning the car around. A couple of the wild peccaries are rooting around in the scrub grass. They gallop along the fence parallel to us, compact gray pigs with surprising speed and razor-sharp incisors.

Ruby takes pictures out the window.

When we pull in to the raft company in Terlingua, the woman at the desk is not happy with us.

"Your shuttle driver went home," she says.

"I'm sorry," I say. "We're an hour late. It's a long way from Montana, and we forgot about the time zone change."

"I don't know if he'll come back," she scolds me.

She calls him. He returns in five minutes, unperturbed. By that time, we have filled our water jugs and made room to squeeze four people in the backseat so he can ride along. We shake hands.

"Jim," he says. He looks about my age. He has that desert rat demeanor—grizzled stubble, sunstruck face, cutoff shorts, a faded T-shirt, like he's landed in an eddy and has no interest in entering the main flow again anytime soon.

"You're paddling the Great Unknown," he says when we start down the road toward Lajitas. "No one goes out there."

The raft company he works for specializes in short trips that concentrate on the spectacular canyons and rapids. One-day outings, overnights. Nobody connects the dots across dozens of miles between canyons, through the open Chihuahuan Desert. Because it is so little traveled, stories build up, the reach takes on a mythic quality—hints of drug traffic, desperate smugglers, lawless borderlands.

Once in a great while something spectacular happens to cement the reputation. Tourists get shot at. Somebody gets robbed. The Great Unknown. Jim says it with a smile, but it's clear that our trip is an unusual departure from the beaten path and that our ability to pull it off is in some doubt.

"I'm from Pittsburgh," Jim tells me when we strike up a conversation.

He spent his adult life running a gas station in partnership with his brother. Around the age of fifty, he couldn't stand it anymore. "I had to try something different," he says. He traveled around the country for a couple of years, took up work when he needed money, moseyed from here to there. Then he came to Big Bend to hike.

"I couldn't believe this place," he remembers. "It blew my mind. I went back to Pittsburgh, took care of a few things, and came back down. I've been here ever since."

Jim runs shuttles for the river company, does odd jobs here and there. He rents a "rockdobe" house outside of Terlingua, stays year-round.

"Once in a while, I'll work on a car if I really need the money," he says. "Mostly I just do what I need to and call it good. I'm thinking about getting trained as a raft guide."

I don't say anything, but I'm thinking about all the humanity stressing out about how to make mortgage payments, send kids to college, pay credit card debt, all the people going off the cliff into bankruptcy. All of that is pretty well off the radar for Jim. It reminds me of the Indian people I met at one of the conferences, when the conversation turned to the Great Depression.

"Yeah, we heard about that," they said, like it happened in a universe far, far away.

A lot could happen in the world that Jim would watch from his Big Bend remove, a distant and quite happy spectator.

The backcountry of Big Bend is really quiet. Parks like Yellowstone and Yosemite bear the mantle of heavy-handed administrations. Permits, fees, forms, regulations burden every hike or campsite registration. For most of Big Bend, however, including the river, it's as simple as filling out a three-by-five card and dropping it in the box with ten dollars. There is no ranger checking out your gear, stipulating campsite locations, going through the list of rules.

We drive upriver past Lajitas on Texas Farm Road 170. Our tired, overburdened Honda van strains over Big Hill, known as the steepest incline of any paved road in the country, and we pull off at a nondescript launch above Colorado Canyon.

There I experience a time warp.

Fifty-Six

Roughly a dozen resident pairs of peregrine falcons live in the canyons of the Rio Grande in Big Bend. Brought to the verge of extinction by the scourge of pesticides and DDT in the 1950s and '60s, they have slowly reestablished themselves over the decades, assisted by legal protections and breeding programs. They nest and roost in the sheer cliffs, from which they dive after prey—mostly small birds and ducks. The fastest bird on earth, peregrines have been clocked at nearly 200 miles per hour in a dive.

—CHIHUAHUAN DESERT RESEARCH INSTITUTE, ALPINE, TEXAS

The same impression of explosion I experienced on our arrival in 1995—when Eli and Sawyer were energetic toddlers and Marypat toted her bean-bag-sized belly in front of her—strikes home within minutes of turning off the Honda's engine near Colorado Canyon fourteen years later. Three boats emerge, including a ducky kayak that needs inflating and a folding canoe that requires assembly. The same sprawl of colorful debris litters the ground. This time, in addition to the usual trip gear, it is sprinkled with school back-packs, iPods, headphones, the clutter of teenage essentials, most of which will be left in the van.

This time around, the Rio Grande is clipping along at a healthy flow. During the fall months, northern Mexico was inundated by waves of tor-rential rain. The dams along the Rio Conchos couldn't cope. Floodgates had to be opened wide, releasing a gush of water through Big Bend like nothing seen here in a generation. The river lodged debris forty feet up bridge abut-ments, backed half a mile up tributary canyons, and completely drowned the tamarisk and cane thickets that choke much of the river corridor.

Mudflats plug the mouths of sidestreams. At this put-in, the camp-ground, a newfangled composting outhouse, and the boat ramp have been obliterated. From the turnoff, the launch is a hundred-yard portage across a muddy riverbed strewn with boulders and drying pools. Several park camp-grounds and pumping stations were wiped out downstream. The state high-way is still stained with mud in the low spots, and the river has only recently subsided to a level where canoeing is allowed.

For a moment, a kaleidoscope of memories swirls around me. The last time we were here, the anemic river and the little boys ramming around in the prickly pear, peeing themselves, and that impossible pile to fit into our seventeen-foot boat. All of the riverbanks and lakeshores over the years, each cluttered with expedition debris. Blackflies on Kasba Lake, mosquitoes on the bank of the Yukon outside of Dawson, a short-tailed weasel whisking through the packs in northern Manitoba.

Our family huddled under a tarp in a hailstorm, or swimming the Yellowstone, or wading chest-deep up the Churchill River through rapids in Saskatchewan. Warding off hypothermia with a birchbark fire and hot cocoa in a freezing drizzle. Catching frogs on a sandbar. Slamming through whitewater on the Salmon. The musk ox on Yathkyed Lake. The polar bear at dawn. The kids bent over a camp game in lingering summer light.

"C'mon you guys, let's get this stuff together," Marypat cajoles the kids, who are stretching and wandering aimlessly through the piles of water jugs, boat bags, dry sacks. They start picking up stuff, trudge toward the river. Ruby lays out the kayak and attaches the foot pump. I wake from the clutch of memory and try to remember how the folding canoe goes together. Jim watches the scene unfurl with a better-you-than-me look on his face. When we get everything clear of the car, he fires it up and takes off.

"See you in a couple of weeks," he says. "Watch for the wall shots!"

"What's a wall shot?" Ruby asks.

"Where the river runs straight into the bank and makes a sharp turn," Marypat explains. "I guess this canyon is known for them."

The first night's camp is on the Mexican side, only a few miles below the put-in, at the mouth of a canyon. It doesn't feel quite as abrupt as walking off of a plane in Cancun, but the leap we have made is still stunning. From the predawn arctic of our Montana driveway to shorts and sandals in a seventy-degree campsite in Mexico in less than three days, with a wind-buffeted, economically devastated, north–south transect of the country in our wake.

Ruby talks Sawyer into a sunset dunk in the river. She comes up sputtering. "That's pretty cold!" She hops around, shaking water out of her hair.

"It's dam water," I remember. "Hasn't had time to warm up yet."

Eli joins in. They stroke to the far side, below a small rapid, and clamber around in the cliffs, climbing barefoot.

"I'm not putting a rain fly on the tent," Marypat announces.

We collect driftwood, which is in copious supply, cook our dinner over the fire pan. The sun drops over the canyon rim. A planet pricks the twilight. I pull on a light jacket. The first canyon wren sings its descending, fluted song from a rock wall behind camp.

In the tent, stars are thick through the mesh netting. I lie there on my back, the marathon drive still tingling in my nerves, the highway hum fading, feeling the firm ground beneath my pad, another river making noise in the distance. The night sky is full on, a dense quilt of stars and planets, the Milky Way a river running through it. This is a very dark quadrant of sky. Pictured from space, this part of Texas and northern Mexico is utterly black at night.

"Kind of cool talking to Jim," I say. "He let a landscape pull him in, gave up a life he was tired of and started new."

"He doesn't have kids," Marypat reminds me.

"True, but it's still a nice contrast to the material culture and everyone feeling desperate to hang on to some illusion of lifestyle."

"I liked him," Ruby says.

"Yeah, it's cool what he did," says Sawyer. "But it would also be good to have some options."

"People forget that they have options like the one he took," I say. "They get trapped by debt or put blinders on, and the idea of moving somewhere because the land grabs you, and working things out, seems completely impossible. Hell, I forget those options. You just get so pulled in by everything. It takes meeting a person who's doing it to remind you."

"Good night, Dad," Ruby says. "I'm going to sleep before you start whale breathing."

"And Dad," Eli adds. "Just chill in the morning. We don't have to make a lot of miles. Take it easy getting up."

I lie there for a long time thinking about the entire editorial staff of a magazine I write for being laid off a few weeks earlier. About my parents, whose retirement savings lost half their value in two months. About a friend who had invested with Madoff's scheme and who, overnight, went from feeling quite comfortable about his future to not being able to cover his mortgage.

Marypat and I have been drawing up plans to expand our vegetable garden, put up more food. We've started baking bread every week. Marypat got a library book out on building a backyard chicken coop.

Every magazine I write for is scaling back, getting thinner, losing ad sales, depending on staff writers for articles. I've been at it long enough and have contacts enough to stay somewhere in the loop, but it's sketchy. All of it, the entire premise, feels sketchy. Our month-to-month financial juggling act staggers on. It's all well and good to count your wealth in time with your kids and the flexibility to take trips, until you can't put food on the table. And Sawyer's hope for options is just that. All of our hopes are just that.

I ignore Eli's advice and leave the tent in the chill dawn. It is my time of day. I'm in no rush, but the crack between night and day is my sanctuary, a coffee-infused still spot before the downriver enterprise lurches on. The first sun fires up an ocotillo plant on the rim of the canyon. The spiny arms light up like a wild, thin sprig of hair. Canyon wrens greet the day. When the sun finally strikes camp, the very first thing it hits, like a spotlight, is the tent. I know how happy this makes Marypat, who likes nothing better than a good morning lounge, snuggled deep, warming in the sun.

In Ruby's sixth-grade year, she and Marypat went to Spain for a soccer tournament. It sounds excessive. It was excessive. But Ruby played for a boys' soccer team coached by a charismatic Lithuanian who is crazy about the game.

Those kids played together for years. Ruby ended up being the only girl, but it didn't seem to matter. She was just one of the gang. Nobody remarked on it. They became a solid unit, won some tournaments. The coach kept threatening to find a European tournament to take the team to.

Then, one fall, he followed through. "I've found a tournament in Spain," he announced. "We have all year to save pennies. We're going."

Marypat and Ruby did just that. Everyone on the team did. They hid a big glass jar and started putting money in it. Babysitting money, reffing money, money Marypat made on contract sewing jobs or beadwork, birthday checks. I never thought they'd pull it together, but by the following spring, they'd put aside enough to bankroll the trip. One night they sat together on the living room floor and poured out the jar full of cash. It came to more than three thousand dollars.

The entire team, along with a gaggle of parents, took off for Barcelona. Although Ruby's team thought nothing of playing with a girl, she was the only girl in the entire tournament and became something of a sensation.

On bus rides, the boys from other teams constantly harangued her. "Can I be your boyfriend?" they asked her. "Can I sit with you? You are so beautiful!"

After the first bus trip, the rest of her team put her in the back of the bus and formed a wall to protect her. At the games, cries of "La Nina!!" kept coming from the sidelines. Boys from other teams all wanted their pictures taken with her after the games.

"It was crazy," she told me later. "I couldn't wait for that part to be over."

Most of the kids flew home right after the tournament, but Marypat figured they'd come that far, they should stay another week and travel.

"Ruby was totally fun to be with," Marypat told me. "She was always up for stuff. She was flexible. She could entertain herself." They went to museums, took a trip to Montserrat, stayed in youth hostels, ate bread and cheese three times a day, started talking with a lisp, Barthelona-style.

"It was like traveling with my sister," Marypat said.

Fifty-Seven

Had a good solstice breakfast with eggs and solstice bread. It was overcast and a little breezy. We saw two wild horses—one black and one brown. Made it to Santa Elena Canyon, which is really cool.

—RUBY, GROUP JOURNAL

According to the geologic creation story, until roughly one million years ago, more or less yesterday, the Rio Grande stayed true to the trend of the Rio Grande Rift and flowed south into Lake Cabeza de Vaca, named for the Spanish explorer who blundered around this section of the New World, circa 1528, planting the flag, enduring capture by Indians, and experiencing epic doses of misadventure. But well before that, a million years before, a dramatic event took place on the geologic stage. Around that time, the Rio Grande drainage was captured by a neighboring watershed and turned hard east, carving a new path to the Gulf of Mexico.

Stream capture is a dynamic event despite the fact that it happens incrementally, grain by grain, over millions of years. The upper tendrils of watersheds erode headward, gnawing away at the divide that separates them from the next valley over. Eventually, depending on the topography, that divide is breached, worn down, and finally the entire drainage pattern can shift into the new channel, captured from its old course.

Geologists believe that the river we paddle through Big Bend was captured just so and that it has been busy eroding its new path, carving through canyons, finding its way, ever since. These days, it is a stuttering process. While the river volume through Big Bend has been replenished by Mexican tributaries, irrigators and towns downstream of the park rob the flow again, a replay of the raids upstream of El Paso.

In the early years of this century, it went dry again before reaching the Gulf. A huge sandbar formed near the mouth of the river. The channel was dredged. The river flowed to the sea again, but within a year went dry once more. The sandbar reformed. The Rio Bravo, as it is known in Mexico, only intermittently meets the saltwaters of the Gulf.

On the cosmic scale, the matter of a river reaching the sea is neither here nor there, of little weight. To me it feels like an amputation of potential, with ripple effects extending across the arid watershed and far beyond, impacting every species, the climate, the ocean currents; a spectrum of ripple effects from the well-being of microorganisms to the march of geology. It feels especially poignant because it is a consequence of greed and mismanagement by my species, a consequence I share responsibility in. If you buy the concept that the earth is a living, interconnected organism, what have we done when we drink a river dry, and what does it say about our abuse of limits?

On December 21, winter solstice, we camp a few miles above Santa Elena Canyon, on the Texas side. It is a sweet site, paved with a sloping bed of patterned shale, backed by a high, steep slope sparsely vegetated with ocotillo, agave, prickly pear. The tent nestles on a sandy bench just above the river under an acacia tree.

Winter solstice has always been our surrogate Christmas, our pagan festival. We send solstice cards rather than Christmas cards. For years we have rented Forest Service cabins on December 21, where we spend the darkest night in the mountains, light luminaria, eat a festive dinner, open presents, howl at the moon. Christmas remains, but it is a social day, a family day. Solstice is the holiday with meaning.

Our trip preparations were rushed and last minute, but Marypat still managed to come up with festive touches. She included little gifts to be opened each morning, along the twelve days theme—gourmet hot chocolate one day, a book to read aloud the next, miniature puzzles, floating candles. We also planned a few special meals to celebrate with. Marypat brought a loaf of her patented solstice bread for breakfast, and we concocted special menus for both solstice and Christmas dinners. Our solstice menu features bratwurst, mashed potatoes, coleslaw, and stuffing; not bad for a night on the river.

Three days in, the trip has achieved that embedded feeling. After Lajitas, the river enters Big Bend National Park and turns away from the road. By this time we are fully apprised on the subject of wall shots. Repeatedly the river shunts around corners and runs smack into a rock wall or muddy bank. If you aren't ready to brace away or angle properly, riding the line at the edge between current and eddy, it gets dicey.

The rapids haven't been particularly difficult. We stopped only a couple of times to scout anything, but Marypat and I swamped a canoe on a corner that took us by surprise, where a deadfall jutted out from shore and the boat broached against it. It's always something ignoble like that, a moment of inattention, an unassuming corner, the wrong stroke, a mistimed lean.

"That was retarded!" Eli said, which is exactly how it felt.

Sawyer and Eli pulled in to help us regroup. Ruby stroked up with the ducky. No harm done, except to our bruised paddling self-esteem. Marypat and I take some pride in the fact that we have never capsized together in a canoe. We have had some very, very close calls, some miraculous recoveries, like this one, to maintain that record, but after the swamp, the streak has another asterisk next to it.

We are alone on the water. In one camp, Eli discovers a set of longhorn cattle horns, a span four feet across. There are agates in the gravel. In this volcanic terrain, it's not surprising, and they are very different from the

Yellowstone variety, more apt to be streaked with red. The collection of keepers builds.

We pass what looks like an old adobe settlement on the Texas side. The buildings are full of flood debris, mud to the windowsills. It turns out that it was a thrown-together movie set for some spaghetti Western.

On the Mexican side, a small house perches at the top of a black rock escarpment, directly above the river. It is an imposing spot. High-water stains mark the brink of the wall, but the flood didn't crest over.

A dog barks at us. There is a pump in the river for irrigation, a clunky bicycle leans against the house. A garden flourishes inside a fence, and what looks like a spring behind it seeps out of the hillside. No one around. Although pavement provides access to towns on the Texas side, I know that, for these people, unless they make an illegal crossing, it is hours on appalling four-wheel dirt tracks to get anywhere for anything.

"Wonder where they ride that bike," I say when we coast past the base of the river-polished cliff. The kids look the place over. I can see the wheels turning. *What if I grew up here?*

At Lajitas, we stop to replenish water. It's a half-mile hike into town from the river access. I troop up the empty road in my river shorts and Hawaiian shirt carrying two five-gallon jugs. There used to be a funky trading outpost here, a bar, some marginal enterprises scattered around, hippies and desert rats living off of tourist and boater trade. All that has disappeared. In recent years, a developer took over, bought up property, and put up an ostentatious complex of hotel, swanky restaurants, upscale condos, a golf course.

It is the equivalent of the Yellowstone Club in Montana, where people build hundred-million-dollar ten-thousand-square-foot homes with eleven bathrooms and heated driveways, and then occupy them two weeks every year—the Yellowstone Club, which, as part of the economic crash, is undergoing bankruptcy proceedings and has been revealed as another mirage promoted by hucksters who should go to jail.

"If I go down and rob the Town Pump of fifty dollars," a friend said to me recently, "I'll go to jail for years. But developers who pillage the countryside and bilk millions from people go free. Go figure."

It's the same here. The Lajitas project is in dire straits. I can't find anyone around. Finally, I wander into the dark lobby of the hotel. A young woman behind the desk identifies me as not-a-client from thirty yards. She smiles anyway. I like her for that.

She directs me to a spigot outside for water. I fill the jugs, hoping the water is safe, and start back, forty pounds of sustaining liquid lengthening each arm. I see a Mercedes sedan idling in the parking lot, a couple in the front. I wander over, tap on the window. A woman opens it, looks out at me, eyes skeptical. What scam is this? her expression asks.

"I'm floating the river with my family," I say. "I just filled up some water jugs. Do you think I could grab a ride with you to the river? It's just down the road."

She pauses, looks at the man behind the wheel. He shrugs. They don't seem like they have any pressing engagements. Maybe tee time or a condo tour; maybe they've come all the way here on a whim only to find this hollow sham and have nothing but time. Maybe they wish they were doing something vaguely adventurous.

"Hop in," the man says.

At the river, a pair of border patrol agents lurk around, studying my family from fifty yards. Khaki uniforms, that idle tension, shifting weight from foot to foot, guns in holsters. Homeland Security on the job. I decide to ignore them. I thank the couple. They pause there, looking over the scene, then drive back up the road.

One bend down, on the Mexican side, an adobe shrine of some sort pulls us in. We stop and wander around. A man herding goats clatters through the mesquite on horseback. He pays us no attention, works the herd up a steep, loose bank. He dismounts there, waiting for some stragglers. When they don't follow, he starts chucking rocks behind them to spook them uphill.

The afternoon is gusty and chilly. We cross the park border. The signs have been washed away. More wall shots, some small riffles. We beat into the wind until we make our miles and find the tiled camp with an aspect that looks good for evening sun.

"Brats sound awesome," Ruby says, pulling on long pants and shrugging into a fleece. I give her a big hug, mostly to warm myself up.

Last time, we camped a few bends farther along, in Mexico. By then we had figured out packing the canoe. One of the boys sat on an ammo can in front of the bow paddler. The other sat in a small director's chair crammed in the middle of the load.

Sawyer was still in diapers. Eli used the plastic potty contraption with mixed results. Cloth diapers dried on the load in the boat or hung from tent guylines in camp. The boys' favorite occupation was throwing rocks in the water. For hours, Eli and Sawyer stood side by side, tossing stones into the muddy river. Periodically during the day, we filled a plastic bucket with rocks for the boys to throw from the boat. They also trailed rubber toys on tethers tied to the canoe thwarts. They reeled them in—orca whales, rubber ducks—talked to them, flung them back out.

Throughout the day we fed them licorice, candy, gum, dried bananas, suckers, crackers and cheese. Food diversion was key to making our miles. In camp, we explored up side canyons, scrambled into the slickrock, found thorns in every conceivable way. Looking back, I can't believe we pulled it off. The daily labor, the constant need for diversion, the nursing, changing, pooping, waking up crying, falling down, eating sand, dirty diapers, cleaning up, entertaining, carrying, picking up, soothing, playing. More than a decade later, I can't imagine it.

Toward dusk that evening with our little boys, fourteen years back, we noticed a pair of riders on the cliff above us. Our red canoe was turned over on shore. Our bright tent sat in a grove of acacia trees. The riders were silhouetted against the gray sky. They made their way along the edge of cliff, well above. Several times they stopped together, looking down at us.

Then they turned down toward our camp. They took their time. It was steep, prickly, rocky terrain. But they came on steadily. The boys picked up on our anxiety. They watched the riders.

"Horsey," Sawyer said.

"Two," Eli corrected.

As they came nearer, we could make out a large man on a big horse and a much smaller, older man on a donkey. They came resolutely toward us. We could hear the skitter of hooves against loose rock, the creak of saddle. The big man shifted easily with his horse's gait. They sat lazily, comfortably, looking us over. What drove them, I couldn't say—curiosity, territoriality, something to do, friendliness, mischief?

Suddenly they were in our camp. The horse was massive. The big rider ducked through the vicious thorns of mesquite and acacia trees. Lethal branches whacked against his leather chaps. The horse shied away from the blue tent, our bright clothing. The boys huddled against my legs.

You could see the quick assessment being made. Our little family, the small boys, a pregnant woman. The large man bent low under a branch, managed to tip his hat, and kept right on riding. The old man on his donkey, who I have thought of as Sancho Panza ever since, trotted through behind. He grinned sheepishly at us, big gaps in his teeth. At a small wash, his donkey balked. He dismounted, jogged across, mounted up again, his boots almost hitting the ground. They rode up the bank, out of sight.

"That was interesting," I said.

"Yeah. And a little spooky," Marypat agreed.

This time, we see no one around when we coast past that spot, looking ahead for the maw of canyon. Arroyo San Antonio comes in, running with a respectable flow for this part of the world. We get caught in a shallow side channel and have to wade our boats down a steep, rock-filled drop. It is overcast, cool, the light gray. A wild horse stands above us on the hillside. A great blue heron flaps downriver, exotic birds flit in the underbrush—warblers, pyrrhuloxia, phainopepla, black phoebe; some of the birds here are species found nowhere else in the United States. Consequently, Big Bend is a popular destination for birders who want to add to their life lists.

The first miles of the day are filled with that heightened expectancy. Our first dramatic canyon lies ahead, featuring the biggest rapid of the trip. Few people have run it since the floods, and we don't know what to expect.

The limestone wall of Mesa de Anguila rises above the river. Around a corner, the opening comes to view, a portal in the rock, the viselike opening that is both beckoning and fearsome, a descent into shadowed unknown regions. At rock gates like these, I always think of John Wesley Powell going down the Green and Colorado Rivers in wooden dories in the late 1800s. Going first, entering these dark gates, knowing nothing of what roaring tumult, what sublime beauty, what bliss and calamity await around the bend.

We know what lies before us, at least generally. We're reasonably assured that we can do it, but the thrill and the dread still well up in response, and midmorning our three boats coast on the quickening current through the narrow pass, into the tall canyon walls. The wider world slips away and a more intimate, rock-held universe pulls us in under a slit of sky.

"Hooo-eee!" Ruby shouts. "This rocks!"

Fifty-Eight

—Names of rocks and features on a whitewater map
of Rock Slide Rapid in Santa Elena Canyon

Rock Slide is the rapid in Big Bend everyone knows. It is a unique obstacle, rated a Class IV rapid on the Class I–VI whitewater scale, with I being benign and VI being lethal. It is unique because it doesn't fit the mold. Most river turbulence is caused by a constriction in the channel, where the river volume pinches down and wild waves and currents result, by a sudden drop at a ledge or falls, or by boulders that wash in from a side tributary and create a rocky barrier the river has to find its way through.

Whitewater is tremendously variable. Every rapid on every river is an individual entity, characterized by the effects of volume and gradient and channel profile, by bedrock type and sediment load, by vegetation and seasonal climate regimes. Still, most rapids conform to one of these three general categories and fit certain patterns that render them intelligible. Coming up on a ledge drop or a boulder garden or a narrows, you know what to be looking for, and you have some inkling of the kinds of problems that typically crop up.

The Rock Slide is none of the above. It has formed because Santa Elena Canyon is so sheer and narrow at that spot that boulders peel off of the limestone walls and fall directly into the river. Many boulders, some huge, have done that. The result is a random labyrinth that happens to have a river boiling through it.

At high water, holes develop that equal anything in the Grand Canyon. Because it is so littered and chaotic, logjams routinely hang up and block passages. At very low water, the route requires a combination of paddling moves punctuated by short portages to cross gravel bars and navigate between tight boulders. At moderate water levels, like the one we enjoy, it is runnable after careful scouting and strategizing.

"We've heard that the Texas Gate is clogged with debris," the raft company folks told us, "but that's all we know."

Many years back, I rafted Santa Elena Canyon with a group of college students. The water was moderately high and pushy. The skill level of the group was low. We elected to portage the entire rapid, a Herculean effort, humping heavy boats and gear through a slope of rockfall boulders the size of small cars. It took us the better part of a day to move less than half a mile.

When we came through with the two boys and Ruby in the womb, the river was very low. The only available run was through the Texas Gate, a narrow opening on river left to avoid a huge, midstream, undercut boulder. Then we had to carry across a small gravel bar to the next pool and navigate through a tight squeeze of limestone to the bottom.

Making the move into the Texas Gate was the crux. The water was so shallow that it was difficult to get any purchase with our paddles. We backpaddled away from the boulder. Water sucked under it. The bow of the canoe thunked into the waterworn rock lightly before we could make the cut, but we managed it.

Just behind us, a guided raft with two passengers had showed up. We helped them through the portage. Where we were able to slip through the second narrows, the raft guide had to unload, tip his boat on its side, and push it through. Sawyer and Eli watched all this transpire, wearing their tiny life jackets and river shorts, standing at the bottom of a vise of rock with a slit of warm blue sky overhead. Who knows what they thought? They don't remember the event.

This time, the river slicks us into Santa Elena, down into the depths toward the Rock Slide. It feels like skiing powder, that same dynamic whoosh of speed and balance, water pillowing around rock corners, narrow slots of tributary canyon breaking away, the day going dusky. It is a sweet water level—fast and exhilarating. The canyon is magic—tight and intimate, cool, smelling of rock. And it is ours.

All of these journeys have their blood-hot moments, focused lasers of energy. The musk ox confrontation on the Kazan, the moonrise below Younts Peak, and this entrance to the canyon with the unknown turbulence ahead. We are all tingling with it, the pulse of water, the carved crevasse of rock, the coming challenge.

These spikes of experience, moments of danger and beauty, are what we come for, these reminders to wake up. We are inoculating our children with it. I want them injected with this lust more than any vaccine on the market. Even if it isn't the path they take, even if our addiction to wilderness doesn't become theirs, it shoots them through with passion and resourcefulness and intrepid energy.

The rapid materializes suddenly. Around a bend, the river channel is choked with huge boulders. It looks completely impassable. At the sight of it, instinctively, we all backpaddle. The bows of the boats grind into a gravel bar. Everyone piles out. Ruby straddles the canoe, pulls our bow well up.

"How the hell do you get through?" Sawyer says.

The boulders are worn and polished by floodwaters, fluted limestone, cold stone as smooth as skin. For a time, we all clamber through them, distracted by the playground of rock. Eli takes a climb straight on, with speed, going directly for the top, muscling his way up. Sawyer loses himself in the process, zones in, explores. Ruby takes a climb moment by moment, surprised by things, often distracted. For a time, they work up the slope, through tunnels, pop out on top where they perch, watching each other.

"Up here, Norbert!" Sawyer calls to Ruby. "You can do it. Don't be a wimp."

Marypat and I make our way above the river, more focused on the challenge. Clumps of fresh debris hang up in rock crevices thirty feet above us—wads of vegetation, tree trunks, river cane.

"Criminy," I say. "Imagine this thing thirty feet higher."

"That I'd like to see," Marypat says. "From a distance. Like from a helicopter!"

There are many vantage points to scout from. The Texas Gate is indeed blocked by logs, which the river strains through, impassable. Our only option is the Mexican Gate. Below that, the rocks are clumped in a tight pattern, but the flow eddies through at a sedate pace and with room for our boats to pass.

Eighty percent of the river flows smack into the midstream boulders, hulking blocks with dire currents working under them. In order to sneak past, we will have to hug the Mexican shore and at the last second make a strong move away from the rocks into a small eddy. There we might pause before lining up for the gate and working on down. It is a tight fit. If we miss, the boats will broach against the rock. We could capsize. No telling what the currents would do with our gear or with us.

"I wonder about lining down to the eddy," I muse. I study the shoreline for good points from which to lower the canoes on ropes down to the eddy. It looks possible, but not easy.

"Looks messy to me," Marypat says.

"No way, Dad," Eli weighs in. "Look at the rocks you'd have to get around. Let's just do it."

"I think it looks pretty gnarly," Ruby joins the debate. "I don't really want to paddle this part. I think Mom and Dad should do the canoes."

"What do you think?" I look at my partner.

She shrugs.

"I'll stand right here," Eli hops onto a barely exposed rock at the head of the eddy. "If you guys have trouble, maybe I can reach out and grab your stern as you go by."

"If the canoes go through fine, I'll do the ducky," Sawyer says.

Marypat and I climb up the shoreline, stopping at several points to mark our route mentally. We point things out to each other, make sure we're on the same page.

"That sleeper there." I point to a smooth, submerged boulder. "Let's hang right next to it and then get our angle ready to backpaddle into the eddy." Marypat studies the move, looks further down.

"We have to be making our cut even before we get past Eli," she says.

At the canoes, we stretch, give each other a chesty, life-vest hug. I climb to the stern, kneel on the pads. Marypat steps in, picks up her paddle,

AL AND RUBY FRAMED BY THE MEXICAN GATE IN ROCK SLIDE RAPID.

swivels her head downstream. The canoe swings around, enters the flow. I
see the three kids tensed at the eddy downstream. I look close ahead, find
my first marker rock. We slip past it. The current is faster than it looked.
The next landmark flashes by, I pry the stern toward shore. Marypat starts
backpaddling, easy at first, more emphatically as she slides past Eli. He is
poised in a crouch, ready to make a grab for us. But it isn't necessary. The
stern of the canoe catches the eddy, the bow grazes the rock, a kiss. Marypat
backs us in, smooth as parking in a garage.

"Hot diggity," Ruby shouts. She takes the canoe and hoists it into the
sand on the edge of the eddy just above the rockbound gate. "Do it again!"

"Same old, same old," I say as we jog back up.

The second time doesn't go quite as smoothly. We get pulled too far out, then overcorrect and have to paddle hard into an upstream eddy to collect ourselves.

"Okay," Marypat breathes. "Let's do this right."

A little clumsy, but successful, we horse the second canoe into the eddy. Eli pulls us to safety. Sawyer goes upstream for the kayak.

He bobs down like a pro, composed and on target, grinning at us as he turns the stubby boat in.

From there, the run is anticlimactic. Through the gate, we can eddy behind boulders at will, play back and forth across the boulder-strewn pools, find slots we thread the boats through. It is a thing to savor, this serene pause among the boulders, thinking about the splash they must have made, thinking about the roil of flood, thick with mud, lumpy with tree trunks, bellowing in these depths.

Then on, dawdling around cool, fluting corners, the soaring walls ramping fifteen hundred feet above, the trill of canyon wrens, the sharp flight of peregrines. There are places that deserve the word *sublime*. This is one.

We make camp at Fern Canyon. The floods deposited a steep plug of sand and mud at the mouth, but beyond that the slickrock canyon bends back magically. Banks of maidenhair fern drape down rock walls at freshwater seeps. Clear pools shimmer in basins of rock. Ruby starts a contest, straddling a stream, working her feet along the smooth walls, staying dry. Sawyer and Eli follow.

Several short cliffs slow us up, but the kids attack the obstacles, make quick work of them. Marypat and I hoist ourselves up. An overhanging pour-off finally thwarts us, but not before Sawyer shucks down to his boxers and works his way into a very compromised position over a cold, stagnant pool. Ruby and Eli wait to follow if he succeeds, or to laugh at the calamity if he falls.

"Scheisser!" he yells, and makes a gangly leap back to safety. "Not good," he concludes. Ruby holds her sides.

"Aw, Soy-Boy, I really wanted to see you hit that nasty water," she says.

"So sorry to disappoint you, Norbie!"

On the way back, Ruby discovers a mud hole above camp. She and Sawyer spend an hour mucking around in their underwear. At one point, they appear above camp, mud-stained to the crotch. "If you hear us yelling," Ruby calls down, "it means we're stuck in quicksand and need help!" And they disappear again.

Eli can't resist joining them. Then Marypat takes the camera. Her laugh echoes in the rocks.

Just before dark, I head back up the canyon to collect freshwater in a five-gallon jug. Precious water. Hunkered over a clear, deep pool below a seep,

I ladle liquid into the plastic container. A timeless pose, a timeless need. Water drips out of a crack between limestone layers. It may take decades, even centuries, for the water to work down a thousand feet of rock and finally squeeze out, feeding the ferns, feeding my family. The sound of water trickling out of the face fills the alcove.

All the people, in all the places, whose days are devoted to this one thing, gathering water, hauling it home, careful not to waste. The canyon is shadowed with the coming night on this shortest day. A rock wren scoots past, skimming above the canyon floor.

After dinner, Marypat brings out floating candles sent to us by my sister in Massachusetts. It is warm. Stars fill the river of sky overhead.

"Another ritual," Eli moans. The boys shuffle to the river's edge, bumping shoulders, making light of another quirky request from Marypat.

"C'mon, you guys." Marypat brings us into a huddle. She hands out the white, round balls of wax. "Everyone makes a wish and we put them in the river, see which one lasts longest."

Now that it's competitive, the interest gathers. We each ponder our wish. The air is still. The river murmurs past our feet. The candles spark to life. One by one, we set them afloat, where they bob in the slight currents near shore. For a time, nothing happens. The candles go nowhere. Then the microeddies catch hold. Sawyer's candle zooms off upstream. Eli's follows. They troop along, urging their candles forward. Ruby's heads downstream, bumping softly through the shallows.

All of the candles last longer than we expect. They make erratic journeys, get stuck in pools, race upstream, head to deeper water, move down again. Ruby's lasts and lasts. One by one, the rest of the candles go out, but hers rotates through an eddy, in and out of little caverns of rock, through small turbulence.

Marypat is pulled in by the bright little spark's staying power. She starts cheering it on. It rocks on a wave, fades. Marypat groans. Then it revives and she cheers. She hangs on every move the little pinprick of light makes. The boys get restless. Eli threatens to chuck a rock at it.

"Don't you dare!" Marypat warns.

It is very dark, very quiet down in the bottom of Santa Elena at the edge of Mexico. Ruby's light survives wave after wave. Finally it sails out into faster current. It moves quickly, still lit, dancing away from us, and then winks out. Marypat gazes into the darkness after it. She takes Ruby's arm, hugging it to her side, and walks with her into camp.

Fifty-Nine

I took Ruby (4 mos.) on a horse-pack trip in the Spanish Peaks for five days. We took three of Sue's horses for four of us, plus Ruby. Ruby loved the backpack and I only had to carry her in front to nurse for one short stretch. It was very cozy in the tent, just Ruby and me. She got to the top of her first peak and we could see the Grand Tetons way in the distance.

—MARYPAT, RUBY'S BIRTH BOOK

Sunlight washes the mouth of Santa Elena. We stroke toward it. It is still sublime in the depths, but goose-bump chilly, like being in the basement of the desert. One after the other, our canoes cross into the bath of light, the warmth, emerging from the gap of rock. The nature trail at the mouth of the canyon is closed. Flood wreckage lies about, the footpath is under yards of mud, yellow crime tape drapes across the buried trunks of tamarisk. A family wanders around on the bench of newly deposited sand. Two kids in T-shirts stand on the bank, watch us pass. Ruby waves.

Homeland Security, and the immigration quagmire, has rendered the already sketchy life on the Mexican side of the border untenable. In tiny traditional villages like Santa Elena, just downstream of the canyon, a quiet settlement at the isolated northern fringe of Mexico, life withers away.

For generations, people on both sides of the river paid scant attention to the international barrier. Mind you, for residents whose families have been here for centuries, the border remains a matter of heated dispute. Historically, families lived on both sides of the river. Ancestors are buried in cemeteries that are now in Texas. Traditional grazing lands, buildings, ferries, and subsistence businesses straddled the countries, and, until recently, residents paid only passing attention to the political line in the sand.

When we came through in 1995, you could stand on the Texas side and hail a rowboat from Mexico to take you across to Santa Elena. No one checked papers. There you might enjoy home-cooked *comidas* and cold cerveza in a cantina or stroll the town plaza under shade trees. Mexican villagers came across routinely to pick up groceries and supplies in Terlingua and Study Butte. No longer. Not since 9/11.

More immediately for us, the floods seem to have wiped out Cottonwood Campground, where we plan to resupply with water. The green blotch of treed bottom that gives the campground its name is there. I watch for the river access road and water pump I remember from last time, when we came to shore and were greeted by a retired couple in an Airstream. They doted on the boys, coddled Marypat, drove us to the water spigot to fill our jugs. There were roadrunners and white-winged doves.

The access is wiped out; the pump is gone. By the time we realize we've missed it, we are well below what's left of the campground, separated by a thorny barrier of mesquite. Marypat and I grab an empty jug and walk into the thicket. The kids fling javelins of cane at each other. The riverbank is furrowed with flood channels, vegetation beaten into flattened mats. The Rio Grande sprawled half a mile out of its banks, stomping everything in its path.

We duck through the shady, spiky grove of half-buried trees. Insects clack in the midday heat. I tear through spiderwebs. Finally, what's left of the campground opens in front of us. New outhouses have been erected, campsite pullouts regraded. There is one car in sight. The water spigot has a sign that reads Non-Potable Water: Do Not Drink. We fill the jug anyway. I kick myself for not getting more of that limestone-filtered water from Fern Canyon.

"If we run out, we can iodine this stuff," I say.

"Hopefully not," Marypat says. "I hate that iodine taste."

We enter the Great Unknown, the untraveled gap between canyons. No dragons appear. The expansive desert has its own appeal, not the least of which stems from the fact that no one comes here.

The river widens, ripples over shallows. Last time through it was so warm and dry we spooked huge catfish out of stagnant pools, repeatedly went aground on bars. This time, Sawyer sterns one of the canoes. Eli takes a turn in the ducky. A thousand-foot scarp of limestone angles away from the river into Mexico. It rises sheer out of the desert, formidable and dark, water-stained rock without breaks.

Volcanic topography juts out on the Texas side. Cerro Castellan, the Mule Ear Peaks, the Chisos Mountains. A light-phase redtail soars against the washed-out sky. Black phoebe sit in the shrubs. Blue-gray gnatcatchers buzz at each other. A prairie falcon flies the river corridor.

On the topo map, seventeen miles from Fern Canyon it says Buenos Aires. Several small black squares represent building ruins. On land, a firm, smooth bench of sand provides camp. The kids decide to explore the far shore. Eli takes the stern. Sawyer, tall and skinny as a stork, hops in the bow. Ruby flops into the middle. In four strokes they ferry across, park, and disappear up a dry drainage. Their voices float in the distance, strident and thin.

Behind camp, away from the river, everything is sharp—the rocks, the plants, the stings of insects, the light. The ruins of Buenos Aires rust in the air above the river. Broken rock walls, gnarled wood beams, discarded wire, a tin can, rusty, bent spikes—all of it camouflaged, brown and ocher and sandstone, fading into the colors of desert. Someone thought it had good air, gave it a name. Someone chose this spot in the middle of gaping space to build structures, to stage an enterprise; this dry arroyo under the beating sun, with the river below and the lonely, tortured beauty heaving against the horizon.

"I'd say my beard is pretty legit," Eli says, looking at me by the fire. "Actually, I think I might have as much beard as you do."

"You're not setting a very high bar," I agree. "Hell, I can barely grow eyebrows."

I reach out and rub Eli's jaw. He does the same to me. Our eyes joust. We haven't arm wrestled in probably two years. Neither one of us has made the challenge. Neither one of us wants to embarrass the other, or be embarrassed by losing. Soon enough it'll be a moot point.

A two-burner camp stove sits in a dry bag, ready for use. I keep thinking about pulling it out. Part of me enjoys the ease and cleanliness of it, the spiffy technology of it, but dry driftwood from the flood lies everywhere. Every night we pull out the heat-warped old fire pan, turn it to block the breeze, and cook over a fire. Fires have a pace to them. Cooking over the licking orange tongues, feeding the flames, moving pots to adjust heat, making hot drinks, watching the coals.

We pull up seats, rub our bare feet in the sand, fiddle with the fire.

"We found a dead cow over there," Sawyer says, "sunk to his butthole in mud."

"I felt bad," Ruby adds. "I know how it feels to get stuck, not to be able to move. It would be terrible."

"Yeah, you were in just about butt deep the other day," Sawyer remembers.

Ruby rubs her chin, flashes him the middle finger. "You are a butthole, buddy," she taunts.

"Sometimes I kind of miss poopy diapers and baby drool, don't you?" Marypat asks me.

"Ruby's still a drooler, right Norbie?" Sawyer throws in.

She chucks a dirt ball at him. A clod lands on the lid of the dinner pot.

"Quit, or we'll put mud in your bowl."

The light goes gray, then dark. Our headlamps are in our pockets, ready to shine our way to bed later. Wind buffets camp. Sparks from the fire fly in hot horizontal lines through the dark. Stars flood the sky, serene and sharp, right to the horizon. Orion, Cassiopeia, the Pleiades. It stays warm enough for shorts until we button up camp and go to the tent, and it is too warm for down sleeping bags. Sand works through the netting, sifts onto our faces. We still haven't put the rain fly on once.

An owl wakes me before daylight. I escape the gritty closeness of sleeping bag, slap sand off of the breakfast pack, start a flame, fill a pot, settle into a seat with a view downstream. No different from home. But also different in every way from home. At home, I don't know what the wind, the stars, the river say. Here, the air stills with the dawn. The land feels combed, rearranged. A few planets linger near the western horizon.

Ruby pads out in bare feet, looks around, hitches a seat up next to mine. "Is today Christmas?" she asks.

"Tomorrow," I say. "Tonight is Christmas Eve."

"Look!" She points into Mexico. A pinto stands on the riverbank, quivering with attention. A spindly colt hovers at her side. They shy back at the sight of us, prance out of sight, then return. Another horse joins them, looks us over, and makes its way to the river to drink. The pair follow, still nervous. They drink quickly and trot away.

"Are they wild?" Ruby asks.

"Probably not, but the livestock around here is pretty wild to start with. It's not like they hang out around people much."

VOLCANIC LANDSCAPE RISES ABOVE THE RIVER VALLEY ON THE TEXAS SIDE.

On Christmas Eve, we camp on a long, midstream island with the international border drawn down the center of it on the map; balanced between countries, but nothing more than a nice spot for a tent to us.

Our pace on the river is easy. The current alternates between slow pools and rippling current, pulsing down shady aisles. Landmarks thrust up, erupting from the ground. Every bend is another vantage. Black Dike, the Sierra del Carmen, Elephant Tusk. Somewhere we stop for lunch, hunt in the gravel for agate, take a siesta.

Marypat and Eli share a canoe for the day. They talk. Eli reveals that he is no longer a virgin.

"You didn't know that, Dad?" he says in camp. He tries for nonchalance, doesn't quite manage it.

"How would I know that?"

"I just figured you knew."

"I also asked him how many times he's tried drinking," Marypat adds.

"And what did you say to that?"

"Four or five," he says.

"Hundred," Ruby adds. Eli chucks a stone toward her.

"Dad, I'm seventeen years old," he says. "You go to parties, people drink, people smoke weed. Didn't you do stuff when you were my age?"

I grunt. I'm not about to reveal the things I did at his age.

Sawyer grabs a bat of driftwood, hits a stone out over the river. Ruby and Eli stand up. They move to a bench of gravel, start up a game of stick/rock baseball.

"Think he's telling the truth?" I ask Marypat.

"About what?"

"You know what. Think he lost his virginity? It's the kind of thing you might bend the truth on."

"I never thought that," she says. "Seems entirely possible to me."

"If he'd been in my boat, we never would have gotten to that subject," I say, "true or not."

"Maybe you should ask more questions, then just listen."

Sixty

Day 7, Thursday, Christmas:

Weather: Hot all day, with a few clouds in the afternoon

Wildlife: Red-tailed hawk, turtles, great-horned owl, pigeon hawk

Logistics: 14 miles to a camp within a mile of Mariscal Canyon

ELI, GROUP JOURNAL

By now the load is diminished enough that a low-slung chair fits in the middle of the hardshell canoe, surrounded with packs and dry bags. When the ducky paddler gets bored, they have the option of clipping the rubber boat to the stern line and climbing in as a passenger. On the flatwater stretches, especially in a wind, the temptation to lounge is compelling.

I prefer the hardshell canoe, the same boat we paddled across Canada when we were pregnant with Eli. I have thousands of miles of history with it. The folding canoe is convenient to transport and paddles well enough, but it isn't the same. Aluminum ribs get in the way, joints in the tubing fill with sand, the seats are uncomfortable, the hull flexes and bends. It is a boat that has its place and has served us well, but given a choice, it's not a contest.

I'm in it on Christmas day. The bent-shaft paddle is light in my hands. The grip rides against the permanent paddling calluses in my palm. I paddle on the left, my preferred side. My right hand on the grip controls the subtle angles of the blade. I always stern on the left in whitewater. The hull flares and tapers before me, the load tucked in place, clipped to thwarts, lashed down, precise as a load on a packhorse. It is a beamy boat with enough rocker to be nimble in current and a bit maddening to keep on track across lakes.

My dry box lies between my feet, full of maps, journal, binoculars. A small dry bag crammed with wind shirts and rain gear lies behind my seat. The day's food is in a small pack behind the bow seat. A packing system we've refined and adapted over three decades.

The river has revealed itself over the days. How it moves, its idiosyncracies and foibles. Mile by mile, we learn about each other. Wall shots, barely submerged shallows, the chutes along the banks. Every third or fourth stroke is a J stroke, a slight, momentary flick to correct direction. I paddle in time with Ruby, who sits in the bow this morning. A shallow riffle pulls us near shore. I pry the stern to angle away, we take two fast, strong strokes together to avoid the overhanging tamarisk. An alley of current picks us up.

I line up with it, look downstream for the deepest braid of river.

In each stroke, every read of river, the seeds of lessons from the continent hum in the synapses. The restless water below sandstone cliffs on Lake Superior, the tight willowy bends of the East Gallatin River a mile from home in Montana, the brawny current of the Kazan galloping down a tundra straightaway, the iron waters of northern Minnesota, banks of permafrost above the Arctic Circle in the Yukon Territory, the turbid green of the Colorado in canyon country—water running off the back of Turtle Island in the dusky sensory memory lodged in my rotator cuff and elbow tendons, synthesizing into the way this boat moves down this river on this Christmas morning.

It was cold last night. In the gray dawn we stayed in our bags, opening a few presents, waiting for the sun. Marypat baked coffee cake in the Dutch oven. Flycatchers went to work in the underbrush. It was midday before we loaded canoes.

Elephant Tusk juts out at the flank of the Chisos to the north. The river swings us around to different views of it. On hairpin bends, Mule Ear Peaks rise like a gun sight upriver. A few wild cattle graze in Mexico, a horse or two. Big Bend turtles slip off of muddy logs.

On a long straightaway, I keep the boat near the Mexican shore in deeper water, almost underneath the overhanging branches of tamarisk that survived the floods. A pair of red-tailed hawks clatter out of the low branches. One of them swoops ahead and lands again. We coast almost underneath before it spooks. We slow, nosing the boat along, repeatedly playing tag. The wide surprise of wings, the pale flash of red, the patented scream.

A great horned owl roosts in a scrubby tree on the far side. A pigeon hawk jukes and dives above it. The owl is stoic, oblivious as a landlord before nagging tenants, shifts its talons on the branch, hunches lower. The falcon hovers above the tree, dives and pulls up, circles the owl's head. Marypat drifts directly below the roost, shooting up with her camera.

Mariscal Canyon rises into the sky below our Christmas night camp. The kids slosh upriver to the head of a swift chute and ride it down, bobbing in the waves, bumping over rocks, slopping in to shiver around the fire. Their wet footprints dry on the rocks. Park Service literature warns against swimming. In addition to the usual park service overprotectiveness, the implication is that the water coming from Mexico cannot be trusted.

Ruby, Sawyer, and Marypat head up a limestone butte rising behind camp. "Let's go on an adventch!" Ruby cajoles Sawyer into the hike. They chatter at each other all the way up the slope, drop out of sight on some investigation. Marypat climbs steadily toward the view. She hunkers at the top, silhouetted against sky, looking downstream into the depths of canyon and off over the prickly undulations going purple with sunset.

Once, when the kids were toddlers, we took a hike on some land north of the Yellowstone River in central Montana. Marypat led up a slope through ponderosa pine looking for a view. We went slowly, but the kids trudged upslope, complaining and bored. At the brow of the hill, Marypat and I pointed south into the Beartooths, over to the river valley. The view meant something to us. We had been to those places, camped in those meadows, climbed peaks, and paddled floods. Eli and Sawyer threw sticks at a target. Ruby jumped back and forth over a prickly pear.

On the way down, I followed a shallow valley through pine needle duff. I came to a dry pour-off at a rock band. "Uh-oh," I called. "Looks like we have a problem!"

Eli sprinted over to have a look, Sawyer right behind. Ruby toddled up. "A problem!" Eli shouted. He and Sawyer scrambled down. Ruby demanded to go the same way. The boys scampered off down the cluttered draw.

"Hey, another problem, over here," they yelled, diving into a thicket of deadfall that obstructed the valley. Marypat jogged after them. Ruby tugged at my hand. "C'mon, Daddy, a problem!" she insisted.

Ruby's adventures have grown out of that impulse to seek the most gnarled, obstructed, difficult path in lieu of plodding along a trail to some vaguely defined goal.

She asks her friends over to spend the night. Inevitably, part of the agenda is to go on an adventure, preferably in a storm, usually after dark. We only get the highlight reel. "We bushwhacked off the ridge to Church Street," Ruby tells me later. "We went behind the construction yard and skinny-dipped in the creek. A car went by just when we were getting back into our underwear!"

She comes home sopping wet after jumping the fence and swimming in the city pool after dark or after being chased out of the creek by a curmudgeonly neighbor, or stomping clods of ice from her clothes after digging a snow cave at the bottom of the toboggan hill.

She finds foxes and rabbits and strays. She runs into homeless people, gives them money. She always needs a hot shower. She is always flushed with daring. I'd rather have her off on an adventure than at soccer practice or music lessons—those manicured, parent-led, safe activities.

When Ruby and Sawyer return from the bluff, they entertain themselves chucking mud balls and rocks at each other. Eli goes over and takes it up, zinging a sidearm line drive at Sawyer.

"Drives me crazy when they do that," I say. "What happens when they get an eyeful of grit or bean each other with a rock the size of my fist?"

"It's what I grew up doing," Marypat says. "The wrestling and fighting, it was endless. I remember when my dad would yell at us. My younger brother, Andrew, and I would keep wrestling, only in incredibly slow motion, like that would make us invisible. Anything to keep going."

Baked ham, stuffing, and three-bean salad for Christmas dinner. No one is bleeding or pissed off.

"Oh my god, I love three-bean salad!" Ruby gushes. "Why don't we have this at home? When we get home, I am making three-bean salad."

Dishes by starlight and headlamp. The fire dies to a red glow. The mountains are black cutouts in the fling of stars. River curls and hurries past the ends of our boats, phosphorescent in the blackness. A dove calls from Texas, a sound full of ache and urgency.

Where else should we be this holy night?

Sixty-One

Cabeza de Vaca ("head of cow") sailed from Spain with the Narvaez expedition in 1527, occupying the office of treasurer. They reached Florida in 1528, where the expedition split forces in order to cover more ground. De Vaca's group met with various disasters as they pushed west along the gulf. They were reduced to just four men after a shipwreck off the coast of present-day Texas, where they were captured and imprisoned by Indians. They escaped after one year, and for the next eight years de Vaca and his companions wandered around the lower Rio Grande Valley, living with and trading with Indians. De Vaca developed a reputation among Natives as a healer. Eventually, de Vaca met up with Spanish soldiers and made his way back to Spain in 1537. Later in life he was stationed in Argentina, where he became a strident advocate for Native rights and a critic of the treatment of Natives by colonial powers. His political views eventually got him exiled to North Africa in 1546.

Indomitable and fearless as Ruby usually is, she has her insecurities. Paddling whitewater is one of them. The only real rapid in Mariscal Canyon is called the Tight Squeeze, and it's Ruby's day in the kayak when we run it. The rapid is another rock pile with the current ripping between two tightly spaced boulders. We stop upstream and troop down the gravel bar to scout it.

Ruby fidgets with her life jacket. She goes off to pee.

"Nothin' to it, Norb," Sawyer reassures her. "Just brace away from the rock and stick close to the outside. You'll be through like a champ."

"You guys go first," she says.

It's best when the river does the work for you. Lined up on the outside edge of the passage, Sawyer and I hardly have to maneuver. We draw away from the rock with current piling into it and blast through clean, then pivot into an eddy behind a rock the size of a one-car garage. Marypat and Eli follow suit.

I climb to the top of the boulder with the camera. Ruby looks lonely and jittery settling into the rubber kayak. Her run looks off from the start. She clings to shore on the approach. An eddy above the constriction catches her boat and she whips into it inadvertently. Before we can say anything, she paddles back into the current, but now it's tough for her to stay away from the bad spot. Ruby digs hard, but the red kayak slides up against the boulder, her upstream tube goes under. She flips out.

The boat is pinned on the rock. Ruby is shoved up against it. The current won't let her free. She battles in the confined space caught up against the boat and the rock, river tugging her down. I start scrambling down off of the boulder. It is a matter of a few seconds, but interminable. Finally she kicks off, stiff-arms herself free, and swings away. She swims through the gap, still holding her paddle. The boat bobs out, follows her down.

"Ahhh, that was so stupid," she says. "I hate it when that happens! I finally got mad and got myself out of there." But she is shaky and cowed when she drags the boat up and empties it of water.

"You want me to do the ducky?" Eli offers.

She shakes her head. "We're through the hard part."

Deeper in Mariscal Canyon, past the rapids, Sawyer points with his paddle at the cliffy walls. "What the heck are those things?"

A dozen exotic-looking animals perch on the steep canyon ledges. They look like transplanted goats from Asia or Africa, orange-and-white-and-black patterned, with long horns. They seem completely out of place, and yet entirely at home. The mixed herd moves easily up through the rock bands, turning to look down at us. Their coats shine in the warm sun. They look healthy as hell.

Exotic is precisely what they are, and transplanted—a species of oryx native to northern Africa and hunted nearly to extinction there. Several thousand of these goatlike animals were brought to Texas and featured as expensive targets on game ranches. Adults can stand three feet tall at the shoulder and weigh more than four hundred pounds. They have beautiful horns. They do very well in desert environments, capable of going weeks between water holes.

Eventually, and some would say, inevitably, some of the oryx escaped from the hunting ranches. They have settled into a comfortable niche in Big Bend, where they compete quite successfully against the endangered, and indigenous, desert bighorn sheep.

The day has gotten warm. Our boats, red blips, slip along the canyon bottom. The oryx watch us pass. No doubt there are studies under way to determine what to do about this mishap of entrepreneurship. In the meantime, we refuse to let villagers from Santa Elena go to Terlingua to buy a sack of flour, but some Texan with big-game ambitions can import African animals and then let them slip away, setting off a chain of environmental ripple effects no one has a handle on. Oops.

Midcanyon, a trail winds down to the river along a tributary valley. Marypat found the dotted line on the map a few days back and has been amping up for a hike ever since. We park at a sandy beach, grab water bottles, start up the vague trail.

"Looks like about ten people a year come here," I say.

There are no footprints. The path is sporadically marked by low cairns. Game trails lead off here and there, confusing the route. It is hot. More than once we lose the track, spread out and explore, find it again.

"Wow," Eli says. "Imagine this place in August!"

The rock is spiky and rough, every plant and bush has spines or thorns. Blind prickly pear, with tiny hairlike spines as fine as fiberglass. Your garden-variety prickly pear, some plants taller than me and as big around as a minivan. Hedgehog cactus. Walking-stick cholla. Fishhook barrel cactus. In the dry washes, catclaw acacia grab at our shirts. Mesquite bristle with inch-long thorns. The leaves of agave plants are tipped with tough, needle-sharp points that could drive through bone.

There is no shade. A mile up, descending to a dry wash, I step over a tarantula. The spider is the size of a small mouse, brown and hairy, legs the width of pipe cleaners spoking out. It hunkers in some rocks in the middle of the trail.

FRIENDLY NEIGHBORHOOD TARANTULA.

"Oh, God!" Ruby says. "That's bad. I hate spiders, and that spider is really gnar." She makes a six-foot detour around the hairy guy.

"They are poisonous," I say, bending over, "but hardly anyone gets really sick from their bite. People pick them up all the time. Want to try?"

"No thanks," all three kids chorus, stumbling back.

Spiders are their collective phobia. None of them can stand the things. Ruby won't even go in the bathroom if a tiny spider is hanging out on the far corner of ceiling. They think nothing of picking up snakes, playing with frogs and salamanders, catching most bugs, but spiders are another issue entirely.

"In the fall around here, the tarantulas migrate by the thousands," I continue my natural history lesson. "The roads can get greasy with squished tarantulas."

"Nice, Dad. Thanks for that," Ruby says. "And I was thinking I could maybe live here someday, until just now."

The heat reflects off the ground, saps our energy. We share sips out of the two water bottles. Any one of us could drink all of it at any time. The trail leads up a ridge toward the skyline. Marypat really wants to make the top, but the rest of us mutiny.

"For what?" Eli says. "Let's go back for a swim and some lunch."

Marypat turns and looks toward the top. A man-sized yucca juts out in profile. Hiking is her passion. Yes, she loves the river, but give her a mountain to climb, a trail to explore, and the flame of ambition fires up in her eyes.

"Let's go to the next rise," I offer.

Sawyer joins us. Ruby and Eli perch on a rock to wait. We drink the last of the water. I think how short the tether is that water holds us by. We are two miles from the canoes, the river, jugs of water; we have each swallowed several cups of water on the hike. And yet the last of the water draining away starts up a clock. I am parched in less than half a mile.

- -

"We have to camp there!" Eli points to a tent-sized flat rock jutting into the river just out of the canyon. "It's perfect."

"Yeah, and when the wind comes up, our tent cartwheels into the river with all the sleeping bags," Marypat says.

"We'll weight it down really well," he argues. "We have to camp there."

"Sleepwalking could be a problem," Sawyer observes.

ROCK ISLAND CAMP AT THE BOTTOM OF MARISCAL CANYON.

It has taken us half the day to meander through Mariscal Canyon, including the hike. Most river tours gear everything up and drive for hours for a canyon float that lasts less than a day. Hardly anyone does more than an overnight. Snapshot backcountry tourism. No one has to sleep on the ground, pee on a bush, put up with storms. No one has to brave the Great Unknown. No one has even a slim chance at achieving river rhythm.

In camp, the winds do start to gust. I check the tent, but it seems protected and anchored on its perch. The kids spend the remaining daylight working barefoot back up the wall of the canyon along a narrow, polished ledge above the river to a cave they spotted on the way down. Marypat strolls up a Mexican draw with a well-used horse trail along it. We still haven't used the stove once. I cook in a rocky crevice protected from the wind and blowing sand.

In the tent, we give each other back rubs. Sawyer straddles Marypat. Once he has her really relaxed, he ambushes her with a startling karate chop to the base of her neck. She jerks out of her reverie with a shout, then starts to giggle uncontrollably.

"Don't you worry," he says. "I know lots of good back rub tricks."

Sixty-Two

Closed Canyon. Mirror Canyons. Arch Canyon. Fern Canyon. Cow Canyon. Arroyo Venado. Glen Draw.

— NAMES OF SIDE CANYONS ALONG THE RIO GRANDE ON A TOPO MAP OF BIG BEND

In every canyon stretch there are narrow tributaries to explore, and they are irresistible. Repeatedly we leave the boats tied to bushes, enter these cracks in the rock, follow where they lead. Every one is plugged with mud from the floods. Fresh deposits, drying in the heat, cracked into acres of polygonal plates, some still with shrinking pools of water. They fill the side canyons for a quarter mile or more.

RUBY WALKS THROUGH A *LAND BEFORE TIME*.

"It's like *The Land Before Time* movies," Ruby notes.

The sun slips over the rim, cool shadows swoop in. There is rarely any water. Sometimes a shady pool resists evaporation; a *tinaja*, or water hole, where animals come to drink in the protected depths. Occasionally a spring seeps out of the wall, supporting an outburst of ferns and mosses.

Often as not, a sheer or overhanging pour-off stops us a few bends in. Sometimes there is a route around. Always the kids compete to find one, and when they do, they stand above us, arms raised, grinning, with the next evocative bend of canyon opening before them.

There are only rare signs of humanity. A trail, an old rock wall, a thrown horseshoe, a fire scar. Sometimes we come upon abandoned candelilla wax camps. Fifty-five-gallon metal drums, charred wood, scraps of rusted metal, dried-out plants. One of the borderland enterprises, for a time, capitalized on rendering wax from the candelilla plant, an ingredient in everything from chewing gum to floor wax.

Beginning in the early 1900s, the primitive industry was centered in the Big Bend region. Processing camps set up in side canyons or washes cut huge stacks of the candelilla plant, boiled the stalks, and skimmed off the wax. Loaded into burlap sacks, the wax was largely transported by burro. The advent of the national park, which restricted access to plants, and, more recently, the immigration clampdown, have brought the industry to a halt in Big Bend. While candelilla is still harvested and rendered in northern Mexico, it's become a negligible industry, another option for local survival cut short.

In one small canyon, a fifty-foot pour-off stops us almost immediately. We mill together in the cool disappointment. Our hands reach to stroke the sensuous skin of water-polished rock. Here, periodically, torrents of muddy water pulse over the lip, hurling boulders, scouring bedrock, tearing out vegetation, accomplishing erosion on fast-forward. Today it is chilly and hushed, dry as dust.

"Hey, check this out," Sawyer says, scrambling up a sidewall to a piece of climber's webbing. "There's a little ladder," he calls down.

In a crack of limestone, a piton anchors a short ladder that allows passage to a bench above and past the dry waterfall. The route leads through a lethal, bristling thicket of lechuguilla agave spikes and along pitted limestone as thorny as cactus. The canyon continues on and on, around bends, between sheer walls. We jog forward with it, urgent with discoveries, and finally break into an open plateau full of sun.

Marypat and I pick our way to a low summit. The Rio Grande scribes a huge bend behind us, another tier of limestone cliff rises to the south. Something moves. A spooky, scrawny horse watches us from across the wash; wild, or half-wild and belonging loosely to someone, somewhere. There is no road, no trail, no house or shack or corral, no sign of anything man-made, just a horse in the sun looking like it's been a while since the last good grass.

Another day, another canyon. Bigger than most. The streambed is wide, littered with boulders and outwash. A mile in, we walk through a slot in the canyon floor, a tight alley of river-fluted rock. We can put our arms out and touch both walls. Small pools of water gleam in the pockets of shadowed rock. Our voices hush for no reason other than it seems like a sanctuary.

We emerge again, walk into sunlight. Several huge boulders rest on the canyon floor, perched improbably on smaller rocks that act like table legs, as if they dropped neatly onto the supporting pillars. There is something familiar about them.

"We've been here before, Marypat." I point to one prominent, elevated boulder. "Do you remember that? We have a picture at home of the boys sitting under that rock. Remember?"

"You're right," she agrees. "They could stand under there then. Can you believe that?" And she marshals the kids to sit under the same rock. Even sitting, Sawyer has to bend his neck to get underneath.

"I think it's time for Ruby's ceremony," Marypat suggests. "I've been looking for a spot for the last few days. What about back there in that cool little slot of rock? I brought the stuff with me."

For the third time, our family takes up the compass points. Ruby straddles a small pool in gray rock. I think what a little girl she was when we circled around Eli. Each of us holds the symbol of an element. Marypat casts the circle. It is the most dramatic spot yet, held together in the clasp of flood-polished rock, with canyon wrens echoing in the background and the immensity that ripples outward from our knot of family a palpable hum. Mother Earth.

The awkwardness I felt at the start of these ceremonies has evaporated. We have come so far from acknowledging the powers of the elements, being grateful for the most basic amenities, the things that literally keep us alive. Now, to do so requires us to make up the ceremonies that used to be part of everyday life. Now we have to remind ourselves of the weather, the sun, the blessing of rain.

Here, this day in the desert, surrounding Ruby, we honor the forces that surround us—sun, wind, water, earth. We honor this girl, her flame, her blood, her future, her birth. Marypat steps forward with her engraved bracelet. They kiss. Ruby slips it on. We clasp together in a family embrace of bad hair and river grit and goose-bumped skin.

If this isn't church, nothing is.

Sixty-Three

Summer 2003—Eight years old and Ruby has some amazing legs! She climbed Sphinx Mtn. in a day, a 10–12 mile hike to a 10,000' peak. We bushwhacked up to Ramshorn Peak and then climbed Mt. Blackmore, outside of town. She also did an 18-mile mountain bike ride on forest trails. At the end of summer she did her first backpack, carrying her own sleeping bag, pad, clothes, and water. I hope we can keep her interest up.

—MARYPAT, RUBY'S BIRTH BOOK

The border our canoes balance along feels like no man's land. In more than a hundred miles, we have seen a man herding goats, a couple of border patrol agents, a family at the mouth of Santa Elena Canyon. Mile after mile, there is no sign of humanity. A few scraggly cows and horses, some ruined buildings, garbage here and there.

I generally welcome the lack of human clutter on a trip, but here it feels hollow, an ache with a vague filament of tension running through it. The river carries us forward through what feels like a DMZ or the taboo space between gang territories. Away from the river corridor, at a safe, survivable remove, life goes on, as if behind a curtain. People tend gardens, barter services, boil candelilla plants, raise children, tend goats.

On the map, there are villages marked here and there in Mexico, old ruins on both sides of the river; occasionally we pass a building that looks recently inhabited, but nothing moves. One afternoon we coast past a sandbar with fishing poles propped up on forked sticks and bobbers floating in the current, but no one in attendance.

When we climb to the tops of hills, it is like standing on an atoll in the middle of the Pacific. The desert is oceanic, waves of dry air, limestone breakers, distant mountains like clouds. A place full of spirits, invisible powers as palpable as wind.

On our earlier descent we also felt tension in the air, but back then, pre–Homeland Security, it was a vibrant current. One afternoon that February, we stroked past a line of pickup trucks and men parked on the Mexican side of the river, pointing north. Expectancy hummed in the air. No women to be seen. Serious men, a few boys, waiting vehicles. Something pending. We paddled by, made no eye contact, didn't wave. The air felt thick as gauze. Sawyer and Eli, little boys from another universe, looked soberly at the scene.

It isn't until we approach Rio Grande Village and the ruined Hot Springs resort that we see a few people this time. It is early morning when we arrive at the mineral springs, quite chilly. I am more ready for a bath than

I can ever remember, and the cold has nothing to do with it. Ten days of sand, mud, river gunk, charcoal, camp dirt, body odor, unwashed clothes.

The Rio Grande sweeps around a bend. An out-of-place palm tree sits back from the river alongside the dilapidated ruins of the old resort. Fresh mud deposits coat everything, but the old foundations of the hot springs sit squarely above the river, brimming with steaming water. Our boats nose to shore in an eddy.

Although the building is gone, the containment wall remains, pooling the clear, hot water several feet deep. It bubbles up constantly and drains out from one corner. The cold river runs past the other side of the wall.

"Oh my god," I sigh, sliding under. "It feels so good it hurts."

I can almost viscerally feel my pores open, the layers of grime and sweat exfoliate.

"This must be what a snake feels like when it sheds," I say. "Brand new."

A man by the name of J. O. Langford capitalized on the natural hot springs here in the early 1900s. He built his family home on top of the hill overlooking the river and hired a German stonemason to construct the bathing pools. He built changing rooms and established a rustic resort. Langford advertised a twenty-one-day cure for whatever ailed you, combining soaking in the springs and drinking the mineral waters.

For a time, it was extolled as a restorative getaway with curative powers for victims of asthma and tuberculosis and arthritis. It was a period when sanatoriums and mineral springs were the rage. Whether they were effective against those ailments, I have no idea, but when they feel this good, who the hell cares?

The resort is long gone. Langford and his family were driven out, spooked off by border unrest and financial difficulties, but the road comes within walking distance of the springs. Locals and tourists regularly come down to soak.

We aren't there long before a short, somewhat gnomelike man comes stumping down the trail. He has a salt-and-pepper beard down to his chest and some gaps in his smile; could be fifty-five or seventy. He nods at us, strips down to his green Skivvies, and takes his place in a deep corner.

He turns out to be a font of local lore. He tells us the story of the springs, the ebb and flow of border disputes, Mexican army raids, Indian battles, and the continuing legacy of bureaucratic heavy-handedness, whether in response to immigration or exotic animal species. He blames the establishment of the national park for the demise of border equanimity. Homeland Security has only made a tenuous situation disastrous.

"They promised the people of Boquillas a bridge," he says. "They promised electricity, talked about commerce. Never happened. They bulldozed the ancient Santa Elena cemetery on the Texas side. Now Santa Elena is down to four families. Places like San Vicente, which used to be a real village, are just a few holdouts living on catfish and beans.

"They spend thousands to reintroduce desert bighorn sheep, conduct bullshit studies, and come up with management plans, but kill off the exotic African goats that are already thriving here."

But it's his story that captures our attention.

"People call me Peanut," he admits.

"I run a concession stand in North Yarmouth, Maine, all summer," he tells us. "I'm known for my roasted peanuts. I have a corner in town, and I go to the county fairs around New England. But every winter I come back here. I built myself a house on a flatbed truck and park my rig up a dirt road outside the park. I ride my motorcycle, soak in the hot springs, read up on things that interest me.

"I got sober in '81, kicked drugs for good in '86. Got addicted to Big Bend instead. Come fall, when the tourists dry up, I can't wait to get back. In the spring, before I head north again, I make a run over to northern Arizona to pick up raw peanuts."

Upstream of the hot springs on the Mexican side, a man appears on a donkey. He lifts his feet high as the donkey picks its way through the fast current. Once in Texas, he swings off the small animal and posts himself next to the trail to the hot springs. He does not actively solicit, keeps his distance. He hunkers there alongside the river, waiting to make deals.

"Times are really desperate for villagers," Peanut tells us. He strokes his long, wet beard against his chest as he talks. "He's probably from Boquillas. They get by selling little figures made of wire, wooden carvings, walking sticks made from cholla cactus. He could get you marijuana, peyote, mescaline. It's risky for them to even come across the river, but what are they supposed to do? You could get just about anything you want through someone like him."

More people arrive at the hot springs. A few stop and interact with the man. I see nothing change hands. The pool gets crowded. When a family with three boys who look like linemen from a Texas football squad arrive, we decide to canoe on. Peanut nods good-bye.

Drifting through Hot Springs Canyon I think about the economic devastation in our country. People losing homes, going bankrupt to medical bills, having their retirement income vanish overnight, returning to demeaning jobs in their seventies. I think about the failed hype common investors have been victimized by, the seduction of lifestyles fueled on debt.

I think about my children, whose futures lie in the balance, facing the confusing map of their prospects. For them, to have a landmark named Peanut on the charts isn't at all a bad thing. Yes, they also have college education to think about, sports scholarships, SAT tests, grades, career paths, job prospects, security. But Marypat and I are not particularly great role models when it comes to conventionality.

And here is a man with a simple, honest occupation, a passion for place, time to philosophize over history and current events while soaking in riverside hot springs in his underwear. He's overcome a few personal demons, come to an equation that he finds fulfilling. What's a 401(k), a diploma on the wall, and a vacation condo compared to that?

"You could do worse than live a life like Peanut," I say to no one in particular.

Sawyer glances at me, nods, gives me one of his goofy grins. "Whatever you say, Dad. But you won't catch me wearing green whitey tighties, no matter what happens."

I hate the intersections with civilization during a trip. They are rife with potential for strain. Temptations are suddenly available. Options present themselves. Turbulence enters what was, just a mile upstream, unruffled water. It is easy to backslide.

At Rio Grande Village, more KOA than settlement, Eli suggests changing our itinerary. He knows I am planning on calling the shuttle service to confirm our pickup.

"What if we move it up a day?" he says. "Then we could get back with at least one day before school starts again. Maybe we could go skiing. We could get homework done," he throws in.

"Yeah," I say. "Homework. Right."

"Really," he pushes. "I can't do math in the car. And we have ski passes and haven't skied all vacation."

Ruby and Sawyer watch the proceedings. I can see them waffle. I feel the same pressure. Marypat resists.

"I have no interest in rushing to the end," she says.

This temptation to push up the finish is a strange phenomenon. We extol our adventures, love the wilds, want nothing more than to be out, but when an option to end a day ahead presents itself, the pull of creature comforts, the release from camp routine, weather, the vagaries of life in the open, are tremendously tempting. I can fall prey to it. Eli is especially prone to it.

"Whenever I end early I feel like I've demeaned the trip," I say.

"Demeaned? What are you talking about?" Eli says. "I just think we could get home a day early and go skiing."

"That's what you say." I feel some heat, along with the temptation to give in. "But really, you just want to get off the river, and it always feels like you've compromised when you do."

Eli looks at me like I'm certifiable.

"What if we move the pickup to early morning," Marypat says. "We can either camp at the take-out or just upstream and get a jump on the drive home. But I don't want to come out a day ahead."

Marypat is clear about her priorities. She is not fooled by creature comforts. She knows that lure is as fleeting and hollow as costume jewelry. She remains steadfast. Her purest joy is on the trail.

The other reason I hate civilized stops is that they are inevitably discombobulating. It takes me half an hour and I walk half a mile to find the tiny convenience store that sits about one hundred yards from our boats through a screen of shrubs. Then I can find nothing that we need. We were hoping for camera batteries, some toilet paper, perhaps a treat. No batteries. I can't bring myself to buy miniature marshmallows. We end up with toilet paper.

They do have a phone. I call in, move the pickup to early morning.

Eli is sullen when we regain the river. He hangs back in the red ducky.

"He'll get over it," Marypat says.

Hot water bubbles up along the Mexican side. Another ruined hot springs structure pulls us in, where we find some steaming streams and a pool with a miniature hot waterfall that pours on our heads. The community of Boquillas sits along the river. Adobe buildings, a dirt road, some goats.

A little girl stands on a volcanic outcrop overlooking the river. She wears a pink T-shirt, faded jeans. She watches us going past in our canoes. We look at each other. She waves, says hi. We wave back at her.

An older woman sits nearby, busy with her hands—braiding, sewing, mending, something. Then I notice a young woman perched in a hanging natural basin on the cliff face. What I presume is hot water pours into the tub, filling it, spilling out into the river. She is bathing. Her long, wet black hair glistens in the light. She looks demurely over the rim of the rock bath at us.

"Now that is a bathtub to die for," I say.

As we approach Boquillas Canyon, three young men launch a cheap rubber raft from the Mexican side and head for Texas. It is the kind of raft you get when you turn in the coupons from thirty cartons of Marlboros. The paddles are stubby, plastic sticks. The raft tubes are as thin as a kid's pool toy. They flop into the boat and flail at the water.

Eli is still well back, and he drifts up on the young Mexican men.

"*Hola*," I hear them say.

"*Hola*," he says back.

They pass each other. They must imagine the lives they each lead. Ten feet away, with much, probably, in common, but across an unbridgeable divide.

Right at the mouth of the canyon, a battered aluminum canoe rests on the Texas shore. A pair of local men have set up shop. They hunker next to a table-sized boulder. Long jeans, button-up shirts, dark faces, straw hats. They beckon to us, hold up figurines of twisted wire, a walking stick. We wave and drift on.

Sixty-Four

Ruby: You are my best friend. I will never forget about you. Love, Lizzie.
—FRIENDSHIP CARD

Ruby is big and strong and coordinated. That became clear early on. One spring, on a family biking outing, when she was maybe five, we were on a country road near Bozeman looking for newborn bison calves. The boys had graduated to ten-speed bikes by then, while she was saddled with a heavy, one-speed starter bicycle. At one point, all three were laboring up a steep hill. The boys geared down. Ruby kept pumping. The boys started to weave across the roadway. Ruby put her head down. The boys stopped, panting. Ruby stood up and kept climbing, little legs like pistons, right past her chagrined brothers.

When Ruby was in grade school, watching her play soccer or compete in running events could be agonizing. That she was a physical presence was never in question. That she had terrific potential was a given. But about half the time the ball came her way, she was busy holding hands and chatting with a teammate, and her goal in a running race was to meet someone fun.

My impression was that she shared none of the angst we experienced on the sideline. She was playing a fun game, and she was being with her friend. Likely as not, after a race, her summary of the highlights started with the conversations she had with other runners.

"Ruby!" the boys would chorus. "You're supposed to pass those people, not talk to them. You're supposed to win."

Ruby's history as an athlete is a study in cultural mixed messages. That history is revealing about her, but also about the confusing input girls in our society get.

Even as she got into middle school, and as her athletic potential continued to burgeon, she was truly torn. She would run in the pack, stay with her friends, rather than run her strongest race. The point was to have fun, be nice, experience solidarity, and only secondarily to compete.

At one cross-country meet, she stayed neck and neck with her friends throughout most of the run. About two-thirds of the way along, she had to stop and tie her shoe, which cost her a lot of ground. No problem. She turned it on, caught back up, and settled right back into her chatty pace to the finish line.

"Why don't you run the way you did catching up all the time?" Marypat asked her.

"I don't want anyone to be mad at me."

"It's a race, sweetie. If people get mad because you beat them, that's their problem."

Ruby shrugged.

It was the same way when she took up Nordic skiing; it was all about the fun, the socializing. Competing was only marginally on her radar. I couldn't fault her priorities. I loved her sensitivity, but it was still agonizing.

The boys never experienced that dilemma. Sure they had fun, they enjoyed the camaraderie on a team, their best friends were their teammates, but it was very clearly about winning.

Ruby's emphasis on friendship is fundamental. She and her friends make books for each other full of hearts and poems and pictures. They put together elaborate, time-consuming presents. She made a photo collage for a friend that was mounted on an old porch door full of window panes. It took her weeks. The thing probably weighed seventy pounds and took up half a bedroom wall.

On Eli's trip, she talked the whole time about meeting the new girl moving in across the street. As soon as we got home that summer, that's where she went. Within days, Katie was signed up on the same soccer team and the same cross-country team, and they were comparing notes on the teacher they would share in fifth grade. Katie is still in Ruby's intimate circle of friends.

When Ruby decided to ski up a level after several years in her Nordic program, she was motivated by her need to train hard, but also, more importantly, to stay with another friend who was skiing up. Her attitude was slowly evolving, though. The drive to win came into play more and more often. Her coaches made it clear that on the racecourse she was to focus. All the training, working out five days a week, time at the gym—it was about that finish line. Friends hugged you afterward or commiserated with you afterward.

The year she skied up, she ended up qualifying for Junior Nationals. She finished in the top nine skiers of the Intermountain Region and went to California to race against the best skiers in the country. There she qualified as an All American in two out of four races, finishing in the top fifteen.

Still, when she came home, all she could talk about was the friend she met, a young girl from Utah.

Sixty-Five

As a woman, I have no country. As a woman, I want no country. As a woman, my country is the whole world.

—Virginia Woolf

I wake in the pale new day. A bright planet persists against the early gray light through the mesh of the tent ceiling. A mourning dove coos. The crack between worlds, that time of uncertainty and doubt, and also of calm understanding and revelation. Things drift, time comes unmoored.

The Kazan, the Yellowstone, the Rio Grande, the Seal braid together. I lie with my family on the sand. Their faces are serene, untroubled. Marypat sleeps on her back, her hands across her belly.

The sweep of the journeys converge in a jumble of images. Northern lights at the brink of Kazan Falls. Reading our fourteen-year-old river journal entry in the tent. Moonrise below Younts Peak, at the first snowfed drops of the Yellowstone. A panic of blackflies. Ruby's ceremony in a cathedral of side canyon. Sawyer rousting the tent in one of his midnight sleepwalking missions. Musk ox grazing behind camp. Face-to-face with an Inuit skull on Thirty Mile Lake. The torment of wind, the blessing of sunrise, swimming through waves together, sharing food, bear tracks on the trail. Ruby playing air guitar, Eli whittling a stick, Sawyer jumping naked out of the canoe.

These final days, the kids have taken over the hardshell canoe and eschewed the inflatable kayak. The rubber ducky tags along on the stern line like a pet puppy. One of them lounges in the middle of the canoe while the other two paddle. They are comfortable in the stern or the bow, competent handling the boat, adept at reading water.

The miles drop away, the end nears. Boquillas Canyon, full of wild burros braying up sidestreams, canyons to walk up. The downstream boundary of the national park comes and goes. A ranch house on a bluff in Texas, cool-looking, somnolent, full of stories. More river bends, turtles, flycatchers, yucca the size of people, pillars of rock, more sky and wind and the lift and fall of land swelling into the distance.

Marypat and I have come back together, teamed up in a boat. We drop into the accustomed rhythm. It doesn't require discussion or thought. Our paddles land in the water together. We read each other's body language, react to strokes, go long stretches in silence as we have so many days on so many rivers, looping a wake through the continent—all the places we have stopped to rest, pitched camp, built fires, watched the river, all the places we have felt the pulse of the earth.

Neither of us brings it up, but both of us are thinking that the return to our paddling partnership is bittersweet. We don't discuss it, but we both think about the next phase, when Eli leaves home, when they all leave home, and when we will be adrift together again, how welcome and sad, how bruised and bountiful that will feel. What trips we might yet share, how much we will miss them.

We listen to the banter from the other canoe. The talk of soccer coaches, teachers to avoid, scandals, friends they miss, plans for mischief. They ram their way along, half bawdy teenagers, half playful children. The tension of town life has ebbed away, the confusion of social pressures, competition for friends, demands of schoolwork, plans for the future.

They exist here in river time the way they have since birth. They fall into it together the way Marypat and I drop into sync in a canoe. It is as simple as sleep, as profound as moonrise. It is not something we have given them, but a thing they have earned. All we did was put them there.

The planet fades in the tide of coming day. I dress and leave the tent. I find some dried tamarisk and dead grass, light a match, add driftwood, set a blackened pot full of water over the yellow flames. There is no hurry. Sunlight hits El Pico, the dominant peak on the Mexican side, visible from fifty miles. Coffee comes.

Mug in hand, I stroll across the gravel flats etched with flood channels. I hold up redstreak agates in the low sunlight. Some I put in my pocket to show Marypat. Some will come home with us, go into the tumbler, shine with memories on our windowsills and around the garden, luminescent reminders. I roll the cool, smooth stones in my pocket, think of their travels. A great blue heron immigrates across the river, lands in some quiet shallows, pays no attention to the line drawn on our maps.

I hear the tent zipper. Ruby steps out, holding a book. She slides her feet into sandals, hugs herself against the chill, heads for the fire. She feeds the flames, settles into a chair, opens her book. I make my way back to share my finds. I bend down to her raised face, feel the sleepy warmth of her cheek against my two-week beard.

Ruby's trip ends at the La Linda bridge. As soon as the canoes grind against shore, the trip feels over. Chores kick in. We disassemble the folding canoe, drape it over rocks to dry, wipe the rods clean of grit. The odd bits of remaining food consolidate into one small bag. In an hour, the load is reorganized, repacked, cleaned up.

Downstream, the river bends ninety degrees. The old mining operation squats on the hill above. Rusted vehicles, barrels, belts, corrugated metal buildings, the slow decay of abandonment. Town is vacant. Houses, a cantina, a basketball court, streets, some cars and trucks all testify to the settlement that once thrived on this northern frontier.

The day wanes. Ruby and Sawyer wade to Mexico across shallows at the bend. They clamber up the steep bank and start thumping sections of overhanging sand, speeding up erosion. Chunks of muddy bank whump into the river, Sawyer scampers back to safety. Ruby eggs him forward, doubled over laughing.

Marypat and I stroll up toward the quiet, two-lane highway where our car will meet us early in the morning. The bridge that once connected La Linda and its mining industry to America is fenced off, barricaded with concrete, bristling with barbed wire. The view opens wide. Dirt tracks arrow south through the hills, along streambeds, past crumbling buildings. It is probably nine hours to civilization, driving south on horrendous roads. Nothing moves in the town.

Several miles from the settlement, alone on the landscape, stands a white church. It shines in the sunlight, radiant, a beacon. In the distance, rampant against the horizon, the dome of El Pico also gleams with light.

"It would be cool to come back and keep going, do the lower canyons," I suggest. I realize that my image of that future trip doesn't include kids. Marypat nods. We start back, holding hands, tracking a cactus wren through the creosote.

It is New Year's Eve. A thin crescent moon rises in the evening sky with a planet nearby. The mood is subdued. It will likely be the quietest New Year's in memory and the earliest to bed. But we will have stars to the horizon. Everyone's thoughts turn north—the drive, friends, a chance to ski, going back to school and work.

"I want to take a bath in body lotion," Ruby says. "My skin is like fish scales."

"I have some more candles," Marypat says suddenly.

No one complains this time. There is no reluctance, but instead a mute recognition of closure. We circle together, each hold a round, white ball of wax. Everyone makes a wish. We light the wicks, set them in the current.

The candles don't dillydally this night. All five set off in the serene flow, bobbing and twinkling in a loose constellation. They stay lit, diminishing in the darkness, approaching the bend; then, around the bend and out of sight, all five heading into the long unknown.